THEOLOGY IN SEARCH OF FOUNDATIONS

Theology in Search of Foundations

RANDAL RAUSER

OXFORD
UNIVERSITY PRESS

OXFORD
UNIVERSITY PRESS

Great Clarendon Street, Oxford OX2 6DP

Oxford University Press is a department of the University of Oxford.
It furthers the University's objective of excellence in research, scholarship,
and education by publishing worldwide in

Oxford New York

Auckland Cape Town Dar es Salaam Hong Kong Karachi
Kuala Lumpur Madrid Melbourne Mexico City Nairobi
New Delhi Shanghai Taipei Toronto

With offices in

Argentina Austria Brazil Chile Czech Republic France Greece
Guatemala Hungary Italy Japan Poland Portugal Singapore
South Korea Switzerland Thailand Turkey Ukraine Vietnam

Oxford is a registered trade mark of Oxford University Press
in the UK and in certain other countries

Published in the United States
by Oxford University Press Inc., New York

British Library Cataloguing in Publication Data

Data available

Library of Congress Cataloging-in-Publication Data

Rauser, Randal D.
Theology in search of foundations / Randal Rauser.
p. cm.
Includes bibliographical references (p.).
ISBN 978–0–19–921460–0
1. Knowledge, Theory of (Religion) 2. Foundationalism (Theory of knowledge) I. Title.
BT50.R28 2009
230.01–dc22   2009010606

Typeset by SPI Publisher Services, Pondicherry, India
Printed in Great Britain
on acid-free paper by the
MPG Books Group, Bodmin and King's Lynn

ISBN 978–0–19–921460–0

1 3 5 7 9 10 8 6 4 2

To Rae Kyung,
My Archimedean point

Acknowledgements

This book traces its roots back ten years as an idea for a doctoral thesis. Though that thesis was submitted in 2002, I did not consign it to the dusty halls of a research library, but kept labouring on the first half in a seemingly endless process which eventually transmogrified into the present work. As one might expect with a ten-year gestation period, many people have contributed to the composition of this work. I will make a brief mention of the primary players (in so far as my flawed memory will enable me to recall them) in order of historical appearance. To begin with there was my thesis adviser, the late Colin Gunton. The world lost a truly great theologian (and gardener) with Colin's untimely death in 2002 and I am saddened that he could not see this work come to fruition. I also thank my two thesis examiners, John Colwell and Alan Torrance, who in grilling me on my thesis contributed to the development of the present work. Thanks go next to Lucy Qureshi, my first editor at Oxford University Press, who was unflagging in her positivity and magnanimous in her patience with a young professor struggling to juggle a book contract with a flood of new course preps. I am also in the debt of the two readers provided by Oxford, shrouded as they are in the fogs of anonymity, for identifying lacunae in the argument, and flagging many lapses of reason, amateurish errors, and other potential embarrassments. The work is much stronger for their diligence and forbearance. Next, I thank my former student Rick Shott, who offered helpful comments on a number of chapters. I also gratefully acknowledge the work of my second editor at Oxford, Tom Perridge, who shared Lucy's patience and positivity as he saw the manuscript through to completion. Of late I am in the debt of Lizzie Robottom and Jenny Wagstaffe and all the staff at Oxford who laboured diligently to ensure that *Theology in Search of Foundations* would become the next sensation to fly off the shelves of Waterstones and Barnes & Noble. At this point I will depart from my chronological progression by acknowledging the contribution of my family, a contribution which has framed the entirety of the project at a subtler but perhaps more profound dimension. Thanks to my parents, parents-in-law, daughter, and extended family for their prayers and support. And let me not forget my two dogs, Semi (d. 2005) and Sonny, who in their *joie de vivre* have reminded me of the value of pausing from work to chew a rawhide bone. But, most importantly, I thank my wife Rae Kyung, with whom I am overjoyed to have an intimate knowledge of acquaintance. It is to her that this work is dedicated.

Contents

Abbreviations

CDA	conceptual-dependence argument
JDA	justification-dependence argument
F&M	Freud and Marx
A/C	Aquinas/Calvin
IIHS	internal instigation of the Holy Spirit
JTB	justified true belief
CF	classical foundationalism
T-D	Tarksi-Davidson

Introduction

Whatever Happened to the Polemicist?

> It is the winter season for rigorous Christian teaching.
>
> Thomas Oden, *After Modernity… What?*

Every autumn the academic world begins to post jobs for the coming year, with a modest number of theological posts among them. But while one may readily find universities seeking candidates to fulfil such varied posts as 'womanist spirituality', 'queer deconstructionism' and 'Gnostic Christianity', one is not likely to see any postings like the following:

Seeking full-time professor of Didactic and Polemical Theology. Must have a keen desire to pursue truth and defend biblical orthodoxy, be able to communicate concisely with analytic rigour and a minimum of technical verbiage. Experience debating with heretics would be an asset.

Indeed, this job posting would be more likely to amuse or anger than to attract potential applicants. At least that is the case for most theologians. At the same time, Thomas Oden is one stubborn exception, as he avers that 'what today's seminary most needs is a polemicist, trained in the rough-and-tumble give and take of old-fashioned scholastic Protestant polemics'.[1] But this is surely an anomalous opinion. Though polemicists may once have freely roamed the halls of seminaries and universities like buffalo on the prairie, they have since largely disappeared. The radical shift is captured in Hilaire Belloc's poem 'Lines to a Don':

---

[1] Oden, *After Modernity… What?* (Grand Rapids, Mich.: Zondervan, 1990), 171.

> Don different from those regal dons
> With hearts of gold and lungs of bronze
> Who shout and bang and roar and bawl
> The absolute across the hall.[2]

While the polemicist once thrived in this robust theological environment, the more sedate, relaxed atmosphere of contemporary theology has a low tolerance for roaring and bawling theologians.

But what precisely is different about constructive theology in the present age? Part of the difference arises from a change in the standards of civil exchange. Whereas Luther could be cheered by his colleagues even as he farted and spewed the most vulgar epithets, we now take at least as much interest in the theologian's courteous demeanor as the content of his argument. Martin Marty is a barometer of the times when he evocatively asserts that the conservative/liberal divide has been superseded by the divide between 'mean' and 'non-mean'.[3] What is more, today we widely repudiate the legitimacy of coercion as a means to settle theological disputes. So we frown upon both those who curse and insult their opponents and those who invoke the power of the magistrate to have their opponents tortured and executed.[4] What is more, the indisputable nature of these standards for us only serves to highlight the chasm between contemporary theology and the vigorous polemicists of an earlier age.

But as important as these points are, they do not exhaust the differences, for even the vintage polemicist tutored to be kind and tolerant (and even able to navigate a Starbucks menu as a condition of coffeeshop theologizing) would still face significant resistance in the current climate. In my view, the most important difference between the bawling theological dons of an earlier age and the polite academics of today is rooted in epistemology. Theologians of the past believed in their ability to discern the essence of orthodoxy and develop

---

[2] Belloc, 'Lines to a Don', cited in Simon Blackburn, *Truth: A Guide for the Baffled* (Oxford: Oxford University Press, 2005), xvii.

[3] Cited in Krista Tippett, *Speaking of Faith* (New York: Viking, 2007), 161.

[4] On the issue of coercion and the settlement of theological disputes see Oden's comment on irenics as the complement of polemics (*After Modernity ... What?*, p. 173).

theological theories that had a reasonable chance of being (more or less) correct; that is, they believed in theology as a (critically realist) science. But theologians today no longer hold those bold expectations and are just as likely to dismiss those who do as intolerant and naive. If one were to focus on a single epistemological issue which would illumine this shift, I would propose the topic of foundationalism, for this brings us to the heart of a nexus of shifting views concerning the nature of justification, knowledge, truth, and reality. And so, that will be our task. But how ought we to examine the shift of theology with respect to epistemological foundationalism?

We will divide the journey ahead into three sections, beginning with a discussion of classical foundationalism in Chapters 1–4. Since this epistemological theory dominated academic theology from (at least) the Enlightenment until the mid-twentieth century, this section will largely provide the stage setting for the current state of theology. We will begin in Chapter 1 with the background story of how three philosophers—René Descartes, John Locke, and Immanuel Kant—sought to re-establish theology in light of a fracturing of authorities—and inadvertently ended up as theology's gravediggers. Unfortunately, as we will see in Chapter 2, theologians of the time did not recognize the dangerous implications of these philosophies. Instead, some sought to defend the cognitive-propositional status of theological claims by marshalling the deductive and inductive evidence demanded by Descartes and Locke, while others sought a more radical Kantian retreat to subjectivity in which doctrines were reduced to symbolizations of experience. With this background in place, we will turn in Chapter 3 to summarize the key epistemological concepts necessary for understanding the argument, including *reason*, *faith*, *truth*, and *knowledge*, and key debates between *internalism* and *externalism*, *methodism* and *particularism*, and the three distinct accounts of noetic structure: *foundationalism*, *infinitism*, and *coherentism*. Based on this fine-tuned understanding of the epistemological issues at stake, we will turn in Chapter 4 to a final evaluation of the central problems with classical foundationalism.

With an account of the demise of classical foundationalism in place, we will turn in Chapters 5–8 to consider the current state of contemporary theology, in which non-foundationalist epistemology dominates. The discussion will begin in Chapter 5 with an overview of non-foundationalist approaches to justification, knowledge, truth, and reality. Next, we will turn to consider how some of these themes are expressed in the non-foundational theologies of Stanley Grenz and Nancey Murphy. Chapter 6 will focus on a critique of non-foundationalist positions on justification, knowledge, truth, and reality, as well as the particular proposals offered by Grenz and Murphy. From here we will return in Chapter 7 for a second pass at non-foundationalism in the work of Bruce Marshall. Marshall's proposal is distinctive from those surveyed in Chapters 5 and 6 in so far as it eschews overt anti-realism and incorporates the doctrine of the Trinity at the centre of its account. A critical analysis of Marshall's proposal will occupy Chapter 8, and will concern both problems with his Trinitarianism as well as those which beset his form of non-foundationalism more generally. At this point we will have completed our critical survey of the non-foundationalism that dominates in contemporary theology.

The failure of both classical foundationalism and non-foundationalism raises the question of what kind of epistemology we ought to develop for theology. It will be the task of the final two chapters to present some suggestions for the way ahead. In Chapter 9 I will commend Alvin Plantinga's moderate (externalist) foundationalism via an overview of Plantinga's Reformed roots, common-sense realism, and proper-function account of the warrant of Christian belief. Finally, in Chapter 10 I will apply this model more explicitly to contemporary theology by arguing for a view of doctrine as true description as against Kevin Vanhoozer's theory of doctrine as dramatic prompt. I will argue that this position grounds both rigorous epistemic virtue and the possibility of ongoing ecumenical advance.

At the centre of this study is the role of theology as a science of the supernatural. Almost eight hundred years ago Thomas Aquinas confidently described all the sciences as handmaidens to theology.[5] Today the idea may seem quaint, if not ridiculous. Nonetheless, it is my conviction that theology could one day occupy this status again. But

---

[5] Aquinas, *Summa Theologiae*, Prima Pars, 1.5.

if it does, it will not be because theologians remember how to insult their opponents with abandon, and still less because they invoke the power of the magistrate. On the contrary, it will be because they will abandon various subtler scepticisms and instead become again the most passionate and rigorous seekers of the God of all truth.

1

Descartes, Locke, Kant, and the Crisis of Justification

Let us suppose that I, like Mohammed, go into desert places to fast and pray; what things can happen to me which will give me the right to believe that I am divinely inspired?

W. K. Clifford, 'The Ethics of Belief'

That a Christian thinker should feel called upon to render an epistemological 'apology' for the fact that his mind cannot divorce itself from his faith is perhaps a sign of the times.

William Reiser, SJ, ' "Knowing" Jesus: Do Theologians have a Special Way?'

In *The Gravedigger File*, a clever take on the *Screwtape Letters* theme, Os Guinness describes a meeting with a university don on a misty November evening in the streets of Oxford.[1] According to Guinness, the don handed him a dossier of memos which revealed a diabolical plot to subvert the Western Church from within by encouraging it to adopt ideas and practices that, while appearing trendy and important, are actually inimical to its survival. The lesson is that the Church that uncritically strives for relevance ensures its own obsolescence, thereby becoming its own gravedigger. This unfortunate story of the modern Western Church could just as well be told of academic theology, for theologians have often adopted methods to defend and communicate theology which threaten to make them into gravediggers. Thus, it makes sense to begin our survey of theological method by

[1] Guinness, *The Gravedigger File: Papers on the Subversion of the Modern Church* (Downer's Grove, Ill.: InterVarsity, 1983).

considering the impact of certain philosophical trajectories concerning the way theologians have approached the justification of their
discipline.

Over the next four chapters we will see that the epistemology of
classical foundationalism has been especially influential in adjudicating questions of the justification of theology (though the extent
to which it has served as gravedigger is yet to be determined). We
will begin in the present chapter with a brief survey of the struggles theology faced when the medieval consensus of Christendom
crumbled. This tumult will provide the context by which we will
consider the influential rearguard attempts of René Descartes, John
Locke, and Immanuel Kant to secure the theologian's waning authority. Descartes was deeply concerned to further the extent of medieval
scientia through the radical method of critical doubt. Locke was more
pessimistic; indeed, so convinced was he of the severe limitations of
scientia that he focused instead upon the rational regulation of opinion. But Kant was the most pessimistic of all as he severely chastened
reason in order to provide room for faith. While Descartes, Locke,
and Kant all sought to provide a rational ground for theology, with
the benefit of hindsight we can see the fully corrosive effects of these
efforts, a fact which provides a solemn warning for the would-be
apologists of every generation. After laying out in this chapter the
challenge of an increasingly sceptical and secular society, the rest of
this book will chronicle the long and contorted process by which
theology has sought to re-establish its integrity and authority.

PUTTING CHRISTIANITY ON THE DEFENSIVE

Upon visiting the Sistine Chapel, one is immersed in the
grand Judaeo-Christian narrative—from the creation of Adam on
Michelangelo's unforgettable ceiling to the haunting depiction of
Christ's Last Judgment on the altar wall. This experience provides a
powerful visual reminder of the time when theology was still duly
honoured as the queen of the sciences. If the Sistine Chapel represents the medieval world, our secularized world might instead call to
mind the image of a cathedral that has been converted to high-end

apartments. Though our world might share certain superficial similarities with Christendom, we now live in an almost entirely secular
world. Today not only has theology been demoted from its throne,
but in many cases it has been evicted altogether from the realm
of *scientia* (as represented by the precincts of the modern university), with its former regal quarters now occupied by more putatively
'objective' enquiries including the social, psychological, and historical
study of religion.[2] Far from being the queen of the sciences, theology
now exists at the periphery of respectable intellectual existence as a
disciple that appears at best to be engaging in self-indulgent expostu-
lations upon highly tendentious and obscure religious doctrines, and
at worst to be propagating a dangerous and sectarian ideology.[3]

Needless to say, the days are long gone when a fierce debate concerning the procession of the Spirit or the two natures of Christ could
grip the public imagination and shake the university. In the current
situation theologians must ask how theology lost its intellectual credibility and how it can be returned to a place of authority, not so much
for the sake of theology itself as for the sake of the Church and the
world. The question really concerns, as Kristen Heyer puts it, how
theologies can once again 'go public'. Heyer notes that this question
forces us to ask whether the search for public relevance is necessary or,
on the contrary, whether it might actually pose a distinct danger for
the integrity of theology.[4] Though the question of theology's public
status is not the same as the question of foundationalism, the two
issues certainly overlap. In order to address these questions, we must
first consider how theology lost its privilege and the extent to which
this demotion in status is due to Christian academics playing the
unwitting role of gravediggers.

---

[2] Luke Timothy Johnson observes: 'In the academy, what once sat enthroned as
the queen of the sciences now has to argue for a place at the table spread for the
study of religion among the human sciences' ('Explaining God Away', in *Commonweal*
(Dec. 20, 1996), 18).

[3] See Sam Harris, *The End of Faith: Religion, Terror, and the Future of Reason*
(London: Free Press, 2004).

[4] Heyer, 'How Does Theology Go Public? Rethinking the Debate Between David
Tracy and George Lindbeck', *Political Theology*, 5/3 (2004), 308; cf. Lesslie Newbigin,
Truth to Tell: The Gospel as Public Truth (Grand Rapids, Mich.: Eerdmans/Geneva:
WCC, 1991).

Fracturing the Consensus

According to Ellen Charry, the first millennium of the Church was dominated by a 'sapiential theology' which seamlessly integrated knowledge and goodness in keeping with its Hebraic and Hellenistic origins: 'In a Hellenistic environment, knowledge is true if it leads us into goodness, making us happy and good. The idea that knowing good things makes us good implies continuity between the knower and what she knows. It is not simply to be cognizant of the truth but to be assimilated into it'.[5] As a result, sapiential theology sought to gain the knowledge of God by which people might live in the truth. By contrast, our world today is remarkably fractured. Charry traces the fracturing of theology to the rediscovery of Aristotelianism in the twelfth and thirteenth centuries, at which point theology adopted a highly technical, rigorous, and specialized approach that subtly switched its primary focus from *sapientia* to *scientia*. As a result, the medieval scholastic was constrained to search for *scientia*, a knowledge which is both incorrigible (it cannot fail) and indubitable (it cannot be doubted) and which, while formally excluding first principles, included all the deductions from intuitive first principles.

Whether or not Charry's analysis is wholly correct, it is manifestly clear that medieval scholasticism did introduce a heightened emphasis upon technical knowledge—a shift that brought mixed results. On the one hand, the focus on *scientia* promised impressive advances in technical knowledge, with the methodical labour of syllogisms thrusting up the systems of medieval scholastic theology like great cathedrals. On the other hand, this narrowing of theology to a technical, deductive method also made the discipline more vulnerable to intellectual challenges. And so, while scholasticism represented perhaps the apogee of technical systematization, it also heralded a loss of the integration of wisdom that made it more vulnerable to the successive storms that began to roll in with the Renaissance, Reformation, and Enlightenment. Each of these past storms battered once unified opinion, leading to truths once unquestioned now becoming

---

[5] Charry, 'Walking in the Truth: On Knowing God', in Alan G. Padgett and Patrick R. Keifert (eds.), *But Is It All True? The Bible and the Question of Truth* (Grand Rapids, Mich./Cambridge: Eerdmans, 2006), 145.

doubtful. Ironically, of all these events, the Protestant Reformation is arguably the most critical. And if one were to identify a single moment to encapsulate the Reformation, it would probably be Martin Luther's memorable stand at the Diet of Worms, culminating in those immortal words: 'Unless I am convicted by Scripture and plain reason—I do not accept the authority of the popes and councils, for they have contradicted each other—my conscience is captive to the Word of God. I cannot and I will not recant anything, for to go against conscience is neither right nor safe. God help me. Amen'.[6] Anticipating this response, Luther's cross-examiner Eck had already warned: 'Martin, how can you assume that you are the only one to understand the sense of Scripture? Would you put your judgment above that of so many famous men and claim that you know more than they all?'[7] The years following would bear out Eck's warning as new radical directions were soon being taken by Carlstadt, the Zwickau prophets, and the Swiss Brethren. Within a century Christendom had effectively dissolved into a dizzying array of factions ranging from Catholics, Lutherans, Calvinists, and Anglicans to Congregationalists, Anabaptists, Baptists, Socinians, and countless smaller sects.

Over the next century the chaos continued to worsen as Europe sank into a series of bloody wars and sporadic massacres, spurred on by the credal hardening of ever more nuanced theological distinctives. At the same time, a new authority emerged which sought agreement not through private revelation and military action but rather through hypothesis formation, evidence, and rigorous testing. Wolterstorff describes the tumult created by the myriad of competing scientific, political, and religious authorities: 'Some, such as the new mechanistic and mathematical sciences, were in ascendency, others were in decline; and flashpoints of tension leaped about from place to place'.[8] In the minds of many educated elites, the waning authority

---

[6] Cited in Roland H. Bainton, *Here I Stand: A Life of Martin Luther* (London: Penguin, 2002), 185.

[7] Ibid. Nicholas Wolterstorff observes: '[I]t was especially Luther's rebellion against the magisterium that caused this new perception and fracturing. Luther succeeded in persuading a great many Europeans that the tradition of the councils, popes, and Fathers was filled with fault lines' (*John Locke and the Ethics of Belief* (Cambridge: Cambridge University Press, 1996), 6).

[8] Wolterstorff, *John Locke*, p. 7.

of theology was becoming increasingly obvious. It is a sad irony that those who sought to invigorate and defend theology often brought certain assumptions to the task that inadvertently sped its demise. Whatever minor battles these gravediggers may have won, they were slowly but surely ensuring that theology would lose the war.

ENTER THE GRAVEDIGGERS

Today it is enormously difficult to think of a time when virtually all people within a given society were of one mind concerning fundamental religious and metaphysical issues. Indeed, if anything, members of contemporary pluralist society face what Peter Berger calls the 'heretical imperative', which is the fact that today one cannot help but be a heretic relative to one or another creed.[9] The reality created by contemporary pluralism is that one must now defend and argue for positions that were once assumed. Thus, the Catholics found that they had to defend their view of justification to the Lutherans; the Reformed had to defend their view of baptism to the Anabaptists; and Christians everywhere had to defend their views of the Trinity and atonement to a growing list of free thinkers, deists, and sceptics. With the status of theology increasingly being called into question, a number of thinkers emerged who were set on restoring theological credibility, with René Descartes, John Locke, and Immanuel Kant standing among their first rank.

Descartes: From Bracing Doubt to Reason Triumphant

To call the early seventeenth century in Europe a tumultuous time would be a distinct understatement. Indeed, there are few other periods in European history to rival it for social and intellectual ferment. Chaos threatened from the ongoing wars of religion; old authorities were shaken by the rise of a disconcerting heliocentric and mechanistic science; and the rediscovery of ancient Greek scepticism reinforced

[9] Berger, *The Heretical Imperative: Contemporary Possibilities of Religious Affirmation* (Garden City, NY: Anchor, 1979).

the growing conviction that doubt was the new norm of belief. The spirit of the time is captured in Michel Montaigne's controversial book *Apology for Raymond Sebond*, which defended a position known as 'conformist fideism'.[10] Convinced that the issues of truth, justification, and rationality swirling around religious belief were irresolvable, Montaigne advocated admitting one's doubts but continuing with Christian practice *as if* one believed. Conformist fideism struck a chord with many, as it appeared to maintain the doubter's intellectual integrity even as it indemnified him against the social, economic, and legal risks of outright apostasy. The popularity of Montaigne's work suggests that this kind of doubt was not uncommon.

Though he is often lauded as the father of modern philosophy, Descartes's place in the history of philosophy has long been a matter of controversy. According to the standard story, Descartes was the first modern thinker, being one who heralded the shift from the medieval age of authority and trust to the modern age of individualism and doubt.[11] By this account, prior to Descartes theologians argued from an authority grounded in a fundamental trust in one's teachers and traditions. Thus, despite all their syllogistic rigour, the medieval scholastics uncritically accepted the authority of their forebears. Descartes definitively upset this approach with his method of doubt.[12] And thus he set out to re-establish certainty by firmly grasping the nettle of scepticism, thereby outflanking the doubter with more systematic and rigorous doubt: 'Reason now leads me to think that I should hold back my assent from opinions which are not completely certain and indubitable just as carefully as I do from those which are patently false. So for the purpose of rejecting all my opinions, it will be enough if I find in each of them at least some reason for doubt'.[13]

[10] Terence Penelhum, *God and Skepticism: A Study in Skepticism and Fideism* (Dordrecht: Reidel, 1983), ch. 2; cf. C. Stephen Evans, *Faith Beyond Reason: A Kierkegaardian Account* (Grand Rapids, Mich./Cambridge: Eerdmans, 1998), 16–17.

[11] On this shift see Jeffrey Stout, *The Flight from Authority: Religion, Morality, and the Quest for Autonomy* (Notre Dame, Ind.: University of Notre Dame Press, 1981).

[12] For this background see Michael J. Buckley, *At the Origins of Modern Atheism* (New Haven, Conn.: Yale University Press, 1987), 68–99.

[13] René Descartes, *Meditations on First Philosophy*, trans. and ed. John Cottingham, rev. edn. (Cambridge: Cambridge University Press, 1986), 12.

Descartes began with a thorough introspection of his own beliefs, leaving open the possibility that each one could be 'utterly false and imaginary'.[14] Had Descartes stopped here he would have been left in scepticism, but his razing of the superstructure of belief ultimately was intended to reveal a single Archimedean point which could serve as an adequate foundation for a new construction of knowledge. As he put it, 'Archimedes used to demand just one firm and immovable point in order to shift the entire earth; so I too can hope for great things if I manage to find just one thing, however slight, that is certain and unshakeable'.[15] Augustine had rebutted the sceptics of his age by claiming that even if we cannot know if we are awake, 'three times three is nine and the square of rational numbers must be true, even if the human race be snoring away!'[16] But this was not sufficient for Descartes, who, in his relentless search for error, speculated that a supernatural (malevolent) being could deceive him every time he set out to reason (e.g. by adding two and three).[17] Since it seems that I cannot know whether this prima facie incredible state of affairs is *impossible*, I cannot be certain of mathematics or logic, and so this cannot provide a foundation totally secure from possible error.

While Descartes recognized that this sceptical acid could eat through even the unshakeable certainty of mathematics, he had a more positive assessment of his own consciousness. Hence, he found respite in the *cogito, ergo sum* (which is actually a reworking of Augustine's *Si fallor, sum*—'If I am mistaken, I am'). Having deduced his existence from his ratiocination, Descartes then turned to introspect the contents of his mind, discovering at the outset an idea of a most perfect being. Since a most perfect being that fails to be actualized in reality would be contradictory, this being must exist. And since he is perfect he would not deceive us, from which it follows that our cognitive faculties must be reliable. Despite the fact that God serves as the guarantor of our cognitive faculties in the argument, Descartes's method represented a radical anthropological shift. As Jennifer Hecht

[14] Descartes, *Meditations on First Philosophy*, p. 15.

[15] Descartes, *Meditations on First Philosophy*, p. 16.

[16] Augustine, 'Against the Academicians', in *'Against the Academicians' and 'The Teacher'*, trans. Peter King (Indianapolis, Ind.: Hackett, 1995), 75 (3.11).

[17] Descartes, *Meditations on First Philosophy*, p. 14.

puts it, '[s]keptics questioned every aspect of our ability to know that outside world. Descartes flipped the argument: it wasn't that the magnificence of the world proved God exists, it was that inner knowledge of God could prove that the world exists. Consciousness is suddenly esteemed higher than the universe'.[18]

The traditional story ends with the footnote that Descartes never succeeded in escaping the sceptical problematic he instituted, for if a demon can deceive us into thinking that $2 + 2 = 5$, how do we know that the inference from thoughts ('I' think) to a substance that thinks (I am) isn't just another demon-induced fallacy? Thus, we find ourselves locked in the infamous Cartesian circle: by doubting everything, Descartes set in play the obligations that somehow both knowledge and justified belief must be impervious to error, even as he failed to meet these obligations.[19]

The traditional understanding of Descartes's project is correct on some points. Descartes was revolutionary in the extent to which he believed *scientia* could be extended to cover a relatively wide range of beliefs.[20] (This expectation, once in the mind of Christian apologist and sceptic alike, would create an onerous precedent for later theologians.) Further, Descartes's method of doubt led to not simply a refutation of scepticism but a prima facie distrust of all received tradition. He was convinced that when we pursue *scientia* our thinking is often clouded by the encrustations of tradition: 'These prejudgments are in good measure mistaken; and they inhibit our ability to distinguish reliably the certain from the uncertain. So how do we free ourselves from these mistaken *praejudicia*, so as to be able to construct a *scientia* of pure intuition and deduction—a body of certitude?'[21]

The interpretation comes up short in failing to recognize how in key respects Descartes was very traditional. The common assumption, as Wolterstorff observes, is that Descartes's method advocated a full-blooded scepticism: 'The history of Descartes- interpretation makes it abundantly clear that Descartes invites being interpreted as

[18] Hecht, *Doubt: A History* (New York: HarperSanFrancisco, 2003), 317.

[19] See Barry Stroud, *The Significance of Philosophical Skepticism* (Oxford: Clarendon, 1984), ch. 1. Wolterstorff maintains that Descartes is not arguing in a circular manner, but rather simply fails to ground his conclusion (see his *John Locke*, pp. 201–2).

[20] Wolterstorff, *John Locke*, p. 188.   [21] Ibid.

holding that the goal of the Therapy is to free the mind from almost all assent—to vacuum it of almost all belief'.[22] But in point of fact Descartes never really meant to throw our basic beliefs into question. Rather, his doubt was strictly methodological and, in keeping with the medieval focus, aimed at the specific intra-systemic goal of *scientia*.[23] As such, his adoption of scepticism so as to refute the sceptics was a quintessential ivory-tower exercise, very far from the existential 'Cartesian anxiety' with which it has often been associated. Far from true doubt, it was simply an extension of the scholastic pursuit of *scientia*.[24]

Descartes's philosophy reinforced the rationalist claims of Spanish Jesuit theologians Thyrsus González de Santalla and Miguel de Elizalde that revelation can be demonstrated through rational proofs.[25] And Protestant apologist Philippe de Mornay maintained that the theologian is obliged to argue from principles generally accepted by all—a claim that echoes Cartesian attempts to ground knowledge in universal, rational proofs.[26] Subsequent to Descartes, a growing number of theologians sought to establish rigorous rational demonstrations of Christianity. Leibniz's disciple Christian Wolff invoked logical proofs in *The Method of Demonstrating the Truth of the Christian Religion* in order to demonstrate not only the existence and perfections of God but also the fallenness of humanity, the necessity for divine revelation, and the premise that the Christian Scriptures

---

[22] Wolterstorff, *John Locke*, p. 189.

[23] On page 191 of *John Locke and the Ethics of Belief* Wolterstorff quotes Descartes as stating that no sane person truly doubts the existence of things like an external world. Wolterstorff then illustrates the function of doubt within Descartes's system by quoting Harry Frankfurt: 'Consider the example of a mathematician who is, let us say, attempting to construct a system of arithmetic. If he has so far failed or neglected to establish that "$2 + 2 = 4$" is a theorem of his system, he will quite properly refuse to assume in his inquiry that the equation is true. This is hardly a case of scepticism, and it would be inane to argue, as it has been argued occasionally against Descartes, that the mathematician's refusal is insincere or that his project is absurd because it is psychologically impossible for him to cease believing that $2 + 2 = 4$' (p. 193 n).

[24] Wolterstorff, *John Locke*, p. 181.

[25] Avery Dulles, *A History of Apologetics* (1971; San Francisco: Ignatius, 2005), 156. Further, Dulles observes that in the preface to his *A Demonstration of the Gospel to His Highness, the Dauphin* Pierre Daniel Huet 'explains that the gospel can be proved by reasons as valid in their own order as geometrical demonstrations are in the mathematical order' (*A History of Apologetics*, p. 171).

[26] Ibid. 157.

are that revelation.[27] Robert Boyle reflects these rationalist ambitions of *scientia* with his celebrated lectureship, instituted with the goal of 'proving the Christian religion against notorious infidels, viz., atheists, theist, pagans, Jews, and Mahometans'.[28] The great weakness of this approach would emerge gradually as atheists, theists, pagans, Jews, and 'Mahometans' became less and less deferential to the earnest Christian apologist's proofs.

Locke: Use Your Reason Responsibly

While Descartes was concerned with the relatively narrow ivory-tower project of *scientia*, John Locke sought to develop a broad and inclusive programme for the rational regulation of belief. As with Descartes, Locke's philosophy has often been misunderstood; perhaps the most pervasive misunderstanding of Locke is as a vigorous empiricist who counterbalanced the Continental rationalism of Descartes, Spinoza, and Leibniz. Contrary to this Hegelian reading of European philosophy, Locke was also strongly rationalistic, though his assessment of the limits of rational proof is more sober than Descartes's. Thus, while Locke believed that human beings could attain *scientia* in pure mathematics and morality, he denied that there could be any *scientia* of nature: 'The heart of Locke's argument is that a body of genuine knowledge of nature—a true *scientia*—would require a grasp of the essences of substances; however, our place in nature makes it impossible for us to attain such knowledge'.[29] Locke believed that our knowledge of nature is limited to generalizations based on experience and thus necessarily falls short of *scientia*. He denied that belief is a component of knowledge, asserting instead that knowledge is distinct from belief in being the certain perception of a fact. Locke's gradation of knowledge places the certainty of intuition at the top, followed by demonstrations from intuitive first principles, and then sensitive knowledge, in a descending range of probabilities.[30]

---

[27] *A History of Apologetics* 192.
[28] Cited ibid. 177.
[29] Wolterstorff, *John Locke*, p. 29.
[30] Wolterstorff, *John Locke*, p. 45.

Given that knowledge is very hard to come by, most of the time we will have to content ourselves with belief. As such, it is very important that we seek to regulate belief properly. However, Locke recognized that a rigorous regulation of belief in *all* matters is neither practical nor proper and thus he advocated that we focus our efforts in belief regulation on issues of maximal importance or 'concernment'. As Wolterstorff puts it, '[f]or any proposition of maximal "concernment" which is not intuitively or demonstratively known to be true, Reason is to determine the probability of the proposition on satisfactory evidence, and we are to place a level of confidence in the proposition proportioned to what Reason tells us is that probability'.[31] In this way Locke transformed Descartes's fireside reflections into an epistemic deontology of entitlement with wide social implications.

Locke's epistemology, like that of Descartes, arose out of the tumult of his contemporary society. Locke sought to adjudicate the proliferation of religious sects, each with its own creed and authority, by appealing to the rational man who apportions belief to the evidence and withholds belief when rationality dictates. Locke duly warned: '[I]f strength of Perswasion be the Light, which must guide us; I ask how shall any one distinguish between the delusions of Satan, and the inspirations of the Holy Ghost?'[32] As this comment suggests, the appeal to strength of conviction (or 'perswasion') is inadequate to ground belief:

Because the Mind, not being certain of the Truth of that it does not evidently know, but only yielding to the Probability that appears in it, is bound to give up its Assent to such a Testimony, which, it is satisfied, comes from one, who cannot err, and will not deceive. But yet, it still belongs to *Reason*, to judge of the Truth of its being a Revelation, and of the signification of the Words, wherein it is delivered.[33]

Locke recognizes that *scientia* is an unrealistic standard for religious belief, particularly for the lay person: 'The greatest part of mankind

[31] Wolterstorff, *John Locke*, p. 180.
[32] John Locke, *Essay Concerning Human Understanding*, ed. Peter H. Nidditch (Oxford: Clarendon, 1975), 703–4 (4.19.13).
[33] Ibid. 694 (4.18.8).

want leisure or capacity for Demonstration; nor can they carry a train of Proofs; which in that way they must always depend upon for Conviction, and cannot be required to assent to till they see the Demonstration'.[34] But scepticism was not a real danger, for Locke shared Descartes's confidence that where Christian belief was concerned the demands of reason could be met. After all, since God was eminently reasonable, he would always provide sufficient evidence to justify rationally that which he asks us to believe:

Faith is nothing but a firm Assent of the Mind: which if it be regulated, as is our Duty, cannot be afforded to any thing, but upon good Reason; and so cannot be opposite to it. He that believes, without having any Reason for believing, may be in love with his own fancies; but neither seeks Truth as he ought, nor pays the Obedience due to his Maker, who would have him use those discerning Faculties he has given him, to keep him out of Mistake and Errour.[35]

Locke took the position that while there could be rational assent to the propositions of revelation, one could never be rationally certain of those truths. Rather, one could only judge a proposition as more or less probable relative to the evidence for it as a divine revelation.[36]

Locke defends Christian belief in *The Reasonableness of Christianity*, though, in keeping with his philosophy, that defence fell far short of Cartesian *scientia*. Given that logical proofs are inappropriate and unobtainable, we must ground our faith in appropriate belief rather than knowledge: 'Hearing plain Commands is the sure and only course to bring them to Obedience and Practice. The greatest part cannot know, and therefore they must believe'.[37] Locke then asserts that rather than follow 'abstract reasoning', 'the Instruction of the People were best still to be left to the Precepts and Principles of the Gospel'.[38] Although the laity may not be able to have *knowledge* of faith, the core of Locke's proposal is that it is possible to develop a rational faith in accord with reason, based upon the

[34] Locke, *The Reasonableness of Christianity*, ed. John C. Higgins-Biddle (Oxford: Clarendon, 1999), 157 (14).
[35] Locke, *Essay Concerning Human Understanding*, pp. 687–8 (4.17.24).
[36] Ibid. 667–8 (4.16.14).
[37] Locke, *The Reasonableness of Christianity*, pp. 157–8 (14).
[38] Ibid. 158 (14).

historical personage of Jesus Christ. Thus, in the absence of proof and certainty, one must diligently regulate one's belief about important religious matters by the rigorous pursuit of evidence and argument. Locke's programme for rational religion is well summarized under his famous maxim: '*Reason* must be our last Judge and Guide in every Thing'.[39]

Locke's rationalistic, evidentialist approach to faith had a significant impact upon theology by shifting the focus from proofs to probabilistic evidence. Moreover, rather than limiting his scope to a narrow discussion of *scientia*, Locke sought a comprehensive treatment of all matters of faith and belief. As with Descartes, Locke was fitting into a pre-existing stream that downplayed the idea of rigorous proofs, as unrealistic, while continuing to affirm the importance of evidence.[40] Consequently, a number of seventeenth-century apologists, including Caspar Hurtado and Domingo Banez, advocated the defence of the faith through probabilistic arguments.[41] After Locke, some of the greatest apologists adopted a probabilistic defence of the faith, notably including Joseph Butler. Not surprisingly, there was a significant diversity of opinion among advocates of probabilistic apologetics in terms of which evidence was most likely to establish the rationality of Christianity. With the Enlightenment's emerging historical consciousness, French and English apologists in the eighteenth century gradually shifted their emphasis from philosophical to historical evidence.[42]

Locke certainly did not invent evidentialism; long before his work theologians and philosophers had referred to evidence as the ground of a rational faith. Even Pascal proposed that while arguments from miracles and prophecies could not command the conviction of a proof, they were sufficiently strong 'that one cannot say it is unreasonable to believe'.[43] Locke's significance comes in an extension and intensification of this evidentialist supposition and the corresponding requirements for the regulation of belief. As such, it became a first truth for some that faith depends on the imprimatur of reason. As

---

[39] Locke, *Essay Concerning Human Understanding*, p. 704 (4.19.14).
[40] For instance, Gregory of Valencia (d. 1603) argued that the evidences for (Catholic) Christian faith falls short of demonstrations (Dulles, *A History of Apologetics*, p. 154).
[41] Ibid. 155.   [42] Ibid. 197.   [43] Cited at ibid. 164.

Samuel Clarke put it,' 'tis evident there can never possibly be any Authority upon Earth, sufficient to oblige any man to receive any thing as of divine Revelation, which it cannot make appear to that Man's own Understanding (sincerely studying and inquiring after the Truth) to be included in that Revelation'.[44]

While the adverse impact of Locke's evidentialism was initially attenuated by the widespread assumption that the evidence supported Christianity, within a few generations that assumption would be under direct attack by atheists and agnostics. And with this doubt the suspicion began to grow that theologians had failed to provide the necessary evidential grounds to entitle them to hold their religious beliefs and engage in their discipline. The transformation of evidentialism into an objection to Christianity (and theology) arguably reached its apogee in mathematician and amateur philosopher William K. Clifford's famous essay 'The Ethics of Belief'. Clifford appears to see every belief as a possible threat:

No real belief, however trifling and fragmentary it may seem, is ever truly insignificant; it prepares us to receive more of its like, confirms those which resembled it before, and weakens others; and so gradually it lays a stealthy train in our inmost thoughts, which may some day explode into overt action, and leave its stamp upon our character forever.[45]

According to Clifford, believing is a serious business and as such we had better be sure that we do it responsibly. Indeed, one might think that belief regulation becomes for Clifford almost an obsession when he shrilly warns: 'Whoso would deserve well of his fellows in this matter will guard the purity of his belief with a very fanaticism of jealous care, lest at any time it should rest on an unworthy object, and catch a stain which can never be wiped away'.[46] Clifford memorably summarized his position in a jolting maxim of epistemic propriety: 'To sum up: it is wrong always, everywhere, and for anyone, to believe anything upon insufficient evidence'.[47] Unfortunately, by this time a

[44] Clarke, 'The Scripture Doctrine of the Trinity', in *Classics of Protestantism*, ed. Vergilius Ferm (New York: Philosophical Library, 1959), 132.

[45] Clifford, 'The Ethics of Belief', in his *Lectures and Essays*, ii (London: Macmillan, 1901), 169.

[46] Ibid. 171.

[47] Clifford, 'The Ethics of Belief', p.174. For a critique of Clifford's principle see Peter van Inwagen, 'It Is Wrong, Everywhere, Always, and for Anyone, to Believe

growing number were convinced that Christianity lacked the sufficient evidence.

For much of the twentieth century theology has continued to labor under the yoke of the Cartesian and Lockean 'defences' of Christianity. Consider, for instance, early twentieth-century Catholic theologian John Brunsmann's claim that fundamental theology is essential to 'demonstrate with scientific accuracy that the religion which is embodied in the Catholic Church is based on divine supernatural revelation and that, consequently, the belief which the Church demands in the revealed truths which she proposes, can be fully justified before the tribunal of reason'.[48] Brunsmann seems rather unaware of the extent to which the purportedly neutral tribunal of reason was shaped by Descartes and Locke. Regardless, his assumption results in the rationality of Christian faith depending upon the shock and awe of irrefutable proofs and overwhelming evidences:

Belief in supernatural revelation is not rational unless the credibility of that revelation has been demonstrated with sufficient evidence. Before we can make an act of faith in divine revelation, we must be certain that such a revelation has actually taken place. Fundamental Theology presents in scientific form solid and convincing proofs of this fact, the acceptance of which is a necessary condition of real faith.[49]

Thus, Brunsmann assumes that the public justification of theology depends upon the identification of rational proofs to ground theology; indeed, such evidences even provide the *necessary condition for real faith*! Given that a growing number of theologians would share Clifford's scepticism that theology could produce the required proofs and/or evidences, theology would begin to look increasingly like Humpty Dumpty after his fall—and all the apologists and fundamental theologians couldn't put systematic theology back together again.

Anything upon Insufficient Evidence', in his *The Possibility of Resurrection and Other Essays in Christian Apologetics* (Boulder, Col.: Westview, 1998), 2–44.

[48] Brunsmann, *A Handbook of Fundamental Theology*, i, trans. Arthur Preuss (St Louis, Miss./London: Herder, 1928), 5.

[49] Ibid. 6–7.

Kant: Putting Reason in its Place

Perhaps you are thinking that things cannot get much worse. Well, it is time now to turn to Immanuel Kant, who was awoken from his slumbers by David Hume. (In retrospect, one might wish that Kant had kept sleeping.) The Humean argument that shook Kant consisted of a secularized version of Malebranche's occasionalism combined with a healthy dose of Lockean scepticism regarding our ability to gain knowledge of substance. According to Hume, reason is not so much a special faculty that enables us to grasp the nature of reality as it is a matter of habit that reflects our own psychological make-up. To take one example, when it comes to beliefs about causation, Hume argued that we never actually witness efficient causal relations; thus, all our causal beliefs are rooted not in reason but in habit. (For instance, my belief that the fire will burn my hand reveals my own psychological dispositions, but nothing about the nature of fire or flesh.) But even as Kant recognized that Hume presented a debilitating challenge to the pretensions of reason, he remained dazzled by the explanatory power of Newtonian science. So how does one bring these two together? How do you explain our ability to predict with reason if reason is but a habit rather than a penetrating insight into the nature of things?

Kant responded by proposing his famous 'Copernican shift'. Just as Copernicus argued that intractable astronomical problems could be addressed by making the earth go around the sun, so Kant proposed that intractable epistemological problems could be addressed by making the world conform to the mind. That is, instead of thinking of knowledge as the mind's adequation to reality, we ought to think of it as reality's adequation to the mind. As a result, the only world we can speak of is that which conforms to our innate cognitive categories. For Kant, time and space were the two most fundamental categories; but even though they are essential for thought, we cannot infer their objective reality beyond our experience. The same is true for the twelve additional structuring categories of the mind by which Kant proposed we order all experience. To take one example, Kant proposed that causation is a mental concept. That being so, he could address Hume's dilemma by affirming causal relations relative to our essential categories of thought without affirming causation in the world. Kant could concede Hume's point while still providing a privileged place for Newtonian science within the structure of our minds.

What about the knowledge of God? After all, if everything is of necessity structured by the categories so that there can be no experience of the world in itself, then it would seem that *there can be no revelation* of God. Not surprisingly, Kant's dichotomy had a devastating impact upon theology. Kant, however, saw this as a radical means to re-establish theology. In his words: 'I have therefore found it necessary to deny *knowledge*, in order to make room for *faith*'.[50] In contrast to theologians like Aquinas who believed that some truths of God can be known by reason (e.g. that God exists), Kant was consistent in asserting that one could know nothing of God by reason. But even if we could not know God through theoretical reason, Kant allowed for knowledge of God through practical reason—the reasoning of ethical action. This amounted to restoring theology as a subset of ethics, a task which Kant pursued in his *Critique of Practical Reason*. Within this book Kant develops an important axiological argument for God's existence, reasoning from the current lack of justice in the world to a posthumous establishment of justice and a divine judge to guarantee it.

And so Kant put the kibosh on unrestricted human reason and in that sense he offered modest relief to the theologian. But at what a cost! The theologian may have been rendered an equal with the scientist, but that simply meant we could say strictly *nothing* about God for the simple reason that God could say nothing to us. Any theologian insistent on an object of theological discourse would have to find a creative new way to reintroduce that object.

CONCLUSION

Looking back, we can see the extent to which Descartes, Locke, and Kant all operated unwittingly as gravediggers for the theological

---

[50] Immanuel Kant, 'Preface to Second Edition', in his *Critique of Pure Reason*, trans. Norman Kemp Smith (New York: St Martin's, 1929), 29.

enterprise. In the upheaval left by a fractured tradition, each sought a new ground of stability. If there is one theme shared by these three great philosophers, we find it in the forging of a general climate of scepticism regarding the pretensions of theology. This sceptical climate is evident in the low estimate of tradition held by Descartes and Locke. Rather than seeing wisdom in tradition, both viewed it as a source of prejudice warranting critical doubt. As Wolterstorff writes, 'Descartes insisted, we must free ourselves from these *praejudicia*; we do so not by working through our intellectual inheritance in dialectical fashion but only by submitting the whole of it to the Therapy of Doubt. To the things themselves, said Locke!'[51] Kant then enters with an even more sombre note. As sceptical as Descartes and Locke, he nonetheless denied that we could escape the categorical limitations of our minds. In response to Locke's naive 'To the things themselves' he would reply 'To the things *for us*'. In the midst of the bickering between these great minds, the traditional discipline of theology would be left to languish. Hence, while each offers a form of scepticism, they are all complemented by a growing *pessimism*. Since Descartes's scepticism is narrowly limited to the academic's formal pursuit of *scientia*, there is a radical shift with Locke, who is convinced that there is little we can know with certainty, and thus that our primary focus must be upon the regulation of belief in accord with reason. Finally, Kant abandoned *any* attempt to know the world, and with this the increasingly difficult task of theology was finally rendered impossible.

[51] Wolterstorff, *John Locke*, pp. 224–5.

2

Justifying Theology in Reason and Experience

No man has a right to hang the millstone of his philosophy around the neck of the truth of God.

Charles Hodge, *Systematic Theology*

We have to get over our monomaniacal fixation on truth and on what's the case when dealing with the Bible.

Nicholas Wolterstorff, 'True Words'

It is the early 1930s and a young entrepreneur is concerned to secure the future of his fledgling aviation company. After receiving counsel from friends that airships are the future of aviation, he invests heavily in his own fleet, only to watch his fortune go up in flames when the Hindenburg goes down in flames. Sadly this entrepreneur would discover that instead of securing his company's competiveness, his capital investment would actually speed its demise. In retrospect, Descartes, Locke, and Kant were selling airships which inadvertently sped a similar demise for Christian theology. The first wave of airships came with those theologians who accepted the Cartesian demand for *scientia* through rational arguments and the Lockean regulation of belief in accord with the quality of evidence. This is where we will begin our survey, as we consider the attempt to justify theology through natural theology and the inspiration and inerrancy of Scripture.

While both of these avenues to theological justification assumed a substantial cataphatic ground for theological discourse, it is precisely this that Kant challenged. Thus, a new wave of airships went on sale as (to switch metaphors) theologians now sought to nurture their discipline in the pale light of austere Kantianism. Showing great innovation with the meagre resources of near-absolute apophaticism and the continuing demand of universal reason, they carved out space for a mystical, experiential ground for theology. We will evaluate this approach to theological justification by critiquing the work of John Baillie and David Tracy. Through this survey we will be able to gain an initial assessment of the problems with and prospects for the various attempts to justify theology via classical foundationalism.

JUSTIFYING THEOLOGY IN PROOFS AND EVIDENCE

Traditionally, theology has been concerned with the development and defence of doctrines and the theoretical frameworks by which we understand them. Against an evidentialist backdrop, one is obliged to seek a priori (rational) or a posteriori (evidential) grounds by which to justify theological claims and methods. The assumption is thus that theology can only be justified as a public-knowledge discourse if one can offer adequate evidence for it. The Cartesian assumes that these grounds have to be compelling proofs, while the Lockean is content with belief held relative to the strength of solid evidence. However, historically these neat categories have rarely been recognized; indeed, many theologians have mixed and matched Cartesian and Lockean themes in their justification projects. So, rather than attempt to identify token Cartesians and Lockeans, we will focus on the general project of defending theology through rational argument, first in proofs and evidence which support natural theology and then in those which defend biblical inspiration and inerrancy.

And this Everyone Understands to be God

When there is no longer widespread agreement on theological particulars, one must retreat to generally demonstrable truths. Thus, the dissolution of religious agreement in the West gave a new impetus to develop rigorous defences of the existence and nature of God as the ground on which to defend specifically Christian claims.

In essence, theism *simpliciter* became the outer court prior to entry to the Christian sanctuary. The more sceptical and pluralist the culture became, the more natural theology assumed a new level of urgency. The precedent was laid in medieval scholasticism when natural theology reached new heights with the work of theologians like Anselm (*Monologium*; *Proslogium*) and Aquinas (*Summa Contra Gentiles*). Once Christianity began to fracture during the Renaissance and Reformation, the function of these arguments began to shift from being an offensive and evangelistic appeal to the sceptic to a defensive justification of the theologian.[1] As a result, arguments for the existence of God assumed a new importance that saw their placement at the beginning of theological enquiry instead of posterior to discussions of the divine attributes.[2] The new order is vividly captured in the Puritan classic *The Existence and Attributes of God*, where Stephen Charnock observes: 'It is fit we should know why we believe, that our belief of a God may appear to be upon undeniable evidence, and that we may give a better reason for his existence'.[3] Charnock reflects a widespread confidence when he refers to the quality of his evidence: 'For the first, every atheist is a grand fool. If he were not a fool, he would not imagine a thing so contrary to the stream of the universal reason of the world, contrary to the rational dictates of his own soul, and contrary to the testimony of every creature'.[4] For Charnock, the evidence for God's existence is available to every rational individual, while atheism simply contradicts the overwhelming evidence of reason: 'Men that will not listen to Scripture, as having no counterpart of it in their souls, cannot easily deny natural reason, which riseth up on all sides for the justification of this truth'.[5]

Given that reason supported Christianity from 'all sides', cumulative-case approaches were especially popular, by which theologians would marshal a number of convincing proofs for God's existence

[1] As Avery Dulles observes, following the Renaissance '[f]or the first time in history, orthodox Christians felt constrained to prove the existence of God and the possibility and fact of revelation' (*A History of Apologetics* (1971; San Francisco: Ignatius, 2005), 206).

[2] Thomas Oden, *Systematic Theology, i. The Living God* (San Francisco, Calif.: Harper & Row, 1992/Peabody, Mass.: Prince, 1998), 134.

[3] Charnock, *The Existence and Attributes of God* (1682; Grand Rapids, Mich.: Baker, 1996), 26.

[4] Ibid. 25.   [5] Ibid. 27.

and attributes. For instance, nineteenth-century Baptist theologian Augustus Strong begins with an argument that the truth-conduciveness of both induction and deduction (and thus all reason) depends upon God: '[H]e who denies God's existence must tacitly assume that existence in his very argument, by employing logical processes whose validity rests upon the fact of God's existence'.[6] Next, Strong erects a number of impressive a posteriori and a priori arguments on this foundation that combine to form an unanswerable cumulative case for God.[7]

While some theologians considered their arguments for God's existence to constitute proofs, others were more modest, believing them merely to be sufficient to make faith rational. Theologians likewise held a range of views on which doctrines of special revelation could be rooted in natural theology. For instance, seventeenth-century theologian/philosopher Samuel Clarke ambitiously proclaimed that natural theology establishes God's existence and identity as creator and revealer:

There is *One* Supreme Cause and Original of Things; *One* simple, uncompounded, undivided, *intelligent Agent*, or *Person*; who is the Author of all Being, and the Fountain of all Power. This is the *Great Foundation* of all Piety; the *First Principle of Natural Religion*, and every where supposed in the *Scripture Revelation*.[8]

A. A. Hodge was even more optimistic, declaring that 'Natural Theology ascertains for us an infinite, eternal, wise, and absolutely righteous and benevolent personal God'.[9] Indeed, Hodge went on to add that natural theology

ascertains also that man created in the divine image is morally corrupt and judicially condemned. It reveals to us man needing divine help, yearning and hoping for it, and therefore not incapable of it, as are the finally lost demons. Therefore all the perfections of God, and all the miseries of men, lead to the rational hope that at some time and in some way God may be graciously

---

[6] Strong, *Systematic Theology* (Valley Forge, Pa.: Judson, 1907), 59.

[7] Strong, *Systematic Theology*, p. 111 ff. Similarly, A. A. Hodge invokes a battery of cosmological, teleological, moral, and ontological arguments for God's existence, and the necessity of revelation in light of original sin (*Outlines of Theology*, enlarged edn. (London: Banner of Truth Trust, 1972), 44–5).

[8] Clarke, 'The Scripture Doctrine of the Trinity', in *Classics of Protestantism*, ed. Vergilius Ferm (New York: Philosophical Library, 1959), 141.

[9] Hodge, *Outlines of Theology*, p. 61.

disposed to intervene supernaturally for man's help, and reveal his character and purposes more fully for man's guidance.[10]

So, according to Hodge natural theology grounds not only the existence and attributes of God, but also the fall of humanity and salvific intent of God, resulting in a fully rational hope.

Impressive though these arguments may be, nonetheless many theologians today dismiss them as theological equivalents of a Rube Goldberg machine: a system of labyrinthine complexity that accomplishes nothing.[11] Such dismissals are due in no small part to the famous attacks upon the enterprise by David Hume and Immanuel Kant. Unfortunately, it is an underreported fact among theologians that neither Hume nor Kant provides a compelling critique.[12] Others reject natural theology because it fails to achieve the Cartesian gold standard of rational proof and universal assent. Millard Erickson thus asserts: 'If the arguments are valid and are adequately presented, any rational person should be convinced'.[13] But here too the objection is less than convincing, for we do not demand universally compelling proofs for other arguments, so it is inconsistent to penalize natural theology for failing to achieve this gold standard. Alvin Plantinga made the point in the preface to the 1990 edition of his classic work *God and Other Minds*:

There may be plenty of good arguments for theism even if there aren't any that start from propositions that compel assent from every honest and intelligent person and proceed majestically to their conclusion by way of forms of argument that can be rejected only on pain of irrationality. After all, no philosophical arguments of any consequence meet *that* standard.[14]

---

[10] Ibid.

[11] There are always exceptions, of course; a minority have maintained vigorous optimism regarding the potential of natural theology. See, for example, R. C. Sproul, J. Gerstner, and A. Lindsley, *Classical Apologetics* (Grand Rapids, Mich.: Zondervan, 1984). For a critique of Sproul et al. see Kelly James Clark, *Return to Reason* (Grand Rapids, Mich.: Eerdmans, 1990), 47–53.

[12] But see John Earman, *Hume's Abject Failure: The Argument Against Miracles* (Oxford: Oxford University Press, 2000); Plantinga, *God and Other Minds: A Study of the Rational Justification of Belief in God* (Ithaca, NY: Cornell University Press, 1990), 2–38.

[13] Erickson, *Christian Theology*, 2nd edn. (Grand Rapids, Mich.: Baker, 1998), 185.

[14] Plantinga, 'Preface to the 1990 Paperback Edition,' in *God and Other Minds* (Ithaca, NY: Cornell University Press, 1990), pp. ix–x; see also Stephen T. Davis, *God, Reason and Theistic Proofs* (Grand Rapids, Mich.: Eerdmans, 1997), ch. 5.

The fact is that natural theology is alive and well on planet Earth. For evidence of the fact one need only peruse the latest issue of *Philosophia Christi* or *Faith and Philosophy* or one of the many recent monographs published in the field.[15]

The problem is not natural theology per se but rather its inability to shoulder the full demands of modernist evidentialism. Pascal observed that the arguments of natural theology are simply not adequate to ground belief of the strength that the Christian requires: 'The metaphysical proofs of God are so remote from men's reasoning and so complicated that they make little impression. And when they are of service to some, it is only for the instant during which they see this demonstration. But an hour later they fear they have been mistaken.'[16] Even if the arguments were much stronger than they in fact are, it is still doubtful that they would suffice to ground belief. As James Beilby observes, '[o]ne cannot base "firm and unwavering" belief in Christianity on an argument the conclusion of which is that the probability of theism on the public evidence is 0.9, or even 0.999.'[17] Thus, if we really are obliged to calibrate our faith to the strength of our evidence or proofs, we will be forever teetering between pious conviction and conformist fideism.

Our best hope to ground faith in natural theology is probably found in the work of Richard Swinburne.[18] In the great tradition of seventeenth-century apologetics, Swinburne argues for the existence of God, the possibility and actuality of revelation, the triunity of God, and the resurrection of Christ, all based on natural reason. But while the cumulative argument is an enormously impressive achievement, when one multiplies the probabilities from the various arguments together one encounters the problem of dwindling probabilities.[19]

[15] For example, William Lane Craig and J. P. Moreland (eds.), *The Blackwell Companion to Natural Theology* (Oxford: Blackwell, 2009).

[16] Blaise Pascal, *Pensées*, ed. and trans. Roger Ariew (Indianapolis, Ind./ Cambridge: Hackett, 2005), 55–6.

[17] Beilby, *Epistemology as Theology: An Evaluation of Alvin Plantinga's Religious Epistemology* (Aldershot: Ashgate, 2005), 140.

[18] Among Swinburne's many important books are *Responsibility and Atonement* (Oxford: Clarendon, 1989); *Revelation* (Oxford: Clarendon, 2007); *The Christian God* (Oxford: Clarendon, 1994); *Providence and the Problem of Evil* (Oxford: Oxford University Press, 1998); *The Resurrection of God Incarnate* (Oxford: Clarendon, 2003).

[19] Plantinga, *Warranted Christian Belief* (Oxford: Oxford University Press, 2000), 272–80. For further debate see Timothy McGrew, 'Has Plantinga Refuted the

In order to calculate a series of probabilities they must be multiplied, and this leads to a diminishing cumulative probability with each multiplication. (For instance, if the probability of p is 0.9 and the probability of q is 0.9, then the probability of p and q is 0.81.) As a result, the more doctrines we seek to establish on the ground of natural theology—the existence of God, revelation, the Trinity, incarnation, resurrection, and so on—the lower the total, cumulative probability. To make matters worse, Swinburne observes rather modestly that on the very first point—the existence of God—the total evidence only makes the truth of the proposition 'more probable than not'.[20] But if our starting point is that a minimal *theism* is only more probable than 0.5, how low does the cumulative probability drop when we factor in revelation, the Trinity, incarnation, atonement, and resurrection?[21] While this seems to be a serious problem for evidentialism, one should not conclude—as many theologians have—that natural theology is thus of little value. Even if natural theology fails to provide arguments of the rigour demanded by Descartes and Locke, it still may fulfil other crucial functions.[22]

The Justification of an Inspired Text

Important though natural theology may be, without an equally vigorous defence of specifically Christian revelation it would be of little use to the theologian. Thus, many theologians have sought to extend persuasive arguments to Scripture, reasoning that '[b]ecause the Bible *is* God's word . . . it provides humanity with an Archimedean vantage point of timeless and unchanging truth; therefore, we possess

Historical Argument?', *Philosophia Christi*, 6/1 (2004), 7–26; Alvin Plantinga, 'Historical Arguments and Dwindling Probabilities: A Response to Timothy McGrew', *Philosophia Christi*, 8/1 (2006), 7–22; Timothy McGrew and Lydia McGrew, 'On the Historical Argument: A Rejoinder to Plantinga', *Philosophia Christi*, 8/1 (2006), 23–38.

[20] Richard Swinburne, *The Existence of God*, rev. edn. (Oxford: Clarendon, 1991), 291.

[21] The problem exists even if we grant Swinburne's claim that the probability that God became incarnate as Jesus and that Jesus rose from the dead is 0.97 (see his *The Resurrection of God Incarnate*, p. 214).

[22] As Pascal observed, '[t]here is enough light to enlighten the chosen and enough darkness to humble them. There is enough darkness to blind the reprobate and enough clarity to condemn them and leave them without excuse' (*Pensées*, p. 70).

indubitable certainty as it concerns the knowledge of God'.[23] While classic Protestants and Catholics would agree on Scripture's inspired and inerrant authority, they have differed over the perceived need for an authoritative interpreter of that inerrant authority: while the Protestant focuses upon the Spirit's guidance and Scripture's perspicacity, Catholics have sought an epistemological guarantee in the authority of the magisterium.[24] Within Catholicism, the Enlightenment demand for certainty spurred on the development of papal infallibility,[25] culminating in the Vatican I Declaration.[26] While one may debate the extent to which infallibility was promulgated as a response to modernity, ever since Vatican I Catholics have appealed to its epistemological authority—as when Karl Keating reasons: 'For men to be saved, they must know what is to be believed. They must have a perfectly steady rock to build on when it comes to official teaching, and that is why papal infallibility exists'.[27]

Even if we grant that natural theology provides powerful evidence that there is a God who could be expected to reveal his will to human beings,[28] what evidence do we have to think that this revelation is found in the Christian Scriptures? This question has often been answered through the amassing of internal and external evidence drawn from a variety of sources, including the character of the writers, the quality of the writings, the unity of the Scriptures, the fulfilment of predictive prophecy, and evidence for specific miracles attested therein (notably the resurrection).[29] For instance, in his

---

[23] Steven B. Sherman is here summarizing the early views of Clark Pinnock (Sherman, *Revitalizing Theological Epistemology: Holistic Evangelical Approaches to the Knowledge of God* (Eugene, Ore.: Pickwick, 2008), 33.

[24] While Millard Erickson claims that there is a functional equivalency between papal authority and Protestant views of scriptural authority (*Christian Theology*, p. 272), in my view papal infallibility more closely parallels the Protestant doctrine of scriptural perspicacity.

[25] Pascal observed: 'We like certainty, we like the Pope to be infallible in faith and for grave doctors to be so in morals, in order to be reassured' (*Pensées*, p.140).

[26] See Hans Küng, *Does God Exist?*, trans. Edward Quinn (Garden City, NY: Doubleday, 1980; New York: Vintage, 1981), 25.

[27] Keating, *Catholicism and Fundamentalism: The Attack on 'Romanism' by 'Bible Christians'* (San Francisco: Ignatius, 1988), 231.

[28] As Swinburne argues in *Revelation: From Metaphor to Analogy* (Oxford: Clarendon, 2007), chs. 5–6.

[29] If successful, such evidence could address the problem of 'how to know that *this* book, the Christian Bible, is in fact the expected revelation' (Nancey Murphy,

Baker Encyclopedia of Christian Apologetics[30] Norman Geisler defends scriptural inspiration through both inductive evidence and deductive proof. In the entry 'Bible, Evidence for' Geisler confidently asserts that the amassed evidence for the Bible's claim to be inspired is simply 'overwhelming'.[31] Among this evidence Geisler cites the exemplary character of the writers, for '[t]hey taught the highest standard of ethics, including the obligation to always tell the truth'.[32] In addition, Geisler appeals to the evidence of miracles and the unity of the Scriptures, which is all the more remarkable given that the Bible consists of writings composed by dozens of men spanning centuries. Geisler claims that this unity is so profound that it can only be plausibly explained through the planning of a divine mind.[33] When all these arguments are put together we conclude that the Bible 'alone, of all books known to humankind, needs a God to account for its unity in diversity'.[34] Geisler provides further proofs for scriptural inspiration in the entry 'Prophecy, as Proof of the Bible', where he cites the enormous improbability of Christ fulfilling Old Testament prophecies by chance: 'That forty-eight predictions might meet in one person, the probability is 1 in 10^{157}'.[35] Obviously, with such dizzying improbabilities at play, the only *rational* conclusion to draw is that Jesus was in fact the divine fulfilment of these prophecies, a fact that allows us

Beyond Liberalism and Fundamentalism: How Modern and Postmodern Philosophy Set the Theological Agenda (Valley Forge, Pa.: Trinity, 1996), 14).

[30] Geisler, *Baker Encyclopedia of Christian Apologetics* (Grand Rapids, Mich.: Baker, 1999).

[31] Geisler, 'Bible, Evidence for', in *Baker Encyclopedia of Christian Apologetics*, p. 93.

[32] Ibid. But how does one reconcile approval of genocide and human sacrifice (the implications of *cherem* warfare) with 'high standards of ethics'? Geisler offers no help here. So, he is vulnerable to critics like Christopher Hitchens: 'Then there is the very salient question of what the [ten] commandments do *not* say. Is it too modern to notice that there is nothing about the protection of children from cruelty, nothing about rape, nothing about slavery, and nothing about genocide? Or is it too exactly "in context" to notice that some of these very offenses are about to be positively recommended?'(*God is not Great* (New York: Twelve, 2007), 100).

[33] Geisler, 'Bible, Evidence for', pp. 94–5.   [34] Ibid. 95.

[35] Geisler, 'Prophecy, as Proof of the Bible', in *Baker Encyclopedia of Christian Apologetics*, p. 613. Not surprisingly, Geisler rejects all attempts to 'postdate' prophecies.

to accept the authority of Scripture with supreme confidence.[36] Thus, we may conclude that the Bible alone can prove its own claim to be the unique and inspired divine Word.[37]

Conservatives have viewed inerrancy as epistemologically necessary to defend and justify theology. Thus, even though discussion of this theologumenon has abated in recent years (peaking as it did in the late 1970s[38]), inerrancy appears to retain a disproportionate importance in a number of Evangelical-institutional confessions. For instance, the two confessional requirements for membership in the Evangelical Theological Society are biblical inerrancy and the Trinity—in that order. And the Chicago Statement on Biblical Inerrancy[39] has been compared in importance by some Evangelicals to the Creed of Nicaea. The epistemological necessity of inerrancy arises from the need to ensure that one's beliefs truly are incorrigible. As Millard Erickson observes, '[o]ur need for certainty is in direct proportion to the importance of what is at stake; in matters of eternal consequence, we need a certainty that human reasoning cannot provide'.[40] And, as Harold Lindsell puts it, '[f]or anyone who professes the Christian faith the root question is: From where do I get my knowledge on which my faith is based?'[41] Thus, the doctrine of inerrancy has often served as the means to secure the scriptural foundation of Christianity.[42] Jonathan R. Wilson explains the centrality of inerrancy for the articles of faith at Westmont College: 'On more than one occasion, I have heard a Westmont faculty member say that our Articles of Faith begin with this confession because once you have the

---

[36] While Geisler does not explicitly say that these types of arguments are necessary to justify belief in scriptural authority, he certainly does imply that failure to believe in light of this evidence is a sign of irrationality.

[37] Geisler, 'Bible, Evidence for', p. 95.

[38] But see G. K. Beale, *The Erosion of Inerrancy in Evangelicalism: Responding to New Challenges to Biblical Authority* (Wheaton, Ill.: Crossway, 2008).

[39] The statement was produced in 1978 by a cadre of Evangelical and fundamentalist theologians including J. I. Packer, James Boice, and Norman Geisler. It is reprinted in Wayne Grudem, *Systematic Theology: An Introduction to Bible Doctrine* (Grand Rapids, Mich.: Zondervan, 1994), 1203–7.

[40] Erickson, *Christian Theology*, p. 273.

[41] Lindsell, *The Battle for the Bible* (Grand Rapids, Mich.: Zondervan, 1977), 17.

[42] Ibid. 18.

inerrancy of Scripture, the rest of our faith follows ineluctably'.[43] So, it is hardly surprising that conservatives have vociferously defended this doctrine, since the loss of it will threaten to destabilize the entire edifice of belief.

Since inerrancy would have little credibility if it were a mere ad hoc postulate, inerrantists have grounded the doctrine's epistemological necessity in conceptual necessity, claiming that it follows necessarily from biblical inspiration. The claim is that in virtue of his omniscience and omnipotence God is able to prevent any errors from entering an inspired text, while divine omnibenevolence ensures that he would wish to do so. Erickson explains:

If God is omniscient, he must know all things. He cannot be ignorant of or in error on any matter. Further, if he is omnipotent, he is able to so affect the biblical author's writing that nothing erroneous enters into the final product. And being a truthful or veracious being, he will certainly desire to utilize these abilities in such a way that humans will not be misled by the Scriptures. *Thus, our view of inspiration logically entails the inerrancy of the Bible.*[44]

Similarly, Lindsell claims: 'Inspiration involved infallibility from start to finish. God the Holy Spirit by nature cannot lie or be the author of untruth. If the Scripture is inspired at all it must be infallible. If any part of it is not infallible, then that part cannot be inspired. If inspiration allows for the possibility of error then inspiration ceases to be inspiration'.[45] These claims to the conceptual necessity of inerrancy are so strong that Lindsell seems to suggest that 'All inspired texts are inerrant' is an analytic truth of the same order as 'All bachelors are unmarried'. It is difficult to conceive a more robust defence of inerrancy than this. If successful, the argument would be sufficient to ground the truth of every claim in Scripture from the account of a floating axe head to that of a rising Messiah.[46]

[43] 'Toward a New Evangelical Paradigm of Biblical Authority', in Timothy R. Phillips and Dennis L. Okholm (eds.), *The Nature of Confession: Evangelicals and Postliberals in Conversation* (Downers Grove, Ill.: InterVarsity, 1996), 154.
[44] Erickson, *Christian Theology*, p. 251; emphasis added.
[45] Lindsell, *The Battle for the* Bible, p. 31.
[46] Conversely, William Culbertson could warn that '[t]he root from which all heresy springs is a faulty view of the inspiration and inerrancy of the Word of God' (cited in Lindsell, *The Battle for the Bible*, p. 152).

On the downside, if one assumes that inerrancy is epistemologically essential, and one comes to doubt that Scripture is inerrant, then one might find the whole edifice of belief thrown into doubt. In *Misquoting Jesus* Bart Ehrman recounts how, as a young theological conservative, his faith came to depend upon the full, inerrant inspiration of Scripture.[47] As a result, when he discovered that in Mark 2 Jesus referred to Abiathar being high priest during the time when Ahimelech was high priest, he found his whole faith under threat. Determined to meet the problem head-on, Ehrman wrote a detailed if implausible paper attempting to resolve the error. At the end of the paper the professor wrote one comment that pierced to Ehrman's heart: 'Maybe Mark just made a mistake'.[48] That simple comment marked the first step on Ehrman's journey toward agnosticism. For him at least, inerrancy had failed at the point when it was most needed.

Can Inerrancy Justify Theology?

Unfortunately, all the great efforts to justify theology by appeal to inerrancy founder on the fallibility of hermeneutics and the absence of the autographs. The hermeneutical issue involves two problems. To begin with, we face the general problem that an inerrant text does not ensure inerrant interpretation. If I read Scripture with the inerrancy doctrine of J. I. Packer and Wayne Grudem, but have not proper hermeneutics, my interpretation is a resounding gong or a clanging cymbal. But then what good is it to defend the claim that everything the Bible asserts is true, if one fails to understand what it is asserting? Jehovah's Witnesses hold as vigorously to an inerrant biblical text as any fundamentalist Christian, and yet it has done them little good. Indeed, it is revealing to observe how quickly conservatives have been forced to recalibrate inerrancy to specify the 'correct' range of legitimate interpretations; consider, for instance, when the Chicago Statement on Biblical Inerrancy tacitly implies a six-day creation and universal flood as a corollary of inerrancy (article 12). And to

---

[47] Ehrman, *Misquoting Jesus: The Story Behind Who Changed the Bible and Why* (New York: HarperSanFrancisco, 2005), 11.

[48] Ibid. 9.

make the range of legitimate interpretations of the inerrant text even clearer, the Chicago Statement on Biblical Hermeneutics was released a few years later in order to outline the legitimate boundaries in interpreting the inerrant text.[49] But once such ancillary requirements have been added, inerrancy has lost its epistemological punch.

A second hermeneutical problem arises with the empirical observation that a commitment to the necessity of establishing inerrancy predisposes one to misinterpret and thus abuse the text. This type of distortion arises when theologians feel constrained to redress every apparent error in the text to the point where they adopt very doubtful interpretations of the 'problem' passages. For instance, in addressing whether the cock crowed once or twice prior to Peter's denial, Harold Lindsell argued that Peter in fact denied Jesus *six times* with the cock crowing subsequent to both the third and sixth denials.[50] While this may be *possible*, it seems rather like the propositional tail wagging the narrational dog. John Perry thus concludes: '[T]he constraints of modern philosophy caused evangelicals to care so much about detailed inerrancy that all apparent difficulties must be reconciled, no matter how great the exegetical sacrifice'.[51]

In an echo of Maslow's famous observation that when your only tool is a hammer everything looks like a nail, for the inerrantist every linguistic utterance begins to look like a proposition. As a result, inerrantists tend to de-emphasize the non-propositional portions of Scripture. This is a serious problem, since, as Kevin Vanhoozer observes, '[n]ot every sentence in the Bible conveys a proposition that requires our beliefs. There are commands that require our obedience, and promises that solicit our trust'.[52] On this view, the propositions

---

[49] See Norman Geisler, *Explaining Hermeneutics: A Commentary on the Chicago Statement on Biblical Hermeneutics* (Oakland, Calif.: International Council on Biblical Inerrancy, 1983).

[50] See Lindsell, *The Battle for the Bible*, pp. 174–6.

[51] Perry, 'Dissolving the Inerrancy Debate: How Modern Philosophy Shaped the Evangelical View of Scripture', *Quodlibet Journal*, 3/4 (2001), at <http://www.quodlibet.net/perry-inerrancy.shtml>.

[52] Vanhoozer, 'Disputing about Words? Of Fallible Foundations and Modest Metanarratives', in Myron B. Penner (ed.), *Christianity and the Postmodern Turn: Six Views* (Grand Rapids, Mich.: Brazos, 2005), 196. Similarly, Nicholas Wolterstorff writes: 'There are a great many assertions in Scripture, and I am all for raising the question of truth about those. But we also find in Scripture an abundance of questions, commands, optatives, blessings—you name it. If we approach any of these with the

emerge as more important to the justification of the text, whilst promises, questions, and commands are reduced to being a dispensable linguistic husk to the propositional kernel.[53] To make matters worse, as narrative theologians have reminded us, these propositions, promises, questions, and commands all come embedded in a greater literary context. As such, the task of understanding Scripture is much more complex than interpreting a collection of sentences. Gordon Fee and Mark Strauss describe the challenge:

> Some people say, 'Just tell me what the Bible says, not what it means.' The problem with this is that 'what the Bible says' is in Hebrew and Greek, and there is seldom a one-to-one correspondence between English and these languages. Before we can translate a single word, we must interpret its meaning in context. Of course it is even more complicated than that, since words get their meaning in dynamic relationship with other words. Every phrase, clause, and idiom must be interpreted in context before it can be translated accurately into English.[54]

The fact that propositions are embedded has striking implications for the nature of translation. Karen Jobes illustrates the problem when she contrasts the word counts in the original Hebrew (Masoretic) and Greek New Testament texts (545,202 words) with various English translations, including the NIV (726,133 words), the NASB (782,815 words), and the NRSV (895,891 words).[55] These wildly variant totals are due in large part to the phenomenon of 'implicature'; that is, the implied or assumed meaning in statements. In each case, the translator must decide whether to make the implicature explicit in the translation. The problem is

question "Is what's said true?" we are trying to force square pegs into round holes' ('True Words', in Alan G. Padgett and Patrick R. Keifert (eds.), *But Is It All True? The Bible and the Question of Truth* (Grand Rapids, Mich./Cambridge: Eerdmans, 2006), 35).

[53] Hans Frei, *The Eclipse of Biblical Narrative* (New Haven, Conn./London: Yale University Press, 1974); cf. Stanley Grenz and John Franke, *Beyond Foundationalism: Shaping Theology in a Postmodern Context* (Louisville, Ky.: Westminster/John Knox, 2001), 50.

[54] Fee and Strauss, *How to Choose a Translation For All Its Worth* (Grand Rapids, Mich.: Zondervan, 2007), 31.

[55] Jobes, 'Relevance Theory and the Translation of Scripture', *Journal of the Evangelical Theological Society*, 50/4 (2007), 796.

how to define fidelity for translations in general and for Bible translations in particular because the communicative clues that evoke necessary implicatures in one language must be transferred successfully to evoke equivalent implicatures in another. This means that simply plugging in the equivalent words more often than not will fail to preserve the implicatures intended by the original language to the extent that the cultural frames of the original audience differ from those of the target audience.[56]

It is important not to draw overly sceptical implications from implicature, as if the original meaning were always inaccessible or indeterminate. Nonetheless, it does call into question an overly simplistic conception whereby one grasps atomically simple inerrant statements. To say the least, if a significant element of the text is not accessible to the reader in translation, then it seems reductionistic to make individual proposition units the determinative criteria of the text's authority.[57]

The problem of the autographs is simple enough: We don't have them. And so, we can never confirm whether they were in fact inerrant. Indeed, as Bart Ehrman observes, '[n]ot only do we not have the originals, we don't have the first copies of the originals. We don't even have copies of the copies of the originals, or copies of the copies of the copies of the originals'.[58] When Ehrman learned this as a young man he was deeply disturbed, for '[i]f one wants to insist that God inspired the very words of scripture, what would be the point if we don't *have* the very words of scripture?'.[59] To illustrate the problem, imagine that I want to win a race at the drag strip. My neighbor offers his 1969 Boss 302 Mustang to drive (*sweet ride!*), telling me that when it was new it clocked 13-second quarter miles. Delighted, I climb in and drive the car down to the track, only to discover that at some point the original V8 was replaced by an anemic four-cylinder from a Mustang II. The fact that the car was originally created fast is of little value if it is no longer. Similarly, the fact that Scripture was originally created inerrant is of no value if it is no longer.

---

[56] Ibid. 789.

[57] Unfortunately, the adverse effects of a disproportionate focus upon inerrancy influence other areas of dogmatics as well (see William Placher, *The Domestication of Transcendence: How Modern Thinking about God Went Wrong* (Louisville, Ky.: Westminster/John Knox, 1996), 169).

[58] Ehrman, *Misquoting Jesus*, p. 10.   [59] Ibid. 11.

To get an epistemological pay-off, the inerrantist needs an inerrant text now.

In Ehrman's mind, Scripture's de facto errancy (in present form) provides a defeater for claims to its divine inspiration, since an omnibenevolent God who could inspire the Scriptures also could (and would) have preserved their inspired, inerrant form. Thus, the fact that God did not maintain the text as inerrant suggested that he did not initially inspire the text. Ehrman's argument can be put in the form of *modus tollens*:

(1) If God inspired the original Christian Scriptures then he would ensure that subsequent copies of the Christian Scriptures retained an inerrant form.

(2) God has not ensured that subsequent copies of the Christian Scriptures retain an inerrant form.

(3) Therefore, God did not inspire the original Christian Scriptures.

Since the argument is logical logically valid and (2) is indisputably true, everything depends on (1). One way to put this intuition is that if the autographs are inerrant, then they do not have the property of inerrancy *simpliciter* (that is, just in themselves) but rather another property that we might call *guaranteed inerrancy* (that is, being inerrant and never able to be lost by the community of faith) or *copy inerrancy* (that is, being inerrant in subsequent overlapping copies). Either way, without an inerrant Bible now, the Scripture is no more effective at securing the theologian's epistemic status than a four-cylinder Mustang is at winning drag races.

GROUNDING THEOLOGY IN RELIGIOUS EXPERIENCE

Those who accept the Kantian proscription on knowledge cannot very well appeal to proofs and evidence in order to justify theology, for such arguments assume a grasp of divine reality that is unobtainable to us. While this would initially appear to mark the evisceration of theology, some theologians have instead seen in Kant the opportunity to return to a more adequate, if modest, conception of the theological task. According to these theologians, theology has often tended to view God as just another thing in the universe, when in fact God is the absolute subject who transcends all human categories, and thus can only truly be experienced and known in a sublime, mystical dimension which is then expressed in a rich network of metaphors.[60] On this view, the justification of theology shifts from arguments for a 'God-out-there' to an analysis of the Divine Absolute in human experience. In short, Kant's Copernican shift in theology involves substituting humanity for God as the primary object of study, while doctrines are understood to be metaphors for human religious experience.[61] This approach was pioneered by Friedrich Schleiermacher, who, according to Dulles, established 'religion from the inside outward on the basis of inward emotions and dispositions', thereby turning 'the apologetic sword against traditional orthodoxy'.[62] Lindbeck famously referred to this position as 'experiential-expressivism':

[T]hinkers of this tradition all locate ultimately significant contact with whatever is finally important to religion in the prereflective experiential depths of the self and regard the public or outer features of religion as expressive and evocative objectifications (i.e. nondiscursive symbols) of internal experience.[63]

While a cognitive-propositionalist seeks to meet the demand for justification in public proofs and evidence, experiential-expressivists appeal to a universal, primal experience of reality. Questions remain as to whether it is possible to think at all about a God who transcends every subject/object split and whether such an analysis can

---

[60] Paul Tillich argues for this view in his *A History of Christian Thought* (New York: Touchstone, 1972). Cf. James K. A. Smith's description of the correlationist 'Tübingen' school (*Introducing Radical Orthodoxy: Mapping a Post-secular Theology* (Grand Rapids, Mich.: Baker/Milton Keyes: Paternoster, 2004), 3–7, 157–8).

[61] As Peter Berger observes, 'when the objective certainty of religious definitions of reality can no longer be taken for granted (for whatever sociological and psychological reasons), the individual in quest of some measure of certainty must turn toward subjective sources of verification' ('Secular Theology and the Rejection of the Supernatural: Reflections on Recent Trends', *Theological Studies*, 38/1 (1977), 51).

[62] Avery Dulles, *A History of Apologetics* (1971: San Francisco: Ignatius, 2005), 211. Schleiermacher's method represents a third means to justify theology, as opposed to Cartesian proofs and Lockean evidence (Dulles, *A History of Apologetics*, p. 213).

[63] George Lindbeck, *The Nature of Doctrine: Religion and Theology in a Postliberal Age* (Philadelphia, Pa.: Westminster, 1984), 21.

provide genuine insight into human existence rather than being merely another ad hoc attempt to justify theology.[64]

If experiential-expressivism succeeds, it may offer theology a means to survive and even thrive in light of the Kantian problematic by grounding theology as a rigorous analysis of religious experience. No longer would one be obliged to shoulder the burden of justifying a transcendent deity or a written revelation, for the ground of justification would now be focused upon individual experience. The challenge here is to demonstrate how the transcendent deity is found in human religious experience. A number of experiential-expressivists have embraced the challenge of grounding theology relative to subjective experience. In this section we will unpack the experiential-expressivist conception of God as absolute subject and then consider the proposals of John Baillie and David Tracy.

God as Absolute Subject

While the evidentialist theologian will typically begin by establishing the existence of God, for the experiential-expressivist this is the exactly the *wrong* thing to do. The issue, as Blaise Pascal observes, comes back to divine transcendence:

> If there is a God, he is infinitely incomprehensible, since, having neither parts nor limits, he bears no relation to us. We are therefore incapable of knowing either what he is or whether he is. This being so, who will dare undertake to resolve the question? Not we, who bear no relation to him.
>
> Who then will blame Christians for not being able to give rational grounds for their belief, they who profess a religion for which they cannot give rational grounds?[65]

Thus, a century before Kant, Pascal pointed out that we should *expect* God to be fundamentally unknowable, for if he were knowable he wouldn't be God. (And this is hardly Pascal's discovery; one finds similar statements throughout the Greek Fathers.) But what does it mean to affirm that God is transcendent and incomprehensible? To answer this question, William Alston has helpfully identified an ascending scale of transcendence. The lowest transcendence claim is

---

[64] Berger, 'Secular Theology', p. 53.   [65] Pascal, *Pensées*, p. 212.

infinity, which denies that God is subject to finitude; next is time-lessness, which denies that God is subject to temporality; third is simplicity, which denies that God is subject to composition. But the highest transcendence claim is that God transcends the subject/object split and so is not a being but rather 'Being-itself'.[66] I will refer to this notion of the highest form of transcendence as the 'absolute subject' thesis, since according to this thesis God is not an object or being that is subject to predication, for to predicate anything of him is to treat him as *a* being rather than Being-itself. The absolute-subject thesis leads to a 'no predicate' thesis: the denial that anything positive and non-trivial can be predicated of God.[67]

Paul Tillich famously contrasted absolute-subject theology (which he referred to as the 'ontological model') with a predicate theology (which he called the 'cosmological model'). In addition to arguing that absolute-subject theology is a vibrant and noble tradition, he distinguished two points at which it differs from the cosmological alternative that are relevant for the justification question: the incorrigibility of God and the universality of human experience of God. According to these points, once one recognizes that God is not *a* being but rather *Being itself* it is impossible to doubt God, because God is the universal condition of existence and thought. Every other assertion of reality is an abstraction from Being and as such is less certain than Being. In contrast to this certainty, the best proofs and evidence of predicate-based natural theology are fleeting and dubitable.

In reflecting on absolute-subject theology it would be helpful to begin with the incorrigibility claim. Absolute-subject theologians adopt the no-predicate thesis because predicating anything of God treats God as a being, and thus as *just another thing* in the universe. And once we do this we include God among those things the existence of which can be *doubted*, a consequence which paves the way for atheism. John Robinson explains:

Traditional Christian theology has been based upon the proofs for the existence of God. The presupposition of these proofs, psychologically if not

---

[66] Alston, 'Functionalism and Theological Language', in his *Divine Nature and Human Language: Essays in Philosophical Theology* (Ithaca, NY/London: Cornell University Press, 1989), 64.

[67] See John Hick, *An Interpretation of Religion: Human Responses to the Transcendent* (New Haven, Conn.: Yale University Press, 1989), 246–9.

logically, is that God might or might not exist. They argue from something which everyone admits exists (the world) to a Being beyond it who could or could not be there.

...

The purpose of the argument is to show that he must be there, that his being is 'necessary'; but the presupposition behind it is that there is an entity or being 'out there' whose existence is problematic and has to be demonstrated. Now such an entity, even if it could be proved beyond dispute, would not be God: it would merely be a further piece of existence, that might conceivably not have been there—or a demonstration would not have been required.[68]

If a predicate (including existence) can be applied to God, then it can also be denied of God. As a result, Paul Tillich avers that the view of God as a being leads to a diminution of belief: '[O]ut of this paradoxical situation the half-blasphemous and mythological concept of the "existence of God" has arisen. And so have the abortive attempts to prove the existence of this "object." To such a concept and to such attempts atheism is the right religious and theological reply'.[69] Now, that is a surprising gravedigger thesis: according to Tillich the attempt to establish God's existence through proofs and evidence is the womb of atheism!

Since God is not an object of discourse, but rather the *condition* of any discourse, absolute-subject theology claims that theology must be based not only on an incorrigible ground, but a universal one as well. When one invokes proofs and evidence, one finds that some accept the arguments while others do not. As a result, the justification of theology remains in doubt. But according to absolute-subject theology, the unconditioned subject is the very condition of experience and thought. Thus, Tillich avers that according to Augustine the Truth of God is the *presupposition* of the question of God: 'God can never be reached if he is the *object* of a question, and not its *basis*'.[70] God as the universal ground of affirmation thus dovetails with God as the incorrigible ground of experience: 'Psychologically, of course, doubt is possible; but logically, the Absolute is affirmed by the very act of doubt, because it is implied in every statement about the relation between subject and predicate'.[71] As Robinson puts it, 'God is, by

[68] Robinson, *Honest to God* (Philadelphia, Pa.: Westminster, 1963), 14.
[69] Tillich, 'The Two Types of Philosophy of Religion', in his *Theology of Culture*, ed. Robert C. Kimball (New York: Oxford University Press, 1959), 25.

definition, ultimate reality. And one cannot argue whether ultimate reality *exists*. One can only ask what ultimate reality is like'.[72]

Absolute-subject theology has an ambitious goal and makes startling claims, but if successful it would enable theology to survive and even flourish in the arid Kantian desert. Unfortunately, problems are emerging even at this preliminary stage. For instance, if the no-predicate thesis is correct, then it would seem that we cannot apply the no-predicate thesis to God or affirm that God transcends the subject/object split; in other words, the position seems to be self-refuting. Further, Tillich's charge that the predicate thesis and cosmological model lead to atheism is unconvincing given that his conception of God transcending all predicates, including existence, would oblige him to deny that God exists, a claim which itself looks like atheism.[73] While aware of these objections, the absolute-subject theologian will probably reply that they tacitly assume the very issue of contention; namely, that God can be thought of as a being.

John Baillie: Finding God in Consciousness

Rather than continue a general dialogue on the viability of absolute-subject theology, we will shift at this point to consider whether this model for theology yields positive results, by considering two concrete exemplars of the method. We will begin with John Baillie, a Scottish theologian on the fringe of neo-orthodoxy who expressed a deep dissatisfaction with the discursive defence of God's existence. In his early book *Our Knowledge of God* he commented:

During the last several generations we who preach the gospel have been far too ready to assume that the modern man had developed an immunity against its appeal. We have approached him apologetically. We have made stammering excuses for our intrusion. For the old direct challenge we have substituted the language of debate. Where our forefathers would have

---

[70] Ibid.13.   [71] Ibid.14.   [72] Robinson, *Honest to God*, p. 29.

[73] See George Mavrodes, 'The Gods above the Gods: Can the High Gods Survive?', in Eleonore Stump (ed.), *Reasoned Faith: Essays in Philosophical Theology in Honor of Norman Kretzmann* (Ithaca, NY: Cornell University Press, 1993), 179–203.

confronted him with God's commandments, we have parleyed with him over God's existence and over the authenticity of his claims.[74]

Baillie believed that the shift to apologetics had done little to establish the credibility of Christian belief. Indeed, it had weakened Christian belief by treating it as an afterthought and rationalization rather than the cause and ground of all belief.[75] In short, by placing God as a conclusion of an argument, we render God an object of doubt, when he is in fact 'not an inference but a presence'.[76] Once we recognize that we are *always* experiencing God, questions of justification will dissolve like dew in the desert sun. Baillie made the point as follows:

[T]he only humanity known to us is a humanity which has already, in some degree at least, been confronted with the reality of God and disturbed by the challenge of his holy presence, and...this fact...determines the form and conditions the success alike of theological argument and of religious appeal.[77]

Thus, God is always present to us as the condition of thought. Since the experience of God is universal and incorrigible, shared by all people at all times, arguments for God are wholly redundant: 'The most flawless proof of the existence of God is no substitute for [real faith]; and if we have that relationship the most convincing disproof is turned harmlessly aside. If I may say it with reverence, the soul and God laugh together over so odd a conclusion'.[78]

Baillie developed this thesis further in his Gifford Lectures, *The Sense of the Presence of God*. When he wrote them, theologians were still struggling to meet the logical positivist's demand that all meaningful claims either be analytic or have clear conditions of falsification.[79] Baillie cut through this discussion by denying that faith could be falsified:

The question [What would falsify faith?] is...formally parallel, not to the question as to what would lead me to the reversal of a particular judgment of sense perception or a particular scientific conclusion, but to the

---

[74] Baillie, *Our Knowledge of God* (London: Oxford University Press, 1939), 14.
[75] Baillie, *Our Knowledge of God*, pp. 132–3.
[76] Ibid. 126.   [77] Ibid. 17.   [78] Ibid. 227.
[79] For a classic response to logical positivism see Basil Mitchell, 'Theology and Falsification', in Antony Flew and Alasdair MacIntyre (eds.), *New Essays in Philosophical Theology* (London: SCM, 1955), 103–5.

question as to what would lead me to distrust my sense perception as a whole and consequently to surrender my belief in the objectivity of the corporeal world.[80]

The analogy is illustrative, for it treats belief in God as being as basic and comprehensive as belief in the external world. Neither can truly be doubted, and so to debate with the atheist, no less than the solipsist, is already to have conceded too much.

In *Our Knowledge of God* Baillie argued that human knowledge always includes four dimensions: God, the world, other people, and ourselves. We are not autonomous *cogitos* free to court scepticism seriously; for, others, the world, and ourselves are preconditions of our ability to doubt. For this reason, the act of *doubting* the existence of God is as impossible as doubting the existence of the world, other persons, or our very selves. Falsification is thus a non-issue, since our apprehension of these things will always be more certain than any argument that could be raised against them—indeed, our apprehension of these dimensions is the *condition* for any arguments against them. Of course, some people certainly *seem* to doubt one or more of these spheres, but Baillie responds that such doubt is a form of self-delusion limited to the 'top of our minds' even as it is undermined by the knowledge in the 'bottom of our hearts'. So it goes for the inadequate arguments of natural theology: while they may lead one psychologically to deny the existence of God, logically speaking real doubt is impossible.

Baillie must be given credit for a bold attempt to justify theology irrespective of proofs or evidence. His parallel argument between beliefs in God, other minds, the world, and oneself is ingenious and goes some distance to addressing the question of justification. That said, a basic question remains: Why think a universal precognitive divine encounter underlies all experience? In short, what reason is there to think Baillie's argument is *true*? I can see scant grounds to believe it biblically, theologically, or psychologically. Indeed, it looks suspiciously like an ad hoc posit offered up only to meet demands for justification. Even if one cannot *refute* Baillie's thesis, it reminds one of Bertrand Russell's suggestion that the world was created five

---

[80] John Baillie, *The Sense of the Presence of God*, Gifford Lectures 1961–2 (London: Oxford University Press, 1962), 72.

minutes ago with all the dusty books, crumbling mountains, and apparent memories: while indefeasible, such a claim adds nothing to our knowledge and so is ultimately uninteresting. Philosopher of science Imre Lakatos famously argued that scientific theorizing proceeds with core theories which are supplemented by auxiliary theses that are open to revision or abandonment in order to accommodate new data, all to the end of maintaining the core theory. However, when the necessary revisions reach a critical mass, and the research programme continually fails to predict novel facts, it is deemed degenerative and eventually abandoned.[81] Baillie's core thesis that we perceive God all the time is defended by a battery of (dubious) auxiliary theses (e.g. we experience God even when we are not conscious of doing so), but it does not explain experience, makes no predictions, and thus bears the hallmarks of a degenerative theory.

Even more critically, Baillie's core thesis appears to be empirically vacuous. Consider as an analogy Lindbeck's comment on the concept of a 'universal love' which many pluralists claim underlies all the world's religions: 'The datum that all religions recommend something which can be called "love" toward that which is taken to be most important ("God") is a banality as uninteresting as the fact that all languages are (or were) spoken'.[82] The posit becomes banal because it must be rendered so general and abstract in order to include all religions that it is no longer interesting. If the concrete sense in which love is shared by all the world's religions is trivial, what about the divine dimension that is alleged to underlie all perception? What could it possibly mean to claim an individual always perceives God, irrespective of whether one is eating pizza, swimming in the ocean, giving birth, praying at a revival meeting, watching Eddie at a Van Halen concert, or being violently interrogated at Guantanamo Bay? To accommodate every experience, the concepts 'perception' and 'experience' would have to be so stretched as to be rendered virtually meaningless. But even worse, in addition to banality and triviality, the thesis appears to be false. Stanley Grenz and John Franke charge that '[t]here is no generic religious experience, only experiences endemic to specific religious traditions—experiences the occurrences of which

---

[81] See the discussion of Lakatos in Ch. 5.
[82] Lindbeck, *The Nature of Doctrine*, p. 42.

are facilitated by an interpretative framework that is specific to the religious tradition'.[83] While it may not be easy to prove Grenz and Franke correct, their claim is much more plausible than Baillie's.

Finally, Baillie's proposal raises theological concerns. While Baillie was sufficiently neo-orthodox that he steered away from overt Schleiermachean revisionism, he only did so by refusing to apply his theory consistently to the genesis of doctrinal beliefs. While Baillie wishes to derive doctrine from a universal given of religious experience, he refuses to develop a plausible account of *how* justified doctrinal beliefs are related to universal experience. Instead, he remains in the generalities of simple belief in God and the totality of Christian belief. Were he to have turned to the hard work of explaining how specific doctrines like the Trinity, incarnation, and atonement could be justified relative to a universal given, he would have had to begin the tortured process of doctrinal revision. And at that point the appeal of his theology would significantly diminish.

David Tracy: Limit Experiences and Classic Texts

The core weakness of Baillie's argument centres on the ad hoc nature of its appeal to experience in order to justify theology. In order to revitalize this argument the experiential-expressivist must explain how the universal and incorrigible experience of God is not merely possible but practically inescapable. David Tracy, a leading Catholic theologian, has developed an impressive proposal over several important monographs including *The Analogical Imagination*[84] and *Plurality and Ambiguity*.[85] However, we will focus on his early book *Blessed Rage for Order*, where Tracy develops a theological method to meet the requirements of universal, secular rationality. As Tracy observes (in fine Lockean form), 'the modern theologian ordinarily shares the morality of scientific knowledge of his contemporaries. He recognizes that such a commitment imposes

[83] Grenz and Franke, *Beyond Foundationalism: Shaping Theology in a Postmodern Context* (Louisville, Ky.: Westminster/John Knox, 2001), 49.

[84] Tracy, *The Analogical Imagination: Christian Theology and the Culture of Pluralism* (New York: Crossroad, 1981).

[85] Tracy, *Plurality and Ambiguity: Hermeneutics, Religion, Hope* (San Francisco: Harper & Row, 1987).

the *ethical duty* to provide the proper kind of evidence for whatever claim he advances'.[86] Given this duty, the theologian must forgo the authority of tradition in favor of a universally accessible knowledge which resides in 'common secular faith'. Tracy believes this faith underlies the two sources for Christian theology: common human experience and language, and the Christian texts.[87] The 'morality of scientific knowledge' requires the theologian to correlate universal human experience with the particular Christian texts in a symbolic reinterpretation of Christian doctrine.

According to Tracy, it is crucial to identify a religious dimension to common human experience which serves as the source for doctrinal formulation; to this end, he appeals to the concept of a transcendent, ineffable 'limit-experience': 'By its limit-character, a religious dimension is more accurately described by some such phrase as ultimate ground to or horizon of all other activities'.[88] Limit questions and experiences involve meaning, value, and purpose, and arise in the realms of science, morality, and the tumult of everyday life. In arguing for the limit character of these spheres of life, Tracy hopes to demonstrate the common basis of human religious experience as the means to justify theological discourse: 'The meaningfulness of both religious language and of the form of life it re-presents is grounded in the experience of a basic faith and is mediated cognitively by reflection upon limit-situations and limit-questions'.[89] Religion has a unique role in constituting and analysing these limit experiences in their fullness:

Religious language does not present a new, a supernatural world wherein we may escape the only world we know or wish to know. Rather that language re-presents our always threatened basic confidence and trust in the very meaningfulness of even our most cherished and most noble enterprises, science, morality, and culture.[90]

[86] Tracy, *Blessed Rage for Order: The New Pluralism in Theology* (Chicago, Ill.: University of Chicago Press, 1975), 6; emphasis added.
[87] Tracy maintains the two-source view in later writing (see 'Approaching the Christian Understanding of God', in *Systematic Theology: Roman Catholic Perspectives*, i, ed. Francis Schüssler Fiorenza and John P. Galvin (Minneapolis, Minn: Fortress, 1991), 146).
[88] Tracy, *Blessed Rage for Order*, 108.   [89] Ibid. 119.
[90] Ibid. 135; cf. 132.

With his phenomenological analyses of these three spheres Tracy is intending to establish a religious quality to human experience.[91] As a re-presentation of the universal dimensions of human existence, the Christian religion reveals itself as a higher conceptual articulation of human being which, as such, is fit to meet the morality of scientific knowledge. Thereby theology is admitted back into the university, gussied up in rouge and mascara as the new blushing consort of religious studies.

Tracy's attempt to ground (and so justify) theological discourse by identifying general phenomenological qualities constitutes a subtle (if at times obscure) argument. But is it successful? Many of the objections to Tracy's argument in *Blessed Rage for Order* have focused upon his attempt to identify a reified universal religious experience. Both Baillie and Tracy appear to hold a view of faith that William Lad Sessions refers to as the 'attitude model'. According to the attitude model faith is rooted in a prelinguistic '"horizon of significance", a kind of propositional boundary both between a person and her world and also around them both'.[92] This radically encompassing view of faith conditions the way one exists in the world while preceding propositional expression. Thus, while beliefs and other cognitive attitudes express faith, they 'are relatively superficial manifestations or aspects of faith, not its essential kernel'.[93] Unfortunately, the ad hoc problem remains: as Sessions puts it, by asserting a universal 'totalizing attitude' underlying experience, one is 'thereby cheaply purchasing a kind of universal apology for faith . . . But this answer seems very doubtful'.[94] Indeed, there is little to commend this obscure thesis apart from the need to justify religious belief and theology.

In his more recent work Tracy has conceded the obscurity of appealing to reified and trans-contextual limit experiences: 'The fact that the Christian understanding of God is grounded not in a general theory of theism but in the concrete history of God's self-disclosure

---

[91] T. Howland Sanks, 'David Tracy's Theological Project: An Overview and Some Implications', *Theological Studies*, 54 (1993), 708.

[92] Sessions, *The Concept of Faith: A Philosophical Investigation* (Ithaca, NY/London: Cornell University Press, 1994), 69. While a few reviewers of Sessions's book criticized his articulation of the attitude model as unduly vague, it seems to me that this merely reflects the inherent vagueness with this understanding of faith.

[93] Ibid. 77.   [94] Ibid. 82–3.

as loving agent in the cross and resurrection of Jesus of Nazareth is the theological foundation of all properly Christian understandings of God'.[95] Tracy has since replaced reference to limit experience with the language of 'classic' and 'conversation'. The classic is a sacred and/or highly influential and inspiring text which is recognized as authoritative within a particular cultural and/or religious tradition. As such, one may justify granting theological authority to the Bible by understanding it as the token classic of the Christian community. Tracy's reference to conversation emphasizes the importance of ongoing dialogue across traditions. And so he forgoes appeals to the proofs and evidence of natural theology and inerrancy in favour of the situated authority of the Christian classic: 'The proper "place" for these legitimate concerns on the nature and existence of God is after an analysis of the scriptural-revelational understanding of God. More exactly, on a Catholic understanding, we understand God foundationally in and through Scripture-in-tradition'.[96]

While Tracy's move away from limit experiences addresses some objections, two significant problems remain. The first problem is symptomatic and concerns Tracy's programmatic commitment to doctrinal revisionism. To an extent every theologian is a revisionist as they reinterpret the faith for every new generation. In principle, the theologian's task could require the revision of key orthodox doctrines given new evidence. For instance, the discovery of Jesus' body at an archaeological dig would surely impact on Christology.[97] As such, the objection is not to revisionism itself but rather to the fact that Tracy offers no new data (apart from a vague public morality of knowledge) to justify his abandonment of traditional orthodox boundaries. For instance, Tracy adopts a minimalist Christology in which Jesus apparently represents some type of abstract existential truth.[98] The extent of this revision is evident with Rosemary Ruether's

[95] Tracy, 'Approaching the Christian Understanding of God', p. 37. Cf. 'Each of us contributes more to the common ground when we dare to undertake a journey into our own particularity...than when we attempt to homogenize all differences in favor of some lowest common denominator...[or] are tempted to root out all particularity and call it publicness' (cited in Kristen Heyer, 'How Does Theology Go Public? Rethinking the Debate Between David Tracy and George Lindbeck', *Political Theology*, 5/3 (2004), 313).

[96] Tracy, 'Approaching the Christian Understanding of God,' p. 135.

[97] See Paul Maier, *A Skeleton in God's Closet* (Nashville, Tenn.: Nelson, 2005).

[98] Heyer, 'How Does Theology Go Public?', p. 320.

observation that Tracy's Christology would be acceptable to Jews.[99]
To put it bluntly, Tracy's revisionism of the 'Christ symbol' constitutes
an abandonment of the Church's two-thousand-year-old kerygmatic
confession of the hypostatic union.[100]

At least Tracy does not follow the more radical revisionists like
Gordon Kaufman in abandoning theism.[101] But that may be cold
comfort given that absolute-subject theology leads to a conception
of deity so abstract and distant that God is emptied of any concrete reality save the content poured in by one's chosen symbolic
substitutes. Needless to say, this is a potent recipe for idolatry. In
The Great Divorce C. S. Lewis illustrates the danger through the dialogue between George MacDonald and a liberal bishop who holds
to the absolute-subject and no-predicate theses. MacDonald pleads:
'Come and see. I will bring you to Eternal Fact, the Father of all
other facthood'. The bishop responds indignantly to the repugnant
implication that God might be included within the catalogue of
what exists: 'I should object very strongly to describing God as a
"fact". The Supreme Value would surely be a less inadequate description'. Undeterred, MacDonald asks 'Do you not even believe that He
exists?'; to which the bishop retorts: 'Exists? What does Existence
mean? You *will* keep on implying some sort of static, ready-made
reality which is, so to speak, "there", and to which our minds have
simply to conform. These great mysteries cannot be approached in
that way'.[102] One could substitute for the liberal bishop any number
of experiential-expressivists. While this bishop may appear to hold
a most sophisticated conception of transcendence, as Lewis suggests
it can equally become a way of avoiding God's sheer facticity. Given
human nature, this can amount to a gift card to shop at 'Idols-
R-Us', where we fill in the content with our own chosen conception of God. As Stanley Hauerwas and William Willimon evocatively
observe:

'God' is not an experience we have had but rather a proper name we have
been given. We have become confused into thinking that when we hear 'God'

[99] Rosemary Ruether, review of David Tracy, 'Blessed Rage for Order,' *Journal of
Religious Thought*, 33/2 (1976), 78.
[100] See also Lindbeck, *The Nature of Doctrine*, p. 80.
[101] See Tracy, *Blessed Rage for Order*, pp. 146–7.
[102] Lewis, *The Great Divorce: A Dream* (Glasgow: Collins, 1946), 42.

that we are hearing a description of some vague, allegedly universal human experience ('Everybody believes in God, even those who do not believe in Jesus') rather than a name. 'God' is the name Christians are told to call Trinity—Father, Son, and Holy Spirit. You cannot get this name through long walks in the woods, hugging trees, delving into your psyche, sitting quietly in your room, or getting in touch with your inner child. This God cannot be known other than by revelation. Any other claimant to the name 'God' is an idol.[103]

These are admittedly strong words, but it seems to me that there is an important warning to be heeded here. In short, there is forceful evidence that the absolute-subject and no-predicate theses are in fact effective gravediggers.

If overzealous revisionism is the symptom, the underlying disease is Tracy's uncritical commitment to the Lockean morality of scientific knowledge. Tracy argues that '[i]n terms of modes of argument, fundamental theologies will be concerned principally to provide arguments that all reasonable persons—whether "religiously involved" or not— can recognize as reasonable'.[104] Unfortunately for the theologian, traditional theological claims are profoundly *unreasonable* to many secularists. Tracy asserts that 'fundamentalism and supernaturalism of whatever religious tradition are dead and cannot return'.[105] The theologian must meet the standards of the new scientific morality in order to gain public legitimacy. Here we see clearly the impact of modern demands for evidence and argument to justify theological claims. But are these demands neutral and consistently applied? On the contrary, Tracy can be charged with trading one tradition of authority (that of the Church) for another (that of the secular academy) and thereby effectively subordinating Christianity to an

---

[103] Hauerwas and Willimon, *The Truth About God: The Ten Commandments in Christian Life* (Nashville, Tenn.: Abingdon, 1999), 43.

[104] David Tracy, 'The Necessity and Insufficiency of Fundamental Theology', in René Latourelle and Gerald O'Collins (eds.), *Problems and Perspectives of Fundamental Theology*, trans. Matthew J. O'Connell (New York: Paulist, 1982), 25.

[105] Tracy, *Blessed Rage for Order*, p. 135. As Peter Berger observes, for Tracy '[t]he notion of supernaturalism is used synonymously with "fundamentalism", which is understood as any authoritarian demand for religious assent' ('Secular Theology and the Rejection of the Supernatural', p. 50).

alien faith. As such, while Tracy has been classified as postmodern,[106] his epistemology remains thoroughly entrenched in modernity. For evidence of his modernism one need look no farther than his deep scepticism of tradition: '[O]ne cannot investigate a cognitive claim with intellectual integrity if one insists simultaneously that the claim is believable because the tradition has believed it'.[107] One can picture Descartes nodding with approval.

CONCLUSION

In this chapter I have sought to illustrate that a theology laden down with the epistemological demands of Descartes, Locke, and/or Kant is as apt to take flight as an airline of flammable dirigibles. The traditional approaches of rational-deductive and evidential-inductive argument have yielded an impressive range of arguments for the existence and attributes of God and the inspiration and inerrancy of Scripture, but all remain surprisingly unconvincing to those who are not already committed to the assumptions. If the efforts to ground theology in a Kantian landscape via absolute-subject theology are even more ingenious, they are also less convincing. At this point we might be ready to ask whether we ought to try to justify theology at all. In order to address this question we shall turn in the next chapter to analyse directly those terms that have come to haunt theology: rationality, justification, and knowledge.

[106] See Richard Lints, 'The Postpositivist Choice: Tracy or Lindbeck?', *Journal of the American Academy of Religion*, 61/4 (1993), 655–77.
[107] Tracy, *Blessed Rage for Order*, p. 6.

3

On Foundationalism and Other Concepts

> If only people would be sensible. If only they would submit to the order of reason.
>
> Simon Blackburn, *Truth*

> To describe a position as 'foundationalist' without further explanation is to plunge into a swamp of verbal vagueness.
>
> Nicholas Wolterstorff, *Thomas Reid and the Story of Epistemology*

Call someone a fundamentalist in the 1920s and it was eminently clear what was intended: a Christian conservative, sympathetic with the reaction to liberalism typified by the series of books entitled 'The Fundamentals' that were funded by oil magnate and philanthropist Lyman Stewart. However, in the intervening eight decades the term has been repeatedly broadened, so that today it has lost almost all precision; indeed, as Alvin Plantinga has observed, 'fundamentalist' now means little more than 'stupid sumbitch whose theological opinions are considerably to the right of mine'.[1] The evolution of fundamentalism and its cognates closely parallels that of another set of 'f' words of serious intellectual disapprobation: 'foundationalism' also initially had a very narrow, technical, and specific meaning, and it too has evolved over time until today it means something approximating 'stupid sumbitch whose epistemological opinions are to the right of mine'.[2] Like fundamentalism, the *term*

---

[1] Plantinga, *Warranted Christian Belief* (Oxford: Oxford University Press, 2000), 244–5.

[2] Nicholas Wolterstorff writes: 'The range of positions called "foundationalism" has been expanding by leaps and bounds in recent years, so much so that the expan-

foundationalism is of recent vintage, even if the position to which it refers is centuries old. And here too the expansion in meaning has been dizzying, so that, as Wolterstorff observes, 'there is no one position which is *foundationalism*; there's only an extended family of positions that are foundationalist in character'.[3] Our task in this chapter is to understand that family of positions, as well as a number of other key concepts in the near vicinity.

First a bit of background: The evolution of the term foundationalism can be traced in three basic steps. The term's use begins with W. V. O. Quine's use of it to refer to the epistemology of the logical positivists.[4] The metaphor of a foundation is a powerful one which suggests a basis of belief, a ground, a level of security, and an end to enquiry, all of which the logical positivists were seeking. The next step came as the term began to be used to refer to the type of epistemology of which logical positivism was a token. That position, which has of late come to be called strong foundationalism or classical foundationalism (we shall use the latter term), is the view that knowledge is grounded in indubitable truths (typically limited to rational intuition and sense perception) and that knowledge entails the ability to give an account of how one's beliefs trace back to indubitable truths. For a number of decades the term foundationalism was used to refer to classical foundationalism. For instance, the *Oxford Companion to Philosophy* (1995) defines foundationalism as '[t]he theory that knowledge of the world rests on a foundation of indubitable beliefs from which further propositions can be inferred to produce a super-structure of known truths'.[5] Most recently the term has come to refer to the type of epistemology of which classical foundationalism is a token. The core claim of this type of epistemology is more modest, and simply specifies that the regress of justification must be finite

---

sion is well on the way to the point where the shared property will be little more than *being an epistemological position of which the speaker disapproves*' (*Thomas Reid and the Story of Epistemology* (Cambridge: Cambridge University Press, 2001), 187).

[3] Wolterstorff, *Thomas Reid*, p. 187. For an outline of the two main forms of foundationalism see David Clark, 'Relativism, Fideism and the Promise of Postliber-alism', in Timothy R. Phillips and Dennis L. Okholm (eds.), *The Nature of Confession* (Downers Grove, Ill: InterVarsity, 1996), 10–20.

[4] R. R. Reno, 'Theology's Continental Captivity', *First Things* (April 2006), 28.

[5] Ted Honderich (ed.), *The Oxford Companion to Philosophy* (Oxford/New York: Oxford University Press, 1995), 289.

and cannot be circular. To sum up, classical foundationalism is to foundationalism *simpliciter* as logical positivism is to classical foundationalism; namely, a token instance of the more general type. Not surprisingly, much confusion arises when these tokens and types are conflated.

Probably no single contemporary philosopher is more responsible for perpetuating the confusion of foundationalism with classical foundationalism than Richard Rorty, particularly in his book *Philosophy and the Mirror of Nature*.[6] This is not entirely Rorty's fault, as he wrote the book just as the term foundationalism was beginning to be used to refer to the more general theory of which classical foundationalism is a token. But even with this qualification Rorty's definition is idiosyncratic, for he conflates classical foundationalism with a particular token of classical foundationalism—not logical positivism, but rather an eighteenth-century version of the sense-data theory of perception that was held by Locke and his contemporaries. Thus, Rorty never distinguishes foundationalism from classical foundationalism, leading to the fallacious conclusion that the failure of the latter leaves us without hope in the former. To make matters worse, Rorty then conflates classical foundationalism with epistemology as a discipline:

[T]o think of knowledge which presents a 'problem,' and about which we ought to have a 'theory,' is a product of viewing knowledge as an assemblage of representations—a view of knowledge which . . . was a product of the seventeenth century. The moral to be drawn is that if this way of thinking of knowledge is optional, then so is epistemology and so is philosophy as it has understood itself since the middle of the last century.[7]

Here Rorty equates his target of 'representationalism' with the whole project of theorizing about belief and knowledge. Thus, he concludes that if classical foundationalism fails, then so does the entire project of epistemology and, incredibly, even *philosophy itself*. But this is clearly erroneous. Not surprisingly, as Alvin Goldman has noted, Rorty's conflations undermine his striking conclusions:

⁶ Rorty, *Philosophy and the Mirror of Nature* (Princeton, NJ: Princeton University Press, 1979).
⁷ Ibid. 136.

Rorty's critique of epistemic warrant or privilege...is strikingly abortive. He simply ignores most theories now under serious consideration. He pays almost exclusive attention to a single historical theory that once enjoyed popularity but was long since exploded, as everybody in the field knows. All the currently respected theories, on the other hand, are treated as if they did not exist.[8]

So, it is most unfortunate that many theologians, having only read enough Rorty to be dangerous, have uncritically followed him in dismissing foundationalism.

Our task in this chapter will be focused upon providing a framework to understand a number of central epistemological concepts by which we might locate both foundationalism and classical foundationalism within the wider discussion of epistemology. We will begin with an overview of the meaning of the following key terms: *reason, faith, certainty, truth, knowledge,* and *justification*. Next, we will turn to consider the main theoretical options concerning how justification and knowledge are generated. At this point we will consider the divisions between *internalism/externalism* and *methodism/particularism*. Finally, we will survey the three main theories of noetic structure which provide the ground for justification and knowledge: *infinitism, coherentism,* and *foundationalism*. This will provide the background necessary to consider in Chapter 4 whether classical foundationalism really is dead.

PLACING FOUNDATIONALISM IN CONTEXT

While the last thirty years have seen a rich and illuminating epistemological debate over foundationalism, within theology such discussions have often been clouded by confusion and consequently have tended to generate more heat than light. Perhaps the best way to move the conversation forward is by clarifying some basic terms, beginning with what may be the most misunderstood concepts of all: reason and faith.

---

[8] Goldman, *Knowledge in a Social World* (Oxford: Clarendon, 1999), 27.

Reason and Faith

Obviously the philosophical and theological literature on faith and
reason is vast. For the theologian, the question of how faith relates
to reason is often intimately connected with the question of how
theology goes public; that is, how can a discipline based on faith
justify a place in the public space of those who do not share that faith?
The answer to this question depends in large part on the relationship
between faith and reason. At a popular level, a warfare model of faith
and reason continues to exert influence quite out of proportion to its
intrinsic merit (or lack thereof). Much of the credit for this must go to
village atheists like Richard Dawkins, a brash Englishman who balks
at 'dyed-in-the-wool faith-heads'[9] for whom '[f]aith (belief without
evidence) is a virtue'.[10] Never one to nuance his anti-religious screeds,
Dawkins asserts: 'The more your beliefs defy the evidence, the more
virtuous you are. Virtuoso believers who can manage to believe something really weird, unsupported and insupportable, in the teeth of
evidence and reason, are especially highly rewarded'.[11] Unfortunately,
many Christians have responded in kind, as with the church sign that
quoted Martin Luther: 'Reason is the greatest enemy that faith has'.[12]
To put it bluntly, many on both sides assume that reason is evidence-
based belief while faith is despite-the-evidence belief. This warfare
conception aligns reason with scepticism and faith with credulity as
two extremes of a continuum with no possible point of reconciliation.
Popular periodicals like *Skeptic* and *Skeptical Enquirer* and countless
village atheists perpetuate the notion that reason is tantamount to
scepticism.

This definition is correct in affirming that reason includes scepticism, but incorrect in denying that reason includes credulity (that is,
belief). No doubt Carl Sagan, author of *The Demon Haunted World*, a
book which trades on a warfare model, believed that his beloved Ann
Druyan had a mind, and that the world followed scientific laws, and
that, all things being equal, the man on the street could be trusted

---

[9] Dawkins, *The God Delusion* (Boston, Mass.: Houghton Mifflin, 2006), 5.
[10] Ibid. 199.   [11] Ibid. 199.
[12] For a defence of such prima facie irrational statements see C. Stephen Evans,
Faith Beyond Reason: A Kierkegaardian Account (Grand Rapids, Mich./Cambridge:
Eerdmans, 1998).

for directions. And surely he was perfectly rational to do so. The lesson we should draw is that one can violate reason both by excessive credulity and by excessive doubt. As Alvin Plantinga observes, '[w]e appraise a person's *beliefs*, but also her skepticisms or ... her withholdings, her refrainings from belief. An unduly credulous person may believe what she ought not; an unduly skeptical (or cynical) person may fail to believe what she ought'.[13] Thus, while reason sometimes dictates the withholding of belief, other times it commends belief. Indeed, as Anthony Kenny suggests, one ought to define reason in virtue of the optimal balance between credulity and doubt:

One can err by believing too much or believing too little. The person who believes too much suffers from the vice of credulity or gullibility; the person who believes too little is guilty of excessive incredulity or scepticism. If you believe too much, your mind will be cluttered with many falsehoods; if you believe too little you will be deprived of much valuable information. There is no universally accepted name for the virtue which stands in the middle between the two vices of credulity and scepticism: a name which is sometimes used, and which is as good as any, is 'rationality'.... The rational human being is the person who possesses the virtue that is in contrast with each of the opposing vices of credulity and scepticism.[14]

Thus, according to Kenny, reason may be thought of as an Aristotelian virtue or golden mean between the vices of excessive credulity and excessive scepticism.[15] The reasonable person adopts a prima facie trust in memory, reason, sense perception, the laws of nature, the integrity and reliability of one's teachers,[16] and other basic sources of belief ... including the methods of science. As the famous physicist Max Planck wrote: '[O]ver the gates of the temple of science are written the words: *Ye must have faith*. It is a quality which the scientist cannot dispense with'.[17]

---

[13] Plantinga, *Warrant: The Current Debate* (Oxford: Oxford University Press, 1993), 4.

[14] Kenny, *What is Faith? Essays in the Philosophy of Religion* (Oxford: Oxford University Press, 1992), 6.

[15] Kenny, *What is Faith?* p. 6. Cf. Nicholas Wolterstorff, *John Locke and the Ethics of Belief* (Cambridge: Cambridge University Press, 1996), 62.

[16] Robert Wilken, 'Memory and the Christian Intellectual Life', in *Remembering the Christian Past* (Grand Rapids, Mich.: Eerdmans, 1995), 165–80.

[17] Max Planck cited in Avery Dulles, *The Craft of Theology: From Symbol to System* (New York: Crossroad, 1992), 144.

Not surprisingly, the concept of faith is much more complex than sceptics like Dawkins and Sagan are willing to admit. Indeed, it is doubtful that faith can be analysed into a single concept at all. In his study of faith William Lad Sessions has argued that there are six major types or models of faith. Of these, we briefly outlined the attitude model in Chapter 2 when critiquing Baillie and Tracy. At this point we will focus on two other models: the belief model and the personal-relationship model.[18] According to the belief model, faith is constituted by a strong belief in a proposition on a basis other than evidence for that proposition.[19] Stated as such, the model begs the question of what ground other than evidence one might have for faith. And if there is no ground, then isn't faith *by definition* irrational? This question brings us back to the conception of reason as the mean between scepticism and credulity. Given that reason includes a willingness to believe in the absence of evidence (even belief in the most secure proof requires faith in one's memory, rational intuition, etc.), reason as such includes a degree of faith.[20]

The personal-relationship model brings together the acquaintance dimension of the attitude model with the cognitive dimension of the belief model to create a model of faith that is both personal and propositional. The faith that a spouse has in her beloved or that a student has in his teacher includes intellectual assent, but this cognitive dimension is embedded within the context of personal relationship. Thus, while faith involves cognitive assent to a proposition in the absence of evidence, it embeds this cognitive act in a personal relationship. Sessions memorably describes the intimate relationship within faith between the cognitive and the personal: 'Those who would reduce such faith to propositional belief are mistaken; they confuse the skeletal beliefs held on faith with the entire living organism of faith. But equally in error are those who would dispense with propositional belief; they forget that living organisms

[18] The remaining models are the confidence model, the devotion model, and the hope model (Sessions, *The Concept of Faith: A Philosophical Investigation* (Ithaca/London: Cornell University Press, 1994), ch. 2).

[19] Sessions, *Concept of Faith*, pp. 6–9.

[20] As James K. A. Smith puts it, 'faith and reason are but two varying intensities along a continuum of divine illumination' (*Introducing Radical Orthodoxy: Mapping a Post-secular Theology* (Grand Rapids, Mich.: Baker/Milton Keyes: Paternoster, 2004), 160–1.

need skeletons to support their many vital functions'.[21] In fact, the personal-relationship model could be understood as grounding faith in the evidence of authority and acquaintance, as one comes to believe through the authority of the testifier.[22] As Blaise Pascal observed, '[f]aith truly says what the senses do not say, but not the contrary of what they see. It is above, not against them'.[23]

What is True and What is Real?

Any discussion of knowledge must begin with notions of truth and reality. While we shall return a number of times to refine our conception of truth, we will begin the discussion here by considering the mode of application of the concept of truth. As a first approximation, truth is the property a proposition exemplifies when it describes what is the case. For instance, the proposition 'Paul Tillich was not a one-woman man' is true if and only if Paul Tillich was not a one-woman man (he wasn't). While this view of truth as a property of propositions is intuitive and compelling, it may be too restrictive in so far as there is evidence that the concept of truth can be meaningfully applied to much more than propositions or statements. As David Williams points out, when we turn to Scripture we see that the words for truth (*emet, alethia*) have a much wider application than simply ascribing truth to statements. To be sure, there are passages that presuppose the correspondence metaphor, such as 1 John 1: 8: 'If we claim to be without sin, we deceive ourselves and the truth is not in us' (cf. 1 Kgs. 17: 24; Ps. 119: 43). In this case, to have the truth within oneself means (at minimum) that one knows the truth of one's own character. In addition Williams identifies references that speak of truth as something *personal* and participatory, as in 2 John 1: 4: 'It has given me great joy to find some of your children walking in

[21] Sessions, *Concept of Faith*, p. 34.

[22] Ibid. 42. The tension between faith and reason is more evident on the belief model according to which the belief by definition lacks adequate evidence: 'Unlike rational conviction or knowledge, faith's believing involves going beyond, perhaps far beyond, the evidence—it requires an evidential risk or "leap" ' (Sessions, *Concept of Faith*, p. 57).

[23] Pascal, *Pensées*, trans. and ed. Roger Ariew (Indianapolis, Ind./Cambridge: Hackett, 2005), 54.

the truth, just as the Father commanded us' (cf. Ps. 25: 5). Since one cannot *walk* in a statement about reality, it would appear that truth is being used in a different sense here. In addition Williams points out two cases in the New Testament where the reference to truth occurs in *verbal* form (Eph. 4: 15, Gal. 4: 16). In this case, the word could be variously translated as 'truthing', 'doing the truth', or 'speaking the truth',[24] with the first two possibilities again suggesting a broader concept than mere correspondence between proposition and what is the case. Thus, it is clear that Scripture's predication of truth is not limited to propositions.

Nicholas Wolterstorff points out that English reflects a similarly broad application of the concept of truth: 'Our English word "truth" along with its grammatical variants, maps the Greek word *alethia* and its grammatical variants, as they are used in the New Testament, about as closely as one could wish'.[25] So, should we think of these non-propositional ascriptions of truth as non-literal applications of the concept of propositional truth, or is the concept of truth broader than propositions describing what is the case? Wolterstorff opts for the latter alternative by arguing that the core concept of truth is of 'measuring up in being or excellence'; this concept can be applied to persons ('Tom is a true friend') as well as propositions ('What you say is true'): 'A true friend is one who measures up with respect to the quality of his friendship; true coffee is coffee that measures up with respect to its flavor or composition. When we speak of "a true so-and-so," we are implicitly measuring a contrast between this so-and-so that measures up and other so-and-so's that do not, or would not, measure up'.[26] If Wolterstorff is correct (and I shall assume that he is), then a true statement is but a linguistic example of the broad concept of measuring up in being or excellence.[27]

---

[24] David Williams, 'Scripture, Truth and Our Postmodern Context', in Vincent Bacote, Laura Miguélez, and Dennis Okholm (eds.), *Evangelicals and Scripture: Tradition, Authority, and Hermeneutics* (Downers Grove, Ill.: InterVarsity, 2004), 229–43. Cf. Nicholas Wolterstorff, 'True Words', in Alan G. Padgett and Patrick R. Keifert (eds.), *But Is It All True? The Bible and the Question of Truth* (Grand Rapids, Mich./Cambridge: Eerdmans, 2006), 37–8.
[25] Wolterstorff, 'True Words', p. 39.   [26] Ibid. 42.
[27] Alan Padgett writes: 'Sometimes that truth will be mediated through everyday experience, or common sense, sometimes through the specifics of propositions'

As we have seen, our linguistic concept of truth centres on what is the case. To unpack this a bit further, we should provide a brief overview of the related questions concerning realism and anti-realism. Realism is the view that an entity or class of entities objectively exists (that is, it exists apart from human conceptualization), while anti-realism is the denial that that entity or class of entities exists. One can adopt a realist or anti-realist position on an endless range of entities, including angels, the germ theory of disease, God, or even reality as a whole. Two qualifications of this picture are necessary. First, realism does not entail *naive* realism, and thus the realist's conception of an entity may be quite different from that held by 'the man on the street'. Second, anti-realism comes in two types, which we can call 'simple anti-realism' and 'conceptual-relative anti-realism'. While simple anti-realism denies that the putative entity exists in any sense (e.g. an atheist is a simple anti-realist regarding God), the conceptual-relative anti-realist denies that it exists absolutely, but claims that the entity exists relative to a conceptual scheme. Typically conceptual-relative anti-realism has been defended in an unqualified form as 'the view that whatever there is, is constituted, at least in part, by our cognitive relations thereto, by the ways we conceptualize or construe it, by the language we use to talk about it or the theoretical scheme we use to think of it'.[28] But, as I will argue in Chapter 10, one could be a conceptual-relative anti-realist about some entities whilst denying the truth (or even coherence) of unqualified conceptual-relative anti-realism.

What is Knowledge?

When we turn to the concept of knowledge we find an intriguing diversity of usage that parallels the diversity regarding truth. Keith Lehrer points out that the word 'know' is used in three basic ways: awareness of the truth of belief ('I know that Paris, France has more pavement cafés than Paris, Texas'), the possession of an ability or skill

(' "What is Truth?" On the Meaning of our Confession that Scripture is True', *Canadian Evangelical Review*, 29 (2005), 7).

[28] William Alston, *A Sensible Metaphysical Realism*, Aquinas Lecture 2001 (Milwaukee, Wisc.: Marquette University Press, 2001), 8.

('I know how to confuse undergraduates'), and direct experience or acquaintance ('I know my wife').[29] In addition to personal knowledge, one may also speak of direct acquaintance with the whole range of sense-perceptual experience. Frank Jackson made the point with the thought-experiment of Mary, a woman who has been kept all her life in a black and white room and has never seen colour. During this time she becomes a world-expert neurologist by specializing in the study of the brain events that occur when individuals see red. Though Mary already has comprehensive knowledge of the brain states that are associated with seeing colour, when she finally leaves her room and first sees a rose, she gains new knowledge (of acquaintance) of what red looks like.[30] As with the case of truth, one could choose to argue that propositional knowledge is the sole literal application of the concept, while ability and acquaintance are mere analogical extensions of the concept. But why limit knowledge in this way? Just as we accepted an expanded conception of truth, so we have good grounds to expand our conception of knowledge to accommodate all three.

The first element in propositional knowledge is belief which obtains when one affirms a proposition or (perhaps) is disposed to affirm a proposition. Thus, for me to believe that the Trinity is three coequal divine persons is to affirm the proposition that the Trinity is three coequal divine persons or to have the disposition to affirm that proposition were it presented to me.[31] In addition to belief, knowledge requires the truth of the proposition. But, then, might knowledge consist simply of a true belief? At first blush that may seem adequate, but virtually all epistemologists have rejected this account, instead viewing knowledge as belief in a true proposition plus the ability to provide an account as to why one accepts the

[29] Lehrer, *Theory of Knowledge* (Boulder, Col./San Francisco, Calif: Westview, 1990), 3.

[30] See Jackson, 'Epiphenomenal Qualia', *Philosophical Quarterly*, 32 (1982), 127–36, and 'What Mary Didn't Know', *Journal of Philosophy*, 83/5 (1986), 291–5. Many physicalists have responded to Jackson by arguing that knowledge of qualia is reducible to knowledge of ability.

[31] The addition of disposition is significant for orthodox belief, given that many Christians might not actually affirm the proposition that one God is three coequal divine persons but they do possess the disposition to affirm it were it to be explained to them.

proposition. The core intuition behind requiring an additional criterion is that one cannot stumble upon knowledge by lucky accident. To illustrate, consider a five-point Calvinist who is convinced that all Arminians are closet Pelagians. One day he sees an Arminian at the grocery store and automatically comes to believe 'That Arminian is a closet Pelagian'. Let us assume that while Arminianism does not trivially entail Pelagianism, *this* Arminian *is* a closet Pelagian. While our Calvinist has a true belief, we are reluctant to recognize it as knowledge because he lacked an adequate reason to believe it; he did not have a good account; he believed for the wrong reason; he simply *got lucky*. This tells us that knowledge involves another element in addition to true belief; let us adhere to convention and refer to that element as *justification*. Thus, it follows that for a true belief to be knowledge the person must be justified in holding it. So, according to our preliminary assessment, knowledge consists of justified, true belief.

While there is a vast literature on the concept of justification,[32] we can restrict ourselves here to making a tentative distinction between subjective and objective justification. The concept of subjective justification is based on the observation that people often have reasons or grounds for their belief that are valid relative to their total set of background beliefs but may or may not be good reasons or grounds *all things considered*. Thus, consider Orson, a Mormon who was raised in Salt Lake City with the belief that the angel Moroni revealed a number of ancient texts to Joseph Smith in the 1820s. Is Orson's belief justified? What if he holds the belief in light of a two-year mission trip in Peru replete with charismatic experiences, a four year BA from Brigham Young University, and a summer internship at FARMS, the Mormon apologetics organization? In light of this broad base of experience I would be inclined to affirm Orson's belief as justified. At the same time, I believe there are a number of historical, theological, and philosophical objections to Orson's beliefs that, if he were aware of them, would constitute defeaters for those beliefs. In light of this fact, it would seem that I should view Orson's justification as, in some sense, substandard. I would suggest that we put it this way: Orson is

---

[32] See, for one example, Richard Swinburne, *Epistemic Justification* (Oxford: Clarendon, 2001).

subjectively justified, meaning that he is justified non-culpably and relative to his knowledge base. At the same time, he is not justified objectively given that there are defeaters to his belief.[33] We reach the lower threshold of subjective justification when we have secured a link between belief and our knowledge base and we are not aware of any defeaters to the link or knowledge base. The higher threshold of objective justification is reached when there are in fact no defeaters to our belief and substantial evidence supports it. Orson illustrates that subjective justification does not guarantee objective justification.

While we will return to the vexed question of justification in the next section, we must first take a brief excursus to consider whether knowledge requires certainty. Philosophers from Plato to Descartes have sought to refute sceptics by identifying items of knowledge that are truly certain, a practice which reinforces the impression that knowledge requires certainty. In order to be clear on what we mean by certainty, we need to distinguish between psychological and epistemic conditions of certainty. We might begin by noting that one may be psychologically certain of propositions that are false. For instance, after you cite Wikipedia to provide irrefutable evidence that ABBA sold more records than Herb Alpert and the Tijuana Brass, I might reply 'But I was *certain* that Herb Alpert and the Tijuana Brass outsold ABBA!'. Psychological certainty occurs when one has a maximal conviction (or, conversely, no significant doubt) in the truth of a proposition *irrespective of whether the proposition is true*.[34] When a belief not only elicits maximal conviction but is also true and not conceivably false, then we refer to it as indubitable.[35] You may have no real doubt that ABBA sold more records than Herb Alpert and the Tijuana Brass, but, even so, it is still conceivably false (for instance, it is possible that Herb Alpert sold tens of millions more records in the Indian subcontinent than you or I ever suspected). By contrast,

---

[33] As Bruce Russell puts it: 'Someone who grows up in a religious society and is taught to listen to the deliverances of an oracle can be epistemically blameless in believing those deliverances even though her belief may not really be supported by the evidence and so is objectively *unjustified*' (cited in Michael Bergmann, *Justification without Awareness: A Defense of Epistemic Externalism* (Oxford: Oxford University Press, 2006), 5).

[34] See Sessions, *Concept of Faith*, p. 56.

[35] The distinction between maximal conviction and indubitability parallels that between subjective and objective justification.

there are other statements that are not conceivably false and so are indubitable, including the following:

(1) $2 + 2 = 4$
(2) No contradictory statement can be true.
(3) The shortest distance between two points is a straight line.

It is important to note that indubitability does not entail incorrigibility. An incorrigible belief is not only one that cannot be doubted but one that could not be false. Thus, lower-grade certainty arises from truth and indubitability while higher-grade certainty arises from incorrigible truth and indubitability.

So, then, is it possible to identify incorrigible beliefs, or ought we to embrace fallibilism, the view that any of our beliefs could be false? Rather than address that question directly, perhaps we should distinguish between 'ivory tower' and 'real world' indubitability (and certainty). Perhaps all our beliefs are fallible, but is that a real cause for worry? Even if we recognize that a belief could in principle turn out to be false (the ivory-tower doubt), we may have no real *practical* doubt that it is true. I, for one, have no doubt that ABBA outsold Herb Alpert and the Tijuana Brass, even though I recognize this is conceivably false. But I don't stay up at night worrying that Herb Alpert might possibly have outsold ABBA. You might say that this is only because the truth about ABBA's and Herb Alpert's record sales lacks existential import. But I have a similar attitude toward a great number of existentially significant beliefs, including the reliability of my memories, sense perceptions, and even the existence of the external world. In each case these beliefs could be false, and yet I don't stay up at night worrying about that possibility. The reason is that these beliefs hold for me a maximal real-world (or practical) certainty, even though most if not all lack ivory-tower certainty.

GETTING IN THE KNOW

The story of the gravediggers in the first two chapters focused on the impact of one particular understanding of justification upon theology. At this point we will clarify the relevant issues by distinguishing three fundamental matters of epistemological debate: internalism versus externalism, methodism versus particularism, and foundationalism versus infinitism and coherentism. We will consider each of these debates in turn.

Internalism and Externalism

We will begin with the debate between internalism and externalism. Internalism is the view that for a belief to be justified one must be aware of the evidence or reasons that support it. That is, the ground upon which one holds the belief must be *internally accessible* to the individual. Plantinga defines the internalist view of justification (though he substitutes the term 'warrant' for justification) as follows: 'Warrant and the properties that confer it are internal in that they are states or conditions of which the cognizer is or can be *aware*: they are states of which he has or can easily have knowledge; they are states or properties to which he has cognitive or epistemic access'.[36] Thus, internalist epistemologies maintain an access requirement according to which justification requires the ability to access the justification for the belief. The strongest form of access involves the individual knowing what evidence makes the belief true. More modestly, one might limit the access requirement to an ability upon reflection to identify reasons or evidences that support the belief.

Plantinga identifies three important internalist motifs. To begin with, the internalist typically holds that justification is deontological in nature so that it involves one meeting basic duties or obligations in terms of believing. 'As the classical deontologist sees things, justification is not by faith but by works; and whether we are justified in our beliefs is up to us'.[37] As a result, the aim of epistemology is not first to attain true beliefs, but rather to hold beliefs on the right grounds. For the internalist, justification is our decision as it is rooted in our own actions to meet our epistemic duties; as Plantinga observes, '[m]y system of beliefs may be wildly skewed and laughably far from the truth; I may be a brain in a vat or a victim of a malicious

---

[36] Plantinga, *Warrant: The Current Debate*, p. 5.   [37] Ibid. 15.

Cartesian demon; but whether my beliefs have justification is still up to me'.[38] The second internalist motif is that the internal nature of justification ensures that one has access to the justification of one's own beliefs.[39] Finally, justification is rooted in our effort to fulfil an objective duty to regulate beliefs by holding them with an appropriate level of conviction relative to our evidence base.[40]

It is interesting to note how closely these internalist motifs reflect the epistemological assumptions of the gravediggers surveyed in Chapter 1 (Locke in particular). The internalist approach to epistemology has been so influential in modern philosophy that many philosophers have simply assumed that justifiably believing or knowing *p* entails being able to produce reasons to think *p* is true. As Bertrand Russell put it, '[w]e must, therefore, admit as derivative knowledge whatever is the result of intuitive knowledge even if by mere association, provided there *is* a valid logical connexion, and the person in question could become aware of this connexion by reflection'.[41] One gets a sense of the domination of internalist theories of justification when one reflects on the fact that the term justification, which is so essential to analyses of rationality and knowledge, appears to assume internalism. This is why Plantinga opts to use the more neutral term 'warrant', for, as he points out, ' "Justification" suggests duty, obligation, requirement; it is redolent of permission and rights; it brings to mind exoneration, not being properly subject to blame— it connotes, in a word (or two) the whole deontological stable'.[42] The influential definition of knowledge as justified true belief (JTB) includes justification, with all its internalist associations, right in the very definition of knowledge. So, it is hardly surprising that theologians have widely (and often uncritically) imbibed an internalist approach to justification. Nor is this limited to the modernistic gravediggers surveyed in Chapter 2, for most contemporary non-foundationalists who vigorously eschew the mistakes of cognitive-propositionalists and experiential-expressivists alike continue to hold an internalist view of justification. Thus, J. Wentzel van Huyssteen writes: 'In theology, as a critical reflection on religion and religious

[38] Ibid. 19.   [39] Ibid. 22.   [40] Ibid. 20.
[41] Russell, *The Problems of Philosophy* (Oxford: Oxford University Press, 1912/1980), 78.
[42] Plantinga, *Warrant: The Current Debate*, p. 4.

experience, rationality implies *the ability to give an account, to provide a rationale*, for the way one thinks, chooses, acts, and believes'.[43] Further, Bruce Marshall (a theologian with whom we will engage at length in Chapters 7 and 8) asserts that 'we regularly suppose that what gives us *the right* to hold beliefs is that we have employed criteria which settle the matter of their truth'.[44]

The alternative approach to justification is known as externalism. While externalists will admit that some of our beliefs require justification, they are emphatic that not all do. Thus, the justification for a large number of beliefs need not be accessible to a person in order for them to be justified in holding the belief. In those cases we need not give an account of why we believe or how we know something in order to be justified in believing it or knowing it.[45] Despite the dominance of internalist approaches to justification, externalism has grown in popularity in the last few decades. One of the reasons relates to a critical weakness with the JTB definition that was identified by Edmund Gettier in 'Is Justified True Belief Knowledge?',[46] a three-page paper which fell like a bomb on the playground of the epistemologists. In this short paper Gettier launched a full-on assault at the seemingly impregnable definition of knowledge as justified true belief.[47] The core of Gettier's argument identified putative cases of justified true belief that intuitively do not count as knowledge (so-called Gettier cases). Recall the case cited above of the Calvinist who believes all Arminians are Pelagians and then comes to believe that a particular Arminian is Pelagian. I concluded that even if the Arminian is a Pelagian, the Calvinist would not know this because his belief is rooted in prejudice. But what if the Calvinist was justified in this

[43] Van Huyssteen, *Essays in Postfoundationalist Theology* (Grand Rapids, Mich.: Eerdmans, 1997), 39; emphasis added.

[44] Marshall, *Trinity and Truth* (Cambridge: Cambridge University Press, 2000), 8 n. 4; emphasis added.

[45] Plantinga writes: '[T]he properties that on this view confer warrant are not such that I need have any special kind of epistemic access to them' (*Warrant: The Current Debate*, p. 6). See also Robert Audi, *Epistemology: A Contemporary Introduction to the Theory of Knowledge* (London: Routledge, 1998), 231–7.

[46] Gettier, 'Is Justified True Belief Knowledge?', *Analysis*, 23 (1963), 121–3.

[47] Plantinga writes: '*Knowledge is justified true belief*: so we thought from time immemorial. Then God said, "Let Gettier be"; not quite all was light, perhaps, but at any rate we learned we had been standing in a dark corner' (*Warrant and Proper Function* (Oxford: Oxford University Press, 1993), 31).

belief? What if he came to believe it not because of an ungrounded prejudice but rather because the Arminian was wearing a T-shirt that said 'Pelagius was right'? Would it then count as knowledge? If the JTB analysis is correct, then it *must* count as knowledge because it meets all the conditions of knowledge.

The strength of Gettier's argument consisted in pointing out that we could conceive of scenarios where all these elements are present and yet the belief does not constitute knowledge. For instance, let's say that the Arminian has no idea who Pelagius was, and that he purchased the shirt at a Broadway musical entitled 'Pelagius Was Right' about a struggling singer named Pelagius who makes it big. In that case, it would seem that the Calvinist does not have knowledge, even though he does have a justified true belief. In essence, the *luck* problem has returned, in this case corrupting the Calvinist's justification. And so, if one could hold a justified true belief and still fail to have knowledge then the JTB account is not adequate as a general definition of knowledge. But if (internalist) justification is not sufficient for knowledge, then what is the missing criterion? More radically, if justification is not sufficient for knowledge, *is it even necessary?*

Gettier's argument led to a re-evaluation of long-assumed internalist conceptions of justification and thus to the development of externalist theories of justification. Hilary Kornblith summarizes the difference between internalism and externalism with the following three questions:

(1) How ought we to arrive at our beliefs?
(2) How do we arrive at our beliefs?
(3) Are the processes by which we do arrive at our beliefs the ones by which we ought to arrive at our beliefs?[48]

Kornblith points out that internalism apportions question (1) to philosophers and question (2) to psychologists, with the two groups pooling results to answer question (3). On this view, epistemology is concerned with the normative criteria that our doxastic faculties and processes must satisfy, while psychology is concerned with the description of these processes as they actually function. With

---

[48] Kornblith, 'Introduction: What is Naturalistic Epistemology?', in Kornblith (ed.), *Naturalizing Epistemology*, 2nd edn. (Cambridge, Mass.: MIT, 1994), 1.

externalism, however, the actual functioning of our doxastic processes is accorded a prima facie normative status; to put it simply, how we *do* function under normal circumstances is how we *ought* to function (though, as we will see, a further stipulation of normativity is required to ensure that beliefs resulting from a common dysfunction are not automatically justified). The externalist approach is thus often termed *naturalistic*, because it focuses on a description of the natural processes by which we form beliefs.[49] In other words, for the externalist, question (1) is answered through an analysis of question (2), so that the core criterion for knowledge is shifted back to doxastic processes shorn of the normative internalist element.

A range of externalist positions have developed in the wake of Gettier's challenge to justified true belief. The extreme wing is represented by W. V. O. Quine, who in 'Epistemology Naturalized' refused any attempt to find a normative criterion for justification or knowledge beyond concrete psychological and, at the most basic level, neural processes. In short, Quine rejected the normativity of belief altogether, thereby reducing epistemology to the descriptions of empirical psychology.[50] However, most externalists have maintained that epistemology cannot be reduced without remainder to the sciences and thus have sought a normative criterion for justification and knowledge. According to the early Alvin Goldman, knowledge requires an appropriate causal connection between the knower and that which is known.[51] More recently Goldman has developed the theory of reliabilism, according to which a true belief constitutes knowledge if it is true and produced by reliable truth-producing cognitive faculties.[52] Robert Nozick offers a different proposal again by suggesting that the criterion is rooted in a counterfactual ability

[49] This type of epistemological naturalism should not be conflated with metaphysical naturalism, as Earl Conee does in 'Plantinga's Naturalism', in Jonathan Kvanvig (ed.), *Warrant in Contemporary Epistemology* (Lanham, Md.: Rowman & Littlefield, 1996), 183–96.

[50] Quine, 'Epistemology Naturalized', in *Ontological Relativity and Other Essays* (New York: Columbia University Press, 1969), 69–90.

[51] Goldman, 'A Causal Theory of Knowing', *Journal of Philosophy*, 64/12 (1967), 357–72.

[52] See Goldman, *Epistemology and Cognition* (Cambridge, Mass.: Harvard University Press, 1986); William Alston, 'How to Think about Reliability', *Philosophical Topics*, 23/1 (1995), 1–29.

to 'track the truth' successfully in nearby possible worlds.[53] Finally, in the view of Alvin Plantinga, which we shall return to in Chapter 9, the missing criterion is the concept of proper function.

Methodism and Particularism

Our second distinction is between 'methodist' and 'particularist' approaches to epistemology.[54] In order to set up these two approaches we can ask which of Kornblith's first two questions ought to preface epistemological enquiry. Those who begin with (1)—How are beliefs justified?—are adopting a particularist approach, while those who begin with (2)—Which of our beliefs are justified?—have opted for methodism. The second question is not directly concerned with whether individuals possess any justification for beliefs (or, as a result, whether they have knowledge). Hence, to accept the priority of (2) tacitly implies one can and ought to identify criteria of justification irrespective of whether one has any justified beliefs. But how can we begin by assuming justified true beliefs if we might not have any? If it is illegitimate for a scientist to assume the veracity of her theory, surely it is equally illegitimate for an epistemologist to do so. The methodist begins with intuitive criteria of justification and knowledge and then examines different beliefs to see whether any in fact meets these conditions. Since this approach sidelines the question of whether we in fact have any justified beliefs, it opens up the possibility of the enquiry terminating in scepticism where none of our beliefs meets the criteria of justification. For a methodist that possibility is demanded by an honest epistemological enquiry. The methodist thus obliges us to countenance global scepticism as a viable possibility. This approach has high stakes, for, as Keith Lehrer warns, '[w]hen one once enters the den of skepticism, an exit may be difficult to find'.[55]

The particularist begins with (1) and seeks to explain justification with reference to common properties or characteristics shared

---

[53] Nozick, *Philosophical Explanations* (Cambridge, Mass.: Harvard University Press, 1981), ch. 3.

[54] See Roderick Chisholm, *The Problem of the Criterion*, Aquinas Lecture 1973 (Milwaukee, Wisc.: Marquette University Press, 1973). The same distinction can be found in Plato's *Theaetetus*, 146d–147c.

[55] Lehrer, *Theory of Knowledge*, p. 2.

by our beliefs. Once those properties are gleaned from specific instances of belief we will have the material to develop a preliminary theory of what justification entails. Since we *begin* by identifying *which* of our beliefs is justified, particularism *already assumes that we have justified beliefs*. So, to sum up, the methodist assumes a priori a certain perspective on the nature of justification and then proceeds a posteriori to investigate which beliefs are justified. By contrast, the particularist assumes a priori that certain beliefs are justified and then proceeds a posteriori to analyse the nature of justification.

At this point you might guess that methodism is closely related to internalism. By approaching the analysis of justification through a method, one implies that every belief we hold requires a reason— every belief must be shown to measure up to internalist constraints. Conversely, particularism is a natural ally with externalism, for it assumes that we can have justified beliefs about our justified beliefs without yet knowing the criteria by which we do so. There seem to be elements of truth and error in each method of analysis. The methodist worries that the particularist's assumption of justification and knowledge is viciously circular. The particularist retorts that we must assume an ability to identify some justified beliefs or the enquiry could never get going. To provide one example, surely I am presently justified in believing that I am now typing at my computer, and if I am so justified, why not use such belief as a starting point for the analysis of justification?

The Origin and Transmission of Justification: Foundationalism, Infinitism, and Coherentism

While the internalist/externalist debate is concerned with the nature of justification (or whatever element plus true belief results in knowledge), the methodist/particularist debate concerns the means by which we identify justified beliefs. Our final debate concerns the origin and transmission of justification. At this point there are three positions: infinitism, coherentism, and foundationalism. Each of these is a theory of noetic structure; that is, a theory of how justification originates in and is transmitted between beliefs.[56] As such, they all offer different responses to what Hans Albert refers to as the 'trilemma' of justification; namely, whether the regress of justification is infinite, circular, or terminated in particular beliefs.[57] We will begin by making some preliminary points, before we turn to consider these three theories.

Upon reflection it would seem that a belief could pass epistemic muster in one of three ways: either it is self-justified, or it does not require justification, or it receives justification from another belief. Say, for instance, that a student taking a university class on the history of contemporary rock music comes to believe that (i) David Lee Roth was the first front man of Van Halen based on the instructor's assertion that (ii) Sammy Hagar became the second front man of Van Halen, thereby replacing David Lee Roth. This is a clear case of coming to believe something as a straight deduction from a prior belief and thus being justified in virtue of that other belief. Most epistemologists recognize that at least *some* of our beliefs are justified by other beliefs. The real question is whether they *all* are or whether there are beliefs that do not receive (or require) justification from other beliefs. The person who concludes that all beliefs receive justification from other beliefs has two noetic theories to choose from: infinitism and coherentism. Infinitism explains the justification of beliefs by way of an *infinite series of justifying beliefs*. For instance, (a) is justified relative to (b), and (b) is justified relative to (c), ad infinitum. However, if one concludes that the set of beliefs that justifies must be finite, then the justification relation must ultimately be *reciprocal* such that beliefs justify one another: in shortest compass: (a) justifies (b) and (b) justifies (a). This second option is called coherentism, appropriately enough since on this view the primary locus of justification is the coherent relation of our various beliefs. Those who reject both of these accounts by holding that *some* beliefs *do not* receive justification from other beliefs, and yet *do* transfer justification to other beliefs, have anticipated our third theory of

---

[56] All three theories are anticipated in Aristotle, *Posterior Analytics*, 1.1–4, 2.19.

[57] See Hans Albert and M. V. Rorty, *Treatise on Critical Reason* (Princeton, NJ: Princeton University Press, 1985), 18, cited in Wolterstorff, *John Locke*, p. 68.

noetic structure: foundationalism. At this point we will assess each theory in more depth.

We will begin with the least popular theory: infinitism. This theory has attracted few defenders,[58] and for good reason since human beings do not, and cannot, in fact *hold* an infinite number of beliefs. Hence, if this is required for knowledge, then it would seem to follow that we cannot know anything. In fact, the problem is even worse, for, as Michael Bergmann has pointed out, each subsequent belief further down the infinitely long chain will be of greater complexity, since each further belief must include its conceptual relation to all previous beliefs. For instance, the person must know that (b) justifies (a), and that (c) justifies (b) which justifies (a), and that (d) justifies (c) which justifies (b) which justifies (a), and so on. Within but a few steps the complexity of belief already begins to slip beyond our cognitive grasp.[59] To put the problem in perspective, Robert Audi observes: 'Imagine the "largest" proposition a supercomputer could formulate after years of work. It could easily be too long to understand and so cumbersome that one could not even take in a formulation of it, being unable to remember enough about the first part of it when one gets to the end'.[60] And yet, this proposition would only put us at the very *beginning* of the series of beliefs that would be required for the justification of *just one* belief. In addition to this infinite regress of increasing complexity, we can note one final objection: as Richard Fumerton points out, the infinitist's regress collapses into *an infinite regress of regresses*.[61] Infinitism thus appears to provide a one-way ticket to a bracing epistemological scepticism.

[58] In 'Foundationalist Theories of Epistemic Justification', in *Stanford Encyclopedia of Philosophy*, Richard Fumerton contends that Peter Klein is the only notable philosopher to hold this position (at <http://plato.stanford.edu/entries/justep-foundational>). For Klein's views see 'Human Knowledge and the Infinite Regress of Reasons', in James Tomberlin (ed.), *Philosophical Perspectives, ii. Epistemology* (Atascadero, Calif.: Ridgeview, 1999), 297–325.

[59] Bergmann, 'A Dilemma for Internalism', in Thomas Crisp, Matthew Davidson, and David Vander Laan (eds.), *Knowledge and Reality: Essays in Honor of Alvin Plantinga* (Dordrecht: Springer, 2006), 137–77; cf. Bergmann, *Justification without Awareness*.

[60] Audi, *Epistemology*, p. 183.

[61] Fumerton, 'Classical Foundationalism', in Michael DePaul (ed.), *Resurrecting Old-fashioned Foundationalism* (Lanham, Md.: Rowman & Littlefield, 2000), 7.

One could try to save infinitism by reworking the internalist requirements, for instance by weakening belief to a disposition to accept a proposition so that one need not *actually* believe every proposition in this infinite series but only have the disposition that one *would* believe every proposition in the series if it was presented to one. However, this is no help given that no finite mind can possibly grasp an infinite series of concepts/propositions and so appealing to *potential* simply begs the question. But never mind the whole set, for even the hundredth belief in the series would already be far too unwieldy to grasp. For these reasons it is widely agreed that infinitism collapses into scepticism. In other words, if we begin with this view of noetic structure, we end up with the stark conclusion that none of our beliefs is ultimately justified (and that of course includes belief in infinitism). Given the severity of these difficulties we shall set infinitism aside.

Technically speaking, the term non-foundationalism should encompass *all* theories that deny foundationalist theories of justification, including infinitism. However, in point of fact the term is used more narrowly to refer to the coherentist approach to justification, as well as pragmatic approaches to epistemology that reject the traditional search for justification.[62] The coherentist account of noetic structure claims that justification is grounded in a finite set of coherent beliefs. There are two basic accounts of coherence justification: the circle and the web. On the circle model, justification is a linear relation between individual beliefs. This approach is structurally like infinitism in so far as the chain of justification continues in a linear fashion without ever terminating. It is unclear *how many* beliefs would be required for justification to arise on this account, but whatever that threshold is, at that point justification transfer occurs asymmetrically and irreflexively from one belief to another until it is ultimately transferred from the original belief back to itself. This notion of circular justification has not appealed to many coherentists for a number of reasons. First, the implication that a belief ultimately

---

[62] Since pragmatism is not a theory of justification but rather a rejection of accounts of justification, we shall defer discussion of it until Chapter 5. For a discussion of the contrast between coherentism and foundationalism see Ernest Sosa, 'The Raft and the Pyramid: Coherence Versus Foundations in the Theory of Knowledge', in his *Knowledge in Perspective* (Cambridge: Cambridge University Press, 1991), 16–91.

justifies itself seems to flout the intuitively compelling principle that nothing can be the cause of its own justification.[63] Second, the account appears contrived, given that we do not actually reason in a circle to justify beliefs. As Audi observes, 'I do not see how to go full circle, unless I *think up* propositions I do not originally believe, hence do not originally know'.[64] Clearly it is important that an account of noetic structure not contradict psychology. Given the fact that justification can only arise if the number of beliefs is sufficiently large, it would appear that justification actually arises holistically from the total *size* and *fit* of the series, a fact which favours the web model. With this model (or metaphor) justification is a holistic property that arises from the total fit of our beliefs. According to this type of coherentism justified beliefs are coherent with our other beliefs while those that are not require further evidential justification.[65]

Most coherentists hold a holistic view of justification. This picture has the benefit of avoiding an infinite regress while making justification an *internal* and *accessible* property of belief: I can find out on reflection whether my beliefs are coherent. While this approach may be more appealing than the circle model, holism still faces challenges. To begin with, there is the difficulty with identifying a golden mean of coherence between the mere absence of contradiction and strict logical implication. Take, for instance, my beliefs that *God is three persons* and that *Hondas are more reliable than Ladas*. Since these propositions do not contradict, they can both be coherently held. Yet there is no obvious link between them (certainly not implication). In virtue of what, then, are they part of a coherent whole? Can I really link them epistemically within my total set of beliefs or must I *invent* beliefs to do so? The apparent need for contrivance here echoes the problem with circular justification. A second problem concerns the *origin* of justification. While holistic coherentism may not be as counter-intuitive as the circular form, it still conflicts with

---

[63] 'Suppose I believe that my dog is an alien from outer space, and suppose I could manage, somehow, to start believing this proposition on the basis—the immediate evidential basis—of *itself*. Surely this belief would not thereupon acquire a greater degree of warrant for me than it had before I executed this dubious maneuver '(Plantinga, *Warrant: The Current Debate*, 77).

[64] Audi, *Epistemology*, p. 184.

[65] Plantinga, *Warrant: The Current Debate*, pp. 78–80.

the intuition that justification is somehow generated in experiences in the world. Analogically speaking, one might argue that we have no more reason to think our beliefs can produce justification internally than we have reason to think ten empty wallets can fill each other with money. Just as an *external* monetary source is required to fill the wallets, so an external source is necessary to justify beliefs. Further, some of our beliefs do not appear to be justifiable relative to the coherence principle, including the belief that *coherence is a source of justification*. Justifying this belief by way of coherence begs the question, but the only other alternative is to leave the basic criterion undergirding the whole theory unjustified.

Foundationalists share the premiss that some beliefs do not require justification from other beliefs. Hence, there are two kinds of beliefs, those that require justification (non-basic), and those that transmit it but do not require it (basic), with the latter generating the sequence of justification. The foundationalist thus agrees with the infinitist that certain beliefs support others via an irreflexive and asymmetric justification transfer from basic to non-basic beliefs; justification never travels from non-basic beliefs to basic beliefs. But he also agrees with the coherentist that the regress of justification transfer must be *finite*. In this way, he seeks to maintain the best of both approaches while sidestepping the objections faced by each.

Stated in bare essentials there is an undeniable plausibility to the foundationalist account of belief formation/justification, and thus it clears the first hurdle of psychological plausibility. As Craig and Moreland put it, '[f]oundationalism just seems to be the way that people actually and appropriately go about justifying their beliefs'.[66] To take but one example, the foundationalist avers that it seems more

---

[66] J. P. Moreland and William Lane Craig, *Philosophical Foundations for a Christian Worldview* (Downers Grove, Ill.: InterVarsity, 2003), 149. Non-foundationalists reply that the intuitive appeal of foundationalism (perhaps even its default status among non-philosophers) is due to the pervasive influence of the theory rather than to common sense per se. Nancey Murphy writes: 'This [foundationalist] metaphor has so thoroughly imbued our thinking that we can scarcely talk about knowledge without hints of it: good arguments are well-grounded and solidly constructed; suspicions are unfounded or baseless; disciplines that explore presuppositions are called foundational' ('Introduction', in Stanley Hauerwas, Nancey Murphy, and Mark Nation (eds.), *Theology Without Foundations: Religious Practice and the Future of Theological Truth* (Nashville, Tenn.: Abingdon, 1994), 9–10.

plausible to claim that justification for one's belief that an apple is red arises from a basic experience of *seeing* the apple (the experience of being appeared to redly and apple-wise) rather than from an infinite regress of beliefs or the coherence of this particular belief with one's noetic web. Similarly, it would seem that one's justification for 2 + 2 = 4 is rooted in a rational intuition of the incorrigibility of the belief. The property of 'proper basicality' is thus predicated at least of beliefs that are justified by immediate experience or rational reflection, and possibly of many more.

But, alas, there is always a dark cloud with every silver lining, and here it is found in the nature of basic beliefs and the means by which they transfer justification. In short, the claim that some beliefs can generate their own justification (or do not require justification) appears to coherentists about as plausible as a perpetual-motion machine. And how is it that a non-doxastic experience can produce a justified belief? This appears to the coherentist to be a suspicious conjuring trick. And so, the viability of the foundationalist account depends in large part on the sense we can make of properly basic beliefs. One final point: while foundationalists are united in their claims to finite and asymmetrical regresses of justification, they are divided on the question of the nature of justification, with some opting for internalist and methodist analyses of justification and knowledge and others opting for externalist and particularist approaches.

CONCLUSION

In retrospect, we can see that the contentious understanding of justification that has dominated the philosophical gravediggers (Chapter 1) and their theological counterparts (Chapter 2) is in large part internalist, methodist, and foundationalist. As such, this survey has provided much-needed clarity on what has too often been assumed in the debates over justification and what, in the coming chapters, must be called into question.

4

The End of Classical Foundationalism

The person who is certain, and who claims divine warrant for
his certainty, belongs now to the infancy of our species.

Christopher Hitchens, *God Is Not Great*

For always to have proofs before us is too much trouble. We
must acquire an easier belief, which is that of habit, which,
without violence, art, or argument, makes us believe things and
inclines all our powers to this belief.

Blaise Pascal *Penseés*

Prior to his conversion, C. S. Lewis had a series of informal debates
with a Christian friend who, as Lewis recounts, repeatedly challenged
the Oxford don's uncritical acceptance of atheism:

He made short work of what I have called my 'chronological snobbery', the
uncritical acceptance of the intellectual climate common to our own age
and the assumption that whatever has gone out of date is on that account
discredited. You must find why it went out of date. Was it ever refuted (and
if so by whom, where, and how conclusively) or did it merely die away as
fashions do? [1]

Thus, Lewis learned that academics are just as liable to become fashion victims as anybody else, albeit their fashions are found in ideas
rather than the accoutrements of popular culture. Given this fact, it is
crucial that we analyse intellectual trends to ensure that they represent
not merely the changing of fashions but real substance. So it is with
the currently unfashionable status of foundationalism, and classical

---

[1] Cited in Kenneth G. Howkins, *The Challenge of Religious Studies* (London:
Tyndale, 1972), 23.

foundationalism in particular. Those who now reject classical foundationalism for the sake of fashion are no better than the gravediggers who once accepted it for the sake of fashion. The issues here are complex and the initial case for classical foundationalism, like the case for corduroy jackets and bell-bottomed jeans, is at least appreciable if not quite compelling. There is no doubt that classical foundationalism exacts a significant theological cost, but in this chapter we will focus on assessing the nature and strength of the various philosophical objections. We will begin with the problem of identifying incorrigible beliefs and universal reason. Then we will consider the claim that classical foundationalism is self-referentially defeating; finally we will address the central problem of an epistemic interface with the world (often termed 'the given'). This will provide the background to reconsider the viability of classical foundationalism.

WHY CLASSICAL FOUNDATIONALISM IS DEAD

Before we begin a close survey of the arguments against classical foundationalism, we should seek to define the position. Here is a classical foundationalist account of justification, where b = a justified belief:

Every b is either (1) properly basic—that is, b is either a self-evident intuition or an incorrigible sense experience—or (2) non-basic—that is, it is ultimately deduced or inferred from beliefs that are properly basic and the individual is aware of how b derives from a properly basic belief.

In assessing this account we will focus first on the incorrigible and universal-methodist criteria assumed by classical foundationalism and then on the austere limitation of properly basic belief to the immediate deliverances of rational intuition and sense perception. We will then consider the internalist demand that one must know how one's beliefs are justified.

A Certain and Universal Foundation

The most important methodist criterion at work in classical foundationalism is that knowledge must be incorrigible: since knowledge begins at the foundations, justified beliefs must be inferred from certain foundations. So important is this criterion that it has often been taken to be the single most notable distinctive of classical foundationalism.[2] But it would be a mistake to connect the thesis with foundationalism *simpliciter*.[3] From the other direction we should not make the mistake of thinking that only classical foundationalism demands certainty or incorrigibility, for many non-foundationalists have held this methodist criterion. That said, it is still undoubtedly true that incorrigibility has been an overriding epistemic desideratum among foundationalists ever since Descartes initiated his search for an Archimedean point. Indeed, given the hegemony of classical foundationalism, some like Richard Rorty have identified the search for certain incorrigibility as the central preoccupation of epistemology: 'The theory of knowledge will be the search for that which compels the mind to belief as soon as it is unveiled'.[4] With a commitment to incorrigibility as a noble epistemic goal, the advocate of classical foundationalism then provides showcase instances of incorrigible beliefs, perhaps the most famous being Descartes's *cogito, ergo sum*.[5] (Of course, even if one's own existence could be established with certainty, this would surely be a slim reed on which to build an entire noetic structure.) All told, classical foundationalism admits two distinct sources of belief as properly basic: rationally intuited first principles (e.g. $7 + 5 = 12$) and the immediate deliverances of sense perception (e.g. I seem to see an apple).

This leads us to the second methodist criterion of universality. According to this criterion properly basic beliefs are so obviously true that they compel universal assent among rational individuals. Roy Clouser calls this the 'everybody requirement' and defines it as

[2] Conversely, the single most significant mark of the current post-modern malaise is a perceived loss of certainty (see Peter Berger, 'Protestantism and the Quest for Certainty', *Christian Century*, 26 Aug.-2 Sept. 1998, pp. 782–96).

[3] As Robert Audi has observed, '[f]oundationalism is committed to unmoved movers; it is not committed to unmovable movers' (*Epistemology: A Contemporary Introduction to the Theory of Knowledge* (London: Routledge, 1998), 208).

[4] Rorty, *Philosophy and the Mirror of Nature* (Princeton, NJ: Princeton University Press, 1979), 163.

[5] Whether the *cogito* acts as a basic intuitive belief or a discursive argument is hotly debated (see Peter Markie, 'The Cogito and Its Importance', in John Cottingham (ed.), *The Cambridge Companion to Descartes* (Cambridge: Cambridge University Press, 1992), 140–73).

follows: '[A] genuinely self-evident belief is one that *all* normal adults see as true once they understand it'.[6] Along with incorrigibility, universality delimits the types of basic evidence that are admissible in the classical-foundationalist court of reason. Evidence for the universality criterion is present when the truth of the belief is readily demonstrable to all rational people. (*Mutatis mutandis* for the Christian theologian: according to classical foundationalism, Christian beliefs can only be justified if one is able to defend their proper basicality by appeal to these two sources, either as properly basic or as legitimate inferences from certain basic beliefs.[7]) The incorrigibility and universality requirements of classical foundationalism have come under severe criticism in the last few decades on two fronts. While some have argued that there are not enough incorrigible beliefs to ground our entire noetic structure, the stronger charge is that in fact *none* of our beliefs is incorrigible. If either claim is successful, the classical foundationalist will have to choose either to embrace scepticism or to abandon classical foundationalism.

The Loss of Certainty

The assumption that knowledge requires certainty has a venerable history dating back to the ancient Greeks, and for good reason. After all, intuitive reflection suggests an intimate relationship between knowledge and certainty. David Lewis comments:

It seems as if knowledge must be by definition infallible. If you claim that S knows that P, and yet you grant that S cannot eliminate a certain possibility in which not-P, it certainly seems as if you have granted that S does not after all know that P. To speak of fallible knowledge, of knowledge despite uneliminated possibilities of error, just *sounds* contradictory.[8]

Thus, it is intuitively plausible to assume that in order to have knowledge one must have certainty. And since the consequence of denying

---

[6] Clouser, *Knowing With the Heart: Religious Experience and Belief in God* (Downers Grove, Ill.: InterVarsity, 1999), 80–1.

[7] See Alvin Plantinga, *Warranted Christian Belief* (Oxford: Oxford University Press, 2000), ch. 3.

[8] Cited in Robert Oakes, 'Theism and Infallibilism: A Marriage Made in Heaven?', *Religious Studies*, 40/2 (2004), 194.

knowledge is a bracing scepticism, there are powerful grounds to seek certainty in our beliefs. So substantial has been the emphasis on certainty in much of the philosophical and theological tradition that a denial of incorrigibility has often been interpreted as tantamount to embracing scepticism. The incorrigible ground of certainty has classically been found in the notion that rational intuition grasps truths that are eternal and thus unchanging and indubitable. Since eternal truths never change, once we grasp them we can *know* they will never change and thus we cannot be incorrect in believing them; therefore we can be certain of them. Rational intuition of such stable truths has long been a goal and paradigm for knowledge, as in the following passage from Augustine's *Confessions*:

I wanted to be as certain about things I could not see as I am certain that seven and three are ten. I was not so mad as to think that I could consider even that to be something unknowable. But I desired other things to be as certain as this truth, whether physical objects which were not immediately accessible to my senses, or spiritual matters which I knew no way of thinking about except in physical terms.[9]

For Augustine, the paradigm of knowledge is that which is incorrigibly certain, in this case the knowledge that seven and three added together make ten. And so Augustine desires that same certainty in all areas, whether concerning 'physical objects ... or spiritual matters'.

A certain belief that is rooted in public evidence is one that is known either intuitively or deductively in the form of a proof that is a deductively valid argument with true premises. The real difficulty comes in identifying sound proofs; indeed, the impregnable certainty that has been sought after by so many is now widely derided and dismissed as a futile and foolhardy goal. The currently dominant fallibilist position is stated succinctly by Lesslie Newbigin, who observes that '[o]nly statements that can be doubted make contact with reality'.[10] Conversely, unshakeable confidence in one's beliefs is widely associated with intellectual immaturity and, as Christopher Hitchens suggests, with intolerance: 'The nineteen suicide murderers

[9] Augustine, *Confessions*, trans. Henry Chadwick (Oxford: Oxford University Press, 1991), 95 (6.4).

[10] Newbigin, *Proper Confidence: Faith Doubt, and Certainty in Christian Discipleship* (London: SPCK, 1995), 52.

of New York and Washington and Pennsylvania were beyond any doubt the most sincere believers on those planes'.[11] Thus, the danger is that those who hold their beliefs with unshakeable conviction suffer arrested intellectual development and are more likely to oppress others. But, setting the ethical concerns aside, the greatest objection to the possibility of certain, incorrigible beliefs comes in the cumulative force of multiple cases of apparently indubitable beliefs that have been shown to be false. If indubitable beliefs can be falsified such that indubitability is not a sure guide to truth, then we will have undercutting defeaters for the putative certainty/incorrigibility of *any* belief.[12]

Two of the most influential examples of 'defeated indubitables' are the discovery of non-Euclidean geometries and Russell's paradox. To take the first, Euclidean geometry was long considered to be the most striking example of incorrigible a priori knowledge, a set of truths on which all could agree regardless of race, religion, or ethnicity. Take, for instance, the luminously compelling parallel postulate.[13] In the nineteenth century, when geometers attempted to deduce the Euclidean parallel postulate from the other postulates, non-Euclidean geometries were inadvertently discovered. As a result, the parallel postulate was modified, resulting in two internally coherent non-Euclidean systems: Lobachevskian geometry, which accepts a many-parallels postulate, and Riemannian geometry, which holds to a no-parallels postulate. As BonJour observes, '[t]his result has by itself been widely regarded, both then and later, as a refutation of the claim that Euclidean geometry provides *a priori* insight into the nature of physical space'.[14] One might have hoped that further work in mathematics would relieve the tension and demonstrate which

[11] Hitchens, *God Is Not Great: How Religion Poisons Everything* (New York: Twelve, 2007), 32.

[12] For a discussion of undercutting defeaters see John Pollock, *Contemporary Theories of Knowledge* (Totowa, NJ: Rowman & Littlefield, 1986), 48 ff.

[13] Euclid's parallel postulate reads as follows: 'If a straight line falling on two straight lines makes the interior angles on the same side together less than two right angles, the two straight lines, if produced indefinitely, meet on that side on which the angles are together less than two right angles' (cited in BonJour, *In Defense of Pure Reason* (Cambridge: Cambridge University Press, 1998), 219).

[14] BonJour, *In Defense of Pure Reason*, p. 220.

geometry is the correct one. Unfortunately, subsequent work has only fanned earlier doubts into roaring flames. As Morris Kline puts it:

The current predicament of mathematics is that there is not one but many mathematics and that for numerous reasons each fails to satisfy the members of the opposing schools. It is now apparent that the concept of a universally accepted, infallible body of reasoning—the majestic mathematics of 1800 and the pride of man—is a grand illusion. . . . The disagreements about the foundations of the 'most certain' science are both surprising and, to put it mildly, disconcerting. The present state of mathematics is a mockery of the hitherto deep-rooted and widely reputed truth and logical perfection of mathematics.[15]

And so mathematics, that discipline which since Pythagoras has ignited the mind with the mystic dazzle of sacred certainty, has also seen its revelations subjected to critical doubt.

If we cannot attain certainty in the eternal realm of numbers, we might hope for unshakeable ground in a retreat to logic. But, alas, the same problems that have shaken mathematics have also bedevilled modern work in logic. Our example begins with the young Bertrand Russell's near-obsessive search for certainty. He initially thought that he had found it when he read Euclid's *Elements* as a child. But, alas, young Russell soon grew discouraged as he wondered why he should accept Euclid's axioms without proof. This concern set Russell on the ambitious road of attempting to ground the axioms of mathematics in logic, a task which culminated in the monumental but ultimately unsuccessful *Principia Mathematica*.[16] Along the way Russell identified a second putative defeater of certainty in the appropriately named Russell's paradox.[17] The paradox was originally developed with respect to classes. (A class is simply a specified collection of objects; for example, the class of unemployed theologians, the class of Pelagian Arminians, the class of prime numbers, or the class of

---

[15] Kline, *Mathematics: The Loss of Certainty* (New York: Oxford University Press, 1980), 6, cited in Clouser, *Knowing with the Heart*, p. 77.

[16] Co-written with Alfred North Whitehead, 1910–13.

[17] William Placher appeals to Russell's paradox as an example of how 'tough-minded philosophers have chipped away at supposed examples of necessary truths' (Placher, *Unapologetic Theology: A Christian Voice in a Pluralistic Conversation* (Louisville, Ky.: Westminster/John Knox, 1989), 32, 33–4). But while Russell's paradox has epistemological implications, it has *no metaphysical implications* about modal necessity.

unread copies of Stephen Hawking's *A Brief History of Time*.) Prior to Russell's work, the great philosopher Gottlob Frege had set out to reduce arithmetic to logic via the theory of classes. It seemed self-evident to this brilliant man (and many others besides) that for every class there is a set of things that are members of it. However, admitting this premise leads to the paradoxical class of all classes that are not members of themselves. As Russell pointed out in a famous letter to Frege, this class is contradictory, for if it is a member of itself then it is not a member of itself. While this problem led Frege to abandon his dream of reducing arithmetic to logic, the epistemological reverberations were significant, for here we had a principle that *seemed* self-evident, and yet turned out to be false—indeed, *necessarily* so.[18] Thus, one could have a belief that *appeared* to be self-evidently true and yet could turn out to be necessarily false. But if we can make these kinds of mistakes, then which intuitive beliefs *can* be completely trusted?

Another important source of scepticism about incorrigible beliefs arises from the influence of the fallibilistic mind-set of science. While science continues to make truly astounding advances in knowledge, it also is predicated on a unique humility. Chet Raymo writes:

Let this, then, be the ground of my faith: All that we know, now and forever, all scientific knowledge that we have of this world, or will ever have, is as an island in the sea [of mystery] ... We live in our partial knowledge as the Dutch live on polders claimed from the sea. We dike and fill. We dredge up soil from the bed of mystery and build ourselves room to grow. And still the mystery surrounds us. It laps at our shores. It permeates the land. Scratch the surface of knowledge and mystery bubbles up like a spring. And occasionally, at certain disquieting moments in history (Aristarchus, Galileo, Planck, Einstein), a tempest of mystery comes rolling in from the sea and overwhelms our efforts, reclaims knowledge that has been built up by years of patient work, and forces us to retreat to the surest, most secure core of what we know, where we huddle in fear and trembling until the storm subsides, and then we start building again, throwing up dikes, pumping, filling, extending the perimeter of our knowledge and our security.[19]

---

[18] For a fuller account see Anthony Kenny, *Frege* (London: Penguin, 1995), 173–7.

[19] Cited in Raymo, *Skeptics and True Believers: The Exhilarating Connection Between Science and Religion* (London: Vintage, 1999), 47.

Science is in principle so committed to fallibilism that it enshrines within its methodology a commitment to falsify scientific hypotheses. Hence, Robert Swenson comments, '[w]hen a musical King of Siam sang: "There are times I almost think I am not sure of what I absolutely know," he could just as easily have been talking about modern science. Science is, after all, only "an orderly arrangement of what seem at the time to be facts" '.[20] As such, science has ample examples of well-established theories being overturned by new evidence. One thinks, for instance, of the tempest that swept over physics courtesy of Einstein.[21] If fallibilism is the lot of science, why should we expect theologians to be more successful?

The Loss of Universal Reason

In the previous chapter we distinguished between subjective and objective justification. With the example of Orson the Mormon, we noted how an individual may be justified relative to his particular knowledge base and still lack objective justification. Perhaps at that point you were led to wonder what good this notion of objective justification is, if *all* judgements about justification are rendered with respect to one or another knowledge base. Isn't *all* justification in that sense relative? And isn't all reason situated and perspectival? Hilary Putnam observes that 'the idea of a "point at which" subjectivity ceases and Objectivity-with-a-capital-O begins has proven chimerical'.[22] But it would seem that the first casualty of a loss of rational objectivity is the concept of universal reason. And if we have no claims that will compel universal assent, then we cannot speak of reason as having the type of probative force that the classical foundationalist demands.

---

[20] Swenson, *More than Meets the Eye: Fascinating Glimpses of God's Power and Design* (Colorado Springs, Col.: NavPress, 2000), 102.

[21] Robert P. Crease and Charles C. Mann, *The Second Creation: Makers of the Revolution in Twentieth Century Physics* (London: Quartet, 1997), 9.

[22] Putnam, *The Many Faces of Realism*, Paul Carus Lectures (LaSalle, Ill.: Open Court, 1987), 2.

The point is made memorably in the essay 'On the Very Strongest Arguments,[23] where George Mavrodes identifies the conditions necessary for a universally compelling proof. He starts with the following definition: '[A]n argument is compelling if and only if it is sound and everyone accepts it'.[24] The problem is that there are numerous reasons why a person might not accept an argument, not the least being failure to *understand* it. Hence, Mavrodes adds the qualification that everyone who comes to understand it accepts it. But what if there are two sound arguments for a particular conclusion, the first being compelling but only comprehensible by a select few while the second is not compelling but is comprehensible by the average lay person? Here we see a conflict between the virtues 'being accessible' and 'being compelling', with neither of clearly greater epistemic value. One may think compulsion is more important, but accessibility may lead to a *stronger* argument in the sense that it gives rise to the greater epistemic good of a wider number of people apprehending truth. To illustrate, let's say the issue is that human-produced carbon dioxide is increasing the world's mean temperature. Which is a better argument for this claim? One that convincingly establishes its conclusion with highly complex mathematical models that are accessible only to a few eggheads, or one that if less than fully compelling, still is simple, accessible, and compelling to the masses? Based on this, Mavrodes further emends the proposed criterion: 'An argument is compelling if and only if it is sound and everyone who understands it accepts it and everyone who studies it understands it'.[25]

But perhaps this populist focus is misguided, for oughtn't we to assess arguments in terms of intrinsic quality rather than mere ability to woo the unwashed masses?[26] With this consideration in mind, Mavrodes proposes a counterfactual quality-control criterion: 'An argument is compelling if and only if anyone who understood it (or studied it, etc.) would know it to be sound'.[27] The problem with this stipulation is that we have no way to know whether any such

[23] Mavrodes, 'On the Very Strongest Arguments', in Eugene Thomas Long (ed.), *Prospects for Natural Theology* (Washington DC: Catholic University of America Press, 1992), 81–91; cf. Peter van Inwagen, *God, Knowledge, and Mystery* (Ithaca, NY: Cornell University Press, 1995), 158.

[24] Mavrodes, 'On the Very Strongest Arguments', p. 83.

[25] Ibid. 86.   [26] Ibid. 88–9.   [27] Ibid. 91.

arguments exist, and even if they *do*, there is no reason to think they are superior examples of knowledge. 'There are lots of things that it seems to me that I know, and that I have no inclination at all to think would be recognized as truths by everyone who understood them, and that seem to me to be just as firmly parts of my knowledge as anything else that I know.'[28] Hence, our search for criteria by which we may identify proofs of universal reason has been frustrated by the limited, perspectival, and value-driven scope of human reason: universally compelling proofs are unobtainable. But then the demand for such arguments as an epistemological necessity is an untenable dogma without foundation.[29]

The Self-Reference Problem

In accord with its methodist criteria, classical foundationalism identifies two properly basic sources of belief: self-evident first principles of reason and incorrigible sense perception. While Descartes provided the type for the rationalist's introspection of luminous first principles of reason, he also laid the foundations for sense perception by interpreting it, along with rationality, as mental.[30] Still, as Rorty observes, it was John Locke who elevated the epistemic role of sense perception:

Our certainty that our concept of 'painful' or 'blue' signifies something real edges out our certainty that we have a clear and distinct perception of such simple natures as 'substance,' 'thought,' and 'motion.' With Lockean empiricism, foundationalist epistemology emerged as the paradigm of philosophy.[31]

---

[28] Ibid. 91.

[29] The thesis is generally applicable. Consider Gordon Fee and Mark L. Strauss's comments on biblical translations: 'One reader picks up a formal equivalent version and reads Paul's letter to the Romans, understanding about 50 percent of what he reads. Another person picks up a children's version like the NIrV and reads the same letter, comprehending about 95 percent of what she reads. One might well ask, who walks away with a greater knowledge of God's Word? The point is that whatever inadequacies an idiomatic version may have are far outweighed by the benefits of hearing and comprehending God's Word' (*How to Choose a Translation For All Its Worth* (Grand Rapids, Mich.: Zondervan, 2007), 41).

[30] See Rorty, *Philosophy and the Mirror of Nature*, p. 51.   [31] Ibid. 59.

Since there is intuitive plausibility to the notion that we have intrinsically private, incorrigible access to our sensations, sense perception joined the first principles of reason as a foundational pillar for subsequent forms of internalist foundationalism.

The austere limitation of basic belief sets up perhaps the most devastating charge against classical foundationalism: that of self-referential inconsistency. The problem is already evident in logical positivism. The logical positivists initially postulated a verificationist criterion of meaning that defined all meaningful statements as either analytic or verifiable. The most fundamental problem with this criterion, as its critics were delighted to point out, is that it is neither analytic nor verifiable and so is not itself meaningful. When a retreat to the weaker criterion of falsification did nothing to alleviate this problem of self-reference, a surprising number of logical positivists gritted their teeth and, with Zen-like determination, attempted to live with the paradox. Since logical positivism could not inspire religious devotion, it was soon reduced to a less than inspiring footnote in the history of philosophy.

Alvin Plantinga has recently argued that self-referential incoherence afflicts all forms of classical foundationalism.[32] The core problem is that the classical foundationalist's belief that all properly basic beliefs must be either self-evident or incorrigible is neither self-evident nor incorrigible, and so is not properly basic. Moreover, no classical foundationalist has yet succeeded in deriving this belief from premisses that *are*; indeed, the task appears impossible.[33] Could one plead that a defence may yet be devised? Even if this is possible, the classical foundationalist's internalist assumptions require an ability to demonstrate the coherence of classical foundationalism *now*. Without that defence, this epistemology remains unjustified.

---

[32] Plantinga, 'Reason and Belief in God', in Alvin Plantinga and Nicholas Wolterstorff (eds.), *Faith and Rationality: Reason and Belief in God* (Notre Dame, Ind.: University of Notre Dame Press, 1983), 59–63.

[33] Alvin Plantinga and Philip Quinn carried on a debate on this issue. See Quinn, 'In Search of the Foundations of Theism', *Faith and Philosophy*, 2/4 (1985), 469–86; Plantinga, 'The Foundations of Theism: A Reply', *Faith and Philosophy*, 3/3 (1986), 298–313; Quinn, 'The Foundations of Theism Again: A Rejoinder to Plantinga', in Linda Zagzebski (ed.), *Rational Faith* (Notre Dame, Ind.: Notre Dame University Press, 1995), 14–47.

The Problem of the Given

The foundationalist's claim that justification terminates in the world suggests that in some sense the world is given for us. 'The given' refers to any allegedly basic encounter with reality which, as such, can initiate this chain of justification, though what precisely is given remains controversial: Wilfred Sellars observes that foundationalists have suggested many possible candidates for the given including sense data and the first principles of reason.[34] The problem of the given arises from the classical foundationalist's demand that every justified belief have a reason and the claim that there are properly basic beliefs. The problem was first articulated in Wilfred Sellars's seminal essay 'Empiricism and the Philosophy of Mind'. There are in fact two issues here that are not always distinguished, which I will call the wide problem of the given and the narrow problem of the given. The wide problem concerns the licitness of moving from experience to justified belief; this problem is faced by all forms of foundationalism. The narrow problem concerns the attempt to identify a class of givenness that has the universal and/or certain/incorrigible qualities of belief that the classical foundationalist requires.

Even when we consider initially the question of which objects might serve as a foundation, we are enmeshed in controversy. We begin with the conflation of the given with the sense-data theory of perception, a practice which has been perpetuated by non-foundationalists like Wilfred Sellars and Richard Rorty. While the primary target of Sellars's essay is the sense-data theory of perception, the argument clearly has relevance to foundationalism *simpliciter*. According to this theory of perception, sense data are the raw given of experience on which knowledge is based. While one may indeed combine the given with a sense-data theory of perception, it is not necessary to do so; and it's a good thing too, for there are severe objections to sense-data theories.[35] On a sense-data theory, perception is explained by the relationship between a mental sense-datum (which we directly perceive) and the reality that it represents.

[34] Sellars, 'Empiricism and the Philosophy of Mind', in his *Science, Perception and Reality* (London: Routledge & Kegan Paul, 1963), 127.

[35] Even so, the theory still has able contemporary defenders. See, for instance, Howard Robinson, *Perception* (London and New York: Routledge, 1994).

Admittedly sense-data theories are initially plausible when applied to vision. Since a person can hallucinate seeing an apple (i.e. seeing a mental representation) one could reasonably extrapolate that actually seeing an apple involves a mental datum that corresponds to a real apple. However, serious problems arise when we try to extend the explanation to the other senses. For instance, there appears to be little promise in explaining olfactory perception of blue cheese by appealing to a 'rancid datum' that represents the smell of blue cheese.[36] The point is made effectively by Nicholas Wolterstorff's example of how sense-data theory purports to explain proprioception of one's leg:

[T]he acquaintance which is an ingredient in my perception of my leg's position consists of my introspective acquaintance with a certain internal object, namely, a sense datum that is a reflective image of my leg's position; it's by inference from beliefs about that sense datum, formed in me by acquaintance with that mental entity, that I come to have knowledge of my leg's position.[37]

Not only is the sense-data theory explanatorily vacuous, but it also begs a number of questions,[38] and so most foundationalists today do not look to it to provide the foundation of givenness.

While it is important to define a candidate for givenness, Sellars's main challenge concerns the possibility that *anything* could serve in that role. As he observes, the central motivation behind each of these suggestions is 'to explicate the idea that empirical knowledge rests on a "foundation" of non-inferential knowledge of matter of fact'.[39] The core claim of the given, as Sellars describes, is in the epistemic relation between non-verbal experience and epistemic belief:

The idea that observation 'strictly and properly so-called' is constituted by certain self-authenticating nonverbal episodes, the authority of which is transmitted to verbal and quasi-verbal performances ... is ... the heart of the Myth of the Given. For the *given* ... is what is *taken* by these self-authenticating episodes. These 'takings' are, so to speak, the unmoved

---

[36] As Putnam retorts, 'This is an *explanation*?' (*The Many Faces of Realism*, p. 8).

[37] Wolterstorff, *Thomas Reid and the Story of Epistemology* (Cambridge: Cambridge University Press, 2001), 85.

[38] For instance, how do sense-data come to represent external objects? And if they are required to represent objects, do we need sense-data to represent sense-data, thereby setting us on an infinite regress?

[39] Sellars, 'Empiricism and the Philosophy of Mind', p. 128.

movers of empirical knowledge, the 'knowings in presence' which are pre-supposed by all other knowledge.[40]

Sellars's work embodies an attack on both 'myths'. On the one hand, he objects to the notion of 'unmoved movers' that move us from the given presentation of experience to epistemic taking. On the other hand, he raises the narrow problem concerning the claim that there could be any self-authenticating foundation of protean takings.

Sellars's central dilemma is that either the putative foundations involve the sensing of particulars, which would not involve knowing (it is non-epistemic), or they involve the sensing of facts, which is knowing.[41] We find the force of Sellars's argument in the claim that all experience/cognition is by definition both conceptually and proposi-tionally structured, for experience *of* means experience *that*, and thus is propositional.[42] As a result, Sellars can conclude that 'it would seem that one could not form the concept of *being green*, and, by parity of reasoning, of the other colours, unless he already had them'.[43] So, these concepts cannot arise out of a pre-conceptual encounter with sense data, or any other epistemic foundation.

Laurence BonJour echoes this line of argument in his influential essay 'Can Empirical Knowledge Have a Foundation?'[44] After assert-ing that the notion of a properly basic empirical belief is deeply paradoxical, BonJour concludes that every belief must depend on other beliefs for its justification. According to BonJour, the only way out of the dilemma is to adopt externalist foundationalism (which he considers an abandonment of epistemology) or by appealing to the claim that basic beliefs simply are given in experience and do not require justification: 'Givenness amounts to the idea that basic beliefs are justified by reference, not to further *beliefs*, but rather to states of affairs in the world which are "immediately apprehended" or "directly presented" or "intuited" '.[45] But this stipulation appears to bring us out of the frying pan and into the fire:

---

[40] Ibid. 169–70.   [41] Ibid. 129.   [42] Ibid. 144.   [43] Ibid. 147.

[44] BonJour, 'Can Empirical Knowledge Have a Foundation?', *American Philosophi-cal Quarterly*, 15/1 (1978), 1–13; repr. in Ernest Sosa and Jaegwon Kim (eds.), *Episte-mology: An Anthology* (Oxford: Blackwell, 2000), 261–73. Cf. Laurence BonJour, *The Structure of Empirical Knowledge* (Cambridge, Mass.: Harvard University Press, 1985), ch. 4.

[45] BonJour, 'Can Empirical Knowledge Have a Foundation?', pp. 267–8.

If these intuitions or immediate apprehensions are construed as cognitive, then they will be both capable of giving justification and in need of it themselves; if they are non-cognitive, then they do not need justification but are also apparently incapable of providing it. This, at bottom, is why epistemological givenness is a myth.[46]

On the former option, this foundationalism collapses into the coherentist or infinitist versions of internalism. On the latter, it collapses back into externalism in so far as the reasons for belief are embedded in non-cognitive experience.

To sum up, the problem of the given is that any beliefs fit to form an *epistemic* foundation must have conceptual and propositional content. However, such content invariably undermines their unique epistemic status. Alvin Plantinga provides a perspicuous description of the dilemma:

[O]n the one hand there is awareness *of* the content, which of course is not a reason for believing anything; it simply is not the right kind of animal to be a reason, since it is not itself a belief or acceptance of a proposition. On the other hand, there is the awareness *that* I am being appeared to thus and so; this awareness is indeed constituted by a belief, but the belief in question is the very belief whose justification we seek, and hence of course cannot justify it.[47]

Let's unpack these comments. When we ask how content might be justified we have two options: the non-doxastic and the doxastic. The problem with saying that something non-doxastic (e.g. a sense experience) *justifies* a belief arises because, as Plantinga observes, *experiences are not reasons to believe*. Only a reason (something propositionally structured) can give you another reason, and a sense experience is not propositionally structured. One can infer from the inadequacy of language that experience does not come codified in a simplistic propositional or linguistic structure. As such, we cannot claim to find a propositional or linguistic structure to justify our

---

[46] BonJour, 'Can Empirical Knowledge Have a Foundation?', p. 269. The only alternative left is to argue that such intuition is semi-cognitive such that it is able to confer justification, but does not itself require it. BonJour however dismisses this as 'hopelessly contrived and *ad hoc*' (ibid. 270).

[47] Plantinga, 'Direct Acquaintance?', in Michael DePaul (ed.), *Resurrecting Old-fashioned Foundationalism* (Lanham, Md.: Rowman & Littlefield, 2000), 59.

beliefs, and so are left with sensations and beliefs, with no way to unite them.

CHECKING FOR VITAL SIGNS

In light of the above considerations it is hardly surprising that Alvin Goldman dismisses classical foundationalism as 'long since exploded',[48] while David Clark adds: 'Virtually everyone agrees classical foundationalism is dead'.[49] But before we call the undertaker we should be warned that not *everyone* agrees that classical foundationalism has been exploded. Today there is a minor renaissance of philosophers, including Evan Fales, Richard Fumerton, and Laurence BonJour, who are defending new forms of classical foundationalism.[50] So, it is worth considering what might be said for classical foundationalism and what implications this might have for theology.

Are There no Universal, Certain Beliefs?

The shattering effect of the loss of conviction is felt far beyond the academy as a growing number of Christians are adopting theological positions that heighten mystery, tentativeness, and doubt.[51] Were we wrong in the beginning to think that incorrigible certainty should be the goal of knowledge? Or does the problem instead lie with a weak, premature abandonment of the search for certainty? Os Guinness suggests the latter through a character in *The Gravedigger File*:

[48] Alvin Goldman, *Knowledge in a Social World* (Oxford: Clarendon, 1999), 27.

[49] Clark, *To Know and Love God: Method for Theology* (Wheaton, Ill.: Crossway, 2003), 156.

[50] Fales, *A Defense of the Given* (Lanham, Md.: Rowman & Littlefield, 1996); Fumerton, *Metaepistemology and Skepticism* (Lanham, Md.: Rowman & Littlefield, 1995); DePaul, *Resurrecting Old-fashioned Foundationalism*.

[51] See Robert C. Webber, *The Younger Evangelicals: Facing the Challenges of the New World* (Grand Rapids, Mich.: Baker, 2002), 83–106. For the impact of this trend on apologetic method see John Stackhouse, *Humble Apologetics* (New York: Oxford University Press, 2002).

I am not suggesting that certainty has disappeared altogether. It has in some places been replaced openly by doubts or (more respectably) rationalized by notions such as 'humility,' 'ambiguity' or the 'confession of triumphalism.' These notions serve as a protective theological solution to mask the deepening erosion of convictions once as clear-cut as Gothic carvings.[52]

From this perspective, the loss of certainty as the normative condition for Christian belief evinces a regrettable 'erosion of convictions' which we have attempted to rationalize by invoking positive dispositions like humility.

Despite these warnings about abandoning the goal of certainty, many philosophers have concluded that the only viable alternative is to embrace fallibilism—the view that a significant subclass or even all of our beliefs are fallible. Fallibilism was at the centre of Karl Popper's asymptotic approach to knowledge, in which the falsification of hypotheses leads us ever closer to the truth, without us ever attaining it. An even more rigorous form of fallibilism is found in W. V. O. Quine's claim that *any* belief, even basic principles of logic, could be abandoned in light of new experience. However, many philosophers would deny that the undercutting defeaters identified above are sufficient to warrant a global fallibilism as opposed to a more modest local fallibilism; that is, one which is limited to particular classes of belief. (For instance, perhaps synthetic a priori knowledge is fallible while analytic truths like 'All bachelors are unmarried' remain secure.) Further, a number of putative candidates for incorrigibility, including the venerable Cartesian *cogito*, still have avid defenders. But even if we reject global fallibilism, whatever infallible beliefs might remain are simply too spartan to provide the classical-foundationalist base of belief. Nancey Murphy wryly summarizes the resulting dilemma:

there appears to be an epistemological corollary of Murphy's law at work: whenever the foundations are suitably indubitable, they will turn out to be useless for justifying any interesting claims; when we do find beliefs that are useful for justifying the rest of the structure, they always turn out to be questionable.[53]

[52] Guinness, *The Gravedigger File: Papers on the Subversion of the Modern Church* (Downer's Grove, Ill.: InterVarsity, 1983), 162.

[53] Murphy, 'Introduction', in Stanley Hauerwas, Nancey Murphy, and Mark Nation (eds.), *Theology Without Foundations: Religious Practice and the Future of Theological Truth* (Nashville, Tenn.: Abingdon, 1994), 11.

As a result, even if one avoids global fallibilism, the areas of belief that are infallible are too meagre to support a suitably rich noetic structure.

One might well affirm the continued need to pursue certainty in light of our fallible limitations. As Colin Gunton puts it, '[t]here may be a quest for foundations, but it must be recognized as one engaged in by fallible, finite and fallen human beings'.[54] Similarly, Pannenberg writes: 'The conditionality of all subjective certainty is part of the finitude of human experience. To claim unconditional, independent certainty is forcibly to make oneself, the believing I, the locus of absolute truth'.[55] Among theologians, perhaps the most influential statement of this type of fallibilism is Michael Polanyi's definition of 'personal knowledge' according to which 'I may hold firmly to what I believe to be true, even though I know that it may conceivably be false'.[56] Once fallibilism is admitted it appears difficult if not impossible to make claims to certainty—for how can we be certain once we recognize that *we could be wrong?* The result, so it would seem, is that one cannot know *anything* with incorrigible certainty.

The Christian fallibilist who embraces this conclusion could also launch an attack on the sceptical alternative by charging that rejecting the demand for certainty relieves us from the pressure of not having attained it. Moreover, practically speaking, the sceptical stance is unlivable, as trying to be a consistent sceptic would be intellectual suicide. As Michael Polanyi has put it: 'To postpone mental decisions on account of their conceivable fallibility would necessarily block all decisions for ever, and pile up the hazards of hesitation to infinity. It would amount to voluntary mental stupor'.[57] Finally, scepticism appears to be intellectually inconsistent, for sceptics are at least firmly

---

[54] Gunton, *The One, the Three and the Many: God, Creation and the Culture of Modernity*, 1992 Bampton Lectures (Cambridge: Cambridge University Press, 1993), 135; see also Newbigin, *Proper Confidence*; Daniel Taylor, *The Myth of Certainty: The Reflective Christian and the Risk of Commitment* (Nashville, Tenn.: W Publishing Group, 1986).

[55] Wolfhart Pannenberg, *Systematic Theology*, i, trans. Geoffrey W. Bromiley (Grand Rapids, Mich.: Eerdmans, 1991), 47.

[56] Michael Polanyi, *Personal Knowledge: Towards a Post-critical Philosophy* (Chicago, Ill.: University of Chicago Press, 1958), 214.

[57] Ibid. 314–15. While the Pyrrhonian sceptic advocated accommodating to experience, this appears both arbitrary and practically unlivable.

committed to the belief that I should doubt corrigible beliefs, a belief
which is itself a prime candidate for corrigibility.

Though global fallibilism is popular, we should be wary about
adopting such a position uncritically. As Douglas Groothius observes,

> [a]ny intellectual quest is sabotaged and hamstrung by quarantining cer-
> tainty at the outset. It is like injuring a horse before a race on the general
> principle that a strong, swift, and healthy steed is too proud to compete fairly
> or honestly. One should assess the strength of a given conclusion on the basis
> of the arguments given to support that conclusion, not by stipulating some
> 'humble' ideal that forswears certitude in principle and in perpetuity.[58]

With Groothius's warning in mind, it is worth noting the emphasis
upon certainty within the biblical sources. Luke wrote his gospel
'so that you may know the certainty [*asphaleian*] of the things you
have been taught' (Luke 1: 4). Peter preached that one could be
certain (*tekmeirion*) of the Messiahship of Jesus (Acts 2: 36). And
Paul expresses the wish that the Colossians might have 'the full riches
of complete understanding' (*plerophoria*—most certain confidence)
(Col. 2: 2). There are many other places in Scripture where certainty
is promised due to God's perfect character and reliability.[59]

In addition to the scriptural witness, one finds a consistent testimony to the certainty of faith in theological history. Thomas Aquinas
described theology as a unique science surpassing all others because
it depends not on human reason but rather divine knowledge.[60] John
Calvin writes: 'The certainty which [faith] requires must be full and
decisive, as is usual in regard to matters ascertained and proved'.[61]
And Louis Berkhof asserts that '[t]he certainty of this knowledge has
its warrant in God Himself, and consequently *nothing can be more
certain*. And it is quite essential that this should be so, for faith is

[58] Groothius, 'Why Truth Matters Most: An Apologetic for Truth-Seeking in Postmodern Times', *Journal of the Evangelical Theological Society*, 47/3 (2004), 448.

[59] Groothius asserts that 'the apostle John would never agree with the statement,
"No human being knows anything for certain," since he evinces certainty that Jesus
Christ is God incarnate' ('Why Truth Matters Most', p. 47). D. A. Carson lists dozens
of passages in Scripture which are concerned with propositional knowledge and
certainty (see *Becoming Conversant with the Emerging Church* (Grand Rapids, Mich.:
Zondervan, 2005), 193–9).

[60] Aquinas, *Summa Theologica*, 1.1.5.

[61] Calvin, *Institutes of the Christian Religion*, trans. Henry Beveridge (Grand
Rapids, Mich.: Eerdmans, 1989), 482 (3.15).

concerned with spiritual and eternal things, in which certainty is needed, if anywhere'.[62] Finally, Karl Barth observes: 'In human uncertainty like any other science, it establishes *the most certain truth ever known*'.[63] Such claims, which could readily be multiplied, are at least prima facie difficult to reconcile with a global fallibilism.

As we noted in the last chapter, we must distinguish indubitable conviction from incorrigible certainty, for an indubitable proposition could be false. I also noted there that it is helpful to distinguish between ivory-tower doubt and real-world doubt and to emphasize that our primary concern should be with the latter. Thus, while we might recognize the formal possibility of global fallibilism, we do not need to concede that it is a *live* possibility. Consider for comparison: I have no doubt that the world was *not* created five minutes ago with all the dusty books, crumbling mountains, and apparent memories, and yet I have no means to refute this possibility conclusively. Thus, even if we admit fallibilism, serious existential implications do not necessarily follow.

One possibility is to retain certainty but interpret it from an externalist perspective such that (as a first approximation) a certain belief is one that is true and properly elicits maximal conviction or indubitability. Far from being a last gasp at some assemblage of Cartesianism, this may provide a plausible interpretation of the biblical and historical references to certainty. Scripture treats certainty as *a gift* which *ultimately resides in God*; our knowledge will always be inadequate this side of the *eschaton* (1 Cor. 13: 12). Our beliefs achieve certainty not because of the percipient's cognitive power but rather because of the wholly trustworthy God who testifies to us and grants certain knowledge as a gift. As Gunton observes, the knowledge of faith 'is guaranteed to—rather than in—the knower because it is given by God'.[64] Certain beliefs depend not on our sure grasp of them so much as on God's grasp on us through these beliefs. Lutheran theology offers a helpful conceptuality to think of this knowledge in

[62] Berkhof, *Systematic Theology* (Edinburgh: Banner of Truth Trust, 1958), 504; emphasis added.

[63] Barth, *Church Dogmatics: Doctrine of the Word of God*, ed. G. W. Bromiley and T. F. Torrance, trans. G. W. Bromiley, vol. i, pt. 1 (Edinburgh: T&T Clark, 1975), 12.

[64] Colin Gunton, 'I Know that My Redeemer Lives', in *Intellect and Action: Elucidations on Christian Theology and the Life of Faith* (Edinburgh: T&T Clark, 2000), 51.

the *finitum capax infiniti*. As Gabriel Fackre observes, '[w]hy should not the real Presence of Christ in the eucharist have its counter-part in the real presence of the knowledge of God in the church and the believer?'[65]

One might add that there are at least two reasons why we do not have internalist epistemic certainty. The first relates, as Pascal observed, to our freedom such that there is sufficient evidence to believe but not so much as to compel belief. Second, as Barth observes, the tenuous nature of our knowledge drives us back to divine dependence: 'The intractability of faith and its object guarantees that divine certainty cannot become human security'.[66] T. F. Torrance provides a vivid metaphor for this relationship of confident dependence: 'I sometimes recall what happened when my daughter was learning to walk, I took her by the hand to help her, and I can still feel her little fingers tightly clutching my hand. She was not relying on her feeble grasp of my hand, but on my strong grasp of her hand, and even my grasping of her grasping of my hand'.[67]

Is Classical Foundationalism Incoherent?

What about the devastating charge that classical foundationalism is self-referentially defeating? Recently John DePoe has argued that Plantinga has not in fact demonstrated the self-referential incoherence of classical foundationalism.[68] After observing that classical foundationalism is not obviously self-referentially incoherent, DePoe suggests that Plantinga might actually mean that it is meaningless by its standard in the same way as is logical positivism. However, DePoe points out that taken as such Plantinga's argument only establishes the contingent falsity of classical foundationalism; that is, the argument is a posteriori, so that we could only come to know classical

---

[65] Fackre, *The Doctrine of Revelation: A Narrative Interpretation* (Edinburgh: Edinburgh University Press, 1997), 222.

[66] Barth, *Church Dogmatics*, i.i. 12.

[67] Torrance, 'Preaching Christ Today', in his *Preaching Christ Today: The Gospel and Scientific Thinking* (Grand Rapids, Mich.: Eerdmans, 1994), 32.

[68] DePoe, 'In Defense of Classical Foundationalism: A Critical Evaluation of Plantinga's Argument that Classical Foundationalism is Self-refuting', *South African Journal of Philosophy*, 26/3 (2007), 245–51.

foundationalism is false empirically.[69] DePoe reconstructs Plantinga's argument as follows (the numbering is DePoe's; CF refers to classical foundationalism):

(11) Plantinga is not aware of a good argument for CF.
(12) Therefore, there probably are no good arguments for CF.[70]

As DePoe then wryly observes, '[e]ven though Plantinga is very knowledgeable about epistemology and truly one of the most brilliant philosophers of our time, the inference from (11) to (12) is certainly dubious and it hardly presents any reasons for someone (perhaps, besides Plantinga himself) to conclude (12)'.[71] As a result, DePoe argues that Plantinga has failed to demonstrate that classical foundationalism is not possibly true; the most it can establish is that we cannot presently see how it could be true. At the very least, it must be conceded that Plantinga's argument does not quite establish self-referential defeat. Thus, it may be that while classical foundationalism remains unjustified, it could still be developed into a viable theory. But we should keep in mind the distance between saying *x* is not self-referentially incoherent and saying *x* is true. There may be no incoherence in the claim that there is a methane snowman on Pluto, yet we need some reason to think this is true. And while there may be no incoherence in classical foundationalism, here too we require some ground to think it true. Even if this theory is not quite a dead option, that hardly means it is a *live* one.

CONCLUSION

The fallibilist should agree that we ought to be extremely careful about magisterial pronouncements about the final viability or otherwise of a given philosophical project, classical foundationalism

---

[69] Nicholas Wolterstorff points out that there is no necessary incoherence, since different forms of classical foundationalism differ as to which beliefs are universal: 'some are such that the belief that the version of classical foundationalism is true does not belong to the sorts of beliefs to which the criterion is meant to apply' (*John Locke and the Ethics of Belief* (Cambridge: Cambridge University Press, 1996), 83 n.). Consequently, this type is not self-referentially defeating.

[70] DePoe, 'In Defense of Classical Foundationalism, p. 249.   [71] Ibid.

included. For instance, a classical foundationalist could adopt a modest particularism by dropping incorrigibility as a general obligation for the base while maintaining an internalist constraint.[72] This type of modified internalist foundationalism is currently being explored by contemporary defenders of classical foundationalism. For instance, Richard Fumerton identifies the criterion of proper basicality as follows: '[O]ne has a noninferential justification for believing P when one has the thought that P and one is acquainted with the fact that P, the thought that P, *and* the fact which is the thought that P's *corresponding* to the fact that P'.[73] In this way, Fumerton hopes to avoid the retreat to an externalist account of proper basicality. While his proposal raises a number of questions (not least of which is the meaning of 'acquaintance'), every theory takes some terms as primitive, and thus it may well be premature to discount this proposal categorically. But if an epistemology of this type could be redeemed, what implications would it have for theology? Given that Fumerton concedes that the possibility of hallucinations undermines the notion that we could be directly acquainted with facts about the external world,[74] his epistemology leads to a form of indirect realism, with direct acquaintance being limited to the immediate deliverances of subjective, mental experience. If this were correct then it would follow that beliefs about God would not themselves be properly basic, since they would be inferences from properly basic mental experiences. At the same time, it is far from clear that this would require revisionism in our beliefs in either revelation or the real world. The revisionism arises rather from certain methodist assumptions. But, regardless, such reflections remain speculative. At present, the prospects for classical foundationalism continue to appear bleak.

---

[72] Keith Lehrer observes that 'a foundationalist might "despair" of finding sufficient beliefs that guarantee their own truth and settle for a more modest foundation of self-justified or basic beliefs that provide a *reason* for their acceptance but without a guarantee of their truth' (*Theory of Knowledge* (Boulder, Col./San Francisco, Calif.: Westview, 1990), 40).

[73] Fumerton, 'Classical Foundationalism', in Depaul (ed.), *Resurrecting Old-fashioned Foundationalism*, pp. 13–14.

[74] Ibid. 16.

5

Philosophy and Theology After Foundationalism

I suppose that before describing the world in English we ought to determine whether it is written in English, and that we ought to examine very carefully how the world is spelled.

Nelson Goodman, 'The Way the World Is'

The way I experience the pen on the table, let alone the cross on the altar, is shaped by my language and previous experience.

William Placher, 'Postliberal Theology'

In the film *Castaway* Chuck Noland (played by Tom Hanks) is on a routine flight in the South Pacific when his plane crashes into the ocean. After four years stranded on an island with Wilson (a volley ball) as his only companion Noland has finally adapted to his surroundings: he is able to spear a fish, he resides in a relatively comfortable cave, and he can readily build a fire. But while life on the island has grown tolerably secure, it has also become increasingly obvious that staying there provides little hope of ever contacting the outside world. Noland cannot remain alone on the island, and so he resolves to leave...or else die trying. Thus, with unshakeable determination, he constructs a large raft and launches it into the roiling surf. After several tense minutes paddling he lifts the makeshift sail, clears the reef, and is helplessly cast upon the mercy of the vast Pacific.

In key respects, Noland's escape from the island parallels the situation of twentieth-century epistemology. At the beginning of the century most philosophers were safely ensconced on the terra firma of classical foundationalism. And just as Noland's adaptation to life on the island only highlighted its inadequacy, so it has been with the successive attempts to redeem classical foundationalism, which have illustrated the inadequacy of attempting to stake all belief on a foundation of self-evident and incorrigible certitudes. Finally, just as Noland opted to launch himself on to the sea on a makeshift raft, so many epistemologists over the last several decades have launched off the island of epistemic foundations. Several decades ago, Otto Neurath captured the move from stable island to open sea in the vivid metaphor of a boat: 'We are like sailors who have to rebuild their ship on the open sea, without ever being able to dismantle it in dry-dock, and reconstruct it from the best components'.[1] Given the magnitude of this shift, we will devote the next four chapters to surveying the philosophical and theological issues raised by non-foundationalism. We will begin in this chapter and the next with an overview of some major philosophical and theological forms of non-foundationalism, focusing specifically on their approaches to knowledge, truth, and metaphysical realism.

The flexibility of the term non-foundationalism[2] becomes evident when one considers the broad range of philosophers who have been identified as non-foundationalist, including Charles Peirce, John Dewey, William James, Ludwig Wittgenstein, Martin Heidegger, Wilfred Sellars, W. V. O. Quine, Donald Davidson, Jacques Derrida, Hilary Putnam, and Richard Rorty. In order to work toward an understanding of non-foundationalism we will begin by exploring how it relates to post-modernism. While the term post-modern has both historical and philosophical connotations, our concern here is with the latter.[3] Given its eclectic and fragmented nature, post-modernism is difficult to define as a philosophical project. Indeed, as William Lane Craig and J. P. Moreland note, it is not so much a unified movement as 'a loose coalition of diverse thinkers from several different academic disciplines, and it would be difficult to

---

[1] Cited in Roger Trigg, *Rationality and Science: Can Science Explain Everything?* (Oxford: Blackwell, 1993), 46–7.

[2] Sometimes the terms anti-foundationalism and post-foundationalism are distinguished from non-foundationalism while at other times they are treated as synonyms.

[3] For a discussion of non-foundationalist themes in the history of philosophy see Tom Rockmore and Beth J. Singer (eds.), *Antifoundationalim Old and New* (Philadelphia, Pa.: Temple University Press, 1992).

characterize postmodernism in a way that would be fair to this diversity'.[4] Indeed, the qualifier 'post-modern' is so broad that many dismiss attempts to distil a post-modern essence as futile. (Scepticism about the propriety of definition is compounded by the fact that many post-moderns reject essentialism, the view that entities— post-modernism included—have identifiable essences.) The best we can do is identify a broad post-modern 'ethos' or 'turn'.[5]

While I take these warnings seriously, we should be careful not to deflate post-modern claims into something as philosophically innocuous as a non-cognitive temperament or attitude. Even the language of a post-modern *turn* presupposes a turn *from* one thing and *to* another which brings us back to the question of essence. Since it is helpful to have at least a provisional definition, I propose that we proceed by identifying a list of common post-modern theses, whilst understanding them more as markers of family resemblance than necessary and sufficient conditions. To that end, Craig and Moreland have helpfully identified seven positions that post-modernists tend to reject: (1) metaphysical realism, (2) the correspondence theory of truth, (3) universal standards of rationality and logic, (4) foundational epistemic justification, (5) universals and essentialism, (6) the primacy of thought over language and the referential use of language, and (7) metanarratives.[6]

When it comes to non-foundationalism, the key mark is (4), the denial of foundations. John Thiel writes:

At most, one can speak of a commitment to a style of philosophizing shared by a number of thinkers, and often in very different ways. Whether this commitment advances the concerns of American pragmatism, sets the direction of the 'linguistic turn,' or fuels the suspicion of theory in a host of contemporary philosophies, it is always critical of the epistemological assumption

---

[4] Craig and Moreland, *Philosophical Foundations for a Christian Worldview* (Downers Grove, Ill.: InterVarsity, 2003), 144–5.

[5] Myron B. Penner, 'Introduction', in Penner (ed.), *Christianity and the Postmodern Turn* (Grand Rapids, Mich.: Brazos, 2005), 16.

[6] Craig and Moreland, *Philosophical Foundations*, pp. 145–9. For other typologies of post-modernism see Richard Davis, 'Can There Be an "Orthodox" Postmodern Theology?', *Journal of the Evangelical Theological Society*, 45/1 (2002), 111; Nancey Murphy and James William McClendon, Jr., 'Distinguishing Modern and Postmodern Theologies', *Modern Theology*, 5/3 (1989), 191–213.

that there are 'foundations' for knowledge, noninferential principles whose certainty and stability ground other epistemic claims.[7]

While the core non-foundationalist thesis concerns a denial of epistemic foundations, token versions of non-foundationalism also frequently include other post-modern elements, especially a rejection of (1), metaphysical realism, (2), the correspondence theory of truth, and (6), the primacy of thought over language.

While non-foundationalists reject foundationalism for a number of reasons (including those surveyed in Chapter 4), one of the most influential is the charge that foundationalism leads to scepticism. As Nancey Murphy and James McClendon observe, '[m]odern skeptics and modern foundationalists have held the same view of knowledge, and one becomes a skeptic insofar as one becomes aware of difficulties in the foundationalist program'.[8] Richard Rorty identifies sceptical concerns as the driving force behind non-foundationalist pragmatism: '[P]eople become pragmatists for the same reason they become idealists or verificationists: they hope to frustrate the skeptic—the philosopher who says that there may be a lot that we cannot know'.[9] From the non-foundationalist perspective, scepticism arises when we divide the world up into various dualistic opposites that must then be overcome. While non-foundationalists have identified many damaging dualisms (e.g. linguistic, modal, metaphysical[10]), epistemologically the problems arise when we distinguish between the world and our knowledge of it, and then divide our beliefs into those that are basic and non-basic, rational and irrational, and incorrigibly certain and corrigibly uncertain.

In light of this concern with scepticism, we can illumine the non-foundationalist programme through the methodist and particularist approaches to epistemology. As we saw in Chapter 3, the

---

[7] Thiel, *Nonfoundationalism* (Minneapolis, Minn.: Fortress, 1994), 1.

[8] Murphy and McClendon, 'Distinguishing Modern and Postmodern Theologies', p. 193.

[9] Rorty, 'Realism/Antirealism and Pragmatism: Comments on Alston, Chisholm, Davidson, Harman, and Searle', in Christopher B. Kulp (ed.), *Realism/Antirealism and Epistemology* (Lanham, Md.: Rowman & Littlefield, 1997), 150.

[10] In addition, there is the linguistic distinction between syntheticity and analyticity, the modal distinction between contingency and necessity, and the metaphysical distinction between thought (mind/soul) and extension (body/world).

internalist foundationalist applies a rigorous method to epistemological enquiry that allows for the possibility of global scepticism. In contrast, the non-foundationalist typically models a particularist method
that grounds epistemological analysis in paradigmatic instances of
rational belief and/or knowledge, thereby ensuring the accessibility
of knowledge. Some non-foundationalists extend the particularist
redefinition to the nature of truth and the world to ensure internal
accessibility to truth and reality; as a result, they reject alethic realism
and metaphysical realism. When attacking alethic realism, the primary target is *correspondence* of belief to fact. When correspondence
has been undermined and scepticism looms, the non-foundationalist
steps in with a new definition of truth. The two primary candidates, the epistemic (belief-focused) and pragmatic (action-/results-
focused), both relativize truth to human interests. In the final step, we
will turn to consider the non-foundationalist treatment of metaphysical realism. Here the particularist element reinterprets reality either
as reducible to our conceptual schemes or as a meaningless postulate
beyond those schemes. Thus, the non-foundationalist defeats scepticism by redefining knowledge, truth, and reality relative to human
concerns and capacities.[11]

DEFEATING DUALISM FOR THE SAKE
OF KNOWLEDGE

These days few theologians are willing to admit that they are dualists,
and even the few that do must find it hard not to blush. James K. A.
Smith sets the mood with his prayer: 'Lead us not into dualism,
but deliver us from Platonism'.[12] The non-foundationalist leads the
charge by arguing that dualism leads to scepticism so that rejecting
dualism defuses scepticism. But how does one defuse scepticism? In

[11] Based on this analysis, one might reinterpret the non-foundationalist reworking
of truth and reality as a modern form of the Protagorean *homo mensura*: 'Of all things
the measure is man, of the things that are, that they are, and of things that are not,
that they are not'.

[12] Smith, *Introducing Radical Orthodoxy: Mapping a Post-secular Theology* (Grand
Rapids, Mich.: Baker/Milton Keyes: Paternoster, 2004), 219.

this section we will consider two types of argument—Rorty's 'alethic apathy' and Putnam's mind externalism—and then reconsider the notion of justification without an epistemic interface with the world.

Rorty's Alethic Apathy

Richard Rorty provides us with the first anti-sceptical argument, a position I call alethic apathy since it is rooted in a deflation of the importance of truth. Rorty believes that scepticism arises from a commitment to a contentious realist conception of knowledge, truth, and reality. But, according to Rorty, by denying alethic realism we do not have to embrace anti-realism; indeed, he emphatically disavows anti-realism as well: '[I]t is no truer that "atoms are what they are because we use "atom" as we do" than that "we use "atom" as we do because atoms are as they are" '.[13] For Rorty, anti-realism is simply the other side of the dualist opposition that needs to be abandoned as unfruitful and ultimately uninteresting. In its place, Rorty offers a down-to-earth pragmatism:

If one takes the core of pragmatism to be its attempt to replace the notion of true beliefs as representations of 'the nature of things' and instead to think of them as successful rules for action, then it becomes easy to recommend an experimental, fallibilist attitude, but hard to isolate a 'method' that will embody this attitude.[14]

Rorty thus advises us to replace grandiose attempts to theorize about 'Reality'and search for 'Truth' with practical values and rules for action.

While many critics have dismissed Rorty's attempt to transcend the realism/anti-realism debate, Jeffrey Stout maintains that we should grant him the benefit of the doubt. While Stout recognizes that Rorty makes prima facie relativistic and nihilistic comments, he argues that we should interpret these as rhetorical excess,[15] and grant interpretative primacy instead to passages like the following:

[13] Rorty, *Philosophical Papers*, i. *Objectivity, Relativism, and Truth* (Cambridge: Cambridge University Press, 1991), 5.

[14] Ibid. 66.

[15] Stout, *Ethics After Babel: The Language of Morals and Their Discontents* (Boston, Mass.: Beacon, 1988), 246.

James, when he said that 'the true is what is good in the way of belief' was simply trying to debunk epistemology; he was not offering a 'theory of truth.' So Derrida, when he says '*il n'y a pas de hors-texte*,' is not putting forward an ontological view; he is trying to debunk Kantian philosophy generally.[16]

Taken at face value, Rorty is proposing not anti-realism but an end to all dualistic realist/anti-realist theorizing. Further evidence for this interpretation comes in the introduction to *Consequences of Pragmatism* when Rorty avers: '[T]ruth is not the sort of thing one should expect to have a philosophically interesting theory about'.[17] Stout comments that here Rorty identifies 'pragmatism not with a new and improved definition but rather with an unwillingness to commit to any'.[18] Further, Rorty interprets the Quine-Sellars attack on intuition and concepts as a rejection of theorization about knowledge rather than a new theory of it.[19] Stout comments:

To be an anti-essentialist with respect to truth is not to offer a quasi-metaphysical thesis—namely, that truth has no essence. It is to hold that once we have learned everything Davidson, Austin, and others like them have to teach us about the behavior of *is true* and cognate expressions, there is nothing remaining to be told about the concept or essence of truth.[20]

Hence, Rorty seeks to wean us from the very notion of a theory of truth or reality in order to avoid the twin dangers of realism (scepticism) and anti-realism (relativism and nihilism). As Philip Kenneson (a Rortian sympathizer) puts it: '[T]he reason I am not a relativist may not bring you much comfort; it is because I *don't believe* in objective truth, a concept that is the flip side of relativism and that is necessary for the charge of relativism to be coherent'.[21] While the realist will suspect that Rorty is living in a borrowed metaphysical

[16] Rorty, cited in Stout, *Ethics After Babel*, p. 248.
[17] Rorty, *Consequences of Pragmatism*, p. xiii, cited in Stout, *Ethics After Babel*, p. 250.
[18] Ibid.
[19] Richard Rorty, *Philosophy and the Mirror of Nature* (Princeton, NJ: Princeton University Press, 1979), 180.
[20] Stout, *Ethics After Babel*, p. 252.
[21] Kenneson, 'There's No Such Thing as Objective Truth, and It's a Good Thing, Too', in Timothy R. Phillips and Dennis L. Okholm (eds.), *Christian Apologetics in the Postmodern World* (Downers Grove, Ill: InterVarsity, 1995), 156.

world, Rorty would counter that concepts like the 'real world' have only practical value.[22]

Putnam's Mental Externalism

Hilary Putnam's externalist interpretation of intentionality constitutes a second non-foundationalist response to the nettle of scepticism.[23] Putnam develops his response by taking the surprising step of socializing intention. Intentionality is that primitive sense of aboutness in virtue of which a belief has a particular content (e.g. it is about Barth's doctrine of election rather than Euclidean geometry). Hilary Putnam defines intentionality as follows:

(1) the fact that words, sentences, and other 'representations' have *meaning*; (2) the fact that representations may *refer* to (i.e., be true of) some actually existing thing or each of a number of actually existing things; (3) the fact that representations may be *about* something which does *not* exist; and (4) the fact that a state of mind may have a 'state of affairs' as its object.[24]

The common assumption is that intentionality constitutes the intrinsic aboutness of our beliefs that transforms sensations into perceptions and links our beliefs to the world. But Putnam argues that the aboutness of our beliefs is not intrinsic to those beliefs but rather is rooted in linguistic reference. And because intentional content is fixed by their extension, our beliefs have a certain guaranteed access to the world.

Putnam's basic argument centres on his famous 'twin earth' thought-experiment according to which there is another world identical to ours save one difference: while water on earth is composed of

[22] Cf. Richard L. Kirkham, *Theories of Truth: A Critical Introduction* (Cambridge, Mass.: MIT Press, 1992), 49; Rorty, *Philosophy and the Mirror of Nature*, p. 280; David K. Naugle, *Worldview: The History of a Concept* (Grand Rapids, Mich.: Eerdmans, 2002), 158.

[23] Putnam, 'The Meaning of "Meaning"', in Keith Gunderson (ed.), *Language, Mind and Knowledge*, Minnesota Studies in the Philosophy of Science, vii (Minneapolis, Minn.: University of Minnesota Press, 1975), 131–93.

[24] Putnam, *Representation and Reality* (Cambridge, Mass.: Bradford, 1998), 1.

H_2O, on twin earth it is composed of XYZ. He then points out that when an individual named Oscar on earth and his exact double on twin earth say 'water', the psychological states that they experience are identical but *the extension is different*: while earth Oscar refers to H_2O, twin-earth Oscar refers to XYZ. Putnam concludes that the two Oscars have different beliefs, from which it follows that *part of the content of our belief remains external to us*: 'Cut the pie any way you like, "meanings" just ain't in the *head*!'[25] While Putnam developed the argument with respect to natural kinds (water), one can readily generalize the point to linguistic communities,[26] leaving the mind seemingly dependent on the social world at every turn.

While the twin-earth experiment goes some distance to addressing scepticism, by making belief only partially dependent on reference, we could still worry about getting the intentional part wrong. Consider, for instance, the archetypal sceptic's dilemma of the brain-in-the-vat, according to which we have no way to know that we are not brains in vats of nutrient fluid receiving stimulations that simulate an external world that does not actually exist. In *Reason, Truth and History* Putnam extends his externalist view of belief to refute this dilemma, beginning with the illustration of an ant whose meanderings in the sand create what appears to be an image of Winston Churchill. Putnam observes that we have strong intuitions to deny that the lines really depict Churchill due to the absence of intention. So, how is it that intention transforms an identical set of lines traced by a human being into Churchill? Putnam responds that the ability to have any intention (including the intention to draw Churchill) entails that one is able to think about the object in question. But '[i]f lines in the sand, noises, etc., cannot "in themselves" represent anything, then how is it that thought forms can "in themselves" represent anything? Or can they? How can thought reach out and "grasp" what is external?'[27] In answer to his own question, Putnam makes

---

[25] Putnam, 'The Meaning of "Meaning"', p. 144.
[26] See Tyler Burge 'Individualism and the Mental', in T. Euhling and H. Wettstein (eds.), *Studies in Epistemology*, Midwest Studies in Philosophy, iv (Minneapolis, Minn.: University of Minnesota Press, 1979), 73–121.
[27] Hilary Putnam, *Reason, Truth and History* (Cambridge: Cambridge University Press, 1991), 3.

the referential determination of mental content complete. This step allows him to charge the classic brain-in-vat dilemma with being self-refuting: '[A]lthough the people in that possible world [of brains in vats] can think and "say" any words we can think and say, they cannot (I claim) *refer* to what we can refer to. In particular, they cannot think or say that they are brains in a vat (*even by thinking "we are brains in a vat"*)'.[28] That is, since the meaning of our thoughts comes from their referents, they cannot fail to have the correct meaning, and so I cannot *fail* to have correct thoughts of the world, since my thoughts come *structured* by that to which they refer. If we were brains in vats, then our intentional thoughts of trees and mountains would just *be* brain states; since we *do* refer to trees and mountains, we are not brains in vats.

Redefining Justification

In place of foundations rooted in the given, Quine bequeathed to us the memorable image of a holistic noetic web where no belief is basic and coherence is the criterion for justification. In his landmark essay 'Two Dogmas of Empiricism' Quine concluded: 'The totality of our so-called knowledge or beliefs, from the most casual matters of geography and history to the profoundest laws of atomic physics or even of pure mathematics and logic, is a man-made fabric which impinges on experience only along the edges'.[29] This emphasis upon belief encountering the world as a whole continues to characterize non-foundationalism.[30] Given that the world cannot justify beliefs, we must look to the totality of our beliefs themselves for justification. As Bruce Marshall puts it, 'the question is whether perceptions themselves *can* play any justificatory role, or whether, should it become

[28] Putnam, *Reason, Truth and History*, p. 8.
[29] W. V. O. Quine, 'Two Dogmas of Empiricism', in his *From a Logical Point of View* (Cambridge, Mass.: Harvard University Press, 1953), 20–46, repr. in Paul Benacerraf and Hilary Putnam (eds.), *Philosophy of Mathematics* (Oxford: Blackwell, 1964), 362.
[30] As Putnam observes, '[w]hat has experiential import is the corporate body of beliefs; this import is not the simple sum of the experiential imports of the individual statements' (*Representation and Reality*, p. 9).

necessary to invoke perceptions for justificatory purposes, that role rather belongs to beliefs about them'.[31]

The first means to justify beliefs is through their coherence with one another; thus, the more coherent a web of belief, the more justified. Rorty writes:

> To say that truth and knowledge can only be judged by the standards of the inquirers of our own day is not to say that human knowledge is less noble or important, or more 'cut off from the world,' than we had thought. It is merely to say that nothing counts as justification unless by reference to what we already accept, and that there is no way to get outside our beliefs and our language so as to find some test other than coherence.[32]

But coherence is not an end in itself, for it leads naturally to the criterion of pragmatism, since ultimately the pragmatic success of our beliefs at aiding survival will be the best testimony to the adequacy of their total coherence. Rorty observes: 'By an antirepresentationalist account I mean one which does not view knowledge as a matter of getting reality right, but rather as a matter of acquiring habits of action for coping with reality'.[33] Together coherence and pragmatism provide an alternative mode of justification to the futile foundationalist attempt to assess the adequacy of our beliefs from some mythical view from nowhere. Thus, we have a refreshingly practical approach to epistemological enquiry as it thrusts us out of the comfortable ivory tower and into the warp and woof of daily living.

TRUTH WITHOUT CORRESPONDENCE

Many non-foundationalists extend this rethinking of knowledge and justification to the concept of truth. In this section we will consider a non-foundationalist critique of the premier form of alethic realism—correspondence truth—and then consider the alethic anti-realist alternative.

[31] Marshall, *Trinity and Truth* (Cambridge: Cambridge University Press, 2000), 88 n. 21.
[32] Rorty, *Philosophy and the Mirror of Nature*, p. 178.
[33] Rorty, *Objectivity, Relativism, and Truth*, p. 1.

Undermining Correspondence

One may categorize theories of truth with respect to their understanding of three elements: the truth bearer, the truth maker, and the relation between them.[34] Though alethic realists have countenanced thoughts, sentence tokens, and sentence types as primary truth bearers, the strongest candidate is the proposition. The primary candidate for truth maker is a fact (that is, an actual state of affairs). Finally, the relation between the truth bearer and truth maker is a form of equivalence or correspondence. Aristotle provides the quintessential realist definition of truth: '[T]o say of what is that it is, and of what is not that it is not, is true'.[35] One may capture Aristotle's alethic realism more concisely with the formulation 'P is true if and only if P is the case' or 'P is true if and only if P'. Thus, according to alethic realism, the truth bearer is true if it is equivalent to a fact or state of affairs. For the realist, this is not an abstruse technicality or a hopeless triviality but rather a systematic articulation of the pre-theoretical and enormously important conception of truth.

At this point we will expand our comments on the three components, beginning with the truth bearer. While discussion of propositional expression is often limited to declarative sentences, clearly other sentences (for example, questions and imperatives) are also meaningful. So, one could identify the essence of the propositional form with gerunds that are expressible through different grammatical moods.[36] For instance, 'John Calvin's complaining about Moltmann's Christology' (perhaps in the interim state) is expressible in three grammatical moods:

DECLARATIVE: John Calvin complained about Moltmann's Christology.
INTERROGATIVE: Did John Calvin complain about Moltmann's Christology?
IMPERATIVE: John Calvin, complain about Moltmann's Christology![37]

---

[34] The deflationary theory is an exception, as it denies the existence of truth bearers.

[35] Aristotle, *Metaphysics* (n.p.: NuVision, 2005), 62.

[36] Clearly a fuller discussion of meaning in language would oblige us to address speech acts, but we can prescind that discussion here.

[37] Kirkham, *Theories of Truth*, pp. 55–6; cf. George Pitcher (ed.), *Truth* (Englewood Cliffs, NJ: Prentice Hall, 1964), introd., pp. 5–6.

While all meaningful sentences express propositions, only declarative sentences (*that* statements) have a truth *value*. (For example, it is true *that* John Calvin complained about Moltmann's Christology.) It is a category error to think that questions and commands could be *true*, since they make no claim as to how things are.[38] According to many realists, we may explicate the basic equivalence relation between the truth maker and truth bearer in terms of *correspondence*: '*P* is true if and only if it corresponds to the fact that *p*'.

While many realists find correspondence to be innocent and illuminating, non-foundationalists charge that the concept is vacuous and leads to scepticism, since we cannot step outside our beliefs to confirm them. The worry is compounded by the dualist distinction between the mind and brain. Thus, Fergus Kerr contends that '[p]ermanent scepticism about other people's thoughts and feelings seems logically demanded by the gaseous [unextended substance] conception of the mind'.[39] Once we accept a contrast between the mind and body, it becomes obvious that there is no way to establish the alethic realist's intrinsic/isomorphic link between the mind and the world.[40] Two problems arise with the attempt to establish an isomorphic relation between truth maker and truth bearer.[41] Colin McGinn illustrates the first problem, the 'explanatory gap' of philosophy of mind, by asking: 'How can technicolour phenomenology arise from soggy grey matter?'[42] That is, how do conscious experiences relate to objective brain states? The typical explanation appeals to a causal process like the following: Prior to my experience of seeing a sunset, light waves hit my eyes and are absorbed by the rods and cones at the back of the retina. This event induces a series of events

[38] Of course one could embed a question or command into a statement and make *that* a statement, as in 'It is true *that* Zwingli said "John Calvin, complain about Moltmann's Christology!"'

[39] Kerr, *Theology After Wittgenstein* (Oxford: Blackwell, 1986), 79.

[40] The point runs deeper than dualism per se, for *any* plausible theory of the mind will view thoughts as radically different from their intentional content. However, the problem is perhaps most obvious, and historically most influential, with a dualist conception of the self.

[41] In the *Tractatus Logico-Philosophicus* Wittgenstein sought to reduce every meaningful utterance to an atomic sentence that is formally isomorphic with a possible state of affairs.

[42] McGinn, *The Problem of Consciousness: Essays Towards a Resolution* (Oxford: Blackwell, 1991), 1.

in the nervous system that triggers a particular brain state that then causes the sensation of seeing the sunset. Hence, the rays of the sunset travelling to the eyes (event A) cause a particular pattern of neurons to fire (event B) which causes my visual experience (event C) replete with 'technicolour phenomenology'. As a result, I grasp the thought that the sun is setting, and this is true because it refers to the actual state of affairs of the sun setting. Hence, there are two links between A and C, two points for the mind/world encounter. On the one hand A causes C through B, while on the other C possesses (intrinsic) similitude with (or represents) A.[43] While the non-foundationalist does not object in principle to the first claim, that the world causes our beliefs, he does object to the claim that we can grasp equivalence *truth* by 'mirroring' the world.[44] Thus, such accounts of reference and truth are dismissed as mysterious, even 'occult'.

The second problem concerning the nature of intentionality is even more troubling, since it does not depend on a dualist theory of mind. George Santayana summarizes the challenge presented by both:

To know reality is, in a way, an impossible pretension, because knowledge means significant representation, discourse about an existence not contained in the knowing thought, and different in duration or locus from the ideas which represent it. But if knowledge does not possess its object how can it intend it? And if knowledge possesses its object, how can it be knowledge or have any practical, prophetic, or retrospective value? Consciousness is not knowledge unless it indicates or signifies what actually it is not.[45]

We can subdivide Santayana's dilemma into the problems of difference and distance. The problem of difference is that our neural states are not like the sensory experience of seeing the sunset, nor is this latter event like the event of the sun setting. What possible similarity

---

[43] For a discussion of these two correlations see John Yolton, *Realism and Appearances: An Essay in Ontology* (Cambridge: Cambridge University Press, 2000), ch. 2.

[44] The medieval Aristotelian dealt with these questions by appealing to the transmission of the form of the object perceived by the medium of a 'sensible species'. On this view, the form of that which is perceived literally infects the mind with the object's qualities, allowing for the causal transfer of similitude (see Anthony Kenny, *Aquinas on Mind* (London/New York: Routledge, 1993)). But apart from a metaphysic like the Aristotelian categories of matter/form, there is no framework to causally link B and C, and thus to explain the similitude of C to A.

[45] Santayana, *Reason in Common Sense*, cited in John Yolton, *Perception and Reality: A History from Descartes to Kant* (Ithaca, NY: Cornell University Press, 1996), p. vii.

could there be between a pattern of neuron synapses and the visual sensation of seeing a sunset, or a private mental event and the actual disappearance of the sun below the horizon? The problem of distance summarizes the separation between mind and world. If, to appeal to an eighteenth-century maxim, there is 'no cognition at a distance', and the world is not literally or virtually *in* our minds, then how can we come to know the world at all?

We might at this point seek criteria that operate at a sufficiently general or abstract level in order to establish the causal and representative requirements of realist reference. However, to do so one must assume a level of similarity between mind/belief and world which is so abstract that the net inevitably captures many other states of the world as corresponding to the belief while providing no plausible criterion to individuate any one of them. The difficulty, as Putnam observes, is that everything is similar to everything else in innumerably different ways:

> My sensation of a type-writer at this instant and the quarter in my pocket are both similar in the respect that some of their properties (the sensation's occurring right now and the quarter's being in my pocket right now) are *effects of my past actions*; if I had not sat down to type, I would not be having the sensation; and the quarter would not be in my pocket if I had not put it there. Both the sensation and the quarter exist in the twentieth century. Both the sensation and the quarter have been described in English. And so on and so on.[46]

The next dilemma arises when we attempt to identify which properties are relevant for linking the mind to the world. Regarding similitude or isomorphism (that in virtue of which we find a mind/world or truth maker/truth bearer fit), our immediate temptation is to respond by saying that event C has an intrinsic quality in virtue of which it represents event A, but this raises the problem of an infinite regress. We begin with the plausible explanation that C represents A in virtue of a property P. But then the question arises: in virtue of what does P link C to A? Appealing to P as the condition for representation explains nothing, forcing us to appeal to $P2$, $P3$, and so on. In short, we face either an infinite regress of properties or a brute fact that leaves correspondence a mystery.

---

[46] Putnam, *Reason, Truth and History*, pp. 64–5.

Alethic Anti-Realism

While one might grant that Rorty's alethic apathy is more subtle than an overt alethic anti-realism, nonetheless the line separating the two positions is thin. Consider how Philip Kenneson commends alethic apathy even as he lapses into anti-realist language:

> If your concept of 'earth' requires that it be the center of the universe for it to count as 'earth,' then on your account, the person who believes in a heliocentric model does not believe in any earth worth having. But if you are open to having your understanding of what might count as 'earth' reshaped, than [*sic*] the answer to this question might be very different. In a similar way, if your concept of 'real' truth requires something like 'how things are in themselves, apart from human interests,' then you will probably insist that a postmodernist account of truth is not an account of truth at all, or certainly not one worth having. But if you are willing to rethink what you understand by 'truth' in order to bring it into line with other conceptions that many contemporary persons have about the character of reality, language, rationality, and knowledge, then it might very well be that a postmodernist reconception of truth might serve some important purposes.[47]

While Kenneson appears to reject the entire realist approach to truth as unfruitful, his alternative sounds like not simply a dismissal of the entire realist/anti-realist opposition so much as a rejection of realism for a competing anti-realist theory. This reflects the tendency of alethic apathy to collapse into alethic anti-realism, a point we shall take up in the next chapter.

Anti-realist interpretations of truth, such as the epistemic and pragmatic, seek to ensure that truth is knowable. The epistemic approach defines truth in terms of epistemic justification, with respect to either coherence or consensus. The coherence criterion interprets truth as the property of coherence in one's beliefs.[48] As Rorty says, 'there is no way to get outside our beliefs and our language so as to find some test other than coherence'.[49] Brand Blanshard

---

[47] Kenneson, 'Truth', in A. K. M. Adam (ed.), *Handbook of Postmodern Biblical Interpretation* (St Louis, Miss.: Chalice, 2000), 274.

[48] For a discussion of coherentism see Ralph C. S. Walker, *The Coherence Theory of Truth: Realism, Anti-Realism, Idealism* (London: Routledge, 1989). The challenge for coherence theories is in defining this property in a way that is neither too constrictive (deductive implication of one's beliefs) nor too broad (absence of contradiction).

[49] Rorty, *Philosophy and the Mirror of Nature*, p. 178.

provides a particularly clear statement of the position that truth consists in coherent belief. Blanshard believes that metaphysical realism leads to scepticism, for if reality exists external to our minds then we could only hope to grasp it by luck. Hence, the sole criterion of truth (coherence) must also be the essence of truth: 'In the end, the only test of truth that is not misleading is the special nature or character that is itself constitutive of truth'.[50] To avoid the alethic relativism of two contradictory systems being true in virtue of their internal coherence, Blanshard argues that there is only one completely coherent and fully comprehensive system of belief.

The second epistemic account of truth, the consensus view, focuses on the projected consensus of rational individuals under an ideal enquiry. Charles Peirce held a consensus view of truth when he wrote: 'The opinion which is fated to be ultimately agreed to by all who investigate is what we mean by truth'.[51] Peirce further explains: 'The truth of the proposition that Caesar crossed the Rubicon consists in the fact that the further we push our archaeological and other studies, the more strongly will that conclusion force itself on our minds forever—or would do so, if study were to go on forever'.[52] While one finds evidence for the consensus view in Rorty's writings, the most notable contemporary defender is Hilary Putnam, who identifies truth with the result of an ideal enquiry: 'We speak as if there were such things as epistemically ideal conditions, and we call a statement "true" if it would be justified under such conditions'.[53] With this definition, Putnam hopes to guarantee that truth cannot remain forever beyond the grasp of enquiring communities.

Pragmatism provides the second major non-foundationalist account of truth.[54] On this view, truth is that which is particularly

---

[50] Blanshard, *The Nature of Thought*, ii (New York: Macmillan, 1941), 268, cited in Kirkham, *Theories of Truth*, p. 105.

[51] *Collected Papers of Charles Sanders Peirce*, ed. Charles Hartshorne and Paul Weiss (Cambridge, Mass.: Harvard University Press, 1931–58), v. 407, cited in Kirkham, *Theories of Truth*, p. 81. Philip Clayton draws on C. S. Peirce to forward an epistemic theory of truth: '[O]ne is justified in calling a theory "true" in anticipation of the convergence of informed ("expert") opinion at the imagined end of the process' (*The Problem of God in Modern Thought* (Grand Rapids, Mich.: Eerdmans, 2000), 33).

[52] Peirce, *Collected Papers*, v. 565, cited in Kirkham, *Theories of Truth*, p. 81.

[53] Putnam, *Reason, Truth and History*, p. 55.

[54] This is also termed the 'performative' or 'instrumental' theory of truth.

useful or effective for achieving ends. William James was one of the more vocal (if inconsistent) advocates of pragmatic truth: '*ideas...become true just in so far as they help us to get into satisfactory relations with other parts of our experience*'.[55] One finds ample evidence for alethic pragmatism in Rorty's writing.[56] For instance, in *Philosophy and the Mirror of Nature* he poses the following choice:

Shall we take 'S knows that p'... as a remark about the status of S's reports among his peers, or shall we take it as a remark about the relation between subject and object, between nature and its mirror? The first alternative leads to a pragmatic view of truth and a therapeutic approach to ontology[57]

According to Rorty, the latter, 'ontological' explanation, which seeks to root truth in the world, is simply an attempt to move truth beyond 'warranted assertability', which he understands to be 'what our peers will, *ceteris paribus*, let us get away with saying'.[58] This infamous statement admits to both epistemic/consensus and pragmatic interpretations. In the former, truth is that which one's peers agree with (consensus), while in the latter truth is that which has the positive effect of fostering agreement amongst one's peers. This ambiguity illustrates that there is significant overlap between the epistemic (particularly consensus) and pragmatic approaches to truth. The unifying theme for all anti-realist theories of truth is the reinterpretation of truth relative to human interests and capacities rather than as something abstract and absolute which might ultimately be unobtainable to us.

---

[55] James, *Pragmatism* (Cambridge: Harvard University Press, 1975), 34, cited in Kirkham, *Theories of Truth*, pp. 92–3. Elsewhere James identifies a true statement as that which agrees with reality (*Pragmatism*, p. 96). However, for James, agreement with reality comes not through a correspondence or equivalence, but through pragmatic efficacy.

[56] Alvin Goldman, *Knowledge in a Social World* (Oxford: Clarendon, 1999), 10–11.

[57] Rorty, *Philosophy and the Mirror of Nature*, p. 175.

[58] Ibid. 176. In response, Dean Zimmerman offered the following limerick:

> 'Truth is what peers let you say',
> It was false said at the APA,
> And so Richard Rorty
> Changed peer groups at forty;
> Now his statements get truer each day.
>
> (Cited in Goldman, *Knowledge in a Social World*, p. 11.)

CALLING OFF THE SEARCH FOR THE 'REAL' WORLD

In addition to retooled conceptions of knowledge, justification, and truth, the non-foundationalist proposes a profound rethinking of the conception of metaphysical realism, the notion that the world exists apart from human conceptualization. Here again we will focus on the positions of Richard Rorty and Hilary Putnam.

Rorty on a World Well Lost

The background for Rorty's dim assessment of the real world lies in the place of the noumenon in Immanuel Kant's anti-realism. To recap, Kant introduced the unmitigated dualism between phenomena of experience and the unknowable noumenal ground of our experience. This dualism raised a nest of contentious problems; for instance, if we can only experience and think of the phenomena, then we cannot refer to the noumenon at all. But the claim that 'the noumenon is that to which none of our concepts apply' certainly *looks* like the application of a concept to the noumenon. As a result, many critics have contended that the very claim that a Kantian noumenon exists is incoherent.

For Rorty, both realism and (Kantian) anti-realism face essentially the *same* dilemma; as Sue Patterson observes, '[it] proves impossible to "get behind" the linguistic mirror to check on how its image reflects the non-linguistic reality because the very getting-behind is itself conceptually framed and hence not a real getting-behind at all'.[59] Rorty complements this observation when he writes: '[W]e shall never be able to step outside of language, never be able grasp [*sic*] reality unmediated by a linguistic description'.[60] Since we have no access to the world behind the mirror (the noumenon of both realism and anti-realism), we cannot establish the correspondence relation, thereby losing the real world; at this point foundationalist epistemology devolves into scepticism. The rejection of metaphysical

[59] Patterson, *Realist Christian Theology in a Postmodern Age* (Cambridge: Cambridge University Press, 1999), 21–2.

[60] Rorty, 'A World without Substances or Essences', in his *Philosophy and Social Hope* (Harmondsworth: Penguin, 1999), 48.

realism arises in a programmatic anti-realist attempt to avoid scepticism by eschewing the realist's dualism between appearance (world-for-me) and reality (world-in-itself). Rorty thus charges that the 'real world' is 'well lost' as an unnecessary vestige which only opens the door to scepticism.

Putnam on a Relative World

While Rorty simply dismisses the real world, Putnam instead argues that everything exists relative to human interests and thus that there simply is no objective world apart from conceptual schemes. To illustrate, picture a room empty save Wolfhart Pannenberg sitting in a chair and reading a 'Sweet Valley High' novel. If Putnam were to ask us how many things are in the room we would respond 'Three: Pannenberg, the chair and the novel'. But according to a mereologist[61] there are actually *seven* objects:[62]

  (1) Pannenberg
  (2) novel
  (3) chair
  (4) Pannenberg + novel
  (5) Pannenberg + chair
  (6) novel + chair
  (7) Pannenberg + novel + chair

So how many objects are there in the room: 3 or 7, or what?[63] Putnam concludes that *there is no single answer* independent of our choice of how to identify an object conceptually: '[T]he idea that there is an Archimedean point, or a use of "exist" inherent in the world itself, from which the question "How many objects *really* exist?" makes

---

[61] Mereology is the metaphysical view that for every two or more particulars there is an object that they constitute.

[62] Cf. Putnam, *The Many Faces of Realism*, Paul Carus Lectures (LaSalle, Ill.: Open Court, 1987), 18–20.

[63] If mereology is correct then the number is actually much greater, for the fabric of the chair and the cover of the book also form an object; and there is the clothing Pannenberg is wearing and his nose and ears (aren't those things?) and the molecules and atoms and quarks of which he and the chair and book are composed, and on and on and on …

sense, is an illusion'.[64] Putnam concludes that existence is relative to a conceptual scheme and the only sense in speaking of 'the world' is as *the world as conceptually structured by human beings*. Thus, there is no God's-eye point of view, no view from nowhere, no objective world. Rather, human beings comprise or constitute the world (at least in part) through their conceptualizing and language. As Patterson puts it, '[i]f knowing (and therefore conceiving) is a part of being, then knowledge not only discovers but also in part constitutes reality'.[65] Thus, we may choose between Rorty's pragmatic dismissal of reality and Putnam's relativization of it. Despite their differences, both dispense with an objective noumenon in favour of a world defined in terms of human interests and experience.

THEOLOGIES OF NON-FOUNDATIONALISM

While many non-foundationalists have been openly hostile to religion,[66] some have adapted non-foundationalism to theological perspectives.[67] In recent decades non-foundationalism has made impressive inroads among Christian theologians, and the reasons are not hard to find, since it marginalizes the Enlightenment primacy of science and focuses on *lived* truth in marked contrast to the cognitive-propositionalism that tends to go with foundationalism.[68]

---

[64] Putnam, *Many Faces of Realism*, p. 20.

[65] Patterson, *Realist Christian Theology*, p. 28. Cf. Putnam: '[T]he mind and the world jointly make up the mind and the world' (*Reason, Truth and History*, p. xi).

[66] Among religion's antagonists are John Dewey, Wilfred Sellars, W. V. O. Quine, and Richard Rorty—though see Jason Boffetti, 'How Richard Rorty Found Religion', *First Things* (May 2004), 24–30.

[67] Such is the case with Putnam (see his *Jewish Philosophy as a Guide to Life: Rosenzweig, Buber, Levinas, Wittgenstein* (Bloomington, Ind.: Indiana University Press, 2008).

[68] Non-foundationalist theology arises from both post-modern and post-liberal influences. See David Ray Griffin, William A. Beardslee, and Joe Holland, *Varieties of Postmodern Theology* (Albany, NY: State University of New York Press, 1989); William C. Placher, 'Postliberal Theology', in David F. Ford (ed.), *The Modern Theologians: An Introduction to Christian Theology in the Twentieth Century*, 2nd edn. (Cambridge, Mass.: Blackwell, 1997), 343–56.

Non-foundationalism appears to evince many other virtues as well, including epistemic humility, holism, and a humble perspectivism. As John Thiel puts it:

Throughout its history, theology has understood itself as faith seeking understanding and so has articulated its contextuality as a dimension of its own disciplinary procedure. Nonfoundationalism encourages theology to be loyal to its age-old reflective strategy, aware of the deficiencies of Cartesian epistemologies, and consistent with its most basic doctrinal beliefs, whether they be ancient or modern in their formulation.[69]

In addition, Colin Gunton observes, '[f][or theologians groaning under the oppression of demands to justify their discipline before the bar of what is supposed to be universally valid scientific method the appeal of non-foundationalism is immense'.[70] Among those exploring non-foundationalism we find narrative theologians (Ronald Thiemann, Stanley Hauerwas[71]), post-liberals (George Lindbeck, William Placher[72]), and post-conservatives (Richard Middleton, Brian Walsh, and Philip Kenneson,[73]).[74] In what follows, we will extend our discussion into a theological context by critically engaging

[69] Thiel, *Nonfoundationalism*, p. 107.

[70] Gunton, *The One, the Three and the Many: God, Creation and the Culture of Modernity*, Bampton Lectures 1992 (Cambridge: Cambridge University Press, 1993), 133.

[71] Thiemann, *Revelation and Theology* (Notre Dame, Ind.: University of Notre Dame Press, 1985); Hauerwas, 'The Church's One Foundation is Jesus Christ Her Lord; Or, In a World Without Foundations: All We Have is the Church', in Stanley Hauerwas, Nancey Murphy, and Mark Nation (eds.), *Theology Without Foundations: Religious Practice and the Future of Theological Truth* (Nashville, Tenn.: Abingdon, 1994), 14–62.

[72] Lindbeck, *The Nature of Doctrine: Religion and Theology in a Postliberal Age* (Philadelphia, Pa.: Westminster, 1984); Placher, *Unapologetic Theology: A Christian Voice in a Pluralistic Conversation* (Louisville, Ky.: Westminster/John Knox Press, 1989).

[73] Middleton and Walsh, *Truth is Stranger than it Used to Be: Biblical Faith in a Postmodern Age* (Downers Grove, Ill.: InterVarsity, 1995); Kenneson, 'There's No Such Thing as Objective Truth', pp. 155–70.

[74] Other significant recent theological engagements with non-foundationalism include F. LeRon Shults, *The Postfoundationalist Task of Theology: Wolfhart Pannenberg and the New Theological Rationality* (Grand Rapids, Mich.: Eerdmans, 1999); Patterson, *Realist Christian Theology in a Postmodern World*; Richard Lints, *The Fabric of Theology: A Prolegomenon to Evangelical Theology* (Grand Rapids, Mich.: Eerdmans, 1993), ch. 6; Dirk Martin Grube, 'Religious Experience after the Demise of Foundationalism', *Religious Studies*, 3/1 (1995), 37–52.

the non-foundationalism of Stanley Grenz and Nancey Murphy. Since both theologians are thoughtful and engaging interlocutors who reject epistemic foundations, alethic realism, and metaphysical realism, their work will provide useful test cases for the prospects of non-foundationalist theology.

Grenz and Eschatological Realism

Until his untimely death in 2005 Stanley Grenz was among the most prolific Evangelical theologians. While Grenz wrote widely in systematic theology, arguably his most important work is found in his model of non-foundational theology, with its innovative integration of Pannenbergian eschatological themes.[75] Though evangelicalism has not been known for theological innovation, Grenz stood at the vanguard of a progressive, post-conservative, and non-foundationalist attempt to revitalize his tradition.[76] Grenz critiques Enlightenment evangelicalism in favour of a *resourcement* of biblical and pietistic roots combined with post-modern and eschatological themes.[77] We will focus here on his book *Beyond Foundationalism*, co-authored with John Franke,[78] an important non-foundationalist in his own right.[79] We will consider in turn the authors' rejection of epistemic

---

[75] See, for instance, Grenz, *A Primer on Postmodernism* (Grand Rapids, Mich.: Eerdmans, 1996); *Renewing the Center: Evangelical Theology in a Post-theological Era* (Grand Rapids, Mich.: Baker, 2000); 'Articulating the Christian Belief Mosaic: Theological Method after the Demise of Foundationalism', in John G. Stackhouse (ed.), *Evangelical Futures: A Conversation on Theological Method* (Grand Rapids, Mich.: Baker, 2000), 10–36.

[76] The growing division between post-conservative and conservative Evangelicals is summarized from the post-conservative perspective in Grenz, *Renewing the Center*, chs. 4–6. For a conservative assessment see Millard Erickson, *The Evangelical Left: Encountering Postconservative Evangelical Theology* (Grand Rapids, Mich.: Baker, 1997); cf. Millard Erickson, *Postmodernizing the Faith: Evangelical Responses to the Challenge of Postmodernism* (Grand Rapids, Mich.: Baker, 1998).

[77] For instance, see Grenz, *Renewing the Center*, ch. 2.

[78] Stanley Grenz and John Franke, *Beyond Foundationalism: Shaping Theology in a Postmodern Context* (Louisville, Ky.: Westminster/John Knox, 2001).

[79] Among Franke's other publications in the area see *The Character of Theology: An Introduction to Its Nature, Task, and Purpose* (Grand Rapids, Mich.: Baker, 2005).

foundationalism, alethic realism,[80] and metaphysical realism,[81] and the implications that their position has for an understanding of doctrine.

Grenz and Franke throw their lot in with epistemic non-foundationalism when they eschew the central foundationalist architectural metaphor of a stratified noetic structure in favour of mosaic imagery:

We ought to view Christian doctrine as comprising a 'belief-mosaic' and see theology, in turn, as the exploration of Christian doctrine viewed as an interrelated, unified whole. And we ought to envision our constructive work as leading to a mosaic of interlocking pieces that presents a single pattern, rather than merely to a collection of beads on a string.[82]

Like the web metaphor, the mosaic image directly counters the appeal to any special class of basic beliefs in favour of a non-foundational holism. Christian beliefs are not like a collection of sequential beads or stratified bricks, but rather like an interconnected mosaic where each tile is only comprehensible (and so justified) in relation to the whole.[83]

At a couple of points however, Grenz and Franke could be interpreted as affirming a foundational epistemic interface with the world, for they concede that 'some beliefs (or assertions) anchor others', and that in this respect at least 'nearly every thinker is in some sense a foundationalist'.[84] Moreover, they affirm the insights of Reformed epistemology,[85] an epistemological school of thought whose major contributors (excepting Nicholas Wolterstorff) are foundationalists.[86] However, it may be that Grenz and Franke have confused

---

[80] Their specific target here is the correspondence theory of truth, though, as with many non-foundationalists, Grenz and Franke take the alternative to be a sort of alethic anti-realism.

[81] Grenz and Franke, *Beyond Foundationalism*, p. 38.

[82] Grenz and Franke, *Beyond Foundationalism*, 51.

[83] Compare Blaise Pascal: 'All things, then, are caused and causing, supporting and dependent, mediate and immediate; and all support one another in a natural, though imperceptible chain linking together things most distant and different. So, I hold it is as impossible to know the parts without knowing the whole as to know the whole without knowing the particular parts' (*Pensées*, trans. and ed. Roger Ariew (Indianapolis, Ind./Cambridge: Hackett, 2005), 62).

[84] Grenz and Franke, *Beyond Foundationalism*, p. 29.   [85] Ibid. 47–8.

[86] On Wolterstorff's views see Andrew Sloane, *On Being a Christian in the Academy: Nicholas Wolterstorff and the Practice of Christian Scholarship* (Carlisle: Paternoster, 2003), ch. 6.

foundationalism with proper basicality. A person may hold a view according to which coherent beliefs are properly basic and all justification subsequently derives from this justification. For instance, a coherentist may believe that *God raised Jesus from the dead* because it is most fully coherent with her other beliefs, while she then comes to hold the further belief that *Jesus rose from the dead*. Pure coherentism views the justification of every belief as deriving wholly from its coherence within one's total noetic structure. However, the impure form allows for local instances of asymmetric, foundationalist justification transfer so long as the *final* (global) source of justification is coherence.[87] As Plantinga puts it, '[g]lobal coherentism is compatible with local foundationalism; the view that coherence alone is the source of warrant is compatible with the view that warrant is sometimes transmitted'.[88] Thus, in both forms coherence is the ultimate and final justification for beliefs. In light of their statements elsewhere, Grenz and Franke appear to be impure coherentists.[89]

Grenz and Franke extend their coherentism and pragmatism beyond justification to encompass knowledge as well.[90] Further, they merge claims about pragmatic justification with claims about truth, particularly as they discuss William James's claim that '[t]ruth is *made*, just as health, wealth and strength are made, in the course of experience'.[91] They conclude that 'coherentism and pragmatism provided ways to leave behind the foundationalist preference for the correspondence of truth'.[92] Grenz and Franke thus see a link between epistemic non-foundationalism and a rejection of correspondence truth. Immediately they add a denial of metaphysical realism by noting that 'the "turn to linguistics" offered the means to overcome metaphysical realism'.[93]

The most interesting dimension of the Grenz-Franke proposal is found in what I call the 'ontological future' thesis. According to this argument, theology promises an advantage over mere *secular* anti-realism by tracing the givenness of the world not to a world which

[87] Alvin Plantinga, *Warrant: The Current Debate* (Oxford: Oxford University Press, 1993), 79.

[88] Ibid. 79.

[89] Compare Grenz, *Renewing the Center*, where he affirms a chastened foundationalism in which some beliefs are 'properly basic' (pp. 200–1, 214) and then endorses a coherentist account where our beliefs form a 'web' or 'mosaic' (p. 205).

[90] Grenz and Franke, *Beyond Foundationalism*, pp. 38–42.

[91] Cited ibid. 41.   [92] Ibid. 42.   [93] Ibid.

'predates' humanity, but to a future world to be created by the Spirit. This argument is clearly inspired by Wolfhart Pannenberg's eschatological metaphysics and epistemology according to which the world ultimately *is* what it will be (and will be known as) in the eschaton.[94] Hence, while agreeing with the post-modern critique of metanarratives, Grenz and Franke maintain the normativity of the Christian story eschatologically.[95] While there is presently no real world or truth makers, they aver that the Holy Spirit is working *from the future* through the Christian linguistic community to create the real world: '[T]he "objectivity of the world" about which we can truly speak is an objectivity of a *future*, eschatological world'.[96] In this view, the task of Christian theology is to explore 'the world-constructing, knowledge-forming, identity-forming "language" of the Christian community'.[97]

According to Grenz and Franke, this backwards creation from the future occurs as the Spirit works through the culture and traditions of the Christian linguistic community and the central scriptural witness. At the same time, it would seem that the relegation of reality and truth to the eschaton allows the Christian to embrace the post-modernist's refutation of metanarratives, at least in the present age. Consequently, Grenz and Franke seek to avoid the oppressive danger of metanarratives with the surprising claim that *there presently is no real world*; the metanarrative will only become true in the perfected age when oppression will be no more. As Grenz writes in *Renewing the Center*: 'In contrast to "totalizing" modernist metanarratives, against which postmodernism rightly rebels, an eschatological theology views the God of the Bible, and not humankind, as the acting subject who unites the diverse moments of time into a single story'.[98]

---

[94] Pannenberg describes the ontological-future thesis as follows: 'The emergence of contingent individual events from the possibility field of the future constitutes ... only the elementary aspect in the creative dynamic of the Spirit, the beginning of its development. It culminates in the integration of events and moments into a unity of form' (*Systematic Theology*, ii, trans. Geoffrey W. Bromiley (Grand Rapids, Mich.: Eerdmans, 1994), 102).

[95] Grenz, *Primer on Postmodernism*, pp. 164–5.

[96] Grenz and Franke, *Beyond Foundationalism*, p. 53.

[97] Ibid. Grenz applies this thesis to anthropology in his *The Social God and the Relational Self: A Trinitarian Theology of the Imago Dei* (Louisville, Ky./London: Westminster/John Knox, 2001), pt. 1.

[98] Grenz, *Renewing the Center*, p. 217.

Grenz and Franke thus develop a counter-intuitive, if intriguing, picture, which consists (at present) of an anti-realist non-foundationalism, though realism will triumph eschatologically. While it is not entirely clear what this means for doctrine, one possible interpretation is that doctrines at present lack a realist reference and thus their primary present function is regulative or ethical for the community of faith (an adaptation of the Lindbeckian thesis). Where this thesis would differ from Lindbeck is in positing an eschatological-realist fulfilment of true doctrine.

Murphy and Pragmatic Theological Science

Our second interlocutor is Nancey Murphy, an innovative theologian and philosopher who labours in the forefront of the discussion between theology, philosophy, and science. Murphy has developed a sophisticated theological non-foundationalism that is richly informed by recent philosophy of science. We will begin with her epistemology and theological method, and then proceed to consider the implications for alethic and metaphysical realism.

Murphy contends that David Hume's attack on the traditional arguments of natural theology initiated a crisis of authority, so that ever since, theologians have attempted to meet the Humean challenge through foundationalist appeals to natural theology, biblical authority, and human experience.[99] Since these attempts to ground theology foundationally have all failed, the justification of Christian theology remains uncertain. In Murphy's view, help comes from the unlikely source of W. V. O. Quine—unlikely because of Quine's unremitting hostility toward religion. Especially significant is Quine's pivotal essay 'Two Dogmas of Empiricism', where he claims to have definitively undermined all forms of foundationalism while embracing holism and fallibilism.[100] Quine showed that any given sentence's

[99] In *Theology in the Age of Scientific Reasoning* (Ithaca, NY: Cornell University Press, 1990), ch. 1 Murphy follows the analysis of Jeffrey Stout, *The Flight from Authority: Religion, Morality, and the Quest for Authonomy* (Notre Dame, Ind.: University of Notre Dame Press, 1981).

[100] So important is this essay (along with Wittgenstein's *Philosophical Investigations*, published in the same year), that Nancey Murphy suggests we date the advent of post-modernity to 1951 (*Beyond Liberalism and Fundamentalism: How Modern and*

epistemological significance depends on a theory or language, leading to the conclusion that a sentence's meaning cannot be a self-contained, atomistic derivation of a prelinguistic phenomenon, but rather is a part of the whole system of belief: the meaning of an individual bit depends upon the whole. Thus, no belief is an island unto itself; rather they are more like lily pads affected by every ripple of the pond. Fallibilism follows from this first point, for the adjustment of any particular belief affects all meanings; hence, it is possible in principle that we could revise or reject *any belief*. From this, it follows that beliefs do not have determinate meanings, but only shifting meanings within the web of belief. But if meaning can change, then no beliefs are analytic and so true *by definition*; all beliefs are fallible and revisable.[101] That is, no belief is properly basic or certain and so immune from rejection. Thus, we must revise our web of belief in the light of ongoing experience. As Quine and J. S. Ullian put it, '[y]our immediate concern must be with the comprehensiveness and coherence of your belief body'.[102] These radical Quinean insights serve to undermine the foundationalist derivation of doctrines from pre-doctrinal prolegomena, even as they point to a new epistemology that is holistic, where theory pervades every belief.

Quine's holistic and fallibilistic epistemology offers a pared-down approach to apologetics and theological method, but in avoiding the sceptical implications of classical foundationalism might it not be sowing its own seeds of scepticism? After all, there are many webs of belief, so how does an individual choose their web of belief? Does this indeterminacy mean that we lose any reason to think our set of beliefs is true? Murphy follows Quine in dismissing this objection as a leftover problem from foundationalism. She counters that we cannot stand outside our total set of beliefs, but can only challenge them one at a time, and then concludes: '[T]he idea that we must

Postmodern Philosophy Set the Theological Agenda, Rockwell Lecture Series (Valley Forge, Pa.: Trinity, 1993), 87).

[101] Nancey Murphy, 'Postmodern Apologetics: Or Why Theologians *Must* Pay Attention to Science', in W. Mark Richardson and Wesley J. Wildman (eds.), *Religion and Science: History, Method, Dialogue* (New York: Routledge, 1996), 107; Placher, *Unapologetic Theology*, pp. 31–5.

[102] W. V. O. Quine and J. S. Ullian, *The Web of Belief*, 2nd edn. (New York: Random House, 1978), 13–14.

somehow justify the whole of our web of beliefs is either a holdover from foundationalist thinking or else an illusion created by a mental picture. We cannot do so, and therefore we need not do so'.[103] Murphy thus surrenders the goal of attaining incorrigible beliefs, while submitting doctrines to the probable reasoning operative in science. Her rejection of the dilemma of scepticism as a false problem reflects the non-foundationalist determination to reinterpret everything— justification, knowledge, truth, reality—in epistemic and coherentist/pragmatic terms.

While Murphy believes that Quine's non-foundationalism effectively counters the threat of scepticism, the worry of relativism also looms. Murphy states the problem as follows: 'We can imagine, alongside our own web, a variety of competing webs, and the question then arises how to choose among them'.[104] How can one respond to the threat of relativism? Thomas Kuhn's theory of paradigm shifts illustrates the dangers of relativism. According to Kuhn, scientific theories are accepted or rejected relative to an entire paradigm. Kuhn runs into trouble by insisting that while each paradigm is internally rational, there are no externally rational criteria to guide the abandonment of one paradigm and the adoption of another. Consequently, his view of science constitutes a form of 'non-rational non-realism', because he denies that the putative entities of scientific theory exist apart from the theory, while he only recognizes the rationality of the process as internal to each particular theory.[105] As a result, Kuhn rejects the notion that we can speak of one particular theory as more closely approximating reality than another (e.g. as if Newtonian cosmology were truer than Ptolemaic). Understandably, this view raises the spectre of relativism.

As Kuhn's philosophy illustrates, we can understand the challenge of relativism in the discernment of rational criteria that transcend individual webs of belief. To respond to this dilemma, Murphy appeals to Imre Lakatos and Alasdair MacIntyre. In *Theology in the*

---

[103] Nancey Murphy, 'Postmodern Apologetics', p. 109. Elsewhere she writes: '[T]here is no "place" in the web for a foundation, so its absence does not lead to skepticism' (*Beyond Liberalism and Fundamentalism*, p. 98).

[104] Ibid.

[105] See Craig and Moreland, *Philosophical Foundations for a Christian Worldview*, pp. 340–1.

Age of Scientific Reasoning Murphy focuses on developing a model for rational theological enquiry based on Lakatos's philosophy of science. Aware of Kuhn's errors, Lakatos offers a more balanced view of the rational basis of scientific enquiry, and by extension a more viable basis for theological discourse. He argues that scientific theories consist of a non-negotiable hard-core thesis that is related to empirical material by a penumbral belt of auxiliary theses. When new data present a challenge to the theory, one alters or abandons the auxiliary theses in order to ensure the continued viability of the hard-core thesis. The picture Lakatos paints is substantially like Quine's web-like noetic structure, where we have deeply embedded (though not basic, let alone incorrigible) beliefs surrounded by an auxiliary belt of beliefs that are the first to be revised with the input of new cognitive data.

Murphy argues that theologians should follow a similar model of fallible, probabilistic reasoning in developing their research programmes. Once the queen of the sciences, theology was expelled long ago from the castle and now labours merely as one more serf striving for a coherent picture of the world. As a result, theologians must constantly adjust understandings of doctrines to new experience, thereby seeking heuristic auxiliary theses to relate data to the core theses. We find a contemporary example in the post-Holocaust abandonment of divine impassibility.[106] Hence, Murphy describes the theologian's task in Quinean fashion: '[T]he theologian can be imagined to be contributing to the reweaving of the doctrinal web as it has been handed on to her, whether this means minor repairs or a radical reformulation to meet an epistemological crisis in her tradition'.[107] As in everyday experience, the penumbral belt of theses (or theologoumena) is more likely to be revised than central beliefs (or dogmas).

Murphy supplements Lakatos's theory with the work of Alasdair MacIntyre, which demonstrates that traditions are rational in so far as they can fail by their own standards of rationality, thereby giving rise

---

[106] Admittedly many theologians would contend with the notion that evil in the world requires the rejection of impassibility. Regardless, the fact remains that post-Holocaust theology reflects this kind of Lakatosian reasoning.

[107] Murphy, *Beyond Liberalism and Fundamentalism*, p. 106.

to an epistemological crisis.[108] While the underdetermination of data may mean that theological doctrines are no more explicitly falsified than are scientific theories, each still faces the threat of degeneration and abandonment. To avoid this danger, the Christian tradition must continue seeking to accommodate itself to new data so as to avoid the fate of innumerable forgotten theologies and religions. To appreciate the point, take the issue of scriptural authority. No longer can the appeal to scriptural authority be justified relative to some foundationalist criterion, be it in relation to natural theology or the inerrancy of the Scriptures or pope. But neither does this mean (as many theologians have assumed) that we need to adopt an understanding of Scripture wholly external to the faith.[109] As MacIntyre points out, every tradition (including the scientific) is constituted by the acceptance of some authority.

How does Murphy's strongly pragmatic and fallibilistic approach to theology affect her views of doctrine? Keeping in mind the close parallel with natural science (one which is necessary given the epistemic superiority of science), our views of doctrine will end up looking like scientific theories—that is, as falsifiable and provisional theories that seek to explain and predict experience. This need not lead to an overt anti-realism, and indeed could be fully critically realist, but it does represent a broadly functional shift in doctrinal assessment. Consider as an example Karen Kilby's explanation of Trinitarian doctrine:

The doctrine of the Trinity, I want to suggest, does not need to be seen as a descriptive, first order teaching—there is no need to assume that its main function must be to provide a picture of the divine, a deep understanding of the way God really is. It can instead be taken as grammatical, as a second order proposition, a rule, or perhaps a set of rules, for how to read the Biblical stories, how to speak about some of the characters we come across in these

---

[108] Ibid. 107. See Alasdair MacIntyre, *Three Rival Versions of Moral Enquiry: Encyclopaedia, Genealogy, and Tradition*, 1988 Gifford Lectures (London: Duckworth, 1990).

[109] Take, for instance, H. L. Mencken's claim that the Bible 'deserves to be set before the young, not as a bugaboo for enforcing the moral ideas of nitwits, but as the rich storehouse of human wisdom and folly, strength and weakness, hope and despair that it really is' ('Searching Holy Writ', in *H. L. Mencken on Religion*, ed. S. T. Joshi (Amherst, NY: Prometheus, 2002), 85.

stories, how to think and talk about the experience of prayer, how to deploy the 'vocabulary' of Christianity in an appropriate way.[110]

On Kilby's proposal, the point of the doctrine of the Trinity is not to provide an accurate description of the nature of God. Rather, it is a theoretical distillation of the scriptural witness with no necessary first-order (descriptive) implications.

CONCLUSION

The fact that Grenz and Murphy take such different approaches highlights the potential for diversity and innovation within non-foundational theology. While both approaches critique the notion of epistemic foundations, Murphy adopts a more obviously pragmatic and anti-metaphysical approach to theological construction. By contrast, Grenz's eschatological realism actually represents a surprisingly ambitious metaphysic slipped in through the back door of the future.

[110] Kilby, 'Perichoresis and Projection: Problems with Social Doctrines of the Trinity', *Blackfriars*, 81/956 (2000), 443.

6

A Critique of Non-foundationalism

[W]hen people thought the Earth was flat, they were wrong.
When people thought the Earth was spherical they were wrong.
But if you think that thinking the Earth is spherical is just as
wrong as thinking the Earth is flat, then your view is wronger
than both of them put together.

Isaac Asimov, *The Relativity of Wrong*

I can respect the men who argue that religion is true and therefore ought to be believed, but I can only feel profound moral
reprobation for those who say that religion ought to be believed
because it is useful, and that to ask whether it is true is a waste
of time.

Bertrand Russell, 'Can Religion Cure Our Troubles?'

Is it more correct to think of our culture as post-modern or hyper-
modern? While the debate on this question will continue, clearly
something has changed at the contemporary university. As Simon
Blackburn puts it,

[i]f you visit a good school, you might find some big words written over
the gate: words such as Truth, Reason, Knowledge, Understanding, or even
Wisdom. If the school is old enough and in another country, you might
find a mention of God, though this word may now be an embarrassment,
or regarded as purely decorative, and if the word was once there, perhaps it
has been erased and something secular substituted. But nobody would want
to erase Truth, Reason, and the rest, would they?[1]

---

[1] Blackburn, 'Robert Brandom, *Reading Rorty*', at <http://www.phil.cam.ac.uk/
~swb24/reviews/Rorty/htm>.

The very fact that Blackburn raises the abandonment of truth and reason as a *possibility* illustrates the extent of the cultural shift. But why would anybody give up on truth and reason? As our survey in Chapter 5 suggests, one non-foundationalist answer is that they are *not* simply *giving up* on truth and reason but rather offering reinterpretations of them in order to address the critical weaknesses of foundationalism. The question then is whether the non-foundationalist offers viable alternative conceptions of justification, truth, and reality. In order to answer these questions we will proceed in this chapter to place the various non-foundationalist proposals under critical scrutiny, focusing in particular on non-foundationalist attitudes toward alethic anti-realism and metaphysical anti-realism. In terms of philosophical positions, I will argue that both Rorty's alethic apathy and Putnam's mind externalism fail to refute scepticism. When we turn to critique alethic anti-realism, we will demonstrate the weaknesses with each of the four possible interpretations: Kantian anti-realism, causal anti-realism, trivialism, and constitutive anti-realism. At this point we will turn to evaluate the respective non-foundationalist theologies of Stanley Grenz and Nancey Murphy.

SCEPTICAL CIRCUMVENTIONS AND ANTI-REALIST TRUTH

We will begin our discussion with an evaluation of Rorty's and Putnam's attempt to overcome dualism and defuse scepticism, through alethic apathy and mind externalism respectively. Then we will consider the problems that arise with alethic anti-realism.

Doesn't Truth Matter?

As Rorty would have it, we can avoid the siren song of scepticism by tying ourselves to the masts of pragmatism and coherence. Can a concern for pragmatism outmode the traditional quest for truth as a mere red herring? If we adopt this approach, might we not be haunted by the scenario that our beliefs, no matter how coherent or useful, still fail on the whole to reflect reality?[2] I will argue that even if we interpret Rorty as holding alethic apathy, this position tends to collapse into anti-realism. To illustrate, we can consider a parallel case, where John Searle claims to transcend the classic debate between theism and atheism by arguing that scientific advances have rendered the concept of God uninteresting since any possible god must be subject to physical laws:

[W]e have gone beyond atheism to a point where the issue no longer matters in the way it did to earlier generations. For us, if it should turn out that God exists, that would have to be a fact of nature like any other. To the four basic forces in the universe—gravity, electromagnetism, weak and strong nuclear forces—we would add a fifth, the divine force. Or more likely, we would see the other forces as forms of the divine force. But it would still be all physics, albeit divine physics.[3]

Searle's attempt to defuse the God question ignores the standard dictionary definition of God as the greatest possible being. If God is the greatest possible being, then it follows that should God exist, that would be the most important fact there could be. So, to place one's primary interest in anything but the supreme reality is surely irrational. Since charity suggests that we attempt to interpret Searle as rational, it is likely that his apatheism[4] actually assumes that *God is not there*. Indeed, Searle's comment that God's existence would have to be 'a fact of nature like any other' could be understood as another

[2] Alvin Plantinga has argued that there is no reason to think that pragmatic beliefs approximate the truth, since for any belief there is a potentially infinite number of scenarios in which that belief is *false* but still adaptive (*Warrant and Proper Function* (Oxford: Oxford University Press, 1993), ch. 12). For further discussion see James Beilby (ed.), *Naturalism Defeated? Essays on Plantinga's Evolutionary Argument Against Naturalism* (Ithaca, NY: Cornell University Press, 2002).

[3] Searle, *Mind, Language, and Society: Philosophy in the Real World* (London: Weidenfeld & Nicolson, 1999), 35. One of the OUP readers suggested that Searle could be interpreted (more charitably) as saying that if God exists then he must operate qua physical force within the universe. Regardless of the plausibility of this interpretation, the key point is that Searle believes the existence of God is not an especially important fact, existentially or otherwise. Admittedly it is not true that God's existence is necessarily of supreme existential import, but for those people concerned with knowing the truth about the world it surely would be of supreme importance to know this fact about what exists.

[4] Apathy about God's existence is described as 'apatheism' by Jonathan Rauch in 'Let It Be', *Atlantic Monthly* (May 2003), 30.

way of saying that God (that is, the greatest possible being) does not exist. As such, Searle's position collapses into atheism, and a rather disingenuous one at that.

The same problem besets Rorty's attempt to carve out a *via media* between realism and anti-realism, for the ostensive importance of truth, like that of God, makes neutrality impossible. The importance of truth is eloquently summarized by Jonathan Weber, the protagonist in Paul Maier's novel *A Skeleton in God's Closet*:

> While gazing across the Old City, Harvard's motto came, suddenly, incongruously, to mind: *VERITAS, truth. Let the Yalies cling to their LUX ET VERITAS*, Jon mused, *their 'Light and Truth.' Truth is enough. Light, without truth, is no light at all*. . . . [N]othing—however ancient, grand, magnificent, or sustaining—must ever, *ever* stand in the way of Truth. Truth in the past, in the present, in the future.[5]

Given that truth is by definition of the *utmost importance*, it is inexplicable that anyone (let alone a tenured professor) should be *uninterested* in it. George Bernard Shaw thus expressed contempt for those unconcerned with matters of truth:

> There is no surer symptom of a sordid and fundamentally stupid mind, however powerful it may be in many practical activities, than a contempt for metaphysics. A person may be supremely able as a mathematician, engineer, parliamentary tactician, or racing bookmaker: but if that person has contemplated the universe all through life without ever asking 'What the devil does it all mean?' he (or she) is one of those people for whom Calvin accounted by placing them in his category of the 'predesinately [*sic*] damned.'[6]

Even if Shaw's statement carries a trace of intellectual elitism, it seems indefensible that an ivory-tower academic who gets paid to sit in his office and ponder the nature of truth could conclude that it isn't worth the bother. Human beings are by nature truth seekers, so that to deny the drive to know the truth is to deny our very humanity.[7] To

---

[5] Maier, *A Skeleton in God's Closet* (Nashville, Tenn.: Westbow, 1994), 256.

[6] Cited in John G. Williams, *Christian Faith and the Space Age* (Cleveland/New York: World, 1968), 69.

[7] Calvin said it well: 'For we see implanted in human nature some sort of desire to search out the truth to which man would not at all aspire if he had not already savored it. Human understanding then possesses some power of perception, since it is

put it bluntly (if bawdily), belief with no interest in truth is as much against our nature as coitus with no interest in orgasm.[8]

Some non-foundationalists have attempted to defend alethic apathy by arguing that the realist conception of truth, including the notion of an objective reality to which our beliefs must be equivalent in order to be true (and so important), evinces not common sense but rather the long shadow of modernity. This seems to be the claim of Richard Middleton and Brian Walsh, who aver that 'the modern project was predicated on the assumption that the knowing autonomous subject arrived at truth by establishing a correspondence between objectively "given" reality and the thoughts or assertions of the knower'.[9] Is there any reason to think that alethic and metaphysical realism are the theoretical vestiges of modernity which, when stripped away, will reveal that Rorty's lack of interest in truth is appropriate? This claim is very wrong-headed. As John Searle points out, alethic and metaphysical realism are not 'views', 'hypotheses', or 'opinions' in anything like the conventional sense: 'I do not, for example, hold the *opinion* that the real world exists, in the way I hold the opinion that Shakespeare was a great playwright'.[10] On the contrary, a conception of the real world and the importance of a true grasp of it is *the backdrop* against which our theories are tested. We may indeed debate theories of realism and truth, but the reality of the world and objective truth stands apart from all our theories.[11]

---

by nature captivated by love of truth' (*Institutes of the Christian Religion*, ii, ed. John T. McNeill, trans. Ford Lewis Battles (London: SCM, 1961), 271.

[8] Jacques Maritain was right to observe: 'Be it a question of science, metaphysics, or religion, the man who says: "What is truth?" as Pilate did, is not a tolerant man, but a betrayer of the human race' (*Reflections on America* (New York: Charles Scribner's Sons, 1958), 79).

[9] J. Richard Middleton and Brian J. Walsh, *Truth is Stranger than it Used to Be: Biblical Faith in a Postmodern Age* (Downers Grove, Ill.: InterVarsity, 1995), 31–2.

[10] Searle, *Mind, Language, and Society*, p. 10. Searle adds: 'I regard the basic claim . . . —that there exists a real world that is totally and absolutely independent of all of our representations, all of our thoughts, feelings, opinions, language, discourse, texts, and so on—as so obvious, and indeed as such an essential condition of rationality, and even of intelligibility, that I am somewhat embarrassed to have to raise the question and to discuss the various challenges to this view' (*Mind, Language and Society*, p. 14). Cf. Paul Boghossian, *Fear of Knowledge: Against Relativism and Constructivism* (Oxford: Clarendon, 2006).

[11] See Michael Lynch, *True to Life: Why Truth Matters* (Cambridge, Mass.: MIT Press, 2004).

Is Reality Guaranteed?

What of Putnam's mind externalism according to which it is not *possible* that my thoughts be wrong because meaning is fixed by reference? It is true that Putnam's H_2O/XYZ thought-experiment has been widely considered to have demonstrated that the meaning of (some of) our beliefs is *partly* external to introspective awareness. And this insight could have important theological applications. For instance, the content of theological concepts could be partially fixed by their external referents in an echo of Thomas Torrance's analogy between concept and icon:

The background is filled in with gold, for it is only in this open perspective reaching out to a golden eternity that Christ may be truly conceived; He cannot be brought within a perspective in which the lines when produced meet at a point in finitude. Here the concept of Christ while definite at one end is infinitely open at the other, but it *is* a concept.[12]

Thus, the icon bears an analogy to the theological concept's openness to its divine referent. This would provide a response to the absolute-subject theologian, who believes that divine transcendence renders non-trivial, positive theological descriptions impossible, leaving only the play of metaphors.

While Putnam's partial mind externalism may have solid potential for theological application, his attempt to *absolutize* mind externalism in order to refute scepticism categorically faces significant objections. To begin with, as Laurence BonJour points out, the success of the twin-earth thought-experiment tacitly assumes that we grasp the content of much of our belief. In his response to Putnam, BonJour refers back to the 'Oscar' twins:

[T]he intuitive appeal and probably even the intelligibility of the example depends on ascribing to the two Oscars accessible thought contents that are identical, perhaps even roughly the content that the locally familiar liquid that appears in lakes and rivers, falls from the sky at times, is good to drink, etc., is wet.[13]

---

[12] Torrance, *Theological Science* (Edinburgh: T&T Clark, 1969), 15.
[13] BonJour, *In Defense of Pure Reason* (Cambridge: Cambridge University Press, 1998), 171.

So, for the argument to proceed we must grasp a good deal of our thoughts. But if mind externalism is only partial, then we could be partially wrong, and with this the questions of truth and realism return.

Three Problems with Alethic Anti-Realism

Given that neither Rorty's alethic apathy nor Putnam's internal realism (as he calls his view) appears to offer a stable third position between realism and anti-realism, we should consider the alethic anti-realist position more carefully. To this end we will consider three central problems with alethic anti-realism. First, while anti-realist theories are generally motivated by concerns to avoid scepticism, they fail to guarantee a more secure access to truth than realist theories. For instance, as Bruce Marshall observes, Putnam's consensus truth criterion of ' "idealized warranted assertability" seems at least as remote and inaccessible a measure of truth as the "correspondence to reality" which, on account of inaccessibility, it was supposed to replace'.[14] To compound the problem, C. S. Peirce's admission that truth can be grounded in non-actual cases of consensus reintroduces the sceptical dilemma that truth remains inaccessible to human knowers.

Second, alethic anti-realism has deeply counter-intuitive consequences for truth, particularly regarding the problem of relativism, for it follows from it that the same proposition could be true for you but false for me.[15] For instance, if it were pragmatically efficacious for Chip but not for Dale to believe 'It is raining today' or even '7 + 5 = 12', then it would be true for Chip but not for Dale. While an anti-realist might attempt to defuse relativism by claiming that there is only one maximally coherent or pragmatic set of truths, pragmatism is relative to certain ends: given one desired outcome it may be pragmatically advantageous to believe *P* while relative to another desired outcome it may be pragmatically advantageous to

---

[14] Marshall, *Trinity and Truth* (Cambridge: Cambridge University Press, 2000), 225.

[15] Donald Davidson, 'The Structure and Content of Truth', *Journal of Philosophy*, 87 (1990), 307–8.

believe not-P. Thus, it appears implausible to posit one ultimate pragmatic standard.[16] As for Blanshard's coherentist claim that there is but one set of maximally coherent (and so true) beliefs, he reintroduces the problem of scepticism, for in order to know any truth it would seem that we must magisterially grasp a proposition's coherent relation to all truth. Moreover, defusing relativism on the consensus view seems to require a purely rational set of individuals who would necessarily agree when presented with the same evidence. Ironically, this claim remains vulnerable to perspectivist critiques of universal reason, for it seems to require that there is only one fully coherent system of belief, but this is surely false. It also depends on the view that there is one true description of reality, a claim with which many non-foundationalists would take issue.

The third problem is arguably the most critical of all: anti-realist conceptions of truth invariably assume realism. This brings us back to the point made above that realism *simpliciter* is not a theory per se so much as the backdrop of theory formation. To illustrate, picture a philosopher on his way to a conference to deliver a paper defending alethic anti-realism. When he finds that he is lost on the university campus, he stops a passer-by and asks whether it is true that the philosophy building is just beyond the quad. The passer-by replies that this is true. Surely in this unguarded moment the philosopher was not simply asking whether his statement would have the pragmatic effect of getting his body into the seminar room, or whether it would fit with a maximally coherent set of beliefs, or whether it would be accepted by an ideal consensus of rational individuals. Rather, he wanted to know whether the statement matched up to reality.[17]

Alethic anti-realism does not simply tread on the toes of common sense and practice; as Kirkham points out, the consensus theory depends on realism, for 'no sense can be given to the notion of ideal circumstances unless we have first made some choice of value

---

[16] Perhaps one could ground a single pragmatic standard theistically.

[17] A more rigorous exposition of these intuitions is found in the 'descriptive argument' (see J. P. Moreland, 'Truth, Contemporary Philosophy, and the Postmodern Turn', *Journal of the Evangelical Theological Society*, 48/1 (2005), 78–9).

at which justification is to aim'.[18] Ultimately the ground for an ideal consensus would be a statement's matching up to reality. In the long term the same goes for pragmatism. Thus, the anti-realist defends his particular theory in the belief that it matches up to reality, and thus informs us of the way things *really* are.[19] This leads to what Craig and Moreland call the dialectical argument: 'Those who reject the correspondence theory either take their own utterances to be true in the correspondence sense or they do not. If the former, then those utterances are self-defeating. If the latter, there is no reason to accept them, because one cannot take their utterances to be true'.[20] It is difficult to avoid Groothius's conclusion that alethic realism 'is part of the intellectual oxygen that we breathe'.[21]

In light of our third point, it would appear that alethic anti-realism is hopelessly self-refuting. However, Richard Kirkham suggests a charitable interpretation of the position that would render it compatible with alethic realism. Kirkham distinguishes three basic projects regarding truth: the metaphysical project, the justification project, and the speech-act project. The metaphysical project, which seeks to identify the nature of truth and thus what it means to say a statement is true, requires alethic realism.[22] The justification project seeks to identify the properties that true statements typically possess, as a guide for judging the truth and falsity of beliefs.[23] Finally, the speech-act project is focused on the locutionary or illocutionary intent evident in ascribing the property of truth to a

[18] Richard L. Kirkham, *Theories of Truth: A Critical Introduction* (Cambridge, Mass.: MIT Press, 1992), 54.

[19] Dallas Willard, 'Knowledge and Naturalism', in William Lane Craig and J. P. Moreland (eds.), *Naturalism: A Critical Analysis* (London: Routledge, 2000), 38–9. Cf. Groothius, 'Why Truth Matters Most: An Apologetic for Truth-seeking in Postmodern Times', *Journal of the Evangelical Theological Society*, 47/3 (2004), 442. Nothing is new under the sun: Socrates used the same argument against Protagoras in *Theaetetus*, 171a.

[20] William Lane Craig and J. P. Moreland, *Philosophical Foundations for a Christian Worldview* (Downers Grove, Ill.: InterVarsity, 2003), 140.

[21] Groothius, 'Why Truth Matters Most', p. 441.

[22] Kirkham further subdivides this project into extensional, naturalistic, and essence analyses (*Theories of Truth*, p. 20).

[23] Ibid. Compare Pannenberg's distinction between correspondence truth and the coherence and consensus criteria of truth (*Systematic Theology*, i, trans. Geoffrey W. Bromiley (Grand Rapids, Mich.: Eerdmans, 1991), 24).

statement.[24] Based on Kirkham's distinctions, many putatively anti-realist metaphysical theories of truth might best be interpreted as viable justification projects that have been conflated with the metaphysical project. As Kirkham puts it, 'the truth-as-justification thesis turns out at best to be a muddled metaphor for a very different thesis and at worst to produce a circular and/or unintelligible analysis of truth'.[25] Thus the anti-realist's choice: persist in a metaphysical application of anti-realism which is fated to circularity or unintelligibility, or admit that the project is in fact epistemological in nature and as such leaves the realist nature of truth untouched.

WHENCE THE WORLD? ANALYSING METAPHYSICAL ANTI-REALISM

According to Walter Truett, the different positions concerning metaphysical realism can be illustrated by the answers three baseball umpires provide for how they call pitches. The first says: 'There's balls and there's strikes and I call 'em the way they are'. The next explains: 'There's balls and there's strikes and I call 'em the way I see 'em'. Finally, the last retorts: 'There's balls and there's strikes, and they ain't *nothin'* until I call 'em'.[26] While the first two positions, representing naive and critical realism, are straightforward, it is much more difficult to interpret the third umpire's position So, we will devote this section to surveying four possible interpretations: Kantian anti-realism, causal anti-realism, trivialism, and constitutive anti-realism.

[24] Kirkham, *Theories of Truth*, pp. 20–1.

[25] Kirkham, *Theories of Truth*, p. 52. Stout anticipates this analysis: 'We might learn, with Putnam, that justification is relative in ways that truth is not. We might learn, with Davidson, that seeing how the expression *is true* functions in sentences of the form "'Snow is white' is true if and only if snow is white" gets us further in the philosophy of language than we might have thought. Or we might learn, with J. L. Austin, how *true* contributes to the force of certain speech-acts' (*Ethics After Babel: The Language of Morals and Their Discontents* (Boston: Beacon, 1988), 251).

[26] Truett's illustration is recounted in Middleton and Walsh, *Truth is Stranger than it Used to Be*, p. 31.

Kantian Anti-Realism

Kantian anti-realism acknowledges the external world (*ding an sich*) as a practical postulate to explain the fact of human existence and experience even as it denies that we can know anything about it (something like the multiverse hypothesis which some cosmologists invoke to explain apparent cosmic fine tuning). The importance of this practical postulate becomes even more pressing once we set aside Kant's assumption that human beings share a single conceptual scheme, for once we recognize different conceptual schemes we need to admit a common reality, a 'causal world' or noumenon, to which they both refer.[27] Rorty appears to express this Kantian anti-realism when he affirms that 'none of us anti-representationalists has ever doubted that most things in the universe are causally independent of us. What we question is whether they are representationally independent of us'.[28] There is no microscope or telescope through which we can peer that gives us a view of the world that is not *our view*. And yet, we must speak practically of a causal world beyond conceptualization. On this view, the umpire is saying 'All I can judge is the ball of my experience; I judge nothing of the ball-in-itself'.

Whatever its attractions, Kantian anti-realism is inherently unstable, for if we can truly know nothing about the noumenon, then we cannot even refer to it as a practical postulate. One may be tempted to retreat to a sort of *via negativa*, by stipulating that only formal and negative properties can be predicated of the noumenon.[29] The problem here parallels that faced by John Hick after he limits all reference to God (aka 'the Real') to negative and formal properties, for it is impossible to *refer* to this reality if we really have no conception of it. And if we stipulate that the Real is *the* being that has no non-formal or positive properties that we grasp we still fail, since the reference remains indeterminate, for there may be many such beings. We can only refer to it if we have experienced it, which would entail

[27] Alasdair MacIntyre, *Three Rival Versions of Moral Enquiry: Encyclopaedia, Genealogy, and Tradition*, 1988 Gifford Lectures (London: Duckworth, 1990), 5.

[28] Richard Rorty, 'Taylor on Truth', in James Tully (ed.), *Philosophy in an Age of Pluralism: The Philosophy of Charles Taylor in Question* (Cambridge: Cambridge University Press, 1994), 22.

[29] A formal property is one that trivially applies to everything, such as *being identical or non-identical with the number 2*.

at least one positive, non-formal property: *being experienced by us.*[30] Similarly, the assumption that our conceptual schemes do not refer to the Kantian noumenon entails the positive, non-formal property of being experienced by us, which contradicts the claim that the world is absolutely unknowable. Hence, the concept of a causal world that we cannot know is both practically unworkable and contradictory. And, as if that were not enough, by asserting that we cannot know *anything* of the world, the threat of scepticism returns *perforce*.

Causal Anti-Realism

Once we recognize the deep difficulties with Kantian anti-realism, we may opt to abandon the *ding an sich* and turn our attention solely to the world of our linguistically constructed experience. But what does it mean to deny any world beyond experience? On one interpretation, this amounts to saying that the world is *created* through language, such that if we did not speak, the world would not exist. This view, which we can refer to as 'causal anti-realism', appears to entail the astounding conclusion that *we create the world through language*: *it exists because we speak*. Or, as the umpire might say, 'I create the ball when I call it'.

Many metaphysical realists interpret non-foundationalist claims in terms of causal anti-realism, and not without textual support.[31] For instance, it is a defensible interpretation of some of Rorty's statements:

Once you describe something as a dinosaur, its skin colour and sex life are causally independent of your having so described it. But before you describe it as a dinosaur, or as anything else, there is no sense to the claim that it is 'out there' having properties. *What* is out there? The thing-in-itself?[32]

Rorty's rhetorical question suggests that there is nothing 'out there' prior to description. After it is described, it exists as causally

---

[30] Alvin Plantinga, *Warranted Christian Belief* (Oxford: Oxford University Press, 2000), 51.

[31] e.g. Alvin Plantinga, 'How to Be an Anti-realist', *Proceedings of the American Philosophical Society* (1982), 47–70.

[32] Richard Rorty, 'Taylor on Truth', p. 23.

independent, but it does not make sense to think of a 'thing-in-itself' existing prior to conceptualization by the human mind. At first blush, one certainly could interpret this as the claim that language creates the world.

Despite this textual support, most realists reject the causal anti-realist interpretation, given the charitable principle that one ought to avoid attributing absurd positions to one's opponents whenever possible.[33] Moreover, anti-realists make other statements that seem to *distance* themselves from this interpretation. So Rorty:

> The trouble with this conclusion is that 'comes from' suggests causal dependence. The picture called up...is of some mighty immaterial force called 'mind' or 'language' or 'social practice'—a force which shapes facts out of indeterminate goo, constructs reality out of something not yet determinate enough to count as real.[34]

Likewise, Philip Kenneson indignantly dismisses the causal anti-realist's interpretation: 'Surely there are some things which are "true" independently of what human beings believe. Your [realist] position makes it sound as if we [anti-realists] *make* these things "true," as if *we* are determining reality. We believe that God exists independently of us'.[35] In so far as anti-realists agree that causal anti-realism is absurd, we ought to seek another interpretation.

Trivialism

Our third possibility swings back to a conservative interpretation— so conservative in fact that the anti-realist's claims end up looking trivial. Coming back to Rorty, the trivialist could point out that

[33] Nicholas Wolterstorff, 'Are Concept-users World-makers?', in James Tomberlin (ed.), *Philosophical Perspectives, i. Metaphysics* (Atascadero, Calif.: Ridgeview, 1987), 233–67. Cf. Andrew Cortens, 'Dividing the World into Objects', in William Alston (ed.), *Realism and Antirealism* (Ithaca/London: Cornell University Press, 2002), 45–6.

[34] In the context, Rorty is critiquing Bernard Williams's interpretation of Wittgenstein as an idealist (Richard Rorty, *Philosophical Papers, i. Objectivity, Relativism, and Truth,* (Cambridge: Cambridge University Press, 1991), 5).

[35] Philip D. Kenneson, 'There's No Such Thing as Objective Truth, and It's a Good Thing, Too', in Timothy R. Phillips and Dennis L. Okholm (eds.), *Christian Apologetics in the Postmodern World* (Downers Grove, Ill: InterVarsity, 1995), 159.

when Rorty refers to the dinosaur he is not speaking of the 'thing-in-itself', but rather of a human *representation*. This fits in with his earlier claim that most things are independent of us causally but not representationally. Taken in this way, Rorty is simply pointing out that human conceptions are dependent on humans making them, a view that has no realist/anti-realist implications. On this view our third umpire only meant to say 'If I had not called the ball, there would have been no call'. When pressed, some non-foundationalists have retreated to this type of triviality.[36] For instance, Hilary Putnam has summarized his internal realism with the apparent tautology 'You can't describe the world without describing it'.[37] And when pushed in debate by John Searle on his famous phrase 'there is nothing outside the text', Jacques Derrida apparently retreated to the benign position that everything belongs to a context.[38] Finally, according to Michael Lynch, trivialism also besets Foucault's work.[39]

Trivialism has two rather glaring problems. First, it is irreconcilable with the fact that the position expressed by the third umpire is widely understood to contradict realism. To say simply that umpire calls depend on umpires or that speech depends on speakers ignores the fact that this position is contrasted with the realism of the first two umpires. Second, this interpretation escapes absurdity by reducing the third umpire's position to triviality. But advocates of the view do not typically understand their position to be trivial or tautological.[40] Rather, they seem to view it as important, surprising, even revolutionary. While anti-realists may occasionally retreat to a trivial position

[36] See Susan Haack, 'Reflections on Relativism: From Momentous Tautology to Seductive Contradiction', in James Tomberlin (ed.), *Philosophical Perspectives, i. Metaphysics* (Atascadero, Calif.: Ridgeview, 1987), 297–315.

[37] Putnam, *Renewing Philosophy* (Cambridge: Harvard University Press, 1992), 123, cited in Cortens, 'Dividing the World into Objects', p. 46.

[38] As Derrida put it, '[t]he phrase which for some has become a sort of slogan, in general so badly understood, of deconstruction ("there is nothing outside the text" (*il n'y a pas de hors-texte*), means nothing else: there is nothing outside context' (Jacques Derrida, *Limited Inc* (Evanston, Ill.: Northwestern University Press, 1988), 136). For Searle's response see *The Construction of Social Reality* (New York: Free Press, 1995), 159–60.

[39] Lynch, *True to Life: Why Truth Matters*, p. 38.

[40] As Cortens puts it, 'we shouldn't count an attempt to articulate the division metaphor as a success unless the position that emerges has a sufficiently "antirealist" or "antimetaphysical" feel to it' ('Dividing the World into Objects', p. 46).

when pressed, it is most doubtful that this is the best normative interpretation of their position.[41]

Constitutive Anti-Realism

While we have thus far failed to identify an anti-realist interpretation that steers between absurdity and triviality, there is one final position to consider, which William Alston calls 'constitutive antirealism'. The constitutive position avoids the absurdity of the causal anti-realist by proposing that our concepts constitute (and so determine) an indeterminate reality.[42] The relativity of motion to framework is illustrative. While it was once assumed that motion is an absolute quality, we now recognize that motion is relative to one's frame of reference. For instance, the judgement that a train is in motion depends upon one's conceptual frame; that is, the train is moving relative to one conceptual frame but is stationary relative to another. To say that our conceptual framework constitutes the train's movement is not to suggest that concepts *cause* the train to move, as if they were equivalent to diesel fuel. Rather, our framework *constitutes* the movement of the train and thus the truth that it is (or is not) in motion. This view thus moves beyond the trivial claim that human representations are causally dependent on human representers and the absurd position that reality is causally dependent on human representers. Instead, on this interpretation the umpire is saying 'I don't create balls, but balls are constituted by my judgments'.

While initially promising, constitutive anti-realism runs into problems that, if less obvious, are no less serious. To begin with, it falls victim to an infinite regress. If all reality is constituted by our conceptual activity, then the claim that everything is constituted by our conceptual activity is also constituted by our conceptual activity. But

---

[41] One possibility is that the occasional retreat to triviality is evidence of bullshit (see my 'Theology as a Bull Session', in Oliver Crisp and Michael Rea (eds.), *Analytic Theology* (Oxford: Oxford University Press, 2009), 70–84).

[42] Alston, *A Sensible Metaphysical Realism*, Aquinas Lecture 2001 (Milwaukee, Wisc.: Marquette University Press, 2001), 17–18. For different approaches see Michael Lynch, *Truth in Context: An Essay on Pluralism and Objectivity* (Cambridge, Mass.: MIT Press, 1998); Michael Murray, 'The God's I Point of View', in Alston (ed.), *Realism and Antirealism*, pp. 79–96.

then it follows that our second-order constituting reality is also constituted by our conceptualizing activity, and so on. The only way to avoid an infinite regress of conceptual schemes or constituting actions is by admitting that some aspect of reality is not constituted by our conceptual activity (e.g. the constitutive anti-realist position itself). So, when Rorty contrasts the conceptually structured 'dinosaur' with the 'thing-in-itself' he would have to face either an infinite regress of conceptually structured realities or an unconceptualized noumenon that is the ground of constitutive structuring.[43] Indeed, as Alston points out, the very notion of different forms of conceptual structuring presupposes an objective (non-conceptualized) reality:

> The different conceptual schemes must be construed as yielding *incompatible* construals of the entities dependent on them. Otherwise there is no objection to taking the entities to be what they are absolutely, not relative to one or another scheme. But they can be incompatible only if they are construals of the *same* entities.[44]

At this point a metaphysically real world stubbornly returns, as we view the constitutive view as *the* correct view of the world that is itself *independent* of human conceptualization. David Naugle's identification of this dilemma in Wittgenstein is illustrative:

> The irony is this: he uses language which presumably connects with reality to suggest that no use of language really connects with reality. He has used the ladder of language to climb to the roof only to deny the necessity of the ladder. But if this is so, then his own system is not simply another way of seeing, but *the* way of seeing.[45]

And so at this point the conceptualization view collapses into an absolute account of how things are. Thus, while some anti-realists may be interpreted as holding to an unqualified constitutive anti-realism, the position itself remains untenable.

---

[43] Alston, *A Sensible Metaphysical Realism*, pp. 32–3.

[44] Alston, *A Sensible Metaphysical Realism*, p. 33.

[45] Naugle, *Worldview: The History of a Concept* (Grand Rapids, Mich.: Eerdmans, 2002), 162. Wittgenstein embraced this tension by proposing that we could kick away the ladder of his philosophy once the argument is grasped (see *Tractatus Logico-Philosophicus*, 6.54).

THEOLOGY AND NON-FOUNDATIONALISM

In light of the challenges faced by non-foundationalist reinterpretations of knowledge, justification, truth, and realism we will now
turn to assess the viability of the theological non-foundationalism of
Stanley Grenz and Nancey Murphy.

Putting Realism Off to the Future?

There is little doubt that Grenz has been an important voice in popu-
larizing non-foundationalist methodologies among Evangelicals. His
relentless drive to critique and challenge evangelicalism is admirable
and refreshing, given that 'progressive Evangelical' has widely been
dismissed as an oxymoron. Further, at key points he has aptly challenged post-modernism, most notably by continuing to assert the
normativity of the Christian metanarrative. At the same time, Grenz's
proposals also face serious problems. We will begin our critical survey
with Grenz and Franke's bold thesis for an 'ontological future', and
then turn to evaluate their relationship to alethic and metaphysical
anti-realism.

The ontological-future thesis faces multiple problems, beginning
with the belief that it can help us sidestep (at least partially) the
post-modern aversion to metanarratives. This belief depends on the
dubious assumption that post-modern offence arises with any claim
to *how things are*, as if claims regarding *how things will be* somehow slips under the radar screen. But post-modernists who object to
metanarratives will find them equally opprobrious even if their purported content has not yet come to pass. So, a metanarrative which
is to become true in the future would still constitute an oppressive
reality as against the present individual's own world-creating. More
basically, any notion of a future metanarrative is really misleading,
since the metanarrative is true now. Grenz might counter that the
real value of his proposal is in its denial of essentialism,[46] for *that* will
only come in the future. But, again, an ontologically future essentialism would be equally offensive to post-modernists. Furthermore, it

---

[46] That is, the view that entities lack an essence (i.e. a set of *de re* necessary
properties).

collapses back into present essentialism, since the present essence of entities consists of a set of kind-essential properties that correspond with a set of kind-essential eschatological properties: for instance, human beings presently exemplify the property *will eschatologically exemplify* p.

The ontological-future thesis raises a number of other questions as well. For instance, if there will be a 'real' eschatological universe which is the transformation of this one,[47] then why cannot states of affairs in the world now be truth makers for propositions? What sense can there be to claim that the truth maker for the proposition 'Jesus died for our sins in AD 30' is an eschatological event? Grenz provides no explanatory framework to understand what it means to say that God acts from the future causally to effect the present. Perhaps one might make these claims coherent by drawing on an eternalist (static) theory of time: the view that all points in time exist timelessly.[48] On this interpretation, the view would perhaps look something like this: the universe exists as a static space-time block and God timelessly affects events at t_1 from the future point t_2.[49] But even if an eternalist interpretation can yield a coherent sense of timeless causation, it still leaves the truth-maker problem unaddressed.

Although the ontological-future thesis appears in one sense like modern system-building, this impression seems to be undermined by Grenz and Franke's radical rejection of alethic and metaphysical realism. As we have seen, they claim that all statements are true by way of social construction. If that were correct then it would follow that 'God is three persons' is not true because it is equivalent to (divine) reality, but because the Christian community constructs reality in a particular way through their language. In addition, it would follow that the truth-value of all theological statements is derived from language users, and thus that this very account of the future is constituted and

---

[47] Stanley Grenz, *Renewing the Center: Evangelical Theology in a Post-theological Era* (Grand Rapids, Mich.: Baker, 2000), 284.

[48] Eternalism contrasts with a presentist (dynamic) theory of time in which only the present exists. On this latter (common-sense) view, the future does not yet exist, and so causal agents cannot exist in the future to affect the present or anything else. The claim that the Holy Spirit acts from the future appears to entail eternalism.

[49] Interestingly, Pannenberg's eschatology appears to collapse into an eternalist view of time, as does Ted Peters's in *God as Trinity: Relationality and Temporality in Divine Life* (Louisville, Ky.: Westminster/John Knox, 1993).

thus made true by the speech of a particular community. This raises an additional problem: Who actually realizes the future? Is it God acting from the future or the community that speaks in the present? More basically, we might ask why some strange conglomeration of the ontological future and present ecclesial reality is necessary to make a statement like 'Jesus died for our sins' true, given that common sense dictates that the occurrence of the event described by the proposition is sufficient. What is more, Grenz does not even begin to address how his eschatological-reality view relates to necessary truths like 'No circle has a corner' or '7 + 5 = 12'. In conclusion, the ontological-future thesis fails to address the concerns of the post-modernist, while suggesting an implausible (and potentially incoherent) anti-realist theory of truth.

Similar hermeneutical challenges accompany Grenz's metaphysical anti-realism. We can jump directly into this interpretative quagmire with the following quote from Grenz and Franke:

There is, of course, a certain undeniable givenness to the universe apart from the human linguistic-constructive task. Indeed, the universe predates the appearance of humans on the earth. To assume that this observation is sufficient to relegate all the talk of social construction to the trash heap, however, is to miss the point. The simple fact is, we do not inhabit the 'world-in-itself'; instead, we live in a linguistic world of our own making.[50]

To begin with, this passage affirms a world beyond human language, given that the universe predates human beings as the given ground of the 'linguistic-constructive task'. But at the same time Grenz and Franke unequivocally affirm that we live not in the given world, but rather the linguistic world we have created. If we take this claim in a straightforward sense, then all assertions, including statements relating to the independence of the world, become yet another part of our linguistic world. Grenz and Franke seem to struggle with this tension as they ask: 'Are we left with nothing but our socially constructed worlds? Is there no actuality to the world?'[51] It's a good question.

[50] Stanley Grenz and John Franke, *Beyond Foundationalism: Shaping Theology in a Postmodern Context* (Louisville, Ky.: Westminster/John Knox, 2001), 53.

[51] Ibid. 271.

Ultimately Grenz and Franke's negation of metaphysical realism brings us to the dilemma between absurdity and triviality. The absurdity looms if we pursue a causal interpretation of the claim that we live in a linguistic world of our own making. If the claim is taken in this sense, then every experience is part of that linguistically constructed world, including the action of the Holy Spirit working from the future. At this point the position would collapse into causal anti-realism, with the radical implications summarized by Francis Watson:

To say that our world is formed out of the communal, linguistic narrative matrix into which we are socialized is to say that language-users (that is human beings) have created that world. But if we create the world through language, it is also the case that we create the (intrasystematic) creator-God through language. The claim that God created the world is intrasystematically true but extrasystematically false in that it was we human beings who created both the world and this intratextual God by means of our language and stories.[52]

Plantinga points out that this absurd claim effectively replaces God as creator with human speakers.[53] What is more, it would follow that human beings exemplify at least two properties traditionally reserved for God: being self-caused, and being the cause of all else that exists. Though radical theological revisionists like Don Cupitt might embrace this consequence,[54] no theologian with a modicum of orthodoxy left could accept such a view. Given these breathtaking implications, I think we must reject the causal-anti-realist interpretation of Grenz and Franke's claims.

But it hardly seems fair to reduce Grenz and Franke's efforts to the trivial claim that human beings only experience the world from a human perspective. Another possible interpretation emerges if we focus on Grenz's use of Charles Peirce, which dovetails nicely with his eschatological, Pannenbergian focus. As we saw in our

[52] Watson, *Text, Church and World: Biblical Interpretation in Theological Perspective* (Grand Rapids, Mich.: Eerdmans, 1994), 139. Cf. Plantinga, *Warranted Christian Belief*, pp. 424–5.

[53] Alvin Plantinga, 'Christian Philosophy at the End of the Twentieth Century', in James F. Sennett (ed.), *The Analytic Theist: An Alvin Plantinga Reader* (Grand Rapids, Mich.: Eerdmans, 1998), 331.

[54] Cupitt, *Creation out of Nothing* (Philadelphia, Pa.: Trinity, 1990).

discussion of alethic anti-realism, Peirce developed a consensus theory of truth according to which truth (and, in turn, reality) depends
on the agreement of a future consensus of rational individuals. This
parallels Grenz's views, although in the latter case that consensus
is apparently forged in some (as yet unclarified) future relationship
between the triune God and the ecclesial community. Peirce's views
suggest that backwards causation operates from the future consensus
to create reality, allowing the eschatologically mediated present existence of truth makers and truth bearers. Unfortunately, this picture
has little to commend it as a viable view of truth and reality, and I
cannot see how it fares any better in the present context. The one
place where Grenz might improve the view is in Peirce's recognition
that some consensus may never be achieved, leading to the possibility
that truth results via backwards causation from a *possible* but *non-
actual* future consensus![55] Perhaps Grenz could avoid this implication
by claiming that God will ensure a future consensus, but this is at best
a marginal improvement on Peirce's views.

What finally is it that compels Grenz (and Franke) to reject
alethic and metaphysical realism in favour of this perplexing alternative? This is difficult to answer, since, like Rorty, Grenz does not
explicitly argue against realism, but instead appears to dismiss it
(along with foundationalism) *tout court* by an apparent *force majeure*.
Such terse handling of the issues gives the impression that there
is a consensus within the philosophical community, which simply
does not exist. In the end, despite the creativity and ambition with
which the project is executed, there is little to commend Grenz's
non-foundationalism.

Is *Everything* Open to Revision?

Nancey Murphy's theological proposals remain among the most
sophisticated on offer today. She is an adept critic of foundationalism
and her call for a chastened rationality is admirable. Further, while
she recognizes an *obligation* to meet public criteria of evidence, her

---

[55] See *Collected Papers of Charles Peirce*, ed. Charles Hartshorne and Paul Weiss
(Cambridge, Mass.: Harvard University Press, 1931–58), vii. 340–4. For a critical
discussion see Kirkham, *Theories of Truth*, p. 85.

anti-individualism offloads this on to the community, thereby easing an epistemic burden that might otherwise lead to scepticism.[56] Her emphasis upon methodological consistency as a guide to theological reflection is important for theologians who are tempted by a premature embrace of paradox. But arguably of greatest importance is her application of a Lakatosian methodology along with a MacIntyrian account of rationality. This provides a basis to distinguish between essential dogmas of the faith (as in C. S. Lewis's 'mere Christianity') and non-essential doctrines or opinions. Moreover, it enables us to evaluate the success of individual doctrines in meeting the challenge of experience. For instance, many theologians would consider the traditional doctrine of divine impassibility unworkable in light of horrific events like the Holocaust. The Lakatosian model provides a framework to assess doctrines critically while adjusting the rest of the doctrine of God accordingly. While these kudos are significant, Murphy's work also raises some serious concerns.[57] We will focus on her Quinean views in epistemology and then draw out the troubling metaphysical implications that follow.

The problems begin when Murphy reintroduces epistemic subordination by tying the public, rational defence of Christian belief to the probabilistic reasoning modelled by science. According to Murphy, this is necessary because, in contrast to theology, 'natural science ... no longer needs epistemological justification but instead, because of its success, prescribes where and in what sense we may talk of knowledge'.[58] This is a strong statement, for Murphy claims that a Quinean–Lakatosian-style enquiry would be *beneficial* for theology and that theology can *only* be rational and justified by modelling itself on scientific procedures that produce appreciable results. Instead of removing the classical-foundationalist yoke of subordination, this merely stipulates that the admissible evidences must parallel the deliverances of science. Murphy's assumption that we are obliged to

---

[56] Murphy, *Theology in the Age of Scientific Reasoning* (Ithaca, NY: Cornell University Press, 1990), 195. For a similar approach to communal justification see the discussion of Linda Zagzebski in Chapter 10 below.

[57] For a critical survey of attempts to justify theology through scientific parallels see Andrew Moore, *Realism and Christian Faith: God, Grammar, and Meaning* (Cambridge: Cambridge University Press, 2003), chs. 2–3.

[58] Murphy, *Theology in the Age of Scientific Reasoning*, p. 26.

recognize science's unique explanatory power and authority begs the question.[59] Further, there is a significant danger that this subordination will distort doctrine, given the preference for interpretations of theological doctrines that are modelled on science and yield pragmatically appreciable results. It seems to me that one sees evidence of this distortion in Murphy's rejection of body–soul dualism in favour of non-reductive physicalism.[60]

More basic problems arise when we attempt to adapt Murphy's Quinean epistemology to theological method. Broadly speaking, Quine's epistemology may be divided into two stages: the coherentism of 'Two Dogmas of Empiricism', that denies pre-conceptual experience and unrevisable beliefs while introducing the holistic web of belief, and the radical externalism of 'Epistemology Naturalized'.[61] The latter is a programmatic extension of Quine's austere naturalism that seeks to remove every sense of epistemic *ought* by reducing epistemology to empirical psychology, and thus eliminating all normativity of belief. This naturalization of epistemology has been popular with few philosophers, and Murphy shows little interest in it.

While Murphy is wise to avoid Quine's externalism, unfortunately significant problems also beset his coherentism, beginning with the claim that we do not grasp any necessary truths (or, more strongly, the claim that there *are* no necessary truths). This claim represents the all-too-common conflation of epistemological limits (epistemic fallibilism) with metaphysical implications (metaphysical contingentism).

---

[59] Or, rather, why think science has a unique authority if one rejects Quine's austere naturalism?

[60] See Murphy, 'Nonreductive Physicalism: Philosophical Issues', in Warren S. Brown, Nancey Murphy, and H. Newton Maloney (eds.), *Whatever Happened to the Soul? Scientific and Theological Portraits of Human Nature* (Minneapolis, Minn.: Fortress, 1998), 127–48. For a critique see J. B. Stump, 'Christians and Philosophy of Mind: A Review Essay on *The Problem of the Soul*', *Philosophia Christi*, 5/2 (2003), 589–99.

[61] W. V. O. Quine, 'Epistemology Naturalized', in his *Ontological Relativity and Other Essays* (New York: Columbia University Press, 1969), 69–90. As Jaegwon Kim argues, Quine's programme entails a rejection of epistemology. Further, though called an externalist, Quine agrees with non-foundationalist internalists that epistemic categories cannot be derived from causal categories (see 'What is "Naturalized Epistemology?"', in James Tomberlin (ed.), *Philosophical Perspectives, ii. Epistemology* (Atascadero, Calif.: Ridgeview, 1988), 381–405).

Apparently the assumption is that if necessary truths are to be known, they must be known infallibly. Since no truths are known infallibly, we cannot know any necessary truths. The obvious rejoinder is that there is no reason to think that we must grasp necessary truths infallibly: the property of *de dicto* necessity has no epistemological implications. So, there is no problem with affirming a fallible grasp of necessary truths. But what sort of necessary truths are there? Quine focuses his critique on moderate empiricism, the position that all knowledge is either contingent-empirical or necessary-analytic. This assumes that no knowledge is synthetic a priori; however, synthetic aprioricity has experienced a revival in recent years.[62] Quine's silence is thus a serious lacuna, for if the synthetic a priori is a source of knowledge, then we have at least one source of knowledge his arguments do not even address.

Problems also arise with Quine's argument that analyticity is unintelligible given its alleged dependence on a vicious circle of terms. For one thing, the grounds on which Quine first rejects analyticity—that is, the opacity of the circle of terms—is illegitimate, since these terms (e.g. synonymy) in fact appear quite meaningful. Quine's argument against analyticity also depends on the rejection of propositions, leaving sentences as the sole truth bearers. If we accept that sentences are the sole truth bearers and no sentence is necessarily true, then there are no necessary truths. This is easy enough to conceive; for instance, the sentence 'All triangles have three sides' would become false if 'triangle' were to come to refer to a square. But sentences are not the sole truth bearers, and thus the shifting of word meaning has no implications for the necessity of the proposition that the sentence 'All triangles have three sides' currently expresses. But even granting that point, one might argue that fallibilism is inescapable whenever we apply definitions to concrete objects in the real world, for it would seem that any such application could be mistaken. For instance, if we defined a swan as 'a large, white, aquatic bird with a long, slender neck', we would find our definition falsified when first we

---

[62] See, for instance, BonJour, *In Defense of Pure Reason.* Alvin Plantinga provides an externalist foundationalist account of aprioricity in *Warrant and Proper Function*, ch. 6.

encountered a black swan.[63] In that case, we might seek incorrigibility by retreating to a more modest claim such as that 'swans are animals'. But even this modest claim could be falsified if, for instance, swans should turn out to be self-replicating robots sent to earth by aliens.[64] This possibility seems to demonstrate that even analytic statements are vulnerable to falsification and revision.

As troubling as such sceptical scenarios might appear, they have no implications for the necessity of analyticity. Indeed, one could establish the necessity of analyticity in one of two ways. To begin with, one could argue via a modified Putnamian externalism that some of the meaning of our concepts is external to us (e.g. the content that swans are *mechanical*). Or one could argue that the original definition remains analytically true but is not actually exemplified in the world since the mechanical birds we call swans are not, in fact, swans. In light of these possible responses, Noam Chomsky is right to conclude that attacks upon analyticity via definition-defeating scenarios like black swans and platypuses are spurious.[65]

Let us not overlook the fact that Quinean contingentism also entails that *there are no necessary truths about God*, including *God is good*, *God is three persons*, and *God exists*. This claim is staggering in its implications and would surely require a powerful theological argument in its favour, which Murphy does not provide. In addition, the denial of necessary truths is incoherent, for it entails that the proposition *There are no necessary truths* is only contingently true. But then it follows on the quantification over possible worlds that this proposition will be false in at least one world. (If it were true in all possible worlds it would be a necessary truth, which would lead to a contradiction.) But propositions are bivalent, so that if the proposition *There are no necessary truths* is false in one world then its negation, *There are necessary truths*, is true in that world. Given the nature of necessity, if there are necessary truths in one possible world then there are necessary truths in all worlds, including

---

[63] See William Placher, *Unapologetic Theology: A Christian Voice in a Pluralistic Conversation* (Louisville, Ky.: Westminster/John Knox Press, 1989), 32–3.

[64] Noam Chomsky, *Language and Problems of Knowledge*, Managua Lectures (Cambridge, Mass.: MIT Press, 1987), 34.

[65] Chomsky, *Language and Problems of Knowledge*, p. 33.

the actual world. Either way, the denial of necessary truths leads to contradiction, and thus is incoherent.[66]

This brings us to the sceptical implications of Murphy's pragmatic view of justification. As we have seen, Murphy follows Quine's attempt to circumvent sceptical objections with the particularist observation that we simply cannot justify our whole web of beliefs. Murphy apparently does not recognize that scepticism originates when we lack a reason or ground to hold a belief true, and Quine's epistemology utterly fails to provide this. To begin with, Quine's whole argument is circular, for he simply assumes the primacy of empirical knowledge over rational knowledge in the same way that earlier philosophers prized rational knowledge over the empirical; as Laurence BonJour points out, 'to conclude ... that any sentence can be rationally given up ... it must be assumed that epistemic rationality is concerned solely with adjusting one's beliefs to experience'.[67] But surely the proposition *All beliefs must conform to experience* is not justified on the basis of experience. So, on what other basis could this proposition be justified? Most non-foundationalists have failed to grapple with this problem. Grenz and Franke claim that 'noncontradiction must be an aspect of any coherence of beliefs'.[68] But if one *rejects* rational intuition and synthetic a priori knowledge, then one must accept the primacy of non-contradiction on an independent empirical basis. Recognizing this, Quine pragmatically suggests a principle of conservatism according to which we should seek to revise our theories by altering the theses at the periphery before deeply embedded theses. But this raises an obvious question: What pragmatic or empirical reason is there to think the principle of conservatism is truth-conducive? It would seem that having rejected a priori intuitions, the only remaining explanation is found in an appeal to emotivism along the lines of 'Yahoo for conservatism!'[69]

---

[66] See my 'Can There Be Theology Without Necessity?', *Heythrop Journal*, 44/2 (2003), 131–46. For an excellent and accessible discussion of God, possible worlds, and modal logic see Jay Wesley Richards, *The Untamed God* (Downers Grove, Ill.: InterVarsity, 2003).

[67] BonJour, *In Defense of Pure Reason*, p. 76.

[68] Grenz and Franke, *Beyond Foundationalism*, p. 39.

[69] While one might defend conservatism by appealing to the psychological difficulties with surrendering deeply held beliefs, that manoeuvre would still lack *epistemic* justification.

But if conservatism is merely a matter of taste, then it would seem that one might, with equal rationality, cheer for a principle of radicalism according to which we ought to begin revising the most deeply embedded beliefs in our noetic structure. The point here is not that we ought to concede ground to the sceptic, but rather that the only non-sceptical justification for conservatism is a foundationalist appeal to the a priori.

The sceptical problem is intensified when we unpack further the full implications of Quine's commitment to the non-foundational equality of all propositions. Murphy summarizes his pragmatism as follows:

When experience necessitates some change in the system, there are usually many ways to revise, including changing the meanings of some terms, revising theories, or even, Quine hazards, revising logic. The decision among these possibilities will in the end be pragmatic—how best to restore consistency with the least disturbance to the system as a whole.[70]

As Murphy observes, since Quine believes that no truth obtains of necessity, he can even countenance 'revising logic'. It would follow from this that some evidence might arise tomorrow which would persuade me to reject the law of non-contradiction and with it the very notion of consistency. But if that is true then there is nothing preventing us from rejecting the law of non-contradiction *now*, and this undermines any reason for surrendering or accepting any belief ever. So, BonJour observes, 'Quine's view can apparently offer no reason at all why the principle of non-contradiction, once it's *a priori* credentials are set aside, should not be as freely revised or abandoned as any other part of the system, making it no less epistemically reasonable to accept the contradictory system'.[71] This presents a further serious problem, since contradictions are explosive; that is, if a contradiction is true, it entails every other contradiction. The sceptical implications of this view are thus absolute.

Fortunately, there simply is no reason (apart from tendentious naturalistic presuppositions) to opt for Quine's radically fallibilist, non-foundational epistemology. Given these problems, it is especially unfortunate that many Christian theologians are now seeking to

[70] Murphy, *Theology in the Age of Scientific Reasoning*, p. 8.
[71] BonJour, *In Defense of Pure Reason*, p. 93.

model theology on Quinean premises, thereby adopting all of Quine's problems even as they edge back to the theological distortions instigated by a commitment to epistemological subordinationism.

CONCLUSION

There is a certain irony in non-foundationalist accounts of theology, for while they are sharply critical of classical-foundationalist revisions of doctrine (e.g. as symbolic representations of pre-conceptual experience), they end up offering surprisingly broad revisions of their own. If Grenz is to be believed, then core doctrines are not true now, but will be made true in the future. If Murphy is correct, then doctrines function more as second-order regulative statements than descriptions of objective reality. Atheist philosopher Simon Blackburn mused about such radical revisions that are proffered by the academic theologian: 'Perhaps contempt for onto-theology is a "Government House attitude", fine for the elite, but to be kept hidden from the ordinary man or woman in the pew'.[72] It seems most unfortunate that an epistemology intended to return the community of faith to its own proper autonomy appears liable instead to introduce yet more of the gravedigger's distorting influences.

---

[72] Simon Blackburn, *Truth: A Guide* (Oxford: Oxford University Press, 2005), 15.

7

Non-foundationalist Trinitarian Theology

> Christians can and should have their own ways of thinking
> about truth and about deciding what to believe.
>
> Bruce Marshall, *Trinity and Truth*
>
> Mackenzie, the Truth shall set you free and the Truth has a
> name; he's over in the woodshop right now covered in sawdust.
>
> William Young, *The Shack*

Human nature seems to predispose us to make sweeping generalizations as a handy way to sort through the inevitable complexities
of actual life. One visit to a city during a spell of poor weather
or one testimony of the unreliability of a brand of car can form
opinions far stronger than the evidence sample would warrant. So
it is with non-foundationalism. After a preliminary survey of some
difficulties we may be tempted to draw rather sweeping judgements about its (lack of) viability. But non-foundationalism, like
the weather of a city or range of cars produced by a manufac-
turer, is diverse and has many possible expressions. Our survey may
have uncovered problems with anti-realist non-foundationalism, but
there are other types. So, in the next two chapters we will turn to
a proposal that draws upon analytic resources untapped by other
non-foundationalists: Bruce Marshall's *Trinity and Truth*.[1] Marshall's
proposal is of particular interest because his case is informed by a
familiarity with contemporary analytic philosophy and a masterful
understanding of the theological tradition. Marshall observes that

---

[1] Bruce Marshall, *Trinity and Truth* (Cambridge: Cambridge University Press,
2000). For another non-foundationalist proposal worth close study see Paul D.
Murray, *Reason, Truth and Theology in Pragmatist Perspective* (Leuven: Peeters, 2004).

there are two major philosophical alternatives by way of which one might respond to theological subordination: the moderate foundationalism of Alvin Plantinga and the non-foundationalism of philosophers like W. V. O. Quine and Donald Davidson.[2] In the next two chapters we will evaluate Marshall's decision to opt for the non-foundationalist path, beginning in this chapter with a consideration of Marshall's critique of foundationalism, in particular the 'interiority' and 'epistemic dependence' theses. Next, we will consider his alternative Trinitarian account of epistemic justification. Finally, we will summarize his account of truth, which presents an intriguing amalgamation of a Davidsonian T-schema theory with Trinitarian theology.

RETHINKING JUSTIFICATION

Marshall recognizes the importance of developing an adequate conception of justification, and so he begins by identifying normative and descriptive dimensions to the term. In the normative sense, '[t]o call beliefs "justified" can mean that they meet tests which establish or secure their truth, and in that strong and normative sense give their holders the right to hold them'.[3] Descriptive justification refers to the actual means by which different communities and individuals seek to justify their beliefs, while normative justification introduces an evaluative judgement on which specific means of justification are in fact successful. Thus, Marshall's normative/descriptive distinction parallels the objective/subjective distinction we drew in Chapter 3. According to Marshall, normative justification reflects the fact that we all have epistemic obligations in the forming and holding of beliefs.[4]

---

[2] Marshall, *Trinity and Truth*, pp. 80–1. Marshall refers to both Donald Davidson and Plantinga as anti-foundationalists. While Plantinga is anti-foundationalist in so far as he rejects universal-methodist criteria of epistemic assessment, he remains a foundationalist in terms of accepting properly basic beliefs that ground the justification/knowledge for all other beliefs.

[3] Marshall, *Trinity and Truth*, p. 7; cf. p. 6.

[4] Ibid. 7. For instance, a child might be meeting her obligations (and thus be descriptively/subjectively justified) by believing what her dad teaches her. At the same

Marshall believes that clear thinking on justification is important so that theologians ensure we have the right to hold Christian beliefs. In this sense, he is distinct from many non-foundationalists, who have expressed ambivalence, if not outright hostility, concerning the question of justification. For Marshall, it is important to ask what epistemic *right* Christians have to hold their beliefs. Marshall's internalist and (as I will argue) voluntarist view of justification leads him to ask: 'By what epistemic right does the church believe in the Trinity?'.[5] The question is all the more important given his deep dissatisfaction with the way that many modern theologians have sought to answer this question by subordinating Christian belief to alien thought-forms.[6]

Marshall's pivotal critique of modern theology comes in chapter 4 of *Trinity and Truth*, where he mounts an ambitious critique of attempts to justify theology with respect to three pivotal theses of modernity: interiority, foundationalism, and epistemic dependence. According to the interiority thesis Christian beliefs are justified in so far as they express inner experiences; the foundationalist thesis proposes that justified beliefs are either self-evident, incorrigible, or derived from beliefs that are; finally, the epistemic-dependence thesis states that the primary criteria for deciding the truth of Christian beliefs are not distinctively Christian. Together, these theses have constrained theologians to subordinate theology to external authorities in a vain plea for intellectual credibility. We will consider Marshall's response in two parts, beginning with his focus on a non-foundationalist approach to justification (*pace* interiority), which emphasizes conceptual holism, coherence justification, and the elimination of the scheme/content distinction. Next, we will consider his critique of epistemic subordination in an argument for the unity of meaning and truth. This will set up the argument to be considered in the final section that Christians *ought* to approach the justification of theology through their own central (Trinitarian) beliefs.

---

time, if her dad is widely known to be a disreputable source of information, then those beliefs will lack normative/objective justification.

[5] Marshall, *Trinity and Truth*, p. 44.   [6] Ibid. 4.

Interiority, Justification, and the Third Dogma

Marshall's critique of foundationalist approaches to theology takes aim at the predominant method of justification in modern theology: the subjective intuitionism of experiential-expressivism. As we saw in Chapter 2, experiential-expressivists seek a universal, incorrigible, and prelinguistic foundation of religious experience in order to ground and thereby justify theological doctrines. Marshall describes this move from common religious experience to theological doctrines as the 'interiority thesis'. In Chapter 2 I argued that experiential-expressivism depends upon an untenable view of divine transcendence which leads to the distortion of doctrine. In addition, it holds to a tendentious view of epistemic obligation which it attempts to meet through an ad hoc appeal to universal religious experience. While Marshall would be sympathetic with these criticisms, his core argument targets the coherence of foundationalism and the scheme/content distinction. Marshall challenges the notion of prelinguistic experience by arguing that experience is always conceptually structured. For instance, he writes that 'having an intentional object is a necessary condition for having an emotion'.[7] The reason, according to Marshall, is that emotions are always objectual. For instance, I am scared *of dogs* or fond *of cats*. There is no such thing as a pure emotion or conscious experience without object which could mediate the knowledge of God. Since being aware of an object entails that one grasps something of the object, emotional experience is always conceptually structured. Further, Marshall argues that the grasping of a concept always entails other concepts and beliefs and thus our ability to perceive an object always entails the possession of an indeterminate number of concepts. Marshall explains:

Having intentional objects requires having both concepts and beliefs. To be afraid of heights I have to intend high objects, and this requires me to have the concept 'high,' which (if I am to have it at all) I must be able to distinguish from the concept 'low'; it also requires me to have the concept of falling, which requires me to have the concepts of up and down, of a material body, of time, and so forth. Only armed with a large battery of concepts can I

---

[7] Marshall, *Trinity and Truth*, p. 74.

intend high places in such a way as to fear them. And I must also have an unspecifiably wide range of beliefs: I must believe that I am a material body, that material bodies tend to fall from high places, and so forth.[8]

Since emotions always intend something, they are dependent upon beliefs. Thus, there simply cannot be a pre-conceptual realm of experience that precedes conceptual reflection and which could provide an experiential ground for theological discourse. It follows that our experience of the world is always conditioned by belief and so we cannot hope to justify our beliefs, theological or otherwise, with respect to a foundation. Beliefs can only be justified by other beliefs.[9]

Marshall's argument thus far reflects the familiar non-foundationalist critique of the given. However, Marshall follows Donald Davidson in warning against the re-entry of foundationalism via what Davidson called the third dogma of empiricism; that is, the distinction between conceptual scheme and empirical content.[10] Though Quine denied that *individual* beliefs can be justified by sense experience, Davidson charges that by continuing to hold to the idea of a conceptual scheme (understood linguistically as a set of declarative sentences that a person holds to be true) Quine in effect conceded that *on the whole* empirical content can be related to the set of concepts/beliefs by which we order it. Thus, Davidson charges that while Quine may deny that we are able to justify individual beliefs relative to a pre-conceptual experience, his view assumes that we can justify an entire conceptual scheme relative to the content of experience. Davidson charges that the resulting scheme/content dualism gives rise to two problems. To begin with, by treating content as a foundation, one opens the door to scepticism, given that the conceptual scheme can approximate reality to varying degrees (and perhaps not at all). Marshall charges that this dualism collapses into

---

[8] Ibid. 74–5; cf. John Thiel, *Nonfoundationalism* (Minneapolis, Minn.: Fortress, 1994), 15.

[9] 'What distinguishes a coherence theory is simply the claim that nothing can count as a reason for holding a belief except another belief' (Davidson, 'A Coherence Theory of Truth and Knowledge', in *The Essential Davidson*, ed. Ernie Lepore and Kirk Ludwig (New York: Oxford University Press, 2006), 228).

[10] For a good discussion see David Naugle, *Worldview: The History of a Concept* (Grand Rapids, Mich.: Eerdmans, 2002), 162–73.

foundationalist justification relative to the raw data of experience, and that this has troubling epistemological implications:

Given this picture foundations become an urgent epistemic need. Since concepts are subject to our manipulation while the evidential given is not, it becomes imperative to anchor scheme in content. Without the sort of justification which arises when scheme is confronted by content, our whole system of belief will end up losing its tie to the world.[11]

Marshall follows Davidson in concluding that we must close the scheme/content distinction in order to defeat scepticism once and for all by undermining the conception of a set of beliefs being justified relative to the content of experience. Thus, while there is a causal link between sensory content and our beliefs, there is no epistemic link.[12] Since only beliefs can justify beliefs, the sole source of justification is found in coherence.[13]

Epistemic Dependence, Truth, and Meaning

According to Marshall, the modern theologian has tended to hold the truth of Christian statements in abeyance while we establish their meaning in order to ensure that that meaning conforms to *Wissenschaft*. For instance, the common-sense interpretation of 'Jesus rose from the dead' is revised in light of the 'modern assumption' that dead men don't rise. As a result, prior to establishing the truth of theological statements, we set about finding a meaning that comports with the *Wissenschaft* (including 'Dead men don't rise'). This leads to the subordination and distortion of belief, where 'Jesus rose from the dead' becomes something radically different such as 'I have experienced the Jesus of faith' even though the body of Jesus remains in the tomb. For those who take Paul at his word (1 Cor. 15: 14) this is a poor substitute for the classic Christian confession.

Marshall seeks to eliminate any possibility of the subordination-ist distortion of doctrine by establishing the conceptual necessity of interpreting meaning by assuming truth. His critique of the epistemic-dependence thesis depends on its alleged procedure of

[11] Marshall, *Trinity and Truth*, p. 83.   [12] Marshall, *Trinity and Truth*, p. 86.
[13] Ibid. 88.

establishing meaning. Marshall analyses the distorting procedure of modern theologians as being dependent upon a critical premise that meaning can be separated from truth, as if we can decide the meaning of a statement prior to deciding upon its truth. Thus, he argues that doctrines have been distorted because theologians have sought to establish their meaning in accord with current notions so as to make them come out as true. While Marshall recognizes that one can separate meaning and truth in limited circumstances,[14] he objects to the practice of doing this as a matter of principle. Instead, our general practice should be to decide whether sentences are true in order to discern what they mean: '[T]he meaning of a sentence is, or is given by, its truth conditions'.[15] When it comes to Christian belief, this means that we cannot explore new meanings of doctrines to ensure that they come out true. Rather, to avoid epistemic dependence, we *begin* with a commitment to truth prior to determining semantic content.

But why think that Marshall is correct that truth and meaning are inseparable? To defend the claim Marshall appeals to Davidson's argument for radical translation. The genesis of Davidson's argument is the concern to develop a theory of interpretation that avoids any circular appeal to meaning. This arises from the question of how an interpreter who knows nothing of a speaker's language could ever begin to interpret it, though the question is applicable to *all* forms of communication. The interpreter cannot presuppose knowledge of the speaker's language or experiences.[16] But once we set aside any claim to prior knowledge of the speaker's desires, intentions, and beliefs, how can we identify the speaker's propositional attitudes? Davidson argues that we must begin by assuming the truth of the speaker's statements; as we begin to posit propositional attitudes, any candidate that would make the speaker's beliefs come out false must be rejected. Thus, a Wycliffe Bible translator named Cliff who discovers a new tribe with an unknown language must begin the translation process by seeking to maximize the truth of what is uttered by the natives so as to 'optimize the fit' between the most important native beliefs

---

[14] Ibid. 98–9.   [15] Marshall, *Trinity and Truth*, p. 91.
[16] Donald Davidson, 'Radical Interpretation', in his *Inquiries into Truth and Interpretation* (Oxford: Clarendon, 1984), 128 ff. Cf. Marshall, *Trinity and Truth*, p. 92.

and his own. So, if an interpreter is to attain a successful translation, he must hold the subject's views true while testing for their meaning.

Davidson explains that this procedure depends upon the 'principle of charity', a principle that is necessary for interpretation. According to the principle, we should always interpret others so that their beliefs come out (largely) true. This principle is necessary because 'any disagreement in belief is only possible against the background of extensive agreement in belief'. Hence, Davidson claims that interpretation depends upon our ability to 'dismiss a priori the chance of massive error'.[17] By implication, when disagreement reaches a critical mass, the interpreter should conclude not that he *disagrees* with the speaker, but rather, following the principle of charity, that his interpretation is false and should be adjusted accordingly.[18] It is important to recognize that this argument applies not only to biblical translators encountering an unknown language; indeed, *every* person faces the challenge of radical translation whenever we attempt to communicate with others. In each case we should not attempt to make our beliefs match up to a foundation external to them but rather must remain dependent upon our beliefs in order to understand the other. Marshall argues: 'It will be impossible, as the different versions of the [epistemic-dependence] thesis attempt in their various ways, to hold for meaning while testing for truth. On the contrary: the very effort to construe Christian beliefs as epistemically dependent will largely determine the meaning one assigns to the sentences which express those beliefs'.[19] Unfortunately, this runs precisely counter to the means of justifying Christian belief that has predominated in modernity.

[17] Davidson, 'Thought and Talk', in his *Inquiries into Truth and Interpretation*, pp. 168–9.

[18] 'We do this sort of off the cuff interpretation all the time, deciding in favour of reinterpretation of words in order to preserve a reasonable theory of belief' (Davidson, 'On the Very Idea of a Conceptual Scheme', in his *Inquiries into Truth and Interpretation*, p. 196). But might there be a case where we successfully interpret only *some* statements in another's conceptual scheme? Davidson counters that in any putative area of disagreement we can conclude that the other individuals are using different concepts, but holding to the same beliefs (and thus same conceptual scheme) ('On the Very Idea of a Conceptual Scheme', p. 197).

[19] Marshall, *Trinity and Truth*, p. 98.

Finally, we should say a few words about how this argument relates to Davidson's critique of conceptual schemes. Intrigued by Quine's famous argument for radical translation in *Word and Object*, Davidson took up his own approach in the pivotal essay 'On the Very Idea of a Conceptual Scheme'. Davidson argues that the identification of distinct schemes is contingent upon the failure of translation. Hence, if we succeed in translation then we conclude that there is in fact one scheme, one set of sentences to which both speakers agree. However, Davidson argues that a failure to translate warrants not the conclusion that the untranslated person holds another scheme, but rather that she *is not speaking* at all. That is, what appears to be verbal behavior is not such after all.[20] In other words, translation failure does not warrant the conclusion that there are two schemes, but rather that there is one scheme (ours) and one instance of non-linguistic behaviour (the 'untranslated' individual). If Davidson is correct then by definition we can only recognize one conceptual scheme.

DEFENDING INTERNAL JUSTIFICATION

Close to thirty years ago Timothy Lull described the doctrine of the Trinity as 'the guilt-producing doctrine' because Christian theologians had widely failed to grant it the centrality that it deserves.[21] If this was true thirty years ago, it is so no longer, for in the intervening decades theologians have placed the doctrine at the front and centre, often applying it to areas ranging far from the doctrine of God. Indeed, today there is a widely held conviction that the doctrine ought to shape virtually every area of knowledge. Colin Gunton expresses the common reasoning: '[B]ecause the trinitarian concepts reflect the being of God, we should be prepared to find them echoed in some way in human thought and in structures of the created world'.[22]

[20] Davidson, 'On the Very Idea of a Conceptual Scheme', pp. 185–6.
[21] Lull, 'The Trinity in Recent Theological Literature', *Word and World*, 2/1 (1982), 61.
[22] Gunton, *The One, the Three and the Many: God, Creation and the Culture of Modernity*, 1992 Bampton Lectures (Cambridge: Cambridge University Press, 1993), 211.

Marshall's proposal comes squarely in the middle of the flurry of Trinity research programmes. Thus far his focus has been diagnostic and critical: theology is in sorry shape due to its dependence upon the interiority and epistemic-dependence theses. But that argument simply intensifies the question: How *are* Christian beliefs to be justi- fied? If the only intermediaries are causal and the only justification is coherence, how should we think about the justification of Christian belief? At this point Marshall introduces his own unique Trinitarian contribution: we must interpret the world in accord with our central beliefs in order to maximize agreement with others. While beliefs can only be justified with respect to other beliefs, we require a coherent account of how Christians meet their epistemic obligations, and Mar- shall finds that account in the doctrine of the Trinity. In surveying this aspect of his proposal, we will begin by unpacking his deontological understanding of justification. Next, we will consider his attempt to meet the challenge of justification through the actions of the Son and Spirit. Finally we will consider his response to the lingering charge of fideism.

Justification and Deontology

Marshall argues that Trinitarian beliefs are essential to Christianity, and thus that Christians must hold them as epistemically primary. Since we must interpret others in accord with what we believe to be true, and since the Trinity is central to our belief, the doctrine should be granted the status of 'epistemic trump' within the Christian noetic web. This means that in the pursuit of coherence justification the Trinity is primary: all other beliefs must cohere with it or be rejected: '[T]he epistemic primacy of the church's narrative identification of Jesus, and with him of the triune God, must be unrestricted; it must range across all possible beliefs'.[23] Our commitment to the Trinity means that we seek to maximize the truth in others by interpreting all reality in accord with Trinitarian beliefs.

While Marshall argues for the necessity of his approach, one could respond that this only intensifies the justification problematic of

---

[23] Marshall, *Trinity and Truth*, p. 117.

'whether the church has the epistemic *right* to regard its own most central beliefs as the primary criteria of truth, and if so, what confers this right'.[24] Marshall recognizes the need to explain the justification of Christian belief. And yet, following the framework just summarized, he contends that the Church's right *is conferred by the very beliefs that theologians have thought needed a foundation*: 'A more satisfying approach to truth rather than taking the church's central beliefs to be especially in need of epistemic support, will take the church's trinitarian identification of God itself chiefly to confer epistemic right'.[25]

Before delving further into Marshall's Trinitarian account of justification transfer, we should understand his view of justification and epistemic right. Internalists typically maintain a parallel between the normativity of belief and the normativity of ethics. While some non-foundationalists, like Quine, reject epistemic normativity altogether, others, like Murphy and Marshall, maintain it. Marshall also finds common cause with the internalist position on epistemic deontology. He thus applies deontological categories to the holding of individual beliefs. Negatively, the one who is justified in believing something is granted the right to believe because she is violating no epistemic duties. Positively, justification is granted when a person has reasons for holding her belief. So Marshall: '[W]e regularly suppose that what gives us *the right* to hold beliefs is that we have employed criteria which settle the matter of their truth'.[26] And so, '[b]eing convinced that a belief is true presumably requires supposing that one has *the right* to hold the belief'.[27] In other words, if one has violated no epistemic duties and has sufficient evidence or reason to hold a belief, one is allotted the right to believe, and so is justified in the belief. Conversely, there are situations where duty dictates that a person *ought* to believe: 'if you believe the premises of a valid argument, you are *obligated* to believe its conclusion'.[28] In particular, '[t]he Christian community's own belief and practice call for an account of the right by which it claims to speak the truth'.[29] Hence, while Marshall rejects

---

[24] Ibid. 108; emphasis added.
[26] Ibid. 8 n. 4; emphasis added.
[28] Ibid. 214; emphasis added.
[25] Ibid. 4.
[27] Ibid. 212; emphasis added.
[29] Ibid. 3.

the Church's adoption of modernistic conceptions of justification, he appears to accept internalist obligations.

While epistemic deontology may support some intuitions, difficulties arise when we press the analogy with ethics. To be ethically culpable for a particular act, an individual must be a moral agent and have committed the act of her own free will, for if one does not freely commit an action, then one cannot be guilty for it. This point raises a difficulty with the ethics/epistemology parallel because we do not have direct control over what we believe analogous to the control we have over which acts we perform. By way of illustration, imagine that you believe Karl Barth to be the premier theologian of the twentieth century. Then an eccentric millionaire approaches you and offers you one million dollars to believe that Don Cupitt is a superior theologian to Barth. He is not simply asking you to sign a statement to that effect, or to make a public profession of it, but actually to *believe* it. I would venture to say that you could not collect, for you simply cannot make yourself believe something just by wishing to.

This brings us to the voluntarist thesis that accompanies epistemic deontology. This is the view that doxastic agents have sufficient control over specific beliefs such that they can be culpable for those beliefs. It would appear that the voluntarist thesis is doxastically untenable, and thus will create problems for Marshall if he depends on it. There is evidence however that Marshall would reject doxastic voluntarism, for he questions the claim that we could have an *obligation* to agree with others given that our original acquisition of language is neither by obligation nor choice.[30] Indeed, Marshall explicitly distances himself from the unqualified voluntarist thesis:

It seems unlikely, though perhaps not impossible, that my desire alone, or even my active quest for forgiveness, could induce me to hold the beliefs without which I cannot trust or be confident in God's forgiveness. Since these beliefs cannot be regarded, epistemically, as either unavoidable or inadmissible, holding them requires a measure of willingness. *But doing so simply because I desire what they promise perhaps demands too much of the will.*[31]

But while Marshall may reject unqualified doxastic voluntarism, I will argue that he reintroduces a modified form predicated upon

<hr>

[30] Marshall, *Trinity and Truth*, pp. 213–14.   [31] Ibid. 207; emphasis added.

the actions of the triune God to enable us to believe. In this way he offers an intriguing means to meet the deontological norms by the very beliefs requiring justification, a sort of doxastic bootstrapping.

Marshall's account of non-foundationalist justification (and by extension voluntarism) emerges in the work of the Son and Spirit. The centrepiece of Marshall's conception of justification is belief coherence or Christological coherence—for the Christian specifically '[c]oherence with the nexus of central Christian beliefs'.[32] However, coherence is supplemented by the Spirit's work (voluntarism), which makes Christian belief pneumatologially effective.[33] We can now consider these two aspects of justification in more depth.

Justification in the Son and Spirit

Marshall's defence of the epistemic primacy of Trinitarian belief begins with Jesus Christ: '[I]f the narratives which identify Jesus are epistemically primary, they are the final and decisive, though of course not the sole, criteria for deciding what count as good reasons for holding sentences true'.[34] Marshall begins with the fact that we know both God and creation through Christ since he is the image of the Father and creator and sustainer of all things. This leads to a Christological theory of justification and knowledge in which Jesus represents every reality within creation and every possibility for creation: '[W]hen the Father wills to create the world, he sees and knows it—indeed sees and knows all possible worlds—in and through his Word in the flesh. The Word in the flesh is, to use the traditional term, the "exemplar" for the Father of all things, real and possible'.[35] As such, the Son is the ground to which all our beliefs must be coherently related.

Based upon this claim, it would appear that Marshall does not reject metaphysical modality and linguistic necessity, but rather seeks to ground them Trinitarianly and Christologically. There is a strong

[32] Ibid. 5.
[33] One might be tempted to interpret Marshall as supplementing his account of coherence justification with pragmatic justification, though he is clear that justification is rooted in the Son's coherence alone.
[34] Marshall, *Trinity and Truth*, p. 143.   [35] Ibid. 112.

theological tradition that recognizes God's knowledge as including modal possibilities. Compare, for instance, Francis Turretin's classic summary of the divine omniscience:

The object of the knowledge of God is both himself (who most perfectly knows himself in himself) and all things extrinsic to him whether possible or future (i.e., as to their various orders and states); as to quantity—great and small; as to quality—good and bad; as to predication—universals and singulars; as to time—past, present and future; as to state—necessary and free or contingent.[36]

However, I am unaware of clear antecedents for Marshall's distinctly Trinitarian casting of the divine knowledge. While Turretin's definitions of omniscience and the ground of possibility and actuality could almost be applied to Aristotle's prime mover, Marshall's focus is upon Jesus' mediation of the Father's will for the truth of creation: '[T]he Father orders each thing, and all things together, around his own Word in the flesh; the Father wills a world which fits, in its totality, with Jesus Christ'.[37] In this way all justified true beliefs are Christologically coherent. Since all truth is grounded in the Word's exemplification of the Father, the Son confers the epistemic right to believe through the coherence of our beliefs.

While Christological coherence is necessary to a Christian conception of justification, it is not sufficient, because this coherence needs to be accessible to humans. The completion of the model comes in the pneumatological efficacy of these beliefs. Marshall thus argues that the Spirit works as a secondary exemplar in the Son to bring creation into the will of the Father, thereby ensuring that every creature partakes in the divine life: 'The Spirit is thus the agent who immediately brings it about that all things receive the life of God by holding together in Christ, and is in that sense the principal agent who moves them to their final goal'.[38] Since these beliefs are the ground of the Spirit's work, they are pragmatically effective. Epistemologically speaking, Marshall argues that the Spirit brings us to affirm the truths of the gospel, central to which is belief in the Trinity. Just as the Son confers epistemic right to believe those truths that are

---

[36] Francis Turretin, *Institutes of Elenctic Theology*, ed. James T. Dennison, Jr., trans. George Musgrave Giver, i (Phillipsburg, NJ: P&R, 1992), 3.12.3.

[37] Marshall, *Trinity and Truth*, pp. 112–13.   [38] Ibid. 114.

upheld within him, so the Spirit acts upon our will, enabling us to affirm those beliefs.

In light of the work of the Spirit, we can return to the question of epistemic voluntarism. From this perspective one could take Marshall to be reinterpreting the meaning of deontology and voluntarism in pneumatological terms. Just as the Son grants us the right to believe, so the Spirit grants us the will to hold certain beliefs. So, while Marshall rejects voluntarism *simpliciter*,[39] he qualifies this rejection:

Without the immediate action of the Spirit, we will lack the willingness to believe in this fashion. But if the omnipotent creator Spirit acts, then we will have willingness sufficient for assent to those beliefs which enable us to cling to Christ, and so even now to have a share, however partial and incomplete, in the life of the Trinity. The Spirit's action, it seems, is both necessary and sufficient for our actual willingness to believe in the Trinity, and so all the more for its possibility.[40]

In acting upon our will, the Spirit enables us to share in the knowledge of God. Marshall thus appears to argue that there *is* a doxastically significant sense in which we can choose beliefs, though it is always pneumatologically grounded. One might worry that the Spirit's working could override free human will. Marshall responds via double causation: we are free so long as the Spirit acts as the primary cause that concurs with the secondary causes of creation, including the free believing acts of human beings.[41] So, as the Spirit concurs with the human will to hold a belief like 'Jesus is risen', holding the belief becomes the individual's 'own attitude and, in some circumstances, *their explicit act*'.[42] That is, the Spirit enables us to act to hold a belief when such a mastery over belief would be otherwise impossible. Marshall summarizes the dual role of Son and Spirit as follows:

As it turns out, the Spirit's epistemic role is not to justify the beliefs Christians hold. Conferring the right to believe belongs rather to the crucified and risen Son. That we have the right to hold a particular set of beliefs does not, however, by itself account for our actually holding them; that we actually believe in Jesus crucified and risen depends wholly on the Spirit's gift of

[39] Ibid. 212.   [40] Ibid.   [41] Ibid. 203.
[42] Ibid. 247; emphasis added.

the willingness to do so. By enjoining these distinctive epistemic roles on the Son and the Spirit, the Father undertakes to give us a share in his own knowledge.[43]

Here Marshall clarifies that the Son finally transfers the (coherent) right to believe. However, our holding beliefs and thus having the operative doxastic will which legitimates the very conferral of epistemic right is mediated pneumatologically.[44]

Escaping the Charge of Fideism

Marshall's argument that the Trinity justifies belief in the Trinity might look like a fideistic begging of the question analogous to Escher's famous picture of a hand drawing itself. To assess the fideist charge, we should begin with definitions. We can define a fideistic belief as one that is either held without evidence when that belief requires evidence (leaving open how 'evidence' is defined), or held despite defeating evidence. In the absence of defeaters, Marshall appears guilty of the first violation: by what right does he privilege Trinitarian belief to trump all and sundry? For those as yet unconvinced of the necessity of assuming Trinitarian doctrine as a necessary condition of interpretation, he invokes the dilemma of justification and noetic structure: if all our beliefs required grounds or reasons, we would face an infinite regress (infinitism) or a belief without reason (scepticism). Thus, the rational person must distinguish when reasons are required. Hence, Marshall appears to hold a position of epistemic innocence until proven guilty. Marshall strongly affirms that the Trinity is properly at the centre of the Christian web of belief. He notes that taking Christian beliefs as primary only terminates justification questions for those (and related) beliefs, and he concludes: 'Apart from foundationalist assumptions, it is not clear that

[43] *Trinity and Truth* 216. This suggests that Marshall does not understand the Spirit's work in terms of pragmatic justification.

[44] Marshall generally says that the Spirit is necessary for our *willingness* but not the actual belief: '[T]here must be a further sense in which we can "decide" to have a Christian view of the world, namely that we can in some fashion choose or opt for the beliefs which structure such a view as a whole' (ibid. 212). But this apparent hedging is unnecessary, as the Spirit's primary act of causing us to believe *is*, on the level of secondary cause, our free act of belief.

central Christian convictions lack any marks ... which beliefs need to have in order to be epistemically primary'.[45] Marshall reasons that the failure of foundationalism leaves the Christian community with the coherence of their beliefs in accord with the epistemic primacy of Trinitarian belief. Here, again, this approach is reminiscent of Murphy's refusal to justify the Christian web of belief via external criteria. In response to that claim I argued that it is not sufficient to say there is no objection to one's web; one must also have positive reasons or grounds to accept it.[46] Marshall clarifies that internal rationality is evident in the criterion of 'inclusive and assimilative power'—that is, the capacity for one's set of beliefs to adapt to or explain countervailing data. This echoes MacIntyre's argument for the growing rationality of traditions as they attempt to assimilate new data according to their own criteria.

Marshall recognizes the possibility of fallibilism in so far as Christian belief could fail to assimilate new beliefs in the future. To illustrate, he speculates on the implications of an epistle being discovered written by Peter to Paul which describes the resurrection as a colossal hoax.[47] This is the dark side of an external appeal to the power of inclusiveness, a condition for which Christian belief would fail to assimilate new data, thus forcing the Christian to surrender these primary beliefs. But how can this possibility be reconciled with Marshall's vigorous affirmation of the *unqualified* epistemic primacy of Trinitarian belief? As he puts it: 'To ascribe unrestricted epistemic primacy to the gospel narrative is thus not simply to hold, as a matter of fact, no beliefs which are inconsistent with it, but to be prepared to reject any possible belief which is inconsistent with it'.[48] If we interpret this absolute claim to epistemic trump at face value, then it follows that when confronted with a defeater the Christian should be justified in simply surrendering belief in the counter-evidence, or the principle of assimilative power, or even the law of non-contradiction, because they are all beliefs which can be trumped by Christian belief. The resolution to the problem is not clear, particularly given that

[45] Marshall, *Trinity and Truth*, p.144.
[46] The infinitist dilemma of course requires us to stipulate that not all beliefs can have a reason, but there should be reasons for one holding an entire web of belief, even if these are something like: 'My parents taught me this and they are trustworthy'.
[47] Marshall, *Trinity and Truth*, p. 167.   [48] Ibid. 119.

for Marshall our standards of rationality are internally framed by the Trinity. What is more, the fact that we could now abandon basic laws of logic like the law of non-contradiction will result here, as it did in Murphy's proposal, in a bracing scepticism.

Marshall's view may lead to irreconcilable tensions, but it is worth considering how one might navigate these waters more successfully. Here we should note that there is no conflict between conceding that a belief is corrigible and maintaining an existentially determinative commitment to that belief.[49] Basil Mitchell provides a helpful illustration that combines fallibility with such existentially determinative commitment:

> Let us imagine a backwoodsman living in a remote part of Quebec, who believes himself to owe unconditional obedience to the King of France. He does not realize that there has not been a King of France for over a century. One day he comes into town and learns for the first time that there is no King of France and there has not been one during his lifetime. His unconditional obedience to the King of France presupposes that there is a King of France and is not to be construed as entailing an unconditional duty to go on believing that there is a King of France in the face of clear evidence to the contrary.[50]

While the backwoodsman could rationally recognize that there is no king of France, prior to recognizing that there is in fact no king of France commitment to the king was existentially determinative for him. Likewise, the Christian could conceivably recognize the falsity of her beliefs, but this side of that recognition her commitment remains absolute. This is a simpler and more plausible account of the relationship between maximal commitment and fallibilism than that which Marshall provides.

TOWARDS A CONCEPTION OF (TRINITARIAN) TRUTH

Thus far Marshall has developed a Trinitarian coherence account of justification while guarding against fideism and the distortion

---

[49] By 'existentially determinative' I mean that the belief significantly shapes the way one lives one's life.

[50] Mitchell, *Faith and Criticism*, Sarum Lectures 1992 (Oxford: Clarendon, 1994), 66.

inherent in epistemic dependence. But Marshall's commitment to the truth of Christian beliefs raises a further question: What does it *mean* to say that Christian beliefs are true? That brings us to the topic of the final two chapters of *Trinity and Truth*.[51]

Truth without Correspondence or Reduction

Marshall draws on Davidson's work to present an alethic-realist alternative to correspondence conceptions of truth. Davidson's views have occasionally been misunderstood as anti-realist because of his rejection of correspondence and realism more generally. However, when it counts, Davidson is willing to identify with realist intuitions, albeit with reservations. For instance, he writes:

I believe in the ordinary notion of truth: there really are people, mountains, camels and stars out there, just as we think there are, and those objects and events frequently have the characteristics we think we perceive them to have. Our concepts are ours, but that doesn't mean they don't truly, as well as usefully, describe an objective reality.[52]

Such a statement should warm the heart of any realist. While Marshall follows Davidson in rejecting the correspondence theory, he too has clarified his views as minimally realist.[53] And so, like Rorty, both Davidson and Marshall are attempting to navigate a middle course between the traditional realism/anti-realism divide. While I referred to Rorty's position as alethic apathy, Davidson's might better be termed alethic agnosticism, given that he replaces Rorty's blatant lack of interest in truth with metaphysical modesty. Davidson is clear that until he sees an illuminating conception of truth he will refuse to identify with either realism or anti-realism.[54] He also

---

[51] Truth has often been overlooked in recent theology. Notable exceptions include Wolfhart Pannenberg, 'What is Truth?' in his *Basic Questions in Theology: Collected Essays*, trans. George H. Kehm (Philadelphia, Pa.: Fortress, 1971), ii. 1–27; T. F. Torrance, *Theological Science* (Edinburgh: T&T Clark, 1969), ch. 4; John Zizioulas, *Being as Communion* (Crestwood, NY: St Vladimir's Seminary Press, 1985), ch. 2.

[52] Donald Davidson, 'Is Truth a Goal of Inquiry?' in Urszula M. Zeglen (ed.), *Donald Davidson: Truth, Meaning, and Knowledge* (London: Routledge, 1999), 19.

[53] See Gary Dorrien, 'The Future of Postliberal Theology', *Christian Century*, 18–25 July 2001, pp. 22–9.

[54] Davidson, 'Is Truth a Goal of Inquiry?', p. 17.

criticizes the metaphysical-realist conception of truth makers, for he warns that descriptions of 'fact' are in danger of lapsing 'into the trivial or the empty'.[55] So, while rejecting Rorty's dismissal of truth, Davidson is convinced that theoretical elements traditionally believed to illuminate truth—namely the truth relation (correspondence) and truth maker (fact)—do not extend our understanding beyond the *function* of truth in language.

Following Davidson, Marshall's critique of alethic realism begins with a predilection for ontological parsimony. Thus, he worries that invoking entities like 'propositions' (truth bearers), 'facts' (truth makers), and 'correspondence' (truth relation) will amount to explaining the familiar with the obscure. So, while truth is an eminently familiar and desirable commodity, explanations of it always seem to invoke more esoteric entities and as such are finally counterproductive. Hence, we discuss propositions and facts *as if* they had a clear meaning and theoretic-independent existence, while correspondence, commonly explicated in vague metaphors like 'mirroring', is even more opaque. If we take a step back we will realize that such an exotic metaphysical apparatus does little to illuminate the nature of truth: 'It seems unlikely that much will be gained by positing as truth bearers entities whose existence and nature is far less obvious than those whose relation we are trying to explain'.[56] This *appearance* of explanation is not unlike the amateur ornithologist who explains the annual migration of the arctic tern by appealing to *instinct*, a term which, behind the explanatory façade, means little more than 'inherited behavior that we do not understand'. In other words, it merely labels the mystery, rather than truly explaining it. There may be some encouragement in such labelling, as when a patient derives some satisfaction when their doctor is able to name their illness, even if medicine is as yet clueless as to etiology, treatment, or prognosis. The same can be said for purported explanations of truth as 'correspondence to the facts'. They may not be particularly illuminating, but at least they have labelled that mystery we call truth.

---

[55] Davidson, 'True to the Facts', in his *Inquiries into Truth and Interpretation*, p. 37.
[56] Marshall, *Trinity and Truth*, p. 222.

While Marshall's metaphysical tastes may be relatively parsimonious, his views appear to be in basic accord with minimal alethic realism. In that respect Marshall's appropriation of Donald Davidson's slingshot argument is significant, since it attempts to demonstrate that the more robust correspondence explanation is ultimately vacuous.[57] The argument is a *reductio ad absurdum*: begin by granting correspondence, and then show that it leads to the absurdity that every true proposition corresponds to every fact.[58] The argument depends on two principles. First, every expression that allows for the substitution of terms with the same extension while maintaining the truth-value of the expression will allow any term with the same extension. Second, in such cases, one may substitute *any* logically equivalent sentence. Based on those premises Marshall explicates the argument:

According to correspondence theories of truth, the sentence 'Northfield is east of Lonsdale' corresponds to the fact that Northfield is east of Lonsdale, and in this the truth of the sentence consists. As it happens, Northfield is the town where St Olaf College is located. Surely, therefore, 'Northfield is east of Lonsdale' also corresponds to the fact that the town where St Olaf College is located is east of Lonsdale. Northfield, it further happens, is the town which is such that St Olaf College is located in it and Yellowknife is in the Northwest Territories. So 'Northfield is east of Lonsdale' further corresponds to the fact that the town where Olaf College is located is east of Lonsdale and Yellowknife is in the Northwest Territories. We can, it appears, keep going for as long as we can keep stating facts, that is indefinitely. If 'Northfield is east of Lonsdale' corresponds to the fact that Northfield is east of Lonsdale, it seems to correspond equally well to the fact that Red Square is in Moscow.[59]

The conclusion is that correspondence reduces to triviality or absurdity. Following the first principle, Marshall begins by substituting the term 'Northfield' with 'the town where St Olaf College is located'. He then adds a conjunctive fact and transfers the correspondence

---

[57] The name 'slingshot argument' originates with Jon Barwise and John Perry, *Situations and Attitudes* (Cambridge, Mass.: MIT Press, 1983).

[58] Even if this argument succeeds, there are some philosophers, like Brand Blanshard, who would embrace the consequence.

[59] Marshall, *Trinity and Truth*, p. 227. For Davidson's formulation see 'True to the Facts', pp. 41–2.

to the conjunctive fact, which reduces correspondence to absurdity. This leads to the devastating conclusion that 'all true sentences correspond to all facts' or 'all true sentences correspond to the same thing—the totality of the real'.[60] As Davidson puts it, '[n]o point remains in distinguishing among various names of the Great Fact when written after "corresponds to"; we may as well settle for the single phrase "corresponds to The Great Fact" '.[61] Since the realist notion of particular beliefs corresponding to states of affairs, propositions, or facts is vacuous, the correspondence theory should be abandoned.[62]

After our critique of alethic anti-realism, we can agree that the 'equivalence thesis' is at the core of any viable theory of truth. While realists flesh out equivalence in terms of correspondence, deflationists claim it is the sum total of all there is to be said about truth, while denying that there is any property of truth per se. Davidson differs from both of these positions, for he affirms the equivalence thesis while denying that truth can be reduced to equivalence. However, his concern is not to explain the *essence* of truth, but rather to identify how truth functions in language. To that end, he suggests that we begin with the formula 'S is true-in-L if and only if p', where S is the description of a sentence, L is a particular language, and p is the sentence. This simple 'T-sentence' form, first developed by Alfred Tarski, shows us how truth functions; hence, the truth conditions for ' "Grass is green" is true' obtain if and only if grass is green.[63] Note that this explanation of truth is purely functional and does not address the essence of truth. Nonetheless, Marshall believes Davidson's functional approach is a desirable alternative to both realist and anti-realist speculation. In contrast to the latter it maintains equivalence, while it differs from the former in its eminent practicality; what more could we need of a theory of truth than an account of how truth *functions* in natural languages?

---

[60] See Marshall's summary and development of Lindbeck's views in 'Absorbing the World: Christianity and the Universe of Truths', in Bruce Marshall (ed.), *Theology and Dialogue: Essays in Conversation with George Lindbeck* (Notre Dame, Ind.: University of Notre Dame, 1990), 69–102.

[61] Davidson, 'True to the Facts', p. 42.

[62] See Marshall, *Trinity and Truth*, pp. 227–33.

[63] Marshall, *Trinity and Truth*, pp. 235–6.

Trinity and Truth

One additional bonus to Davidson's view is that its metaphysical agnosticism leaves it open to a *theological* account of truth. With this in mind, in the final chapter Marshall brings the Tarski–Davidson (T–D) theory into dialogue with a Trinitarian understanding of truth. He begins by enumerating three reasons for extending our analysis beyond the limited scope of the T–D theory. First, Davidson's agnosticism allows it, as he refuses to *reduce* truth to the form of T-sentences. Second, since the New Testament *identifies* truth with Jesus Christ and predicates truth of the Holy Spirit, we can expect a Christian view of truth to be richer than mere linguistic equivalence: 'A Tarski–Davidson approach cannot by itself be adequate for a theological account of what truth is, because it gives us no clue about how to connect truth to a person as its bearer'.[64] Marshall thus believes that a viable theological theory of truth must be *personal*, and, as such, truth bearers cannot be limited to impersonal propositions or sentences. The third reason is Marshall's concern to maintain God's sovereign, asymmetric relation to the world. Speaking of the Son's role as the truth of the Father, Marshall observes: 'Any relations which created reality has to Jesus depend as a whole on Jesus himself'.[65] Marshall takes this to mean that if T-sentences provided the only truth-conditions then truth would be readily accessible by way of equivalence; any individual could grasp truth simply by uttering a sentence that was equivalent to an actual state of affairs. This would effectively 'cut God out of the alethic loop', thereby impinging upon his sovereign being as the source of all truth. In short, if truth were reducible to a T-sentence form, 'we could know the risen Jesus regardless of whether he wanted us to—he would be cognitively at our disposal'.[66] And so we could apprehend the correspondence of the Son to the Father simply by establishing an equivalence relation to the world. For Marshall, this is ultimately a matter of divine sovereignty: 'There is more to the truth than Tarski because the Trinity is not at our disposal'.[67] Marshall thus appears to believe that if truth is fundamentally personal (as rooted in Christ), then all equivalence must be personally grounded in Christ. As a result, Christ is always

---

[64] Ibid. 245.   [65] Ibid. 246.   [66] Ibid. 248.   [67] Ibid. 272.

involved in the personal grasping of truth, if not the truth-conditions themselves.

Here we see Marshall's particularist approach to interpreting reality through the Trinity. One might counter that while one's *true belief* that 'Jesus is risen' may depend on Jesus' action mediated by the Spirit, it would seem that the *truth* of the sentence depends only on whether Jesus is in fact risen (and hence the equivalence of that statement to reality). Marshall is unmoved by this objection; since Jesus is in no way at the disposal of creatures, whatever relation we have to him is *only* because he wills it. It follows that 'the truth of "Jesus is risen," and not only the attitude which holds it true, must depend on Jesus' own will and action. It cannot, by contrast, depend only on his being risen'.[68]

Marshall then turns to epistemology, explicating one's coming to know truth as a fully Trinitarian act by appealing to the classic doctrine of divine appropriations. In one knowing event the Father ensures that a certain state of affairs occurs, the Son presents himself to the knower in that truth, and the Spirit actualizes the individual's will to believe the truth bearer. Hence, each appropriates a different dimension of the numerically singular act. Marshall's example is the paradigmatic belief that 'Jesus is risen' (the numbering is Marshall's):

(6) The Father brings about the true belief that Jesus is risen by raising Jesus.

(7) The Holy Spirit brings about the true belief that Jesus is risen by enabling people to hold this belief true.

(8) The Son Jesus brings about the true belief that he himself is risen by freely presenting himself such that when this belief is held true, it is true.[69]

This provides the model for all our beliefs: as all truth is reflected in Jesus, so his act of self-presentation applies to every true sentence. And so, '[i]f Jesus Christ and the Holy Spirit are, each in his own way, "the truth," then it seems as though the action of each has to bear on what truth is for all sentences and beliefs'.[70]

---

[68] *Trinity and Truth* 248.   [69] *Trinity and Truth*, p. 256.
[70] Ibid. 259.

Surprisingly, Marshall next reintroduces the concept of correspondence truth. However, this is not a propositional correspondence of sentences to facts or states of affairs, but rather a personal correspondence rooted in the intra-divine life. From the fundamental correspondence of the Son to the Father arises our correspondence to Christ, through whom we are made in the image of God. As the Spirit forms our will to believe, he creates this correspondence of persons to Christ and in Christ to the Father, thus providing 'a participated likeness in the incarnate Son's correspondence to the Father'. [71] Truth is ultimately grounded in this relation, a fact which enables Marshall to claim: 'On account of the Son's correspondence to the Father, there would in a sense be truth, even if there were no world, no sentences, and no beliefs'.[72] And so, this personal correspondence subsumes the T–D account into the internal life of the Trinity. For this reason, Marshall claims that everything relates to the Father in his image Jesus Christ, the exemplar of all creation. In this Trinitarian movement the Father sees that the truth-conditions of all things are met, from the greenness of the grass to the rising of the Son. The singular exception to this personal ground of correspondence involves sentences which express evil events or states of affairs: 'It is precisely not the triune God who sees to it that the truth conditions for sentences which follow [an evil] pattern are met'.[73] The T–D account is a sufficient explication of the truth of these sentences because nothing in such truths corresponds to the divine being. So, they appear to represent a sort of black hole in Marshall's theory for which there can be no theological ground. It would seem that Marshall believes this may be the most that we can say about evil.

CONCLUSION

Marshall has followed Davidson in carving out a unique space between classical foundationalism and anti-realist non-foundationalism.[74] In developing his position, he assiduously avoids

---

[71] Ibid. 270.   [72] Ibid. 271.   [73] Ibid. 275.
[74] Marshall interacts with other philosophers as well, including Alvin Plantinga and Michael Dummett, but his novel proposals depend on Davidson in particular.

classical foundationalism's subordination of doctrine, with his argument for the primacy of truth in interpretation and the role of Trinity as trump. This is a refreshing approach toward unapologetic theology, with a robust pay-off. At the same time, he avoids the problems endemic to anti-realism's incautiously unqualified renunciation of alethic and metaphysical realism. Finally, Marshall has developed an ambitious model of coherence justification and truth that is structured in the dynamic triune life of God.

8

A Critique of Trinitarian Non-foundationalism

[M]etaphysics inevitably buries its undertakers.

Ric Machuga, *In Defense of the Soul*

Does the Trinity need to be relevant? What *kind* of relevance does it need to have?

Karen Kilby, 'Perichoresis and Projection'

Once considered practically irrelevant, the doctrine of the Trinity has in recent years been trumpeted for its boundless heuristic potential. Indeed, as David Cunningham has observed, constructive Trinitarian theology has become so popular that it has begun to look like a bandwagon.[1] Cunningham's bandwagon imagery implies that a number of recent proposals are lacking in substance. Such is not the case with *Trinity and Truth*, which, if anything, simultaneously signals the maturation of constructive Trinitarian theology and epistemological non-foundationalism.[2] Marshall proves to be a valuable interlocutor, and a close evaluation of his proposal will illuminate both the strengths and weaknesses with a Trinitarian and non-foundationalist account of theological justification. As we turn to evaluate Marshall's

[1] Cunningham, *These Three are One: The Practice of Trinitarian Theology* (Oxford: Blackwell, 1997), 19.

[2] See Fergus Kerr, Charles Wood, and Bruce Marshall, 'Book Symposium: Bruce D. Marshall, *Trinity and Truth*', *Modern Theology*, 16/4 (2000), 503; R. R. Reno, review of Bruce Marshall, *Trinity and Truth*, *First Things* (Oct. 2000), 53–7; Andrew Moore, 'Philosophy of Religion or Philosophical Theology? A Review Essay of Bruce Marshall *Trinity and Truth* and Alvin Plantinga *Warranted Christian Belief*', *International Journal of Systematic Theology*, 3/3 (2001), 309–28.

proposal we will proceed in reverse order, beginning with his Trinitarian account of truth, and then considering his account of justification and critique of foundationalism, particularly the interiority and epistemic-dependence theses. Finally, we will focus on Marshall's pivotal critique of the given.

MARSHALL ON TRUTH

Our assessment of Marshall's views on truth will begin with a critique of his attempt to clear the decks of correspondence theories as metaphysically extravagant and implausible in order to prepare the way for a Davidsonian minimalism. This will lead us to consider Marshall's surprising attempt to reassert correspondence within a Trinitarian framework.

Is Correspondence Vacuous?

Given that many Christian realists equate alethic realism with correspondence truth, Marshall's acceptance of alethic realism and rejection of correspondence is intriguing. The centrepiece of that rejection comes in the slingshot argument. To recap, the argument claims that commitment to the innocuous correspondence of (1) 'Northfield is east of Lonsdale' to the fact that Northfield is east of Lonsdale collapses into the absurd correspondence of (1) to the fact that Red Square is in Moscow. Marshall seems correct to conclude that if the argument succeeds then the correspondence relation is rendered trivial or vacuous. But does it succeed? First, let us grant for the moment that 'Northfield is east of Lonsdale' further corresponds to the fact that the town where St Olaf College is located is east of Lonsdale and Yellowknife is in the Northwest Territories. Further, let us grant that we can continue to add conjunctive facts indefinitely. Still, Marshall's conclusion that (1) corresponds to the fact that Red Square is in Moscow does not follow, because correspondence is not a transitive relation. That is, even if p corresponds to the conjunctive fact that p and q by way of p's corresponding to a conjunct of that conjunctive fact, *it does not follow that* p *corresponds to each conjunct in the conjunctive fact* including the fact that *q*. Hence, even granting Marshall's initial claim to substitution, the point he requires to reduce to triviality—that (1) corresponds to the fact that Red Square is in Moscow—simply does not follow.[3]

One might respond that the argument still reduces correspondence to 'the one Great Fact' of reality, a conclusion that is sufficiently devastating. To answer this we need to re-examine the assumption we granted temporarily that (1) corresponds both to the fact that Northfield is east of Lonsdale *and* to the fact that the town where St Olaf College is located is east of Lonsdale. Marshall's replacement of the singular term 'Northfield' with 'the town where St Olaf College is located' depends on his first principle, which allows the replacement of singular terms only when they have the same extension. However, this assumption falls victim to the 'failure of substitutivity', which states that co-referential terms that shift referents in counterfactual situations *do not* refer to the same fact (or state of affairs), and thus cannot be substituted.[4] For instance, if St Olaf College moved to Moose Jaw, Saskatchewan, or even (heaven forbid) ceased to exist altogether, then 'Northfield' and 'the town where St Olaf College is located' would no longer have the same extension.[5] But this counterfactual means that they *do not* have the same extension and thus they refer to different facts. Davidson's trivial consequence can only obtain if we *assume* that sentential meaning is extensional rather than intensional, for only if we grant this assumption will sentences lack the requisite responsiveness or sensitivity to context. But granting an extensional reduction of meaning begs the question, and so the slingshot argument cannot get off the ground.[6]

While the slingshot argument may fail, many philosophers still contend that correspondence is trivial and uninformative. Rorty's critique of William Alston's approach to truth is illustrative:

---

[3] I am indebted to Daniel Howard-Snyder for drawing this point to my attention.

[4] Richard L. Kirkham, *Theories of Truth: A Critical Introduction* (Cambridge, Mass.: MIT Press, 1992), 248.

[5] For a succinct clarification of this point see Michael Loux, *Metaphysics* (London: Routledge, 1998), 139–40.

[6] See Jon Barwise and John Perry, *Situations and Attitudes* (Cambridge, Mass.: MIT Press, 1983), 24–6; cf. Marc Joseph, *Donald Davidson* (Montreal: McGill-Queen's University Press), 19–20.

Alston thinks that anybody who agrees that 'what it takes to make a statement true is the actual obtaining of what is claimed to obtain in making that statement' thereby holds a realist conception of truth. This seems to me like claiming that anybody who holds that what it takes to have a substance that puts people to sleep is to have a substance with genuine dormative power thereby holds a realist conception of dormativity. Until Alston comes up with distinct, independent tests for the justifiability of statements and for the actual obtaining of what is claimed to obtain in making those statements, I shall continue to think realism a pseudo-issue.[7]

Rorty's point is that alethic realism is uninteresting and ought to be replaced with a focus on justification. Rorty might score some rhetorical points here in so far as the notion of equivalence *seems* trivial, but that hardly justifies dismissing realism as a pseudo-issue. Notoriously, truisms can become controversial when discussed by philosophers, but rather than seeing that controversy as undermining their plausibility, it can be seen to underscore their importance. Hence, William Alston observes: 'I have been making a lot of fuss about the "realist conception of truth," as if it were some elaborate, complex theoretical conception that is properly a matter for philosophical debate and controversy. But in fact it is a miserable truism'.[8] It is important not to let ivory-tower debates trump common sense. Consider an analogy from language. While it seems luminously clear that language has the power to refer (as I am now doing), theories of reference are notoriously controversial, leading some philosophers to raise doubts about whether language does refer. But clearly language does refer, and we surely should not become sceptics about reference simply because we lack a theory of it. Similarly, we should guard against the temptation to dismiss the truth debate as a pseudo-issue simply because we may lack an adequate theory.

Parsimony and Context

Correspondence may not be trivial, but Davidson can still claim that as an explanation it adds nothing to our understanding of truth. As

---

[7] Richard Rorty, 'Realism/Antirealism and Pragmatism: Comments on Alston, Chisholm, Davidson, Harman, and Searle', in Christopher B. Kulp (ed.), *Realism/ Antirealism and Epistemology* (Lanham, Md.: Rowman & Littlefield, 1997), 159.

[8] William Alston, 'Realism and the Tasks of Epistemology', in Kulp (ed.), *Realism/ Antirealism and Epistemology*, p. 61.

such, one might charge that correspondence theory violates Ock-
ham's ontological parsimony by invoking explanatorily redundant
metaphysical exotica, including propositions, facts, and the correspondence relation. Here a couple points are in order. First, we should
be careful about saddling the alethic realist with more metaphysical
baggage than she ever intended to carry. Alethic realism does not
commit one to a specific account of the proposition/fact relation.[9]
Even so, I would suggest that we can get *enough* pay-off from a
realist conception of truth to move beyond a minimalist focus on the
linguistic analysis of the T-schema.[10]

Second, it should be kept in mind that judgements of parsimony
are relative to world-view. For instance, one would expect a naturalist to reject attempts to explain consciousness by appealing to a
non-material soul as an intolerable violation of parsimony. By contrast, those who already accept the existence of non-material spiritual
beings like God and angels will be more likely to be open to the
existence of souls as well. It is important to recognize that W. V. O.
Quine's and Donald Davidson's austere metaphysical tastes are rooted
in their naturalism.[11] While Marshall does not share these naturalistic
commitments, he does apparently share their overriding suspicion
of metaphysical entities. For example, he refrains from ontologizing
both the truth relation into correspondence and sentence meaning
(truth bearers) into propositions.[12] However, precisely why he holds
these suspicions is not clear.

While the Christian accepts a richer metaphysical framework than
the naturalist, we still require independent grounds to admit specific

[9] Peter van Inwagen, 'On Always Being Wrong', in Peter A. French, Theodore E.
Uehling, and Howard K. Wettstein (eds.), *Midwest Studies in Philosophy, xii: Realism
and Antirealism* (Minneapolis, Minn.: University of Minnesota, 1988), 96.

[10] But see Walter Hopp, 'Minimalist Truth and Realist Truth', *Philosophia Christi*,
10/1 (2008), 87–100.

[11] W. V. O. Quine and Nelson Goodman provide a classic and programmatic rejec-
tion of 'Platonism' in 'Steps Toward a Constructive Nominalism', *Journal of Symbolic
Logic*, 12/4 (1947), 105–22. For a description of Donald Davidson's views see his
'Intellectual Autobiography of Donald Davidson', in Lewis Edwin Hahn (ed.), *The
Philosophy of Donald Davidson* (Peru, Ill.: Open Court, 1999), 3–69.

[12] On the latter he follows the working assumption that 'propositions as eternal
objects are eliminable in Quine's sense; they add nothing to a consideration of the
issue at hand which cannot already be expressed simply by talking about sentences
and the interpretation of sentences' (Bruce Marshall, *Trinity and Truth* (Cambridge:
Cambridge University Press, 2000), 10–11).

entities into our metaphysical catalogue. Interestingly, Marshall himself provides a ground for admitting propositions with his recognition that sentential meanings or propositional attitudes cannot be reduced to sentences.[13] But if the same propositional attitude can be expressed by different sentences and the same sentence can express different propositional attitudes, then we have a ground to admit propositions into our ontology.[14] The importance of propositions becomes evident when we turn to evaluate the slingshot argument. In accounting for the failure of substitutivity, we can say that the sentence 'Northfield is east of Lonsdale' expresses the proposition that *Northfield is east of Lonsdale* while 'the town where St Olaf College is located is east of Lonsdale' expresses the proposition that *the town where St Olaf College is located is east of Lonsdale*. Hence, we have two different sentences expressing two different propositions which correspond to two different facts. This substitution failure demonstrates that ontologizing truth bearers does have an explanatory pay-off.

Marshall's ambivalence regarding propositions is also difficult to reconcile with his recognition of the existence of possible worlds.[15] Although he does not specify which theory of possible worlds he holds,[16] there are two major options: Lewis's nominalist possibilism and Plantinga's realist actualism.[17] I find it doubtful that any Christian could find Lewis's view appealing, as it entails the concrete existence of *all* possible worlds. That leaves the Plantingan view, which involves an ontologically rich modal conception grounded on the concept of a maximal state of affairs.[18] But having admitted states of affairs into our ontology, we already have one serious candidate

[13] Marshall, *Trinity and Truth*, p. 10.
[14] For more on the indispensability of propositions see William Alston, *A Realist Conception of Truth* (Ithaca, NY: Cornell University Press, 1996), 13–22. For a defence of propositions from a critic see William J. Lycan, 'Could Propositions Explain Anything?', *Canadian Journal of Philosophy*, 3/3 (1974), 427–34.
[15] Marshall, *Trinity and Truth*, p. 112.
[16] Marshall briefly notes both Quine's scepticism on the use of the operators 'necessary' and 'possible' and Kripke's defence of them, but does not take a side (*Trinity and Truth*, p. 213 n. 38).
[17] David Lewis, *On the Plurality of Worlds* (Oxford: Blackwell, 1986); Alvin Plantinga, *The Nature of Necessity* (Oxford: Clarendon, 1974).
[18] For Plantinga, a possible world is a maximal state of affairs (see 'Actualism and Possible Worlds', in Michael Loux (ed.), *The Possible and the Actual* (Ithaca, NY: Cornell University Press, 1979), 258).

for truth bearer. And the other primary contender, the fact, is simply an actual state of affairs.[19] Hence, having admitted possible worlds, it appears wholly reasonable to accept both truth makers and truth bearers as metaphysical entities.[20] One final point: the defender of correspondence truth will disagree with Marshall's characterization of facts, propositions, and the correspondence relation as strange. As Craig and Moreland state, 'these three entities all seem to be ordinary and commonsensical, not mysterious or queer'.[21] If the charge of queerness against realist entities has any merit, it is rooted not in the entities themselves, but rather in our lack of familiarity with the metaphysician's technical definitions of them.

Finally, what of the correspondence relation? Davidson's position is essentially agnostic on the nature of truth, while his appropriation of Tarski is purposely limited to the linguistic function of truth.[22] To go beyond this analysis we can first note that identifying the existence of a *relation* between truth makers and truth bearers need not commit one to a particular conception of that relationship. Kirkham writes: ' "Correspondence" serves as nothing more than a handy summing up of a theory in which no such special relation makes any appearance'.[23] That is, while we can recognize that the *existence* of equivalence leads us to say something more about the nature of the relation, it does not commit us to any particular theory of correspondence. The two primary theories of correspondence are congruence and correlation, but nothing obliges us to opt for one or the other. So, one could follow Alston in holding to a minimalist alethic realism which affirms a truth bearer/maker relation whilst taking no position on its specific nature. Further, in so far as one does proceed to offer a theoretical explication of correspondence, it can be noted that

---

[19] For a defence of facts (*pace* Davidson) as irreducible to sentences see Kirkham, *Theories of Truth*, pp. 138–9.

[20] Marshall may also recognize the existence of properties and relations (*Trinity and Truth*, p. 113).

[21] William Lane Craig and J. P. Moreland, *Philosophical Foundations for a Christian Worldview* (Downers Grove, Ill.: InterVarsity, 2003), 141. The 'three things' to which Craig and Moreland are referring are propositions, correspondence, and irreducible intentionality, though facts could just as easily be included here.

[22] 'Convention T embodies our best intuition as to how the concept of truth is used' (Davidson, 'On the Very Idea of a Conceptual Scheme', *Inquiries into Truth and Interpretation* (Oxford: Clarendon, 1984), 195.

[23] Kirkham, *Theories of Truth*, p. 135.

every theory of truth and/or reference faces its own challenges, so correspondence is not uniquely problematic. In point of fact, every theory must treat certain facts as primitive; while Davidson believes that we reach bedrock at the T-schema, the correspondence theorist believes we can further illuminate truth by analysing the equivalence relation in terms of correspondence. Even if we cannot say much as to *how* this relation obtains, we can surely know *that* it obtains. Hence, having admitted truth bearers, truth makers, and the correspondence relation (albeit in a chastened form), we have a respectably robust metaphysic of truth.

Trinity, Correspondence, and Truth

We can now turn to assess Marshall's claim that truth should be interpreted in terms of intra-Trinitarian personal correspondence. In attempting to analyse the concept of truth in terms of the Trinity, Marshall has undertaken a most ambitious task; sadly, it is doubtful that he has succeeded. Marshall's core inspiration is drawn from Johannine Christology, particularly Jesus' claim to be the truth (John 14: 6). But why take this literally, especially when we don't attempt to ontologize Jesus as the way and life (let alone as the gate or shepherd)? While he is aware of this objection, Marshall believes we have good grounds to view Jesus' specific claim to be the truth metaphysically. Marshall's motivation comes from the problem that if mere equivalence were sufficient to make a statement true, then the truth of statements would be automatic irrespective of any divine input. This notion of 'alethic independence' strikes Marshall as counter-intuitive. As Michael Scott observes, '[i]t may seem that while Marshall's argument rightly identifies a divine source of inspiration (or at least access) to true Christian belief, the truth of the belief should be a matter of whether the world conforms to it'.[24] As we have seen, Marshall's alternative account is found in the claim of Jesus' 'self-presentation'. While it may be that Christ provides the condition for coming to know truth, Marshall would have us believe that Christ somehow constitutes the very *concept* of truth, and that obliges us

---

[24] Scott, 'The Truth Conditions of Christian Belief: A Critique of Bruce Marshall', *Journal of Religion*, 85/1 (2005), 48.

to find room for Christic self-presentation within the equivalence relation.

In order to assess the adequacy of Marshall's proposal we can recall his account of the act of justifiably believing a truth:

(6) The Father brings about the true belief that Jesus is risen by raising Jesus.

(7) The Holy Spirit brings about the true belief that Jesus is risen by enabling people to hold this belief true.

(8) The Son Jesus brings about the true belief that he himself is risen by freely presenting himself such that when this belief is held true, it is true.[25]

The problem is that (8) appears to be superfluous to the attainment of a justified true belief in Jesus' resurrection,[26] as the Father's ensuring that the belief is true by raising Jesus coupled with the Spirit's effecting of the will of individuals to believe it provide necessary *and* sufficient conditions for a justified true belief. Instead of illuminating how the Son's correspondence to the Father is the pattern of all truth, Marshall provides opaque references to self-presentation, a term that as yet lacks determinate content. As Scott observes, '[i]t looks as if Marshall's proposal that Jesus' self-presentation is part of the concept of truth for beliefs about the Trinity should simply collapse into the claim that Jesus' self-presentation is a condition of true belief about God'.[27] Scott adds that invoking self-presentation to address the problem 'is akin to insisting that there must be a mysterious quantity in addition to 5 and 7 before they are able to add to 12'.[28] It is, in other words, unilluminating and unconvincing. It is also potentially embarrassing: imagine attempting to explain how Jesus self-presents the truth that 'Fred's mother-in-law blocked his toilet'! As best I can see, Marshall's claim that truth consists of Christic self-presentation is an example of what G. A. Cohen calls 'unclarifiable unclarity'; that is, an obscure claim which cannot be made clear.[29] But then it is surely

---

[25] Marshall, *Trinity and Truth*, p. 256.

[26] (8) is problematic for an additional reason: it appears to entail an epistemic theory of truth, which Marshall explicitly rejects.

[27] Scott, 'Truth Conditions', p. 54.   [28] Ibid. 55.

[29] See 'Deeper into Bullshit', in Gary L. Hardcastle and George A. Reisch (eds.), *Bullshit and Philosophy* (Chicago/LaSalle, Ill.: Open Court, 2006), 129–34.

ironic that Marshall critiques correspondence truth as unnecessary and unilluminating.[30]

MARSHALL ON JUSTIFYING THEOLOGY

At this point we will turn our attention to Marshall's internalist, deontological, and quasi-voluntarist account of justification. We will begin with his pneumatological treatment of the voluntarist problem, and then turn to his Christological account of rights and responsibilities in belief.

The Spirit and the Will to Believe

As we have seen, Marshall's epistemology is structured by a deontological theory of justification in which rights, responsibilities, and duties apply to the holding of specific beliefs. Marshall defends this view by appealing to our intuitions that people are rightly praised or castigated for their beliefs.[31] It is true that people have *some* responsibility for their beliefs. Take Alvin Plantinga's example: 'I take part in a racist lynching: you will not be impressed by my claim that, after careful reflection, I considered that the right thing to do'.[32] But while we would hold Aryanist Alvin's views to be reprehensible, how should we understand the nature and extent of our judgement? At this point it will be helpful to distinguish between 'belief practice', 'belief', and

---

[30] Marshall's account of truth faces other problems, including his attempt to create a buffer between evil and God's knowledge. Since on this view God knows all possible worlds through the incarnate Christ and there is a set of possible worlds that includes evil, then either God is ignorant of evil or he knows evil acts in Christ. Since the former sounds like Aristotle's prime mover, God must know evil in Christ. Given Marshall's views on double causation, it would make more sense to follow Aquinas in arguing that while God is the primary cause of all acts, the evil of evil acts only applies to the secondary causal agent (*Summa Theologica*, 1.49.2). But if this explanation works at all, then it works equally well for Marshall's correspondence theory of truth.

[31] See the section 'Can we control what we believe?' in Marshall, *Trinity and Truth*, pp. 212–16.

[32] Alvin Plantinga, *Warrant: The Current Debate* (Oxford: Oxford University Press, 1993), 17.

'believing'. We may define a belief practice as the doxastic practice which leads a person to come to (and continue to) hold their beliefs; a belief is a propositional attitude which a person affirms as being true; finally, a believing is the state of affairs where a person holds a particular belief. For instance, the racist's belief practice consists of an uncritical acceptance of whatever his neo-Nazi authorities tell him, and a stubborn dismissal of all contrary opinions. As a result, he holds the belief that lynching is commendable. While the deontological assessment of beliefs and practices is uncontroversial, the extension of deontology to believings must be rejected given the fact that this implies a voluntary control over belief that we do not possess.

We can illustrate the problem with doxastic voluntarism by drawing an analogy. We do not criticize a three-hundred-pound man because he cannot now run five miles, but because he has consistently lived a lifestyle that has brought him to the point where he is now physically unable to run five yards, let alone five miles. But while this man is powerless to run any distance, he can choose to implement an exercise schedule and change his eating habits (e.g. eating low-fat yogurt for lunch rather than deep-fried Mars bars from his local fish and chip shop). In this way he may *indirectly* exercise control over his present inability to run five miles by making certain *direct* choices. By the same token, while the racist may not be able to change his beliefs at will, he can choose to alter the way he forms beliefs indirectly by resolving to consider the arguments of minorities and integrationists more carefully, even if only intending to rebut them with carefully reasoned argument.[33] Or, to take another example, suppose that I become convinced that Bill Gates is the Antichrist after reading an article in *End Times Now!* magazine. While it is implausible to judge me culpable for this particular believing, culpability is well ascribed to the processes and dispositions that led me to form such an outlandish belief, such as a tendency to believe assertions on the basis of weak evidence: I ought not to do *that*. And so, the ascription of epistemic guilt to doxastic agents is applicable to belief practices and particular beliefs, but not specific believings.

---

[33] Frank Morison is a classic example of the open-minded sceptic, as he became a Christian while seeking to debunk the resurrection (see his *Who Moved the Stone?* (1930; Grand Rapids, Mich.: Zondervan, 1987)).

The central problem with the attempt to extend moral evaluation to believings is that no matter how epistemically dutiful a person may be, he still does not exercise the direct control over his believings that this deontology requires. In fact, believing is such that we may end up with the opposite result from what we intended or desired. Imagine that I am an iconoclastic Pentecostal who has a certain guilty fascination with the elaborate liturgy of the Catholic Church, and so I choose to stay away from everything and everyone Catholic for fear of being drawn by the papal pull. It would appear to my fellow anti-papists that in shunning all things Catholic I am acting with supreme doxastic wisdom or virtue to ensure I hold the right beliefs. But how can I know? Suppose that keeping everything papist at arm's length causes me increasingly to romanticize Catholicism until I come to believe it is the one true Church. On the other hand, maybe if I were to fraternize with Catholics and observe the mass it would repulse me, thus confirming my anti-Romanist suspicions. I know neither which outcome will obtain, nor which course of action will be more likely to provide the desired outcome. To blame a person for holding a specific belief is like blaming someone with cerebral palsy for spilling their coffee. Just as they lack adequate muscular control to guarantee they will not spill the coffee, so we all lack adequate control over our beliefs to support a believing-based deontology.[34]

Marshall clearly recognizes the difficulties with epistemic voluntarism: 'I have not argued that we can, in general, choose our beliefs at will'.[35] At the same time, with the apparent assumption that the only alternative is a radical Quinean form of externalism, Marshall remains committed to the necessity of epistemic deontology. He is right to counter Quine's attempt to naturalize epistemology: 'Were [the individual] simply a processor of epistemic inputs, who as such had no significant control over her beliefs, presumably we would not blame her'.[36] That is, with the total eradication of ought from our epistemic vocabulary, even broad epistemic virtues would lose any substantive ground. This assumption seems to constrain Marshall to identify a ground for epistemic deontology and voluntarism.[37]

---

[34] As William Alston observes, doxastic voluntarists 'ignore the difference between doing A in order to bring about E, for some definite E, and doing A so that some effect within a certain range will ensue' (*Epistemic Justification: Essays in the Theory of Knowledge* (Ithaca, NY: Cornell University Press, 1989), 130).

[35] Marshall, *Trinity and Truth*, p. 213.   [36] Ibid. 215.   [37] Ibid. 214.

In light of his concern to avoid a Quinean reduction of epistemology, Marshall offers a collection of arguments for limited epistemic control, beginning with the claim that both affective and volitional factors are operative in our epistemic priorities and beliefs.[38] Indeed, we *must* possess a certain amount of doxastic control over our beliefs, since we are readily able to change our set of justified beliefs.[39] Further, Marshall observes that '[w]hen one person makes a remark which, to her surprise, insults or hurts another, we sometimes think it entirely in order to tell the offending party that she should have known better—that she had both the ability and the responsibility to believe that her comment would offend'.[40] It is doubtful however that this can serve as a useful rejoinder to defend epistemic obligation and limited voluntarist control over belief. For one thing, the judgement implies that at some level this individual *did* know that her comment would offend. When Marge says 'Oh Jill, what a *lovely* dress! You really know how to shop the Oxfam sales!' we might say that she should have known that her 'compliment' would offend, but we actually believe that she did know it would offend and thus that she probably *intended* to offend.

Marshall's next example to support a sense of limited control concerns a scientist who believes a theory despite the evidence and who is finally vindicated when the theory is confirmed. Marshall argues that we credit this scientist in a distinctively epistemic manner: '[W]ithout his willingness to stick to the contested beliefs, even when he lacked strong evidence for their truth, the justifying evidence would never have come to light, and a contribution to knowledge would have been lost'.[41] But far from providing a ground for thinking that the scientist exercised control over his believings, this only illustrates that he maintained a state of belief when others abandoned it. If we laud him, it is surely not as an *epistemic* exemplar, but because he displayed courage and honesty. If his actions did elicit epistemic commendation then it would follow that it is an epistemic virtue to believe *p* when others abandon belief in *p* due to lack of evidence, but surely this is absurd.

[38] Ibid. 215.
[39] Ibid. Simply opening one's eyes in the morning will greatly enlarge the number of beliefs we are justified in holding. But since Quine could admit this, it hardly supports Marshall's intended point.
[40] Ibid.   [41] Ibid.

Marshall's most important defence of epistemic deontology and voluntarism comes not with these ad hoc arguments, but rather with the pneumatological context in which he embeds belief. However, even if we accept that the Spirit acts as primary cause to enable us to believe, we still have no reason to think that *we* act volitionally to will particular believings. To see the problem, we can summarize Marshall's argument as follows:

(1) God acts as primary cause to realize our free actions as secondary causes.
(2) God the Holy Spirit (as primary cause) causes me to believe Christianity is true.
(3) I freely choose (as secondary cause) to believe Christianity is true.
(4) Secondary causation is sufficient for a deontologically significant capacity to choose beliefs.
(5) Therefore, I have a deontologically significant capacity to choose beliefs.
(6) Therefore, individual believings are deontologically justified or unjustified.

The point at issue lies with (3), for whether humans *have* the ability to choose their beliefs is precisely what is in contention; therefore, it cannot be a premise. If we did accept Marshall's reasoning then we would have to embrace the following *reductio ad absurdum* for an analogous argument for cardiac control:

(7) God acts as primary cause to realize our actions as secondary causes.
(8) God the Holy Spirit (as primary cause) causes me to have a heart attack.
(9) I freely choose (as secondary cause) to have a heart attack.
(10) Therefore, I have a deontologically significant capacity to have a heart attack.

In this second argument (9) clearly begs the question. By the same token, I would deny (3) and with it a believing-based deontology.

But perhaps our objection misses the mark in another way: might it be that voluntarism is *unnecessary* for a believing-based deontology? Just as we find that we cannot do what we ought to do, so we (often) cannot believe what we ought to believe.[42] There are two problems here. First, this objection depends on the assumption that the Christian doctrine of original sin and grace undermines the principle of ought implies can. But this is based on a misunderstanding, for, as John Hare points out, ought implies can 'does not state that "ought" implies "can" by our own devices'.[43] As such, the principle is fully congruent with compatibilism. This leads us to the second point concerning the failure of the analogy, which can be illuminated with the following simple thought-experiment. All agree that in the prelapsarian state human beings were moral agents who were substantially free to choose the good. This argument requires a similar *doxastic* freedom before the fall (assuming of course a historical fall), but this just appears absurd. When Eve was faced with the choice of biting into the fruit, she faced a real choice as a free moral agent. But when Eve first saw the fruit, *she did not have a choice about whether to believe she was in fact seeing the fruit*; she simply found herself believing it. And when Adam awoke following major surgery, he did not choose to believe there was a strangely alluring creature standing in front of him; again, he simply found himself believing it. What sense could be made of a claim that Adam and Eve *willed* their believings just as they willed to eat the fruit? Surely the onus is on the proponent of prelapsarian doxastic voluntarism to present a credible argument for it. Barring such an argument, there is no reason to think that the doxastic is sufficiently analogous to the ethical to justify deontologically evaluating particular believings. So long as the Spirit is operative in realizing the human will to respond in faith, the principle is maintained.

The Son and the Right to Believe

Marshall explains the epistemological role of the Son deontologically: as the ground of all truth, he appropriates the act of transferring the right to believe. Hence, the justification (right, ground, permission) for holding Christian beliefs arises from the consistency of these

---

[42] Thanks to Steve Holmes for this point.

[43] John Hare, 'Naturalism and Morality', in William Lane Craig and J. P. Moreland (eds.), *Naturalism: A Critical Analysis* (London: Routledge, 2000), 194.

beliefs with epistemically primary Trinitarian belief and the coherence of these beliefs with the other beliefs in one's noetic web. Crucial to the defence of this account is the inductive vindication of Christian beliefs in meeting the necessary criterion of assimilative power. I have two primary objections here. To begin with, it is simply not appropriate to describe our justified beliefs as being held by *right*.[44] When I was in grade 1 I learned that 7 + 5 = 12, but to describe that seven-year-old as having gained the *right* to hold that belief simply appears misguided. Presently I am looking out the window at a brilliant blue sky. Do I now have the *right* to believe it is sunny today? Again, such analyses of belief appear misguided, and attempting to explain them Christologically adds nothing to their plausibility.

Second, while coherence is *a* source of justification,[45] it is not, as Marshall assumes, the primary (let alone sole) ground for justification. As William Alston observes, '[f]rom the fact that I can *justify* a belief only by relating it to other beliefs that constitute a support, it does not follow that a belief can *be justified* only by its relations to other beliefs'.[46] Further, as Alan Padgett points out, even if coherence is necessary for justification, it is still not sufficient, because contradictory propositions such as *The earth is flat* and *The earth is spherical* are *both* coherent with Trinitarian belief, as are many other contradictory propositions. As a result, Marshall's view leaves the epistemic status of the vast majority of one's actual beliefs underdetermined, thus leading to the conclusion that Trinitarian belief is no guide to assessing the vast majority of our beliefs.[47]

Not only does coherence appear not to be sufficient for justification, but it may not be necessary either. Indeed, it appears that some beliefs may be justified even if they are *incoherent* with one's other beliefs, as is the case with revelations that may challenge reason and

---

[44] Marshall, *Trinity and Truth*, p. 212.

[45] At a magic show I witness the smiling young assistant sawn in half by the magician. Clearly it would be unjustified to believe this had in fact occurred in light of my full stock of beliefs, including that I am attending a magic show, that optical illusions are often performed at magic shows, and that people who are sawn in half tend to die. These beliefs would render the belief that the woman was in fact sawn in half unjustified, as it does not cohere with my other beliefs.

[46] Alston, *Epistemic Justification*, p. 198.

[47] See Padgett, review of Bruce Marshall, *Trinity and Truth*, *Scottish Journal of Theology*, 54/3 (2001), 436.

experience. Consider the famous case of Abraham: 'Some time later God tested Abraham. He said to him, "Abraham!". "Here I am", he replied. Then God said, "Take your son, your only son Isaac, whom you love, and go to the region of Moriah. Sacrifice him there as a burnt offering on one of the mountains I will tell you about" ' (Gen. 22: 1–2). Abraham faithfully carried out the task set before him, only to have an angel intervene at the final climactic moment. For his efforts we now recognize him as a knight of faith who is 'justified' *in excelsis*. But note, if Abraham were serving Moloch, and the dastardly deity were to demand the sacrifice of Isaac, the *belief* that Moloch was demanding this would be fully coherent with Abraham's other beliefs. So long as a person believes the demand being made by the respective deity is in character, or at least does not radically contradict character, the belief can be justified by virtue of its coherence with background beliefs. The problem is that Abraham followed a God whom he did not believe to be capricious or malicious, and certainly not one to demand child sacrifice. Consequently, this demand was anathema to his understanding of the holy, loving, just, and merciful God who had promised that his offspring would be as numerous as the stars.[48]

At this point one might retort, so much the worse for epistemic justification. Such is the approach taken by Robert Merrihew Adams, who defends faith as a cognitive virtue even though he contends that it is not knowledge and may even be irrational. This is not a problem, Adams suggests, for 'much of our emotional attachment to *rationality* has to do with our counting on it as a crucial part of our intellectual equipment for controlling our lives'.[49] While desire for control is a significant factor, the central issue concerns the nature of rationality and justification. No doubt Adams would not commend the actions of other fathers who attempt to carry out instructions to sacrifice their sons, and for obvious reasons: while Abraham's actions were indeed in response to a divine command, we would interpret these other instances as cases of cognitive dysfunction (e.g. hallucination). The conclusion seems to be that *if* someone believes he has been

---

[48] Abraham could have believed other things that would address the coherence issue, such as that God occasionally does wholly unexpected things that only *appear* to contradict his plans and promises.

[49] Adams, 'The Virtue of Faith', in his *The Virtue of Faith: And Other Essays in Philosophical Theology* (New York: Oxford University Press, 1987), 19.

asked by God to perform a particular action, that person is functioning properly, and he has in fact been so asked, then *ceteris paribus* his believing he has been asked is objectively justified, even if the request is incoherent given his other beliefs. It is thus possible to view Abraham as an epistemic knight of faith rather than a delusional maniac because we judge his actions to have been carried out in response to beliefs which were *true* and *produced by truth-conducive means* (by way of God rather than a cognitive dysfunction).[50] This suggests that the most basic criterion for justification is not one's present stock of coherent beliefs, but the truth of the belief combined with its production under the appropriate conditions.[51]

There are additional problems with focusing solely upon coherence justification. Consider the isolation problem as it is illustrated in Alvin Plantinga's example of 'Ric the Epistemically Inflexible Climber'. While mountain climbing in the Tetons, Ric is hit by a burst of radiation as a result of which he continues to think he is mountain climbing and experiencing the attendant sensations—seeing a mountain goat, hearing a bald eagle, feeling the warmth of the sun—even after his distraught friends have taken him off the mountain. While his beliefs remain coherent throughout the ordeal, after the radiation blast they are almost totally false.[52] Fanciful, perhaps, but the thought-experiment makes the point that coherence is no sure guide to knowledge: while Abraham arguably has secure knowledge despite incoherence, Ric does not despite his impeccable coherence. Given the close link that we expect between justification and knowledge, this should be a cause for worry. Indeed, it would again appear that

---

[50] Here is a counter-example to the sufficiency of coherence justification. Suppose a Pentecostal pastor tells a young man in the congregation that only men receive glossolalia. A few weeks later a young woman whom this man knows to be a spiritual leader in the church suddenly erupts into tongues. Although believing that she has indeed received this gift would not be initially coherent with his other beliefs, it seems he would be justified in believing it, at least for an initial probationary period where the putative defeaters could be assessed. Ultimately the man would have to seek coherence, for example by concluding that the pastor was wrong or that the woman was pretending (or perhaps possessed by a demon).

[51] Note as well that Marshall cannot claim that the Son justified Abraham, because then coherence would be shown to be irrelevant, as justification would be granted solely by way of Christological fiat.

[52] Plantinga, *Warrant: The Current Debate*, p. 82; cf. Plantinga, *Warrant and Proper Function* (Oxford: Oxford University Press, 1993), 179–80.

the main issue is truth and truth-conducive (reliable) means by which the belief was produced; coherence is a secondary concern.

One final point. Though Marshall vigorously repudiates any subordination of theology to philosophy, this is what appears to happen with his combination of Davidsonian method and deontological epistemology. One sees evidence of this in his metaphysical austerity and the claim that assimilative power is a necessary condition for discourse.[53] If the assimilative criterion is not necessary (and it seems doubtful that it is), then Marshall's defence of it is no more persuasive than the subordination that the classical foundationalist rationalizes as necessary.

Conceptual Schemes and Radical Interpretation

Marshall believes that Davidson's appeal to the interconnection of truth and meaning allows us to prevent recourse to epistemic dependence, while his denial of the scheme/content distinction will ground theological autonomy and circumvent scepticism. To my mind, each of these claims appears doubtful indeed. Davidson's rejection of conceptual schemes has attracted widespread incredulity. Charles Taylor replies:

What is needed is not the Davidsonian 'principle of charity', which means: make the best sense of them in what we understand as sense; but rather: coming to understand that there is a very different way of understanding human life, the cosmos, the holy, etc. Somewhere along the line, you need some place in your ontology for something like 'the Aztec way of seeing things', in contrast to 'our way of seeing things'; in short, something like the scheme/content distinction.[54]

---

[53] Similarly, Ellen Charry charges Lindbeck with subordinationism: 'Now, the integrity of Christian belief resides in its ability to absorb and to be shaped by extra-Christian thought forms, precisely the apologetic move the postliberal stance was designed to challenge!' (review of Bruce Marshall (ed.), *Theology and Dialogue: Essays in Conversation with George Lindbeck*, *Theology Today*, 48/3 (1991), 340).

[54] Taylor, 'Charles Taylor Replies', in James Tully (ed.), *Philosophy in an Age of Pluralism: The Philosophy of Charles Taylor in Question* (Cambridge: Cambridge University Press, 1994), 221. Cf. David K. Naugle, *Worldview: The History of a Concept* (Grand Rapids, Mich.: Eerdmans, 2002), 171–3.

Basically we must decide which is more plausible: Davidson's a priori argument that it is not possible to disagree with others, or Taylor's empirical observation that there are very different ways of looking at the world, some of which may include only partially translatable concepts. Support for Taylor is found in the difficulty with translating jokes and other concepts that are 'lost in translation'. Further support is found in the history of science; for instance, the set of concepts held by a Ptolemaic astronomer will be at least partially incompatible with the set held by a post-Einsteinian astronomer (e.g. an absolute concept of time, the inherent perfection of circular motion, and the incorruptibility of heaven versus a denial of these). Likewise, it seems likely that the Aztec way of seeing things cannot be fully assimilated to our way. In each case Davidson's a priori argument lacks intuitive and empirical support.[55]

We can pursue this question further by taking a closer look at what Davidson understands a conceptual scheme to be. As noted in Chapter 7, Davidson assumes Quine's view of conceptual schemes as sets of declarative sentences to which one assents.[56] This is important because Davidson's attack on conceptual schemes depends on this definition; that is, we must accept the impossibility of failing to interpret the set of declarative sentences held by another while taking them as largely true. However, there are other models of conceptual schemes that one might adopt which would short-circuit the argument.[57] Given that I have already defended a richer ontological framework than sentences alone, I would propose that we think of conceptual schemes as networks of (non-linguistic) concepts that transcend linguistic utterances. Once we accept such an alternative

[55] At the same time, there are transcendent concepts (e.g. the principle of non-contradiction) that govern the engagement between conceptual schemes. I would add this observation to Alasdair MacIntyre's claim that one conceptual scheme can be proved superior to another *on the terms of the other* (see *Three Rival Versions of Moral Enquiry: Encyclopaedia, Geneaology, and Tradition*, 1988 Gifford Lectures (London: Duckworth, 1990)). For a further development of these arguments against Davidson's theory see Alasdair MacIntyre, *Whose Justice? Which Rationality?* (Notre Dame, Ind.: University of Notre Dame Press, 1988), ch. 19.

[56] Marshall apparently views conceptual schemes as networks of beliefs and concepts (*Trinity and Truth*, pp. 82–3).

[57] Michael Lynch, in his *Truth in Context: An Essay on Pluralism and Objectivity* (Cambridge: MIT Press, 1998), ch. 2, also identifies Kantian and Wittgensteinian models.

definition, the argument for alternative conceptual schemes is no longer tied to translation as such, and Davidson's argument becomes a non sequitur.[58]

Marshall has placed great stock in the interconnection of meaning and interpretation as a means to debunk foundationalism. Further, he defends the epistemic primacy of Christian belief by appealing to the criterion of inclusive and assimilative power. This argument, which depends heavily on Davidson's theory of radical interpretation and its close bedfellow the hermeneutic of charity, requires closer examination. The question is whether Marshall has demonstrated a priori that it is impossible to have a largely false set of beliefs. As Michael Devitt points out, Davidson's argument for the necessity of ascribing the balance of truth to a person's beliefs appears arbitrary:

Why does disaster suddenly strike our explanation if we suppose that error goes beyond the Davidsonian limit? I have heard the suggestion that although we can ascribe error in a few areas, we cannot in most. But what differ-ence does it make to my attempt to explain a person uncharitably in, say, semantics that I have already explained him uncharitably in, say, religion and politics? Why does accumulation of error make a difference?[59]

Davidson simply provides no ground to think such truth ascription is necessary, and as a result his principle looks verificationistic, as if he were advocating the move from 'I cannot understand what you say' to 'You are not saying anything'. As Plantinga points out, the principle of charity 'doesn't show that most human beliefs are true; at best it shows something much weaker: that *in order to understand* someone, I must *make the assumption* that most of what she says is true'.[60] One might reasonably suspect that Davidson only achieves apparent understanding by imposing interpretation via a new verification-ism.[61] Fortunately, an externalist proper-functional epistemology (such as we will consider in Chapters 9 and 10) provides a more

---

[58] Ibid. 49.
[59] Devitt, *Realism and Truth*, 2nd edn. (Princeton, NJ: Princeton University Press, 1996), 193.
[60] Plantinga, *Warrant and Proper Function*, p. 80.
[61] Devitt, *Realism and Truth*, p. 192. Davidson recognizes that 'it comes to little more than making translatability into a familiar tongue a criterion of language-hood. As fiat, the thesis lacks the appeal of self-evidence' ('On the Very Idea of a Conceptual Scheme', p. 186). Cf. Lynch, *Truth in Context*, p. 52.

intuitive explanation of understanding while escaping the sceptical worry that either we *have* no meaning or we *assume* or *impose* meaning.

Davidson's functional assumption of meaning reflects a general austerity towards matters metaphysical. Rather than comment on the essence of truth, he develops a truth-functional account. And rather than directly address meaning, he develops a theory of radical interpretation that appears to *impose* it by stipulation. Davidson's view is only defensible if there are no beliefs to come to know apart from interpretation, and this amounts to endorsing both Quine's behaviourist rejection of meaning and Rorty's pragmatic shift from epistemology to hermeneutics. Not surprisingly, Davidson's radical interpretation is counter-intuitive and fails to reflect how we *in fact* interpret others. As Marc Joseph observes:

> In conversation with our fellows, it certainly *seems* that we perceive more than their bare movements and sounds, or even their non-individuative attitudes towards uninterpreted sentences; it seems, indeed, that we do not so much *infer* the significance of someone's utterance from its sound and surrounding circumstances, as much as we *perceive* the recognizable thoughts of the speaker in his words.[62]

Davidson admits that his approach runs counter to our intuitions, but he insists that it brings us to the 'philosophically important' dimension of communication within this austere framework.[63] But without his austere metaphysics we lack any motivation to follow him in dismissing common sense and experience.

As I noted above, a proper-function account of interpretation is simpler and intuitively more plausible.[64] Consider the complexity with Davidson's proposal: the radical translator faces the dilemma that when we encounter a foreign-language speaker who points to a rabbit and utters a sound, we cannot be sure he is referring to what we call rabbits instead of say 'rabbit stages', 'undetached rabbit parts', or any of the infinite number of other possibilities. Davidson proposes to overcome this dilemma by a verificationist rejection of the scheme/content distinction to close the gap in understanding. By contrast, according to the proper-function account we simply say that when *that* type of fuzzy creature is pointed at, a properly functioning

[62] Joseph, *Donald Davidson*, p. 56.   [63] Cited ibid. 57.
[64] Plantinga, *Warrant and Proper Function*, pp. 75–6 n. 16.

adult under normal conditions will come to believe that a rabbit
is being identified, instead of any of the innumerable more exotic
possibilities. Of course, we could be wrong. Perhaps the other speaker
is a foreign metaphysician who *is* referring to undetached rabbit parts
or a prankster who is not referring to *anything*. But it seems much
better to concede the possibility of translation failure than to stipulate
meaning out of existence. Such unusual scenarios are inadequate to
undermine our justification that the individual is referring to a rabbit,
and so if he *is* doing so, then we may *know* that he is (thereby attaining
a successful translation). Fortunately, we are hard-wired for communication so that the regular interpretative boundaries are already set.
Contra Davidson, translation is possible not because we reject the
scheme/content distinction and invoke the principle of charity, but
because we have been created by God to communicate.

THEOLOGY AND THE LINGUISTIC THESIS

At this point we find ourselves back at the non-foundationalist
rejection of the given that we considered in Chapter 4. In rejecting
the given, non-foundationalists widely assume the linguistic thesis,
according to which all thought/experience is conceptually and propositionally structured: experience is always *of* something, so that there
is no 'pure' (that is, non-linguistic) experience.[65] James K. Smith thus
asserts: '[I]t's not a matter of trying to "hook up" to a world "outside"
of language—the world I inhabit is always already *interpreted* within a
framework of signs or a semiotic system'.[66] This thesis has important
implications for Christian theology, beginning, as Smith observes,
with the Christian kerygma:

Even if we are confronted with the physical and historical evidence of the
resurrection—even if we witnessed the resurrection *firsthand*—what exactly
this *meant* would require interpretation, and this interpretative 'seeing' is

[65] See, for instance, Marshall, *Trinity and Truth*, pp. 12–13.
[66] 'Who's Afraid of Postmodernism? A Response to the "Biola School"', in Myron
B. Penner (ed.), *Christianity and the Postmodern Turn* (Grand Rapids, Mich.: Brazos,
2005), 222. Cf. Richard Lints, *The Fabric of Theology: A Prolegomenon to Evangelical
Theology* (Grand Rapids, Mich.: Eerdmans, 1993), 253.

conditioned by the particularities of my horizon of perception. There is no 'neutral seeing' of orange trees or resurrected bodies. Only by means of *interpreting* the resurrection of Jesus do I see that it confirms that he is the Son of God (Rom. 1: 4).[67]

It seems to me that we ought to interpret the linguistic thesis as a linguistic version of the ideational (sense-data) theory of perception in which public language replaces private sense-data as the mediator of all experience. Smith writes: 'Even experiencing a cup "in person" or "in the flesh" demands that I interpret the thing *as* a cup'.[68] In other words, there is no raw, immediate perception of the cup, for all perception is mediated linguistically by interpreting the thing as a cup. Obviously the viability of the linguistic thesis is critical for determining the plausibility of non-foundationalism. In this final section I will undertake two criticisms of the linguistic thesis. To begin with, I will argue that it is false that all experience is linguistically conditioned based upon reflections from sense perception and spiritual experience. Then I will provide a summary overview of an alternative to the linguistic thesis according to which perception is rooted in the grasping of intrinsic properties that constitute what we might call the 'furniture of the universe'.

More than One Can Say

The sense-perception challenge to the linguistic thesis identifies an ineffable dimension of tacit knowledge that precedes and then becomes coextensive with intelligible speech. The point is summarized in Michael Polanyi's maxim: '*we know more than we can tell*'.[69] Thought and experience both precede and exceed our conceptual and linguistic abilities; as Michael Ayers puts it, '*perceptual* knowledge is evidently not a consequence of the subject's grasping a relationship between propositional contents, but derives from a perspicuous cognitive relation to reality itself, the relation itself being a part of

[67] Smith, 'Who's Afraid of Postmodernism', p. 218.

[68] Smith, 'Who's Afraid of Postmodernism', p. 225.

[69] Polanyi, *The Tacit Dimension* (Garden City, NY: Doubleday, 1966), 4; cf. Polanyi, *Personal Knowledge: Toward a Post-critical Philosophy* (Chicago, Ill.: University of Chicago Press, 1958), ch. 5.

the reality presented'.[70] To recall the three types of knowledge surveyed in Chapter 3, it would appear that propositional knowledge emerges from acquaintance knowledge. William Alston illustrates from a mundane case of perception:

When I look at my front lawn, it presents much more content to my awareness than I can possibly capture in concepts. There are indefinitely complex shadings of color and texture among the leaves and branches of each of the trees. That is perceptually *presented* to me in all its detail, but I can make only the faintest stab at encoding it in concepts.[71]

The core problem is that non-foundationalists typically collapse the full range of sense perception into one narrow type. As Alston points out, there is an oft-overlooked distinction between ' "The tree looks green to S", on the one hand, and "S takes the tree to be green" or "S applies the concept of green (or tree) to what S sees" on the other'.[72] The point is that one may experience a property without grasping the associated concept. Once we understand this, we will see the failure of the linguistic thesis.

Robert Audi clarifies this distinction by analysing perception into three distinct relations.[73] Simple perception, the most basic encounter, involves visual, auditory, gustatory, olfactory, tactual, and proprioceptive experiences of the world, including experiences like *seeing an apple.* Such *perceiving of* provides the foundation on which we build beliefs about the world and thus is minimally part of the sensory experience of neonates and conscious animals. The next level of perception, *perceiving to be,* is objectual in nature. At this point, when we perceive the apple we are able to isolate particular properties

---

[70] Ayers, 'Is Perceptual Content Ever Conceptual?', *Philosophical Books*, 43/1 (2002), 17.

[71] William Alston, 'Back to the Theory of Appearing', in James Tomberlin (ed.), *Philosophical Perspectives, xiii. Epistemology, 1999* (Atascadero, Calif.: Ridgeview, 1999), 187. For a rich discussion of sensation and consciousness see David J. Chalmers, *The Conscious Mind: In Search of a Fundamental Theory* (Oxford: Oxford University Press, 1996), 6–11.

[72] William Alston, 'Sellars and the Myth of the Given', at <http://www.ditext.com/alston/alston2.html>, accessed January 2009. Compare Alston's distinction between knowledge of facts and of particulars in 'Back to the Theory of Appearing', p.187.

[73] Audi, *Epistemology: A Contemporary Introduction to the Theory of Knowledge* (London: Routledge, 1998), 15–27.

in our field of awareness, as when we perceive the apple *to be red*. While objectual perception involves a conceptual grasp, it does not require any particular proposition to be believed about the object and it occurs even when one misidentifies an object. For instance, though I may mistakenly perceive an apple as a peach, I could nonetheless have an objectual belief that the misperceived object is red. The third level of perception, *perceiving that*, involves grasping a particular proposition; for instance, perceiving *that the apple is red*. Such linguistically structured perception grasps objects and properties in relation to a propositional attitude. With that framework in place, we can see that advocates of the linguistic thesis ignore simple perception and tend to collapse objectual perceiving-to-be into propositional perceiving-that.[74] Thus, our linguistic experience of the world emerges gradually out of a rich and immediate knowledge of acquaintance.

Surely if our interface with the material world precedes and exceeds our linguistic frameworks, we ought to expect something similar in the personal and spiritual dimensions of existence, as in the profound relationship between mother and baby or a caregiver and her charge. Consider, for instance, Henri Nouwen's reflections on caring for Adam, a severely retarded man at L'Arche community in Toronto. Though Adam could not bathe himself, much less speak, he became a profound spiritual mentor for Nouwen, such that upon his death Nouwen was led to reflect:

Here is the man who more than anyone connected me with my inner self, my community, and my God. Here is the man I was asked to care for, but who took me into his life and into his heart in such an incredibly deep way. Yes, I had cared for him during my first year at Daybreak and had come to love him so much, but he has been such an invaluable gift to me. Here is my counselor, my teacher, and my guide, who could never say a word to me but taught me more than any book, professor, or spiritual director. Here is Adam, my friend, my beloved friend, the most vulnerable person I have ever known and at the same time the most powerful.[75]

---

[74] Compare Donald Davidson's claim that '[a] creature cannot have thoughts unless it is an interpreter of the speech of another' (in 'Thought and Talk', in his *Inquiries into Truth and Interpretation* (Oxford: Clarendon, 1984), 157).

[75] Henri Nouwen, *Adam: God's Beloved* (Maryknoll, NY: Orbis, 1997), 101.

Since Adam could not even grasp the most simplistic sentences, the advocate of the linguistic thesis seems constrained to say that Nouwen was projecting meaning on to an individual who lacked the minimal linguistic abilities necessary for relationship with the world. If we believe on the contrary that a profound spiritual relationship did obtain here, then we have evidence that the linguistic thesis is false: as with sense perception, our experience of personal and spiritual reality both precedes and exceeds language.[76]

The Furniture of the Universe

It is unlikely that reflections on sense perception and relationships will persuade the non-foundationalist to admit a given and surrender the linguistic thesis. But then what exactly is it that is being claimed about our experience of the world? While a large part of this answer will have to await the discussion on proper function in the next chapter, we can offer a preliminary outline of my claim that human beings perceive the world directly. (Here the term perception encompasses sense perception, rational intuition, memory, and other basic sources of belief.) This is not to deny that language plays a pivotal role in our grasping of the world, but it is to deny that language always mediates our experience of the world. Interestingly, my direct-realist views reflect Donald Davidson's distinct distaste for epistemic intermediaries. The difference is that I also include linguistic intermediaries. Further, contrary to the non-foundationalist like Davidson who retreats to a merely causal interface with the world, I submit that our direct relation may be epistemic. As J. P. Moreland puts it,

a knowing subject is not trapped behind or within anything, including a viewpoint, a narrative, an historical-linguistic perspective. To have an entity in the external world as an object of intentionality is to already be 'out there'; there is no need to escape anything. One is not trapped behind one's eyeballs

[76] Michael Scott critiques Marshall's tendency to conflate knowledge of a person with cognitive/propositional knowledge (see 'The Truth Conditions of Christian Belief', p. 50 n. 3).

or anything else. It is a basic fallacy of logic to infer that one sees a point-of-viewed-object from the fact that one sees an object from a point of view.[77]

While the prelinguistic world is structured to varying degrees within a conceptual and linguistic framework, the foundation comes in the direct experience of simple perception.

What precisely is the nature of that direct-realist encounter? While we can only provide the briefest of sketches here, it should be sufficient to note how our position differs from the non-foundationalist. According to Dallas Willard, knowledge arises as thoughts exemplify concepts which in turn have a natural connection with properties exemplified in the world.[78] For instance, when I see green grass, the concept of green that is exemplified in my mind bears an intrinsic relation to the property of green exemplified by the grass. This allows me to perceive the grass as green without exemplifying the property of greenness in my mind or brain. Keep in mind that the concept of green is not a linguistic convention like the word 'green', but rather an abstract entity that bears an intrinsic, natural relation with the property of greenness. Hence, to grasp the concept of green when appeared to 'greenly' is to perceive the property exemplified in the grass. This is very different from the non-foundationalist claim that there is no intrinsic link between properties and the concepts expressed within conventional semiotic systems. Indeed, this notion of an intrinsic link is anathema to many non-foundationalists. Thus, Putnam writes: '[T]he deep systematic root of the disease ... lies in the notion of an "intrinsic" property, a property something has "in itself", apart from any contribution made by language or the mind'.[79] This aversion should not surprise us, given that non-foundationalists often collapse concepts into words, as when the property of redness

---

[77] Moreland, 'Truth, Contemporary Philosophy and the Postmodern Turn', *Journal of the Evangelical Theological Society*, 48/1 (2005), 86.

[78] Willard, 'How Concepts Relate the Mind to Its Objects: The God's Eye View Vindicated?', *Philosophia Christi*, 1/2 (1999), 5–20. Cf. R. Scott Smith, *Truth and the New Kind of Christian* (Wheaton, Ill.: Crossway, 2005), ch. 9.

[79] Hilary Putnam, *The Many Faces of Realism*, Paul Carus Lectures (LaSalle, Ill.: Open Court, 1987), 8. Cf. 'Thought words and mental pictures do not *intrinsically* represent what they are about' (Putnam, *Reason, Truth and History* (Cambridge: Cambridge University Press, 1991), 5). For a general discussion of these problems see John Heil, *The Nature of True Minds* (Cambridge: Cambridge University Press, 1992), 25–30.

is treated as nothing more than the conventional words 'red', 'rojo', 'rouge', and the concrete objects to which they are applied in speech acts. This is very different from my claim that these words are traced back to a simple perception of redness that leads to the grasping of the property of red and eventually propositional belief and linguistic expression.

While we do not have the space to develop and defend a specific theory of perception, it seems to me that the theory of appearing effectively captures the core aspect of immediate presentation in perception while avoiding the problems with sense-data and adverbial theories.[80] At the same time, I am happy to admit that all *theories* of perception remain woefully inadequate. But whatever problems with theories of sense perception remain, they are magnified exponentially once we demand that all perception be draped in linguistic regalia.

Admittedly the notion of grasping properties through intrinsically related concepts will strike many non-foundationalists as naive and untenable. However, we must keep in mind that which kinds of exotica we include within our metaphysical catalogue is determined in large part by our prior world-view. And, as I noted above, it is no secret that many non-foundationalists have been driven by naturalistic presuppositions. For instance, Michael Lynch observes that the switch among philosophers from a Kantian view of conceptual schemes as networks of concepts to a Quinean view of schemes as lists of sentences was determined not by any argument so much as by a shared commitment to naturalism and scientism: 'The fact that languages are public—the fact that they can be dissected and discussed in the open air and are therefore much more palatable to the scientific mind than murky Kantian "categories"—understandably led to a concentration on terms and sentences over concepts'.[81] The behaviourism that results reflects Quine's and Davidson's naturalistic attempt to externalize and so naturalize every potentially 'occult' (aka non-natural) entity, while dismissing whatever cannot be reduced to science.[82]

---

[80] See, for instance, Alston, 'Back to the Theory of Appearing'.

[81] Lynch, *Truth in Context*, p. 35.

[82] As Simon Blackburn observes, '[t]his behaviorist (or anti-privacy) agenda was part of the spirit of the age, and many philosophers besides Davidson were ready to swim along' ('Is That All There Is?', *New Republic*, 21 November 2005, p. 41).

The positing of concepts intrinsically related to real properties does not arise from a mere penchant for all things metaphysical; on the contrary, it arises out of our ability to grasp the world, as well as the very origin and baffling rate of learning from infancy through childhood and onwards. It is, as such, a classic case of a transcendental argument that argues to possibility from actuality. As Willard puts it, the phenomenon of experience forces us back to a given of experience:

Either there is going to be at some point a 'taking as' which does not itself represent anything (even what is 'taken')—which certainly sounds like a self-contradiction...or there is going to be an infinite regress of 'takings.' This inclines one to say that unless there are some *natural* signs—things that refer or represent simply because of what they are—there will be no *signs* at all.[83]

Hugo Meynell refers to the genesis of primitive terms as 'an old philosophical puzzle'. The problem is that every definition must presuppose certain terms, and those terms cannot in turn be defined unless further terms are presupposed, and so on.[84] This leaves us with a paradox of learning (or concept acquisition) that was first stated by Plato in Meno's paradox.[85] Plato argues that either you already know that for which you are looking, in which case enquiry is unnecessary, or you do not know that for which you are looking, in which case enquiry is impossible. Socrates' solution is to reinterpret all putative examples of learning as cases of recollecting something already known. Philosophers still wrestle with this problem.[86] The bewildering rate of language acquisition has forced Chomsky to dust off Platonic innatism: 'The child approaches language with an intuitive understanding of such concepts as physical object, human intention, volition, causation, goal, and so on. These constitute a framework for thought and language'.[87] By contrast, the non-foundationalist cannot offer an adequate explanation for our incredibly rich network of concepts/language. If every belief implies other beliefs, then we

---

[83] Dallas Willard, 'Knowledge and Naturalism', in Craig and Moreland (eds.), *Naturalism: A Critical Analysis*, p. 41.

[84] Meynell, *An Introduction to the Philosophy of Bernard Lonergan*, 2nd edn. (Toronto: University of Toronto Press, 1991), 11–12.

[85] Plato, *Meno*, 80d-e; cf. Plato's parable of the cave, *Republic*, 7.514a–516b.

[86] Noam Chomsky, *Language and the Problems of Knowledge*, Managua Lectures (Cambridge, Mass.: MIT Press, 1988), 4.

[87] Ibid. 32. Chomsky rejects Platonic pre-existence.

must have a formidable set of beliefs to have any, a view that is stated in uncompromising form by Wilfred Sellars: '[W]hile the process of acquiring the concept of green may—indeed does—involve a long history of acquiring *piecemeal* habits of responses to various objects in various circumstances, there is an important sense in which one has *no* concept pertaining to the observable properties of physical objects in Space and Time unless one has them all'.[88] On the non-foundationalist account understanding is fated to remain a supreme mystery.

CONCLUSION

Marshall's Trinitarian theology provides a unique contribution to a range of epistemological questions. At the same time, his view suffers from a number of difficulties. His Trinitarian analysis of truth and justification appears contrived at points and faces critical difficulties. Even more critically, his deontological view of justification ought to be rejected, for it stands as the greatest potential source of subordination. Marshall's view of the Trinity as trump is tendentious and threatens to undermine the nature of theology as a free enquiry. Finally, the linguistic thesis faces multiple problems and must be rejected. It is thus ironic that Marshall writes that 'skepticism, especially when it comes to beliefs about a mind-independent spatio-temporal world, actually depends on foundationalism in order to create the conceptual space in which it can arise in the first place'.[89] After this four-chapter survey of major non-foundationalist proposals, it is beginning to appear that our best hope may be a return to the as-yet still unfashionable precincts of foundationalism.

---

[88] Sellars, 'Empiricism and the Philosophy of Mind', in his *Science, Perception and Reality* (London: Routledge & Kegan Paul, 1963), 148.
[89] Marshall, *Trinity and Truth*, p. 276.

9

Moderate Epistemological Foundationalism

> The spiritually robust man does not need to plough through even one volume of Gifford Lectures before he can confidently recite the Apostles' Creed.
>
> Harry Blamires, *The Christian Mind*

> The Creed of Christian faith rests upon knowledge. And where the Creed is uttered and confessed knowledge should be, is meant to be, created. Christian faith is not irrational, not anti-rational, not supra-rational, but rational in the proper sense.
>
> Karl Barth, *Dogmatics in Outline*

A road diverged in the woods. In the last four chapters we followed the non-foundationalist path and have found the road unpromising as a means of passage to our destination. Now it is time to return to the other fork in the road in order to explore the viability of an account of theological justification rooted in Alvin Plantinga's moderate foundationalism. It will be our task in the final two chapters to develop this alternative. We will focus in the present chapter on an initial exposition of Plantinga's foundationalism, which will set the stage for, in the final chapter, a deeper critical evaluation and appropriation of Plantingan foundationalism for theology.

BACK TO THE FOUNDATIONS

In our reconsideration of foundationalism there are at least two good reasons to focus upon Plantinga's epistemology. First, he is widely regarded as one of the foremost Christian philosophers in the world, and has made stellar contributions to a number of areas of philosophy, including philosophy of religion, metaphysics, and epistemology. His work in epistemology, the results of which are summarized in his magisterial three volumes on warrant and proper function, will be our primary focus in this chapter.[1] I believe that Plantinga's model offers the best overall epistemological framework to ground rationality, justification, and knowledge theologically. Second, Plantinga's model is fully congruent with metaphysical realism and the formation of a rigorous and productive theological method which is responsible to the community of faith. In order to make this case we will begin with an exposition of Plantinga's philosophical and theological roots.

Common-sense Realism

H. L. Mencken once confidently observed:

What I believe is mainly what has been established by plausible and impartial evidence, *e.g.*, that the square on the hypotenuse of a right triangle is equal to the squares of the other two sides, that water is composed of oxygen and hydrogen, and that man is a close cousin to the ape. Further than that I do not care to go.[2]

Mencken's comments express the surprisingly common sentiment that one ought to limit one's believings to the assured results of rational intuition and the physical sciences. Though this heir of classical foundationalism remains popular among philosophically challenged scientists and a smattering of village sceptics, it is becoming less fashionable by the year, and for good reason. To begin with, one cannot consistently hold it, for in doing so one would be obliged to discount beliefs derived from sense perception, testimony, and memory, and this would utterly decimate natural science. In addition, this epistemology is hopelessly arbitrary. Am I really obliged to believe that

---

[1] Alvin Plantinga, *Warrant: the Current Debate* (Oxford: Oxford University Press, 1993); *Warrant and Proper Function* (Oxford: Oxford University Press, 1993); *Warranted Christian Belief* (Oxford: Oxford University Press, 2000). See also Alvin Plantinga and Michael Tooley, *Knowledge of God* (Malden, Mass./Oxford: Blackwell, 2008).

[2] Mencken, 'What I Believe', in *H. L. Mencken on Religion*, ed. S. T. Joshi (Amherst, NY: Prometheus, 2002), 38.

water is composed of oxygen and hydrogen but withhold belief in my memory that I had toast and jam for breakfast?

These criticisms of Mencken's views are reminiscent of the common-sense criticisms raised by the great eighteenth-century philosopher Thomas Reid against Locke and Hume's sense-data theory of perception. According to sense-data theory, we indirectly perceive the world by directly perceiving sense data which represent or mirror the world. Since we have privileged access to sense data, they provide an infallible basis for all non-basic beliefs. Reid launched a devastating critique of sense data (or, as he put it, the 'way of ideas'), beginning with the charge that as an account of perception this theory is explanatorily vacuous. Further, he pointed out that the demand that our beliefs must trace to incorrigible foundations leads to hopeless inconsistency given that the proponents of classical foundationalism must trust their deliverances of reason even as they distrust their other deliverances. Such inconsistency can only be explained as an ungrounded prejudice:

The sceptic asks me, Why do you believe the existence of the external object which you perceive? This belief, Sir, is none of my manufacture; it came from the mint of Nature; it bears her image and superscription; and, if it is not right, the fault is not mine: I even took it upon trust, and without suspicion. Reason, says the sceptic, is the only judge of truth, and you ought to throw off every opinion and every belief that is not grounded on reason. Why, Sir, should I believe the faculty of reason more than that of perception; they came both out of the same shop, and were made by the same artist; and if he puts one piece of false ware into my hands, what should hinder him from putting another?[3]

Here Reid ingeniously lampoons the prejudice of Enlightenment rationalism (and classical foundationalism) for arbitrarily elevating reason over other doxastic processes. Since our doxastic faculties share a common origin, it is arbitrary to pick and choose which we will trust. Reid defends an unapologetically particularist approach to epistemology, beginning with the prima facie justification of common sources of belief including testimony, memory, and perception.

---

[3] Thomas Reid, *An Inquiry into the Human Mind on the Principles of Common Sense*, ed. Derek R. Brookes (Edinburgh: Edinburgh University Press, 1997), 168–9 (6.20).

The fact that none of these is infallible is simply an expression of our creaturely limitations; thus, to demand that we must overcome these limitations is to court scepticism. Reid anticipated Davidson's dislike for epistemic intermediaries interspersed between the world and the knowing agent. But instead of developing a non-foundationalist epistemology, he laid the foundations for a distinct alternative to both classical foundationalism and non-foundationalism.[4]

The work of Thomas Reid has been very influential upon Plantinga and other Reformed epistemologists. To begin with, Reid's epistemology is a form of externalism, since he does not require internal access to the doxastic process and the evidential relations that support a properly basic belief. And so, properly basic beliefs may derive from a wide range of sources. Plantinga contrasts the justification of Reid's foundationalism with internalism as follows: 'What counts for the warrant of the belief in question is not my *believing* that I am appeared to in such and such a way, but simply my *being* appeared to in that way'.[5] Plantinga and other Reformed epistemologists recognized that by adding one or two doxastic processes or faculties to the range operative in human belief formation one could ground theological beliefs with the same immediacy that one grounds other properly basic beliefs. But to develop that conception we shall have to consider the theological background that motivated Plantinga to countenance these additional doxastic resources.

What Proper Basicality is ... and isn't

Many critics of foundationalism remain especially critical of the notion of proper basicality and thus will dismiss any attempt to secure a range of foundational beliefs *tout court*. So, it is important that we clarify some common misunderstandings regarding what proper basicality entails. To begin with, proper basicality does not commit one to any particular theory of perception, including the sense-data

[4] For more on Reid see Wolterstorff, *Thomas Reid and the Story of Epistemology* (Cambridge: Cambridge University Press, 2001); cf. Paul Helm, 'Thomas Reid, Common Sense and Calvinism', in Hendrik Hart, Johan Vander Hoeven, and Nicholas Wolterstorff (eds.), *Rationality in the Calvinian Tradition* (Boston, Mass.: University Press of America, 1983), 71–89.

[5] Plantinga, *Warrant and Proper Function*, p. 184.

theory. Indeed, though I am sceptical of some non-foundationalist arguments against proper basicality, there are strong grounds to reject sense-data theory. On this theory perception is explained by positing a directly perceived mental sense-datum that somehow reflects or 'mirrors' external reality. Admittedly there is some initial plausibility in sense-data theories, at least when applied to vision. For instance, since a person can hallucinate seeing an apple (i.e. seeing a mental representation), one could reasonably extrapolate that actually seeing an apple involves a mental datum that mirrors the real apple. However, as we noted in Chapter 4, when we attempt to extend the sense-data explanation to the other senses, like olfaction and proprioception, it becomes clear that it is explanatorily vacuous. But, again, the foundationalist has no particular stake in the debate either way. Indeed, as I noted in Chapter 8, on a direct-realist view one would be advised to cut out the epistemic intermediaries via the theory of appearing.

A second widespread misconception concerns the notion that for a belief to be basic it must be independent of other beliefs in some particularly implausible way. For instance, George Lindbeck's claim that 'it is necessary to have the means for expressing an experience in order to have it'[6] implies that all beliefs, including allegedly properly basic beliefs, are dependent upon other beliefs. But in what way are they dependent? It would seem that non-foundationalist objections to basicality commonly appeal to two arguments, which I call the conceptual-dependence argument (CDA) and the justification-dependence argument (JDA). The CDA proceeds as follows:

(1) If the ability to grasp a belief depends upon concepts that are not a component of that belief, then that belief cannot be properly basic.

(2) The ability to grasp every belief depends upon concepts that are not a component of those beliefs.

(3) Therefore, no belief can be properly basic.

It would appear that Murphy assumes this argument when she objects to the possibility of an epistemic foundation based upon the 'background knowledge' that conditions all our beliefs:

---

[6] Lindbeck, *The Nature of Doctrine: Religion and Theology in a Postliberal Age* (Philadelphia, Pa.: Westminster, 1984), 37.

[B]eliefs that are in fact usable for purposes of justification often turn out to presuppose beliefs that belong to the higher stories. For example, my belief that I am now seeing a blue book depends on background knowledge that I am viewing it under normal lighting conditions.[7]

Elsewhere she critiques the notion of an epistemic foundation as follows: '[I]f we are to hold to the picture of knowledge as a building, we now have to imagine the foundation partially suspended from a top-floor balcony!'.[8] Similarly, Marshall charges that the implausibility with foundationalism is rooted in the notion that an epistemic foundation of experience 'can have determinate content without depending upon having specific beliefs'.[9] In each case the argument appears to move from the conceptual interdependence of all beliefs to the impossibility of epistemic foundations.

While the JDA is typically not distinguished from the CDA, it does represent a distinct line of argument. Given that non-foundationalists widely accept coherence justification, they hold that beliefs are always dependent on other beliefs for their justification. The first step toward non-foundationalism comes in arguing that beliefs are always *in fact* dependent for their justification on other beliefs. From there it is a short step to argue that doxastic dependence is the *only* way beliefs can be justified:

(4) If a belief derives justification from other sources of belief then it cannot be properly basic.

(5) Every belief derives justification from other sources of belief.

(6) Therefore, no belief can be properly basic.

According to the JDA, for a belief to be properly basic it must not derive *any* justification from other beliefs. Thus, if a belief does receive

---

[7] Nancey Murphy, 'Introduction', in Stanley Hauerwas, Nancey Murphy, and Mark Nation (eds.), *Theology Without Foundations: Religious Practice and the Future of Theological Truth* (Nashville, Tenn.: Abingdon, 1994), 11. Cf. Sellars, 'Empiricism and the Philosophy of Mind', in *Science, Perception and Reality* (London: Routledge & Kegan Paul, 1963), 148.

[8] Nancey Murphy, *Beyond Liberalism and Fundamentalism: How Modern and Postmodern Philosophy Set the Theological Agenda*, Rockwell Lecture Series (Valley Forge, Pa.: Trinity, 1996), 91.

[9] Bruce Marshall, *Trinity and Truth* (Cambridge: Cambridge University Press, 2000), 73.

justification from another belief then it cannot be basic, a conclusion which sets one up to accepting a non-foundationalist account of justification. Once we begin to recognize how intimately our beliefs are related to one another, we can see that maintaining an elite group of independent, untainted beliefs is futile,[10] and thus that the notion of an epistemic foundation is chimerical.

If the first premise of the CDA or JDA were true then proper basicality (and foundationalism with it) would have been dealt a deathblow. While this would be an effective rebuttal of classical foundationalism, the concept of proper basicality per se does not oblige us to accept either premise (1) or (4). To see this we need to be clear on what proper basicality is and isn't. Coffman and Howard-Snyder offer the following definition: 'A particular belief of a person is *basic* just in case it is epistemically justified and it owes its justification to something other than her other beliefs or the interrelations of their contents'.[11] Note first that this minimal definition does not require conceptual independence, for, as Prior observes, 'the fact that you have immediate justification to believe P does not entail that no other beliefs are required for you to be able *to form or entertain* the belief that P'.[12] So, the foundationalist may concede that certain concepts are necessary in order to grasp properly basic beliefs. Kant famously made the point with respect to synthetic a priori knowledge.[13]

Even if the CDA fails, the non-foundationalist could still appeal to the JDA. Indeed, Coffman and Howard-Snyder's claim that a person's basic belief 'owes its justification to something other than her other beliefs' initially appears vulnerable to this argument. If a properly

---

[10] While the CDA and JDA charge that no belief could be properly basic, one could also target foundationalism with a weaker argument according to which while *some* beliefs may be concept or justification independent, nonetheless such beliefs are too few to support our noetic structure.

[11] E. J. Coffman and D. Howard-Snyder, 'Three Arguments Against Foundationalism: Arbitrariness, Epistemic Regress, and Existential Support', *Canadian Journal of Philosophy*, 36/4 (2006), 535.

[12] Prior, cited in Coffman and Howard-Snyder, 'Three Arguments Against Foundationalism', p. 560 n. 21.

[13] Immanuel Kant, *Critique of Pure Reason*, Introd. 1.1. Similarly, as Paul Boghossian and Christopher Peacocke observe, when we grasp the basic theorems of logic '[p]erception of the written proof gives access to that entitlement [to believe it is true], but is not itself part of that entitlement' (introd. to Boghossian and Peacocke (eds.), *New Essays on the A Priori* (Oxford: Clarendon, 2000), 2).

basic belief is that which is epistemically justified according to something other than beliefs, and beliefs always derive some justification from other beliefs, then no belief can be properly basic. But this is based on a misunderstanding, for the claim is not actually that a belief cannot derive *any* justification from other beliefs, but rather that a properly basic belief does not *require* the justification of any other belief in order to be justified. This does not preclude the possibility that every basic belief is in fact *overdetermined* in its justification.[14] As William Alston puts it,

[t]o say that a belief is immediately justified is just to say that there are conditions *sufficient* for its justification that do not involve any other justified beliefs of that believer. This condition could be satisfied even if the believer has other justified beliefs that could serve as grounds. Overdetermination is an epistemic as well as a causal phenomenon. What fits a belief to serve as a foundation is simply that it doesn't *need* other justified beliefs in order to be justified in itself.[15]

Take my belief that I ate toast for breakfast. While it derives its essential, basic justification from my memory that I ate toast for breakfast, it receives further justification from its coherence with my other beliefs, including my perception of sodden toast crumbs in my teeth, a smear of jam on my shirt, and my wife's testimony that I had toast for breakfast.[16] But these additional sources of justification do not undermine the properly basic status of the memory.

Reformed Faith as Knowledge

If it is possible to have properly basic beliefs, might theological beliefs be among them? While Reid's common-sense realism provides the main philosophical inspiration for Plantinga's epistemology, Reformed theology provides the theological framework. Although a consideration of the full Reformed tradition on faith and

---

[14] Coffman and Howard-Snyder, 'Three Arguments Against Foundationalism', pp. 538–9.

[15] Cited ibid. 540 n.

[16] For further discussion see William Alston, 'What's Wrong with Immediate Knowledge?', in *Epistemic Justification: Essays in the Theory of Knowledge* (Ithaca, NY: Cornell University Press, 1989), 72–7.

knowledge, including its Platonic and Augustinian roots, would be both important and fruitful for our understanding of Plantinga,[17] space limits us to a discussion of the unique Reformed assessment of the epistemic status of faith. The Reformed view of faith shares with other major views (e.g. Thomist, Lutheran) both a propositional object and a stance of trust grounded in the one who testifies to the truth (i.e. Christ in the Spirit).[18] As such, while the Reformed view shares similarities with the belief model, it most closely approximates the personal-relationship model defended in Chapter 3.

Plantinga affirms both the personal and propositional dimensions of faith. Regarding the personal dimension he writes: 'I wholeheartedly reject the idea that our chief end is to collect a pocket full of propositions about God. Of course not; our chief end is to glorify God—i.e., perceive and celebrate and delight in His marvelous beauty and glory—and enjoy Him forever'.[19] At the same time, he recognizes that propositions are important; indeed, the most distinctive aspect of the Reformed view of faith is arguably its emphasis upon the epistemic status of faith as cognitive (propositional) knowledge.[20] As Louis Berkhof succinctly put it, '[t]he knowledge of faith should not be regarded as less certain than other knowledge'.[21] Indeed, because of the divine origin of faith, it stands as a particularly strong if not unique source of knowledge. Colin Gunton claims that faith is a knowledge which 'can...be distinguished from many other forms of knowledge as revealed knowledge, that is to say, *knowledge that is guaranteed to—rather than in—the knower because it is given by God*'.[22] While unique, the knowledge of faith is not a *possession* of the knower in the same way as other sources of knowledge. As Gunton

---

[17] See Dewey J. Hoitenga, Jr., *Faith and Reason From Plato to Plantinga: An Introduction to Reformed Epistemology* (Albany, NY: SUNY Press, 1991).

[18] For a lucid summary of Reformed, Thomist, and Lutheran approaches to faith see William Lad Sessions, *The Concept of Faith: A Philosophical Investigation* (Ithaca, NY/London: Cornell University Press, 1994), 160–92.

[19] Alvin Plantinga, 'On Heresy, Mind, and Truth', *Faith and Philosophy*, 16/2 (1999), 192.

[20] See, for instance, Heinrich Heppe, *Reformed Dogmatics*, ed. Ernst Bizer, trans. G. T. Thomson, rev. edn. (London: 1861; repr. London: Wakeman, n.d.), 530–2.

[21] Berkhof, *Systematic Theology* (Edinburgh: Banner of Truth Trust, 1958), 504.

[22] Gunton, 'I Know that My Redeemer Lives', in *Intellect and Action: Elucidations on Christian Theology and the Life of Faith* (Edinburgh: T& T Clark, 2000), 51; emphasis added.

puts it, '[f]aith is a kind of personal knowledge which by virtue of the fact that it is given—passively constituted—*remains outside the control of its* recipient'.[23] Thus, while faith is knowledge, a status it bears because of its divine origin, it is also a type of knowledge in which the full grounds that support the truth of that belief may remain *external* to the knower (e.g. as grounded in the testifier).

In contrast to the Reformed focus on faith as knowledge, Lutheran theologians have typically emphasized the paradoxical nature of faith while downplaying its cognitive claims. For instance, Wolfhart Pannenberg denies that faith is knowledge because, as he sees it, every claim to knowledge must be public and objective and in principle accessible to all.[24] To take one example, on this view knowledge of Jesus' resurrection depends on public, historical evidence: 'Whether or not a particular event happened two thousand years ago is not made certain by faith but only by historical research, to the extent that certainty can be attained at all about questions of this kind'.[25] Pannenberg thus eschews what he perceives to be subjectivist appeals to private sources of belief, instead challenging Christians to measure up to the public facts just like everybody else—and that means reserving true knowledge for the eschaton.[26] As we will see, Plantinga's epistemology supports the Reformed approach to faith.

PROPER BASICALITY AND PROPER FUNCTION

For our purposes, we can roughly divide the development of Plantinga's views on the epistemic status of Christian belief into two stages.

[23] Gunton, 'I Know that My Redeemer Lives', p. 55; emphasis added.

[24] Pannenberg, *Systematic Theology*, i, trans. Geoffrey W. Bromiley (Grand Rapids, Mich.: Eerdmans, 1991), 51–2.

[25] Pannenberg, *Jesus: God and Man*, trans. Lewis L. Wilkins and Duane A. Priebe (London: SCM, 1968), 99.

[26] F. LeRon Shults argues that Pannenberg is not a classical foundationalist, since for Pannenberg fundamental theology serves not a *prolegomenal* justifying role, but rather a *synchronic* justifying role with systematic theology (see *The Postfoundationalist Task of Theology: Wolfhart Pannenberg and the New Theological Rationality* (Grand Rapids, Mich.: Eerdmans, 1999)). It seems to me that Pannenberg's biggest problem is not his view of noetic structure but rather his commitment to internalism and epistemic deontology.

The period from 1967 to 1988 marks his movement to externalism,[27] while that from 1988 to 2000 illustrates the development of his externalism in the terms of proper function. We will consider these stages in turn.

Externalist Foundationalism and Proper Basicality

In *God and Other Minds*, his first significant foray into epistemology,[28] Plantinga defends Christian belief by arguing that arguments for the existence of God are no better or worse than arguments for the existence of other minds. Since we accept belief in other minds as rational, so should we accept belief in God. Plantinga built on this indirect defence of the proper basicality of Christian belief in a series of papers,[29] culminating in the seminal 1983 essay 'Reason and Belief in God'.[30] In this essay Plantinga interprets the Reformed objection to natural theology as involving a rejection of the notion that belief in God is not itself properly basic,[31] and he thus defends the parity between belief in God and other properly basic beliefs.[32] There are two predictable objections to the analogy. First, while we understand the workings of other cognitive deliverances such as sense perception, we do not have a similar understanding of what cognitive mechanism produces belief in God. Second, while the deliverances of sense

[27] See Alvin Plantinga, 'Justification and Theism', *Faith and Philosophy*, 4/4 (1987), 403–26, and 'Positive Epistemic Status and Proper Function', in James Tomberlin (ed.), *Philosophical Perspectives, ii. Epistemology*, (Atascadero, Calif.: Ridgeview, 1988), 1–50.

[28] Alvin Plantinga, *God and Other Minds: A Study of the Rational Justification of Belief in God* (Ithaca, NY: Cornell University Press, 1967).

[29] For instance, 'Is Belief in God Rational?', in C. F. Delaney (ed.), *Rationality and Religious Belief* (Notre Dame, Ind.: University of Notre Dame Press, 1979), 7–27; 'Is Belief in God Properly Basic?', *Noûs*, 15/1 (1981), 4–51.

[30] Alvin Plantinga, 'Reason and Belief in God', in Alvin Plantinga and Nicholas Wolterstorff (eds.), *Faith and Rationality: Reason and Belief in God* (Notre Dame, Ind.: University of Notre Dame: 1983), 16–93.

[31] Although 'Reason and Belief in God' establishes that belief in God *simpliciter* (that is, belief that God exists) may be properly basic, Plantinga believes belief in God is typically a second-order (inferential) belief arising from first-order basic beliefs *about* God, such as that 'God was in Jesus Christ reconciling the world to himself'.

[32] See Terence Penelhum, *God and Skepticism: A Study in Skepticism and Fideism* (Dordrecht: Reidel, 1983), ch. 7.

perception, memory, testimony, and so on arise from universally shared belief-forming faculties, belief in God seems to arise from private and subjective sources.

Plantinga takes up the first challenge by appealing to Calvin's doctrine that human beings possess a cognitive faculty called the *sensus divinitatis* which, when functioning properly, naturally produces beliefs about God upon the occurrence of trigger experiences (e.g. seeing a beautiful sunset). Thus, just as sense perception produces visual and tactual beliefs, so we have a doxastic faculty that produces beliefs about God. But why then do not *all* people have beliefs about God? Plantinga's response is that the *sensus* has been damaged by sin: 'Were it not for the existence of sin in the world, human beings would believe in God to the same degree and with the same natural spontaneity that we believe in the existence of other persons, an external world, or the past'.[33] But when the *sensus* is operating properly (i.e. when its function is restored at regeneration), a person will again begin to form a variety of properly basic beliefs about God. As a result, one acquires properly basic beliefs in God as effortlessly as one acquires sense-perceptive beliefs, leaving the sceptic rather than the Christian as the one who is cognitively malfunctioning.

Not surprisingly, Plantinga's argument has attracted a range of criticism. Some critics have raised the Great Pumpkin *reductio ad absurdum*, which charges that Plantinga's argument can be extended to justify clearly absurd beliefs. For instance, one could posit a pumpkin sense which produces justified beliefs that the Great Pumpkin comes to selected pumpkin patches every Halloween bearing gifts;[34] given that this belief is ad hoc and utterly implausible, we should reject both the pumpkin sense and the *sensus divinitatis*. Three points can be made to defuse this objection. To begin with, having rejected the classical foundationalist's notion of universal reason, Plantinga

[33] Plantinga, 'Reason and Belief in God', p. 66. William Alston suggests that the lack of universal experience of God could be explained by cognitive limitations: 'We are familiar with many areas in which only a small percentage of the population has developed the perceptual sensitivity to certain features of the world—for example, the distinctive qualities of wines and the inner voices of a complex orchestral performance' (*Perceiving God: The Epistemology of Religious Experience* (Ithaca, NY: Cornell University Press, 1991), 169).

[34] Plantinga, 'Reason and Belief in God', pp. 74–8. See also Michael Martin, *The Case Against Christianity* (Philadelphia, Pa.: Temple University Press, 1991), 29–32.

notes that people render judgements of rationality *relative* to their world-view. It would be irrational for a fourteenth-century European villager to embrace heliocentrism, and yet it is perfectly rational for us to do so.[35] This suggests that when it comes to assessing the rationality of a belief and the criteria of proper basicality one cannot speak apart from a particular context that is informed by one's background knowledge and beliefs. As Plantinga puts it, criteria 'should not be presented *ex cathedra* but argued to and tested by a relevant set of examples'.[36] According to Plantinga, Christians make those assessments of rationality, justification, and knowledge *relative to the Christian community*. But does that mean that Plantinga must admit the rationality of belief in the Great Pumpkin? Perhaps in *theory* he might have to concede this, but the point is somewhat academic given that there is no Great Pumpkin doxastic community and thus no genuine followers of this exalted gourd. Nor is there likely to be such a community, since the Great Pumpkin is widely recognized to be a creation of cartoonist Charles Schultz.

But even if a cult of the Great Pumpkin is not likely to arise, there are ample concrete examples of disturbing doxastic communities that could in principle avail themselves of Plantinga's work. Take, for instance, the Heaven's Gate cult, the members of which committed mass suicide in 1996 based on the word of their leader—'Do'—that this action would ensure their resurrection on a spaceship trailing the Hale Bop comet. Could their beliefs be rational? If reason is relativized (at least in part) to one's world-view, then doesn't Plantinga have to concede that Heaven's Gate could be internally rational? In fact, Plantinga could say that *from the Christian point of view* atheists, devotees of the Great Pumpkin, members of Heaven's Gate, and tenured atheistic professors are all malfunctioning. Whether or not they are rational or hold justified beliefs relative to their picture of the world does nothing to the *Christian* assessment of their beliefs. One could simply say that this is the cost of giving up on the Enlightenment project.

---

[35] Compare Wolterstorff's historically situated rationality, as discussed in Andrew Sloane, *On Being a Christian in the Academy: Nicholas Wolterstorff and the Practice of Christian Scholarship* (Carlisle: Paternoster, 2003), 97–110.

[36] Plantinga, 'Reason and Belief in God', p. 77.

It may be that the real problem is not that widely variant sets of beliefs might be prima facie rational, but rather that Plantinga's epistemology secures such rationality as absolute. But that raises the question: Has Plantinga in fact rendered beliefs impregnable to external rational critique? In point of fact, Plantinga does *not* concede this consequence, for he accepts that there still are rational principles (e.g. coherence) that transcend particular systems of belief and function as regulative criteria upon them all. Thus, one's justification is prima facie, and it could be undermined by a defeater.[37] Just as counter-evidence to my belief that I am seeing a pink unicorn may force me to conclude that I am hallucinating, so new evidence could provide a *defeater* for Christian belief (presumably there were many defeaters for Heaven's Gate devotees). Until that defeater could itself be defeated, it would be irrational to accept Christian belief. It may be internally irrational for an atheist (but not a Christian) to accept the occurrence of a genuine miracle. But the evidence could become such that the atheist can no longer plausibly explain the event in naturalistic terms and thus is forced to accept miracles (and by implication reject atheism).

Externalism and Theistic Proper Function

Plantinga provides a book-length summary of the current debates over justification in *Warrant: The Current Debate*. In light of the fact that 'justification' bears deontological and internalist associations, he opts for the neutral term 'warrant'. In the book Plantinga lays the foundation for his theory of warrant by arguing that all other internalist and externalist accounts of warrant (e.g. reliabilism, truth tracking) are beset by a common flaw. The problem in each case is that the theory's stipulated criteria could obtain, and yet due to cognitive malfunction the person could still fail to have warrant. Plantinga uses these counter-examples to argue that proper function is a necessary component of warrant. He formalizes this criterion in *Warrant and Proper Function* as follows:

[37] So, Michael Martin is simply mistaken when he claims that 'Plantinga's foundationalism is radically relativistic and puts any belief beyond rational appraisal once it is declared basic' (*The Case Against Christianity*, p. 30).

A belief B has warrant for S if and only if the relevant segments (the segments involved in the production of B) are functioning properly in a cognitive environment sufficiently similar to that for which S's faculties are designed; and the modules of the design plan governing the production of B are (1) aimed at truth, and (2) such that there is a high objective probability that a belief formed in accordance with those modules (in that sort of cognitive environment) is true; and the more firmly S believes B the more warrant B has for S.[38]

Note first that while warrant may be strengthened by evidence, evidence has no intrinsic or necessary role in providing warrant or knowledge. Neither, for that matter, do epistemic obligations; the criteria to which Plantinga appeals do not directly depend upon the epistemic dutifulness or excellence of the individual.

After positing proper function as the missing criterion of knowledge, Plantinga spends the remaining pages of *Warrant and Proper Function* applying the theory to the main sources of knowledge in a way reminiscent of Thomas Reid. In order to illustrate we can consider a few examples, beginning with sensory perception. Reid's explanation of sensory knowledge is admirably simple: we have been *created* by divine manufacture such that sense experience provides the means by which we directly perceive the world. Thus, belief in an external, spatially extended world of matter is not a naive pre-philosophical prejudice but a fully warranted belief. Indeed, it is difficult to conceive of a more deeply entrenched (and justified) deliverance of our doxastic processes than belief in an external world. Reid thus argued that the sceptic of the external world faces an impossible task as he struggles against the deliverances of his own design:

It would be agreeable to fly to the moon, and to make a visit to Jupiter and Saturn; but when I know that Nature has bound me down by the law of gravitation to this planet which I inhabit, I rest contented, and quietly suffer myself to be carried along in its orbit. My belief is carried along by perception, as irresistibly as my body by the earth. And the greatest sceptic will find himself to be in the same condition. He may struggle hard to disbelieve the information of his senses, as a man does to swim against a torrent; but, ah! it is in vain. It is in vain that he strains every nerve, and

[38] Plantinga, *Warrant and Proper Function*, p. 19.

wrestles with nature, and with every object that strikes upon his senses. For after all, when his strength is spent in the fruitless attempt, he will be carried down the torrent with the common herd of believers.[39]

Plantinga likewise recognizes the means by which we are designed to form beliefs about the natural world and sees this as adequate grounds to have knowledge of the world.

Next, consider our knowledge of other minds. Plantinga attacks Hume's claim that we cannot know we are persons rather than only series of psychological states, not by producing a defeater but rather by pointing out that if we have been designed to form belief in a self and we are substantial selves, then we can know that we are.[40] As for our knowledge of the existence of *other* persons, Plantinga rejects analogical arguments and Wittgensteinian approaches by countering that both fail to recognize the normativity of our regular modes of cognitive function:

[I]t is the person who believes in others only on the basis of analogical arguments (and believes with a strength that matches the strength of those arguments) who is weird or nonstandard. It is part of the human design plan, in fact, to make such ascriptions with very considerable firmness[41]

As these examples suggest, a range of seemingly interminable philosophical dilemmas receive rather straightforward resolutions through Plantinga's epistemology.

Plantinga could rest content with the claim that the *Christian* conception of rationality invokes a designer of our cognitive faculties. However, he goes on to develop a negative apologetic by noting that explaining our design by invoking a finite, created designer (e.g. a super alien intelligence) would simply put the question back to the design of that designer. How do we know that our designer has truth-conducive cognitive faculties that could serve as the ground for our truth-conducive faculties? Given the threat of an infinite regress, we require a necessarily existent and truth-conducive mind; that is, God. Plantinga thus concludes that 'naturalism in epistemology can

[39] Reid, *Inquiry*, p. 169 (6.20).
[40] Plantinga is not claiming that belief in the unity of personhood is *inferred* from the psychological continuity of states, but rather that the latter may be the *occasion* for forming beliefs in the former.
[41] Plantinga, *Warrant and Proper Function*, p. 75.

flourish only in the context of supernaturalism in metaphysics'.[42] And so the only guard against scepticism is found in the thesis that our cognitive faculties are truly designed; a mere *façon de parler* is simply of no use.[43]

Intrinsic Signs and Illumination

In Chapter 8 we adumbrated one of the central questions concerning concept acquisition. At this point we can return to this discussion in the light of proper-function analysis. Non-foundationalist theories of concept acquisition and learning, including causal-historical processes, social location, and conceptual-role semantics, fail to fix awareness of the content internally, leading to the absurd conclusion that we are not aware of the content of our own thoughts.[44] In contrast, the foundationalist grounds understanding in an intrinsic link between the world (properties) and mind (concepts), so that simple perception of the properties of concrete particulars naturally gives rise to mental concepts. So, non-foundationalist objections that foundationalism collapses into an infinite regress are misguided,[45] and are also vulnerable to a *tu quoque*, since the non-foundationalist lacks an adequate account of learning.[46]

---

[42] *Warrant and Proper Function* 194.

[43] Plantinga argues that metaphysical naturalism coupled with evolution entails that the chances that our cognitive faculties produce *true* beliefs as opposed to merely adaptive beliefs is low or inscrutable, leading to scepticism regarding all our beliefs. And since one of those beliefs is that our beliefs are formed by way of naturalistic evolution, the position is ultimately self-referentially incoherent. For more on this argument see James Beilby (ed.), *Naturalism Defeated? Essays on Plantinga's Evolutionary Argument Against Naturalism* (Ithaca, NY: Cornell University Press, 2002). Interestingly, this argument is anticipated in C. S. Lewis, *Miracles: A Preliminary Study* (New York: Macmillan, 1947), ch. 3. Lewis's theistic argument from reason has recently been taken up by Victor Reppert in *C. S. Lewis's Dangerous Idea* (Downers Grove, Ill.: InterVarsity, 2003).

[44] BonJour, *In Defense of Pure Reason* (Cambridge: Cambridge University Press, 1998), 170–80.

[45] F. LeRon Shults writes: 'We need rules to help us get to the right rules. And then we need rules to get at those rules, *ad infinitum*' (*The Postfoundationalist Task of Theology*, p. 33).

[46] See Nicholas Rescher, *Paradoxes: Their Roots, Range, and Resolution* (Chicago/LaSalle, Ill.: Open Court, 2001), 87.

But how exactly do we come to grasp universals? While Plato believed that universals act causally upon our minds, philosophers today believe that universals are causally inert—in which case the problem of understanding returns *perforce*. As atheist philosopher Colin McGinn recognizes, the puzzle of understanding appears to contradict the naturalist's austere metaphysics: 'Let us candidly admit that a priori knowledge confutes dogmatic naturalism: it does indeed call for the attribution of non-natural mental faculties, capable of reaching out beyond space and the causal order. As divine revelation acquaints us with God, so the abstract world is revealed to us by miraculous methods'.[47] But how is the abstract world revealed to our understanding? At this point we can consider a proper-function response informed by the ancient thesis of divine illumination according to which the divine light of Christ (John 1: 9) illuminates our minds to empower understanding. The illumination thesis has been interpreted as referring to either a cognitive faculty specially designed by God that acts *within* human rational intuition or an external doxastic process which concurs with our cognitive faculties. Aristotle's *De Anima*, probably the first treatment of philosophical psychology in western philosophy, suggests both possibilities. In order to explain how we move from experiencing particular substances to intuiting universals, Aristotle distinguishes between two intellects in the rational soul, termed by later commentators the 'passive intellect' and the 'agent intellect'. The passive intellect acts as a receptacle which receives raw sensory input from which the agent intellect abstracts the ideas of intellection (e.g. universal forms) that enable understanding.

Unfortunately, Aristotle was ambiguous in his discussion of the nature of the agent intellect (*De Anima*, 3.5), resulting in two contradictory schools of interpretation. Themistius (*c*.317–*c*.388) argued that both the passive and agent intellects are powers of the soul. So, he interpreted rational intuition as a cognitive faculty possessed by the individual. Thomas Aquinas adopted this interpretation, and thus rejected the need for a cognitive process external to the functioning of the agent that would serve to illuminate the intellect and thus

---

[47] Colin McGinn, *Problems in Philosophy: The Limits of Inquiry* (Oxford: Blackwell, 1993), 98.

facilitate understanding of certain mundane truths that would otherwise remain unknowable.[48] Aquinas understood the agent intellect
to be a cognitive power bestowed by the creator. Anthony Kenny
describes Aquinas' distinction between the agent and passive (or
receptive) intellects: 'If the function of the receptive intellect is as it
were to provide room for thoughts, the function of the agent intellect
is to provide furniture for that room, that is to create objects of
thought'.[49] So, non-natural cognitive processes are not required to
supplement our cognition. Human beings are able to grasp universals
and the logical relations between things in accord with our divine
design.[50]

Alexander of Aphrodisias (*fl.* AD 200) defended the second interpretation, in which the agent intellect is taken to be an external
entity which acts upon the individual to facilitate understanding. This
interpretation provided the rudiments of the theory of divine illumination that was powerfully defended by Augustine when he combined
innatism with external illumination. For Augustine, we begin with
the turn inward to the 'soul that knows itself'. This brings us to
his concept of 'memory', which encompasses what we distinguish
as memory, the unconscious, and self-awareness. In the *Confessions*
Augustine introspects and marvels at the storehouse of experiences
and images he is able to recall at will, including the ability to discern
the truth of words and phrases that he has not encountered through
sense perception:

[T]he ideas signified by those sounds I have not touched by sense-perception,
nor have I seen them independently of my mind. I hid in my memory not
their images but the realities. How they came to me let them explain if
they can. I run through all the entrance doors of my body but do not find
one by which they have entered in. My eyes say: 'If they are coloured, we
have informed you about them.' My ears say: 'If they made any sound, we
were responsible for telling you.' My nostrils say: 'If they gave off any odour,
they passed our way.' The sense of taste also says: 'If they are tasteless, do not

---

[48] Aquinas both used Themistus' commentary on *De anima* and would have been
influenced by this tradition of interpretation through the work of Averroës (see H. J.
Blumenthal, *Aristotle and Neoplatonism in Late Antiquity: Interpretations of* De Anima
(London: Duckworth, 1996), 174).

[49] Kenny, *Aquinas on Mind* (London/New York: Routledge, 1993), 43.

[50] Thomas Aquinas, *The Compendium of Theology*, trans. Cyril Vollert (London:
Herder, 1947), 72–3 (79).

ask me.' Touch says: 'If the object is not physical, I have no contact with it, and if I have no contact, I have no information to give on the subject.' Then how did these matters enter my memory? I do not know how.[51]

Having exhausted every sensible entry point, Augustine reasons along the Platonic lines of innate recollection: 'The answer must be that they were already in the memory'.[52] Augustine adds that 'the memory contains the innumerable principles and laws of numbers and dimensions. None of them has been impressed on memory through any bodily sense-perception'.[53] However, the innate nature of these truths can only be realized in the light of God; hence, we know these truths from within only because of light from without: '[W]hat I know of myself I know because you grant me light'.[54] Our minds are as fields which have been seeded but await the warming rays of the divine light in which understanding may blossom. The knowledge that we rationally intuit is mediated to the soul by the illumination of God in correspondence with the divine ideas:

I did not know that the soul needs to be enlightened by light from outside itself, so that it can participate in truth, because it is not itself the nature of truth. You will light my lamp, O Lord. My God you will lighten my darkness (Ps. 17: 29), and of your fullness we have all received (John 1: 16). You are the true light who illuminates every man coming into this world (John 1: 9), because in you there is no change nor shadow caused by turning (Jas. 1: 17).[55]

Thus, Aquinas and Augustine provide us with two intriguing models by which proper function could be extended to explain the origin of understanding.

Warranted Christian Belief

Dutch Reformed theologians have typically been sceptical of any attempt to provide grounds or reasons for faith through either

---

[51] Augustine, *Confessions*, trans. Henry Chadwick (Oxford: Oxford University Press, 1991), 188–9 (10.10).

[52] Ibid. 189 (10.10).   [53] Ibid. p.190 (10.12).   [54] Ibid. 182 (10.5).

[55] Augustine, *Confessions*, p. 68 (4.15). For further discussion see Robert Adams, 'Divine Necessity', in his *The Virtue of Faith: And Other Essays in Philosophical Theology* (New York: Oxford University Press, 1987), 217–18.

rationalist natural theology or a pre-conceptual divine encounter.[56] Plantinga's argument for the proper basicality of Christian belief comes out of this tradition.[57] Reformed theologians point out that if faith is a secure knowledge, then there is no requirement for the Christian to seek evidential grounds for faith. Since the light of God's revelation has been made accessible to all, if one rejects faith it is not due to lack of evidence, but rather to a sinful and rebellious will. Take the case of Bertrand Russell, who, as John Searle recounts, was asked at an Oxford dinner how he would explain his disbelief in God in a posthumous divine encounter. To the delight of his dinner companions, Russell gave his cool rebuttal: 'Not enough evidence'.[58] But from a Christian perspective Russell's failure to believe arises *not* from epistemic dutifulness, but rather sinful rebellion (e.g. Rom. 2: 21–3). And it is simply misguided to demand arguments when the problem concerns the will. Plantinga does not follow the standard Reformed rejection of theistic arguments;[59] indeed, he developed a valid form of the ontological argument.[60] But he does believe that natural theology is of limited persuasive power: 'I don't know of an argument for Christian belief that seems very likely to convince one who doesn't already accept its conclusion'.[61] This statement does not represent a *lack of interest* in Christian truth, but rather a Reformed

[56] See, for instance, Abraham Kuyper, *Calvinism* (Grand Rapids, Mich.: Eerdmans, 1931); Herman Bavinck, *The Doctrine of God*, trans. William Hendricksen (Grand Rapids, Mich.: Eerdmans, 1951), 64–80. Other Reformed theologians share this suspicion of subordinationism. See, for instance, Karl Barth, *Church Dogmatics*, i. *The Doctrine of the Word of God*, trans. G. W. Bromiley, ed. G. W. Bromiley and T. F. Torrance (Edinburgh: T& T Clark, 1975), ii. I. 5.

[57] See Alvin Plantinga, 'The Reformed Objection to Natural Theology', *Proceedings of the American Catholic Philosophical Association*, 54 (1980), 49–63.

[58] John Searle, *Mind, Language and Society: Philosophy in the Real World* (London: Weidenfeld & Nicholson, 1999), 36–7.

[59] For a discussion of Plantinga's complex relationship to apologetics see Mascord, *Alvin Plantinga and Christian Apologetics*.

[60] In the case of his ontological argument, Plantinga has demonstrated that if it is *possible* for God to exist then God *must* exist; what he cannot establish is that it is *possible* for God to exist (see *The Nature of Necessity* (Oxford: Clarendon, 1974), ch. 10).

[61] Plantinga, *Warranted Christian Belief*, p. 201. This seems unduly sceptical. Take, for instance, the ongoing dialogue Gregory Boyd had with his father that finally led to the latter's conversion (Gregory A. Boyd and Edward K. Boyd, *Letters From a Skeptic: A Son Wrestles with his Father's Questions about Christianity* (Colorado Springs, Col.: Chariot Victor, 1994)).

view of the fall, no doubt reinforced by the scepticism of many of his peers. Hence, while Plantinga does not believe Christianity can be *shown* to be true, he remains convinced that, if it is true, then it can be *known* to be true.[62]

For all his labours, Plantinga has to this point only defended belief in God *simpliciter*. No doubt if this marked the limits of his proposal, the theologian would find it a rather meagre return on investment. However, Plantinga's work has thus far prepared the way for a full account of Christian justification and knowledge, a task to which he turns in *Warranted Christian Belief*.[63] Here Plantinga argues that modern critics of Christian belief tend to posit *de jure* objections that assert that there is something unjustified, irrational, or epistemically derelict about Christian belief, *irrespective of whether that belief is true*. It is a strategic move, for if Christianity is deemed irrational, then the critic need never bother to attack the *truth* of Christian belief (the de facto objection). (By the same token, we need not bother demonstrating the non-existence of Santa Claus if it is assumed that no rational adult would believe in the jolly old fellow.) Plantinga argues that the central *de jure* objection is captured in the Freud and Marx (F&M) complaint according to which Christian belief is either produced by wish-fulfilment (Freud) or malfunctioning cognitive faculties (Marx). Plantinga admits that if either analysis is correct, Christian belief will probably have a very low level of warrant, certainly insufficient for knowledge (even if it is true). But neither Freud nor Marx provides reasons to think that Christian belief is false or that their interpretation of it is correct. Thus, far from demonstrating that Christianity is irrational, these *de jure* objections assume that Christianity is false and then infer its irrationality. Plantinga summarizes the extent to which judgements of rationality and warrant are relative to one's background beliefs or world-view:

What you properly take to be rational, at least in the sense of warranted, depends on what sort of metaphysical and religious stance you adopt. It

[62] This basic position was defended by William Lane Craig in *Apologetics: An Introduction* (Chicago, Ill.: Moody, 1984), 18–25.

[63] For a critique of Plantinga's early focus on theistic belief see William Abraham, 'The Epistemological Significance of the Inner Witness of the Holy Spirit', *Faith and Philosophy*, 7/4 (1990), 434–50. Plantinga responds to Abraham in *Warranted Christian Belief*, p. 200.

depends on what kind of beings you think human beings are, what sorts of beliefs you think their noetic faculties will produce when they are functioning properly, and which of their faculties or cognitive mechanisms are aimed at the truth. Your view as to what sort of creature a human being is will determine or at any rate heavily influence your views as to whether theistic belief is warranted or not warranted, rational or irrational for human beings. And so the dispute as to whether theistic belief is rational (warranted) can't be settled just by attending to epistemological considerations; it is at bottom not merely an epistemological dispute, but an ontological or theological dispute.[64]

In effect, the masters of suspicion have long dominated the discussion by making judgements of Christian belief relative to their presuppositions. The challenge for Christians is to develop an account of rationality and warrant relative to their beliefs.

At this point Plantinga turns to address how Christian belief could be known, by developing the Aquinas/Calvin (henceforth A/C) model: a two-stage doxastic process which he claims is epistemically possible, faces no objections, and is close to the truth if Christianity is true. Plantinga begins with the *sensus*, which he argues is functioning properly in accord with the design plan when it provides properly basic beliefs about God. While Plantinga believes that our ability to have knowledge of God is part of our created cognitive abilities, an additional external doxastic process is also important, which Plantinga refers to as the internal instigation of the Holy Spirit (IIHS). The IIHS is a doxastic process that is designed to produce beliefs about God that could not otherwise be gained given our fallen noetic faculties.[65] That is, the IIHS is necessary to overcome the postlapsarian malfunctioning of the *sensus*.

At this point the extended A/C model moves beyond minimal knowledge of God to fully robust knowledge of Christian revelation. As such, it overcomes the effect of sin on affective and cognitive function by producing personal faith that is both revealed to our minds and sealed in our hearts. This Spirit-led process produces not only belief that God exists but also belief in the '[g]reat things of the gospel', including the Trinity, incarnation, Christ's resurrection, atonement, forgiveness of sins, salvation, regeneration, and eternal

---

[64] Plantinga, *Warranted Christian Belief*, p. 190.   [65] Ibid. p. 180.

life.[66] According to Plantinga, the extended A/C model consists of a three-tiered cognitive process that (typically) begins with the reading of Scripture, whereupon the Spirit enables us to know the truth of what is taught therein:

We read Scripture, or something presenting scriptural teaching, or hear the gospel preached, or are told of it by parents, or encounter a scriptural teaching as the conclusion of an argument (or conceivably even as an object of ridicule), or in some other way encounter a proclamation of the Word. What is said simply seems right; it seems compelling; one finds oneself saying, 'Yes, that's right, that's the truth of the matter; this is indeed the word of the Lord.'[67]

In this way the Holy Spirit remedies the cognitive damage of the fall, making it 'the immediate cause of belief',[68] so that we may grasp the great things of the gospel.[69] The faith that results is both a supernatural gift and knowledge because it meets Plantinga's criteria of proper function.[70]

In so far as the beliefs about Scripture are properly basic, they are in a sense *self-authenticating*, and this speaks to worries of fideism. As Plantinga puts it, '[y]ou might as well claim that a memory belief, or the belief that $3 + 1 = 4$ is a leap in the dark. What makes something a leap in the dark is that the leaper doesn't know and has no firm beliefs about what is out there in the dark'.[71] Thus, faith is not the result of proofs and evidences or the esoteric derivation of precognitive experience, but rather is 'a *gift*, not in the way a glorious autumn day is a gift, but a special gift, one that wouldn't come to us in the ordinary run of things, one that requires supernatural and extraordinary activity on the part of God'.[72]

ON THE IDEA OF *CHRISTIAN* EPISTEMOLOGY

Ever since Karl Barth directed a red-faced *Nein!* in Emil Brunner's direction an unfortunate number of theologians have not been on

---

[66] By contrast, our knowledge of what we might call the 'lesser things of the gospel' (e.g. doctrines such as anhypostasia and the *filioque*) is non-basic.
[67] Plantinga, *Warranted Christian Belief*, p. 250.   [68] Ibid. 256.
[69] Ibid. 244.   [70] Ibid. 245.   [71] Ibid. p. 263.   [72] Ibid. 262.

speaking terms with natural theology. In a predictable overreaction
to the dangers of subordination, these theologians have tended to
emphasize the particular distinctives of Christian belief to an implausible degree,[73] often by attempting to provide a novel interpretation
of some very general philosophical concept in accord with specifically Christian concepts. (Marshall's claim that truth is Trinitarian is
a good example.) Not surprisingly, some of these theologians have
charged Plantinga's epistemology with being insufficiently Christian.
In this section I will defend Plantinga against this charge and then fill
out a Trinitarian account of proper function.

Plantinga and the Possibility of Trinitarian Epistemology

The charge that Plantinga should have developed his epistemology in
accord with particular Christian theological concepts is serious, since
it opens him up to the charge of subordination.[74] While the charge
has rhetorical bite, it is not really plausible, since Plantinga *does* freely
appeal to those theological doctrines that he deems relevant. These
methodological convictions are outlined in the programmatic essay
'Augustinian Christian Philosophy',[75] where Plantinga contrasts two
approaches to relating the disciplines of philosophy and theology.
The 'Thomist' believes philosophy cannot begin with theological
presuppositions, while the 'Augustinian' believes it can. In accord
with the Dutch Calvinist tradition, Plantinga follows the Augustinian
approach, which believes that 'the best way to do these sciences ... is
to use all that we know, including what we know by way of faith
or revelation; according to the Thomist the way to proceed is to
bracket what we know by faith and appeal only to premises we know

[73] One particularly bizarre claim is that Christianity is not monotheistic. For a
critique see Randall Otto, 'Moltmann and the Anti-monotheism Movement', *International Journal of Systematic Theology*, 3/3 (2001), 293–308.

[74] See Andrew Moore, 'Philosophy of Religion or Philosophical Theology? A
Review Essay of Bruce Marshall *Trinity and Truth* and Alvin Plantinga *Warranted
Christian Belief*', *International Journal of Systematic Theology*, 3/3 (2001), 309–28.
For related criticisms see Merold Westphal, 'Taking Plantinga Seriously: Advice to
Christian Philosophers', *Faith and Philosophy*, 16/2 (1999), 173–81.

[75] Alvin Plantinga, 'Augustinian Christian Philosophy', in Gareth B. Matthews
(ed.), *The Augustinian Tradition* (Berkeley, Calif.: University of California Press,
1999), 1–26.

by reason'.[76] Since Plantinga does not recognize such a division of disciplines, it cannot be that he elevates philosophy over theology.

So, the real reason that Plantinga does not engage the doctrines of Trinity and incarnation is because he believes that they do not have any specific implications for epistemology. Among the theological concepts he believes *are* generally relevant for philosophy is 'the proposition that there is an almighty, all-knowing, wholly good and loving person who has created the world and created human beings in his image'.[77] Notably absent from the list is any reference to the Trinity, or indeed any other doctrine unique to Christian belief. Not surprisingly, Plantinga notes that the 'positive Christian philosophy' he advocates could just as well be termed 'theistic philosophy'. Plantinga's low estimation of the relevance of theological doctrines for philosophical issues is hardly unique; indeed, many Christian philosophers hold to an even more meagre list of philosophically relevant theological doctrines. As Peter van Inwagen observes, '[m]uch of philosophy is simply so remote from the concerns of the spiritual life that, like number theory or condensed-matter physics, it does not interact with one's religious convictions'.[78] Indeed, many Christian philosophers would find *too much* doctrine in Plantinga's philosophy.

While Plantinga might be able to weather the initial charge, a reformulated charge objects to the fact that his account of warrant is readily generalizable to many non-Christian religions.[79] Plantinga recognizes the general applicability of the A/C model:

Probably something like that [the A/C model] *is* true for the other theistic religions: Judaism, Islam, some forms of Hinduism, some forms of Buddhism, some forms of American Indian religion. Perhaps these religions are like Christianity in that they are subject to no *de jure* objections that are independent of *de facto* objections.[80]

---

[76] Plantinga, 'Augustinian Christian Philosophy', p. 22.   [77] Ibid. 16.

[78] Inwagen, 'Some Remarks on Plantinga's Advice', *Faith and Philosophy*, 16/2 (1999), 168.

[79] Michael Martin writes: 'Although Reformed epistemologists would not have to accept voodoo beliefs as rational, voodoo followers would be able to claim that insofar as they are basic in the voodoo community they are rational, and moreover, that Reformed thought was irrational in this community' (*The Case Against Christianity*, p. 30); cf. James Beilby, *Epistemology as Theology: An Evaluation of Alvin Plantinga's Religious Epistemology* (Aldershot: Ashgate, 2005), 134.

[80] Plantinga, *Warranted Christian Belief*, p. 350.

Initially, this implication might appear to marginalize Christianity as but one in a broad class of justified belief systems. However, we should keep in mind the particular Christian dimensions to Plantinga's epistemology, including the extended A/C model which covers the range of specifically Christian belief. But the value of that response is limited, since even the extended model can be generalized to non-Christian, and even non-monotheistic, belief systems. For instance, Mormonism (a form of polytheistic materialism) teaches that there is a Holy Spirit that produces knowledge of the faith in the believer upon the reading of Mormon Scripture.[81] As a result, Plantinga's epistemology functions regardless of whether the 'Holy Spirit' is the third person of the Christian Trinity, an impersonal force, or one among a large number of finite gods.

Ultimately, Plantinga's proper-function epistemology is limited to metaphysical systems that accept a trustworthy and capable designer of our cognitive faculties. Thus, as Plantinga observes, it cannot be appropriated to justify 'voodooism, or the belief that the earth is flat, or Humean skepticism, or philosophical naturalism'.[82] Or, to take another example, one cannot assume that the general applicability of proper-function epistemology or the A/C model is any more problematic than the general applicability of a specific thesis in metaphysics or ethics. Such objections surely represent particularism run amok.

---

[81] The key text here is Moroni 10: 4–5: 'And when ye shall receive these things, I would exhort you that ye would ask God, the Eternal Father, in the name of Christ, if these things are not true; and if ye shall ask with a sincere heart, with real intent, having faith in Christ, *he will manifest the truth of it unto you, by the power of the Holy Ghost. And by the power of the Holy Ghost ye may know the truth of all things*' (emphasis added).

[82] Plantinga, *Warranted Christian Belief*, p. 350. Daniel Hill notes that though adherents to other religions will, according to Plantinga's model, be unwarranted in their beliefs, '[n]evertheless, they will be able to mimic Plantinga's defensive strategy in almost every detail, and so will be able to resist any evangelistic attempts to *show* them that their beliefs are unwarranted'. Hill continues: 'In creating an impregnable fortress for the rationality of Christianity, Plantinga may have done the same favor for the other theistic religions too' ('*Warranted Christian Belief*—A Review Article', *Themelios*, 26/2 (2001), 48–9). Pace Hill, Plantinga does not actually allow religions to reside in 'impregnable fortresses', for a defeater could always blast the walls wide open.

Triune Divine Action and Proper Function

While it may not be wise to attempt to interpret fundamental epistemological concepts in terms of Christian theological particularities, it would seem to be proper to reflect more on the nature of proper function from a Christian perspective. In that light, we should say something more about the tension between the two agents in belief formation: the Holy Spirit and the self. The question, in short, is how the Spirit operates as the immediate cause of belief in conjunction with human cognitive faculties. Here we must choose between double-cause/compatibilist and libertarian/incompatibilist conceptions of freedom and divine action.[83] As Paul Helm observes, a Spirit-led proper-function account appears to present a challenge for a libertarian like Plantinga.[84] There is no similar problem with a double-causation view according to which God the Holy Spirit is the primary cause of our believings. John Greco suggests such a reconciliation of the direct act of the Spirit in conjunction with the simultaneous operation of the human cognitive faculty to accept testimony:

[T]he Holy Spirit causes belief by means of the believer's faculties of intellect and will. We may even continue to say that the Holy Spirit is the 'immediate' cause of belief, so long as immediacy is consistent with a role for those faculties. We might say with Aquinas: 'The act of believing is an act of the intellect assenting to the divine truth at the command of the will moved by the grace of God'.[85]

This type of proposal suggests the primary/secondary causal nexus in which knowledge results when our intellect assents to the divine truth as God moves our will and realizes our cognitive function. This account assumes compatibilism, such that God's determining and actualizing of our will to hold particular beliefs and not others

---

[83] For a discussion of the two models of divine action see my *Faith Lacking Understanding: Theology Through a Glass Darkly* (Milton Keynes: Paternoster, 2008), ch. 3.

[84] Helm, review of Alvin Plantinga, *Warranted Christian Belief*, *Mind*, 110/440 (2001), 1113.

[85] John Greco, review of Alvin Plantinga, *Warranted Christian Belief*, *American Catholic Philosophical Quarterly*, 75/3 (2001), 465.

is compatible with the freedom of our will.[86] The double-causation view has the virtue of providing a simple account of belief. It also appears to be attractive, even inevitable, given the formidable problems with doxastic voluntarism. And it is undoubtedly simpler than a libertarian view that postulates a symbiotic relationship between the Holy Spirit and the self.

But can we reconcile libertarianism with a rejection of doxastic voluntarism? To begin with, the libertarian could reject the assumption that God's determination of human belief has any relevance for free will. For instance, God could cause someone to believe that Jesus is God; but that does not determine the person's free response to Jesus any more than it does that of the demons who believe.[87] If that is unsatisfactory, perhaps one could insert an element of libertarian autonomy within believings so that the Spirit grants true beliefs only in response to a (tacit) desire to know the truth in a given situation.[88] While tempting, this view faces its own problems.[89] One could develop this view of tacit desire by attempting to explain the IIHS in terms of prevenient grace. According to this account, there is no *specific* cognitive process that acts on individuals. Instead, the IIHS simply provides a general enabling action akin to prevenient grace.

This brings us to the second point: the Christian could argue that from a Christian view of proper function *the Spirit is always active in conjunction with our cognitive faculties* in what amounts to a theory of divine illumination. We can note that the Christian conception of the Holy Spirit is especially (perhaps uniquely) amenable to an epistemological construal, since the Spirit is understood scripturally

---

[86] This would parallel Marshall's argument that the Spirit is the primary cause of belief.

[87] Presumably there are parameters to the kinds of beliefs the Spirit can cause in accord with a person's free will. For instance, the belief has to be in accord with the person's disposition. To cause a person who hates chocolate cake to believe that he loves chocolate cake would appear to be a violation of the person's libertarian autonomy.

[88] Thanks to Daniel Hill for this objection and its resolution.

[89] Consider the case of a developing neonate. While this child first gains knowledge as a result of the Spirit's action, according to this view that action is only initiated by the Spirit responding to a tacit desire in the child to know a particular truth. But then how can this child ever come to know anything, for knowledge only comes with the desire for knowledge . . . which requires knowledge?

as having a central epistemological role as the one who leads into all truth (e.g. John 16: 13). A central epistemological dilemma that has reared its ugly head time and again concerns the question of how we can have knowledge without the interference of the medium, be it a sense-datum, a linguistic expression, or simply our own perspectival finitude. In this light it is important to remember that the Spirit is understood as the divine person who uniquely reveals the other through self-effacement (as Vladimir Lossky says, the 'imageless Spirit'). Thomas Torrance writes:

He does not show us Himself, but shows us the Face of the Father in the Face of the Son, and shows us the heart of the Son in the heart of the Father. By His very mode of being as Spirit He hides Himself from us so that we do not know Him directly in His own hypostasis, and in His mode of activity as transparent Light He effaces Himself that the one Triune God may shine through Him to us.[90]

This truth of metaphysical knowledge can apply to all divine illumination of mundane, proper-function truth. This is but one possible way to flesh out Plantinga's proper-function model theologically. Undoubtedly we could fine-tune the model further, pushing it in new directions, particularly with regard to these issues of Trinitarian agency and the intersection of divine action and human will. But this should be sufficient at least to defuse initial objections that the model lacks an adequate ability to be conversant with Christian theology.

CONCLUSION

When engaging in historical study of the life of Jesus, N. T. Wright has warned, '[i]f you pin the history to the wall like a butterfly, you may be able to study it analytically, but you mustn't be surprised that it won't fly again'.[91] One might likewise worry that a philosophical examination of faith and knowledge could exert a similar effect upon

---

[90] Torrance, *God and Rationality* (London/New York: Oxford University Press, 1971), 167.
[91] Wright, *The Original Jesus: The Life and Vision of a Revolutionary* (Grand Rapids, Mich.: Eerdmans, 1996), 21.

the theologian. But, contrary to expectations, Plantinga's analysis promises that Christian faith may indeed fly as it was intended, free of the burdens of inadequate epistemology. And he does so in a most surprising way, by elevating the knowledge of faith possessed by the simplest sincere believer to being no less epistemically substantial than that of the great theologian.[92]

---

[92] Plantinga has weathered many other objections in addition to the particularism/subordination charge. Some have critiqued his use of historical authorities, especially John Calvin. See especially Michael Czapkay Sudduth, 'Plantinga's Revision of the Reformed Tradition: Rethinking our Natural Knowledge of God', *Philosophical Books*, 43/2 (2002), 81–91; cf. John Beversluis, 'Reforming the Reformed Objection to Natural Theology', *Faith and Philosophy*, 12/2 (1995), 189–206; Michael Czapkay Sudduth, 'The Prospects for "Mediate" Natural Theology in John Calvin', *Religious Studies*, 31/1 (1995), 53–68; Paul Helm, *Faith and Understanding* (Grand Rapids, Mich.: Eerdmans, 1997), ch. 8. Others have challenged the theological or philosophical aspects of Plantinga's proposal. As an example, Richard Swinburne charges that the proper-function requirement for a designer is counter-intuitive and thus that Plantinga's theory collapses into reliabilism (see *Epistemic Justification* (Oxford: Clarendon, 2001), 206-11). Though I cannot adequately respond to the criticism here, Swinburne's claim seems to me to be false given the plausibility (from a Christian view) that eyes were designed to see and wings to fly.

10

Theology as Foundational and Analytic

> My father used to quote an unanswerable argument, by which
> an old lady, a Mrs Barlow, who suspected him of unorthodoxy,
> hoped to convert him:—'Doctor, I know that sugar is sweet in
> my mouth, and I know that my Redeemer liveth.'
>
> Charles Darwin, *Autobiography*

> God when he makes the Prophet does not unmake the Man.
>
> John Locke, *Essay Concerning Human Understanding*

With the Church's recent emergence from 'Constantinian captivity'
into a secular, pluralistic landscape, and with the prospects for a
mass evangelistic conversion of the academy appearing rather low,
theology now appears fated to continue to struggle as a marginal-
ized, minority discourse. As a result, the theologian must be of two
minds, retaining fidelity to the particular community of faith even
as she engages critically in the public square.[1] Theological prolegomena address how best to actualize these seemingly contradictory
allegiances to particularity and universality, though classical-
foundationalist proposals lean too far toward the universal while non-
foundationalist proposals tend to lean too far toward the particular.
In the previous chapter we considered Plantinga's proper-function
moderate foundationalism as a *via media* between the bracing
universality of classical foundationalism and the stifling insularity
of non-foundationalism. In the present chapter we will complete
the picture by developing a broadly realist account of theology as
the best means to ground the rigour and integrity of theological

---

[1] Kristen Heyer, 'How Does Theology Go Public? Rethinking the Debate Between
David Tracy and George Lindbeck', *Political Theology*, 5/3 (2004), 326.

argument, thereby paving the way for the gone but not forgotten polemicist. I will begin by arguing that a proper-function foundationalism best accords with a cognitive-propositionalist theory of doctrine according to which doctrine aspires to *true description*. I will defend this theory by way of a critique of Kevin Vanhoozer's alternative canonical-linguistic account. In the next section I will argue that cognitive-propositionalism grounds a prima facie theological conservatism that provides a necessary bulwark against unrestrained theological revisionism. In the final section I will argue that cognitive-propositionalism is methodologically congruent with both a rigorous, analytic method of enquiry and a limited doctrinal anti-realism while providing a rich source for ecumenical exploration.

THE MEANING OF DOCTRINE

Every year when I introduce theology students to the Calvinist/ Arminian debate on election there are inevitably a few who vocally express their desire to be 'Calminians'. While the desire is understandable it is also futile, since Calvinist and Arminian accounts of election are logically incompatible. Many Evangelicals appear to hold a similar desire when encountering cognitive-propositionalist and cultural-linguistic accounts of doctrine, desiring the realism of the former and the ethical holism of the latter. Such is the case with the canonical-linguistic theory that Kevin Vanhoozer develops in the hefty tome *The Drama of Doctrine*. In this book Vanhoozer aims to incorporate the best insights from both cognitive-propositional and cultural-linguistic approaches to doctrine. From the realist's perspective, hopes for a rapprochement are reinforced by Vanhoozer's affirmation of alethic realism[2] and Plantinga's epistemology.[3] Indeed, Vanhoozer is emphatic in his concern to avoid the 'epic'

---

[2] Vanhoozer, *The Drama of Doctrine: A Canonical-Linguistic Approach to Christian Theology* (Louisville, Ky.: Westminster/John Knox, 2005), 287 n.

[3] Unfortunately, Vanhoozer's descriptions of both Plantinga's epistemology and foundationalism are confused, as he refers to Plantinga's view as reliabilism (*The Drama of Doctrine*, p. 302) while defining foundationalism as 'an epistemology (theory of knowledge) that likens what we know to a pyramid based on a set of indubitable

subordination of theology to an alien thought system.[4] While such subordination occurs when the cognitive-propositionalist de-dramatizes Scripture by extracting doctrinal propositions from their dramatic narratival context,[5] Vanhoozer warns that any interpretative framework, including cultural-linguisticism, can be used to subordinate theology.[6] Thus, whatever our theory of doctrine, we must always guard against the subordination of Scripture.[7] Vanhoozer is also wary of the reductionism of experiential-expressivist and cultural-linguistic critics of cognitive propositionalism, and thus he strives to maintain the proposition, albeit subordinated to the goal of drawing people into proper participation in the divine drama.[8] As a result, Vanhoozer recognizes cognitive, experiential, and ethical dimensions of doctrine, while situating them all dramatically: 'Doctrine is not merely a proposition, or an expression, or a grammatical rule, but a *prompt*: a spiritual direction for one's fitting performance of the script, and hence a means for continuing the pattern of communicative action that lies at the heart of the gospel as theo-drama'.[9] While Vanhoozer's proposals have elicited high praise,[10] I will argue that the canonical-linguistic theory is critically flawed because it collapses into pragmatism and insularity, and thus is best rejected in favour of a cognitive-propositional account of doctrine. I will begin to defend this thesis by unpacking Vanhoozer's view of concepts, metaphysics, and truth.

Concepts, Metaphysics, and Truth

The debate over the nature of concepts—that is, the basic constituents of thought—is one of the most debated areas of philosophy. Some

---

beliefs' (ibid. 292). The fact that he later refers (on the same page) to this view as '*classical* foundationalism' and then 'classical foundationalism' (no emphasis) suggests that Vanhoozer equates foundationalism with classical foundationalism.

[4] Vanhoozer, *The Drama of Doctrine*, p. 269.   [5] Ibid. 87, 269.

[6] Vanhoozer warns: 'To elevate narrative over all other literary genres is to succumb to the same temptation that besets the propositionalist, namely, of reducing the many canonical forms into one kind only' (ibid. 273; cf. pp. 85, 87).

[7] Ibid. 89.   [8] Ibid. 103.   [9] Ibid. 107.

[10] See, for instance, Terry A. Larm, review of *The Drama of Doctrine*, *Evangelical Review of Theology*, 32/1 (2008), 86–8.

have proposed that concepts are to be understood as mental representations that are part of a language of thought (e.g. Jerry Fodor), a
view that tends to see the mind as analogous to a computer. Others
view concepts as abilities, the means by which we accomplish things
(e.g. Ludwig Wittgenstein). Still others view concepts as abstract
objects that provide the constituents of propositions. In adjudicating
between these competing proposals one ought to seek the explanation
that is most compatible with traditional theological understanding as
well as metaphysical realism, such that it will allow one to affirm, for
instance, that the concept that God is love is rooted in one grasping
the property of God's being love. (Of course one does not need to
know that God exists in order to grasp the property, or else atheists
could know nothing of God.) Vanhoozer is cautious about granting
concepts any overt world-description entailments, apparently fear-
ing that granting concepts a purchase on reality could result in the
subordination of theology.[11] As a result, he appears to opt for a
broadly Wittgensteinian ability approach in which concepts are dramatic 'thought-acts' or *'mental habits that order human experience in
various patterns'*.[12] Vanhoozer's ability approach is evident in the following example: 'The concept "Christmas" does not correspond to an
object in the world but rather to the complex of associations we have
formed on the basis of our experience of that holiday'.[13] Apparently
the point is that concepts do not represent objective constituents in
the world but rather are abilities that enable us to navigate the world,
in this case by grouping a set of social practices and cultural artefacts
(e.g. crèches, candy canes, and carol singing) into a functional group.
Thus, it is simply mistaken to think of concepts as rooted in the
grasping of objective, abstract objects, for they 'are built up out of
our experienced world, not "the world out there"'.[14] Concepts do
not grasp the furniture of the universe, but rather embody cultur-
ally formed practices for ordering experience and interpreting the
world.[15]

   This proposal faces a serious problem, given that Christian theology is *replete* with concepts which resist functional reduction. The
doctrine of God is a particularly striking repository of such concepts,

[11] Vanhoozer, *The Drama of Doctrine*, p. 89.   [12] Ibid.
[13] Ibid. 89–90.   [14] Ibid. 90.   [15] Ibid. cf. p. 285.

including omniscience, infinity, impeccability, and spiration. Instead of affirming that these concepts grasp objective properties, Vanhoozer only allows that 'Christian doctrine encourages certain mental habits rather than others when thinking about God (e.g., one only, perfect, loving, just, maker of all things). *What makes certain concepts theological is their habitual use in relating our thinking about things, persons, and events to the theo-dramatic action*'.[16] According to this statement, we determine which concepts to invoke when thinking about God by identifying which are effective at guiding our interactions with one another. The one place where Vanhoozer appears to assert a realist view of concepts is in the life of Christ. For instance, he seems to accept the concept of Christ's resurrection not merely as a prompt but as a description of a historical event.[17]

In light of his (largely) functional view of concepts, Vanhoozer appears to dismiss *in principle* the possibility that we could come to understand the fundamental nature of reality. This leads him to assume a deep scepticism about metaphysics, which he suspects of subversive, epic thinking:

Transposed to theology, epic takes the form of monological system that unfolds its story from an absolute perspective. Systematic theologies resemble epics to the extent that they appear to be written by impersonal and omniscient narrators who stand nowhere in particular. Many theologies, in their zeal for universal truth, run roughshod over the particularity and diversity of biblical voices (and literary genres) that tend not to fit neatly into a preferred system.[18]

Apparently once one believes that one has identified certain aspects of the nature of (theological) reality, one has assumed the role of 'impersonal and omniscient narrator'. Unfortunately, this leads to the inevitable suppression of other important voices: 'One can virtually chart the history of modern theology in terms of the competition between various "epic" accounts, between various "-isms" or conceptual systems (e.g., existentialism, process theism, feminism, panentheism, liberalism) for naming God'.[19] The implications of Vanhoozer's position are truly striking. While a broadly realist view of metaphysics has been central to Christian theology since the

---

[16] Ibid. 377.   [17] Ibid. 278.   [18] Ibid. 85.   [19] Ibid.

second-century apologists, Vanhoozer views any such project as a distorting constraint on revelation.

The fear of epic theology that leads Vanhoozer to reject a realist view of concepts and metaphysics extends to his treatment of truth. Though he commends alethic realism, he nonetheless appears to stake out an anti-realist position on truth. This is hardly surprising, since his functional view of concepts and rejection of metaphysics together undermine our ability to attain truth as equivalence. In light of that inability, Vanhoozer marginalizes realist truth with a functional pragmatism. Thus, while he affirms that doctrinal truth entails '*adaequatio intellectus ad rei* (the correspondence of mind and thing/subject matter)', he redefines the meaning of *adaequatio*.[20] The view of adequation or correspondence that Vanhoozer rejects looks a lot like the mirroring relation that Rorty repudiates:

'Adequate' here means *equivalent,* a perfect representation, a re-presencing of the thing in one's mind. This philosophical ideal has rightly been called into question by postmodern thinkers who deny epistemology's ability to make good on its claim to yield a complete and exact knowledge of the world. Truth is never fully present to consciousness; rather, our words and concepts always *differ* from what there is. [21]

This passage nicely illustrates the ambiguity characteristic of anti-realist views of truth.[22] If Vanhoozer means that we never know *all truth* (remember his equation of any realist metaphysical statement with omniscience!), then this is trivially true, since only God is omniscient. But if he means that we never know even a single truth, then this is surely too strong, for we know many truths (e.g. 'Jesus is Lord'). And then there is the ambiguity of Vanhoozer's claim that 'our words and concepts always *differ* from what there is'. Straightforwardly interpreted this is trivially true; for example, although bacon tastes

---

[20] Ibid. p. 286.
[21] Ibid. Thus, according to Vanhoozer, '[a] postconservative theology breaks free both from the tendency to treat concepts as pictures and from the impossible ideal of *adaequatio* as a perfect, complete equivalence between language and world, formulation and fact' (ibid.).
[22] Equally ambiguous is the following: 'It is tempting, all too tempting, cavalierly to assume that our system of thought has indeed attained the philosophical ideal of *adaequatio*: that we know the truth, wholly and completely. That way idolatry lies' (ibid.).

salty, the sentence 'Bacon tastes salty' doesn't taste salty. But this is none the worse for the sentence. The fact that Vanhoozer's statements echo the anti-realist's tortured oscillation between triviality and absurdity analysed in Chapter 6 suggests that he shares similarly flawed assumptions.

A closer analysis of Vanhoozer's proposal suggests that he falls into pragmatism, as when he explains the meaning of *adaequatio intellectus ad rei*: 'The adequacy that is truth's measure should not be seen in terms of the philosopher's ideal of complete equivalence but in rather less formal terms: *good enough, sufficient*'.[23] This pragmatic redefinition of truth extends to knowledge, which consists in beliefs that are 'good enough'[24] to provide appropriate prompts in the divine drama. Thus, Vanhoozer seems to believe that a sentence is true in virtue of prompting one to appropriate action. Meanwhile, the performance of wisdom replaces the pursuit of truth as the goal of theology, so that good theology is that which aids good performance.[25] Such statements trade on a disingenuous argument whereby one refutes an ambiguous or erroneous view of realist truth (mirroring) and knowledge (omniscience), and then collapses truth into knowledge and knowledge into practice. Vanhoozer categorically rejects as epic theorizing all theoretical attempts to explain doctrines and opts instead for an imaginative retelling of the theo-dramatic metaphors.[26] Thus, when he applies his proposal to the doctrine of atonement, the criterion for an appropriate theory is found not in a realist theoretical description of God's salvific action but rather in the proposal's ability to enable the Church to become a community of atonement.[27]

Are Doctrines Directives or Descriptions?

In the preceding chapters I have already raised a number of criticisms against various modes of anti-realist and non-foundationalist theology, and many of those apply here as well. However, in light of

---

[23] Ibid. 291.   [24] Ibid. 288.   [25] Ibid. 252; cf. p. 104.
[26] Ibid. 381, 387.
[27] Ibid. 433; cf. Scot McKnight, *A Community Called Atonement* (Nashville, Tenn.: Abingdon, 2007).

Vanhoozer's confidence that his canonical-linguistic theory guards theology against reductionism and reinforces epistemic virtue, we shall begin our critique here. My claim will be that though he affirms the importance of being open-minded and critiquing one's own beliefs,[28] Vanhoozer's theory of doctrine inhibits him from pursuing true epistemic virtue. The problem begins with his pragmatism: since Vanhoozer assesses the adequacy of doctrine in terms of practical effect, he may continue to affirm doctrines regardless of any intellectual/conceptual challenges so long as those doctrines facilitate personal and corporate transformation.[29] The effect is to indemnify all doctrines from rational critique. Second, even if Vanhoozer believes that doctrines have some metaphysical, descriptive function, he cannot consider defeaters, because the only grounds he allows to assess doctrines are internal to Christian faith. Vanhoozer admits two tests for the legitimacy of theology: the canonical criterion evaluates whether the doctrine is congruent with Scripture, while the catholic criterion evaluates whether a doctrine accords with tradition.[30] As is the case with Marshall, Vanhoozer fails to acknowledge any criterion for critical evaluation that is *external* to Christian faith including even *the general rules of logic*. As a result, Vanhoozer presumably could never advise the abandonment or revision of a doctrine that clearly appears to be incoherent or immoral. All Vanhoozer would ask is whether we will choose 'to serve or to subvert the gospel'.[31] While sounding pious, this is actually an egregious surrendering of the theologian's responsibility to the truth. As Michael Lynch observes, 'an unswerving allegiance to what you believe isn't a sign that you care about truth. It is a sign of dogmatism'.[32] Not surprisingly, a narrow dogmatism is evident in Vanhoozer's treatment of atonement, where he does not even acknowledge objections to his view (e.g. objections to the notion of imputation[33]). Of course, this is to be expected,

---

[28] 'A willingness to acknowledge our preferences and biases is one such truth-conducive habit; closed-mindedness, by contrast, is not' (*The Drama of Doctrine*, p. 304).

[29] Ibid. 392.   [30] Ibid. 303.   [31] Ibid. 301.

[32] Lynch, *True to Life: Why Truth Matters* (Cambridge, Mass.: MIT Press, 2004), 3.

[33] Vanhoozer, *The Drama of Doctrine*, p. 390.

given that all potential objections have been dismissed a priori as epic distortions.[34]

This failure of epistemic virtue is ultimately rooted in Vanhoozer's pragmatism. Vanhoozer eschews theology based in 'common human experience', 'sense-data', or 'allegedly objective facts'.[35] (The third denial is the troubling one.) Instead, he advocates grounding theology in 'communicative' and 'cartographic' practices of the canon.[36] Thus, the directive prompt replaces an objective, factual basis for theology. Vanhoozer admits that this looks a lot like pragmatism: '[A]t first blush, it seems that the dramatic definition, with its emphasis on participation or performance, gets no further than a pragmatic conception of truth, where truth is a matter of what works'.[37] But he seeks to defuse this concern by grounding the directive dimension of doctrine in the norm of Christ's history. Unfortunately, this response is hardly sufficient to defuse concerns about pragmatism, since presumably Vanhoozer's claim that our words never fully describe reality includes truths about Jesus Christ (e.g. 'Jesus turned water into wine', 'Jesus rose from the dead'). And this leaves us with the conclusion that claims about Christ, like all others, are only true pragmatically. Moreover, even if truths of Christ's life could avoid pragmatic reduction, this response would still fail to provide a realist reference for doctrines that are not grounded in Christ's life. Even if we concede a broader basis for realist reference according to which doctrines are grounded in God's past, present, and future actions,[38] we still lack any basis for theological reflection apart from the revelation in the economy. This utterly *eviscerates* the doctrine of God, for it leaves us unable to say anything of the metaphysical attributes including omniscience, immutability, impeccability, omnibenevolence, and eternity. In addition, attempts to interpret doctrines as directive prompts are bound to be hopelessly contrived. Given that most doctrines underdetermine the appropriate prompt, most doctrines will be de-emphasized, disregarded as irrelevant to the conduct of the divine drama, or arbitrarily associated with the prompt of

---

[34] Needless to say, such dogmatism fits poorly with Vanhoozer's enthusiastic endorsement of epistemic fallibilism (ibid. 304).

[35] Ibid. 295.　　　[36] Ibid.　　　[37] Ibid. 105.　　　[38] Ibid. 104.

one's choice. This surely is the triumph of both pragmatism and subjectivism.[39]

Though Vanhoozer affirms Plantinga's epistemology, canonical-linguistic theory fits poorly with proper-function foundationalism. To begin with, it contradicts proper function's prima facie realism about Christian doctrines. Of course, a proper-function epistemology does not entail naive realism, but it does mean that we have strong grounds to reject radical reinterpretations of the meaning and function of doctrine, including purportedly canonical-linguistic ones. Moreover, Vanhoozer's claim that we only know God in so far as he is revealed in Christ and Scripture[40] conflicts with the Reformed notion that we have knowledge of God through the *sensus divinitatis*. It is important to keep in mind that the *sensus* works symbiotically with other sources of belief. For instance, one's belief that the sunset is beautiful may trigger the *sensus* to form the belief that God is love. As the Wesleyan quadrilateral suggests, we actually draw theological truths from a wide variety of doxastic sources.[41] Only with this type of commitment to realism and a holistic, multi-source view of the origins and refinement of doctrine will we achieve fidelity to the beliefs of the Christian community coupled with the rigorous enquiry necessary for the public square.

PLANTINGA AND THEOLOGICAL REALISM

Plantinga's epistemology promises the laity the ability to know a full spate of basic doctrines (the 'great things of the gospel') through the

---

[39] Moreover, it is extraordinarily difficult to see how the directive potential would have any role in making a proposition true. For instance, how would a proposition concerning the life of Christ (e.g. 'Jesus rose from the dead') be made true in part by the directive impact that this proposition has in the lives of those who accept it? Wouldn't the fact that Jesus rose from the dead be both necessary and sufficient for the truth of the proposition? Vanhoozer's refusal to countenance defeaters reinforces anti-realist concerns, given that a key mark of simple relativism is the assumption that all the beliefs a person holds are true simply in virtue of the person holding those beliefs (see Lynch, *True to Life*, p. 33).

[40] Vanhoozer, *The Drama of Doctrine*, p. 248.

[41] Steven B. Sherman, *Revitalizing Theological Epistemology: Holistic Evangelical Approaches to the Knowledge of God* (Eugene, Ore.: Pickwick, 2008), 149.

internal instigation of the Holy Spirit. While this does not render the theologian's work unimportant, it does show that her knowledge is rooted in the egalitarian origins of revelation.

Theological Realism and Orthodoxy

In the previous chapter we saw that theologians pressured by the constraints of the modern standards of objectivity and knowledge have often adopted subordinationist distortions of Christian doctrine. A sign of the problem is found in prolegomenal discussions that appear to collapse theology into a wing of anthropology. As Luke Timothy Johnson observes,

> much of what calls itself theology appears to the uninitiated to be less about God than about the politics of identity or linguistic halls of mirrors. What might it mean to speak about God if we ever were to speak about God and if there were a God? Even those who seek to retrieve the theological enterprise find themselves in the infinite regress apparently demanded by academic rigor, talking about other authors who talked about God.[42]

When it comes to constructive theology, the discipline has often been treated more as an art (and a modern one at that) than as a rigorous science. Thus, Thomas Oden reflects: '[F]rom the first day I ever thought of becoming a theologian I have been earnestly taught and admonished that my most urgent task was to "think creatively" so as to make "some new contribution" to theology'.[43] There are a number of factors operative here including the professional need to distinguish oneself with one's own distinctive body of work and the need to legitimate one's place in the university.[44] But whatever the specific factors, theology as an objective science is eclipsed. Plantinga targets this revisionism in part I of *Warranted Christian Belief*, beginning with Kant and contemporary liberal theologians John Hick and Gordon Kaufman.[45]

[42] Johnson, 'Explaining God Away', in *Commonweal*, 123/22, 20 Dec. 1996, p. 18.
[43] Oden, *After Modernity ... What?* (Grand Rapids, Mich.: Zondervan, 1990), 22.
[44] See Randal Rauser, 'Theology as a Bull Session', in Oliver Crisp and Michael Rea (eds.), *Analytic Theology* (Oxford: Oxford University Press, 2009), 71.
[45] Alvin Plantinga, *Warranted Christian Belief* (Oxford: Oxford University Press, 2000), ch. 2.

Plantinga's proposal protects theology against such defensive and pre-emptive revisionism not by removing or revising doctrines, but rather by affirming the proper basicality of Christian belief. As William Alston observes, this clears the way for Plantinga to adopt a refreshingly realist interpretation of doctrine:

[Plantinga] resolutely refuses to compromise, or scale down, the cognitive content of the faith. He insists that it is a matter of objective fact whether there is an omnipotent, omniscient, perfectly good creator of the universe, that belief in God is either true or false in a perfectly straightforward sense of these terms, the same sense in which it is either true or false that snow is white.[46]

Though Plantinga is able to affirm theological realism, nowise does acceptance of this entail a theological naivety, as if Plantinga is obliged to treat theological discourse as if it were indistinct from other kinds of discourse.[47] What it does do is shift the ground from a stance of revisionist suspicion regarding theological statements to a commitment to their meaningfulness and truth.

Given the radically sceptical direction of much modern theological scholarship (of both classical-foundationalist and non-foundationalist strands), coupled with the widespread conviction that the theologian's primary allegiance is to the university rather than the Church, it should come as no surprise that a deep suspicion exists between the academic elites (e.g. professors) and laity, with the clergy often left somewhere in the middle. Proper-function foundationalism provides two ways to contribute toward the healing of this relationship. To begin with, it undermines the elitist mentality of many Christian academics. While some of the suspicion that many clergy and laity harbour towards academic theology traces to an incipient pragmatism and a loss of interest in doctrine among clergy and laity alike,[48] it is also fed by a failure of theologians and biblical scholars to communicate effectively, occasionally reinforced by elitism. Take, for instance, Van Harvey's claim in *The Historian and*

---

[46] Alston, 'Plantinga's Epistemology of Religious Belief', in James Tomberlin and Peter van Inwagen (eds.), *Alvin Plantinga* (Dordrecht: Reidel, 1985), 293.

[47] See William Alston, *Divine Nature and Human Language: Essays in Philosophical Theology* (Ithaca, NY/London: Cornell University Press, 1989).

[48] Alan Wolfe, *The Transformation of American Religion: How We Actually Live Our Faith* (New York: Free Press, 2003).

the Believer[49] that the lay person who has not consulted the experts does not even have a right to a belief about Jesus.[50] In addition, this leads to a de facto Gnosticism in which it is the experts who really know Jesus (the *historical* Jesus)—that is, in so far as he *can* be known. Thus, Marcus Borg recounts how as a student he learned about the great difference between the Jesus of history and the Christ of dogma, a difference which remains unknown among most of the laity: 'I am aware that this is still news for some Christians, even though it has been old hat in the seminaries of mainline denominations through-out this [twentieth] century'.[51]

In order to heal the elite/laity rift we must begin to overcome the division (indeed, the dichotomy) that is reinforced by this type of epistemology. C. S. Lewis describes the way that he came to terms with his own elitism while attending a rural Anglican service:

I disliked very much their hymns, which I considered to be fifth-rate poems set to sixth-rate music. But as I went on I saw the great merit of it. I came up against different people of quite different outlooks and different education, and then gradually my conceit just began peeling off. I realized that the hymns (which were just sixth-rate music) were, nevertheless, being sung with devotion and benefit by an old saint in elastic-side boots in the opposite pew, and then you realize that you aren't fit to clean those boots.[52]

Without naming names, one must wonder how many tenured aca-demic theologians today are not fit to clean the boots of many an old saint in the pew. What Lewis came to recognize is reinforced by Plantinga's affirmation that the IIHS grants to all disciples knowledge of the '[g]reat things of the gospel'. And so, a Christian does not depend on the latest, tentative results of biblical criticism in order to know that the Jesus of history and dogma are substantially one, for

---

[49] Harvey, *The Historian and the Believer: The Morality of Historical Knowledge and Christian Belief* (New York: Macmillan, 1966).

[50] See Plantinga, *Warranted Christian Belief*, ch. 12; cf. C. Stephen Evans, *The Historical Christ and the Jesus of Faith* (Oxford/New York: Oxford University Press, 1996), ch. 11.

[51] Borg, *Meeting Jesus Again for the First Time* (New York: HarperSanFrancisco, 1994), 11.

[52] Lewis, 'Answers to Questions on Christianity', in his *God in the Dock*, ed. Walter Hooper (Grand Rapids, Mich.: Eerdmans, 1970), 61–2.

one can know this directly. There is a striking egalitarianism in this epistemology, as Plantinga marginalizes the intellectual elites who appropriate for themselves the authority to grant dispensations of justified belief. None of this is to deny that theology remains a critically important enterprise, but it must arise organically from within, and retain responsibility to, the body of Christ.

Having recognized that rationality, justification, and knowledge are available to the lay person, the theologian can now dispense with flights of theological creativity and instead reorient herself to the task of developing and defending a body of orthodoxy. This does not mean a blind assent to past or current consensus, but rather a commitment that right doctrine can be known and articulated and that doing so ultimately shapes a more faithful community. Interestingly, this humble task evinces a reversal of the current trend; as Thomas Oden observes, '[t]heology stands today in a comic relation to its subject matter...It is the most humorous of all disciplines because it has worked so hard to disavow its distinctive task. No other discipline has devoted so much energy to doing away with its own subject matter'.[53] It is interesting to note that even among many contemporary Evangelical theologies one will look in vain to discover an evaluative comment on the coherence or orthodoxy of one's theological interlocutors.[54] It is time to refocus upon the central task of theology, and that includes the difficult but important questions of dogmatic essence and boundaries.[55] Few seem willing to assume the mantle of the polemicist who will judge (with conviction *and* grace) a given theology to be heretical.[56] But to reintroduce the place of the polemicist hardly means that our deposit of orthodoxy is sacrosanct and unrevisable (still less that we ought to reinstitute the punitive measures of the gallows for wayward theologians). Such a stance is

[53] Oden, *After Modernity... What?*, p. 185.

[54] An excellent example of this approach is found in Stanley Grenz's survey of recent theologies in *Rediscovering the Triune God: The Trinity in Contemporary Theology* (Minneapolis, Minn.: Fortress, 2004). See my review of Grenz's book in *International Journal of Systematic Theology*, 9/2 (2007), 231–5.

[55] Oden, *After Modernity... What?*, p. 172.

[56] As Oden observes, '[w]hen a theologian forgets the distinction between heterodoxy and orthodoxy, it is roughly equivalent to a physician forgetting the difference between disease and health, or axe and scalpel, or a lawyer forgetting the difference between criminality and *corpus juris*' (*After Modernity... What?*, p. 59).

irreconcilable with a commitment to objective theology and public reason. Nonetheless, the articulation of orthodoxy does provide a context in which the community is to be identified and continually formed.

THE DISCIPLINE OF ANALYTIC THEOLOGY

One of my primary goals in this book has been to lay an epistemological foundation for the rather old-fashioned doctrinal realism that understands doctrines to be cognitive and propositional. This realist view of theology is particularly amenable to a rigorous method of doctrinal construction. One finds such a method in the scholasticism that dominated from Thomas to Turretin (or Anselm to Edwards) and which valued systematic analysis and theological construction.[57] While I could refer to the method of theology proposed here as a form of neo-scholasticism, I will instead adopt the term *analytic theology*.[58] From its origins in the early twentieth century, analytic philosophy was focused upon the analysis of concepts to advance understanding. Bertrand Russell expressed the central analytic conviction when he wrote: 'I have sought solutions of philosophical problems by means of analysis: and I remain firmly persuaded, in spite of some modern tendencies to the contrary, that only by analysing is progress possible'.[59] Analytic philosophy is not limited to the analysis of concepts, however, as is evidenced by the fact that analytic philosophers have undertaken substantial constructive work across the spectrum of philosophy from ethics to metaphysics. Indeed, one could plausibly

---

[57] For instance, Richard Muller writes: 'In the seventeenth century, a theological work was identified as "scholastic" when it belonged to the classroom, echoed the patterns of disputation then typical of education, and employed a refined method of argument to define the terms of debate, the *status quaestionis*, and the resolution of debate with various clearly identified opponents' ('The Problem of Protestant Scholasticism—A Review and Definition', in Willem J. van Asselt and Eef Dekker (eds.), *Reformation and Scholasticism: An Ecumenical Enterprise* (Grand Rapids, Mich.: Baker, 2001), 54).

[58] See Oliver Crisp and Michael Rea (eds.), *Analytic Theology* (Oxford: Oxford University Press, 2009).

[59] Russell, *My Philosophical Development* (London: George Allen & Unwin, 1959), 11.

define analytic philosophy in the way Alvin Plantinga defines philosophy more generally as 'not much different from just thinking hard'.[60]
And thinking hard is of great value when one believes that advance
in the discipline in question is possible. Thus, the great attraction of
analytic philosophy comes in its emphasis upon the importance of
clarity and concision in expression and rigour in argument.

It is that simple and uncompromising approach to enquiry that
has captured the attention of theologians like Nancey Murphy and
Bruce Marshall. Similarly, in the article 'Theology's Continental Captivity' R. R. Reno defends the importance of analytic philosophy for
revitalizing theology: 'Aren't the governing sentiment and thrust of
analytic philosophy—its logic chopping, its punctiliousness about
argument, and its tireless defense of reason—obvious to even the
most casual observer?'[61] For these reasons Reno commends analytic
philosophy as a 'contemporary philosophical scholasticism' which
would provide a valuable handmaiden to theology.[62] It is important
to emphasize that as a method of rigorous enquiry analytic theology
carries no metaphysical baggage, and so is not liable to Vanhoozer's
legitimate worry about epic theology. It should also be noted that
rigorous, analytic theology would tighten the screws on the excessive
interest in unconstrained flights of theological fancy that have little
basis in objective reality. While there is a place for creativity within
theology, it must always subserve the rigours of analytic description
and theorization.[63]

In light of this conception of analytic theology as a rigorous mode
of enquiry congruent with doctrinal realism we can turn to consider
two points of potential tension. To begin with, we will address the
question of whether Plantinga's view of properly basic belief undermines the rigour of an approach to theological description, doctrine,
and theory formation. I will argue on the contrary that it is fully congruent with a rigorous theological method. Second, I will consider the
Lindbeckian charge that a propositional view of theology commits
one to 'timeless, universal propositions' that inevitably undermine

---

[60] Plantinga, *God, Freedom, and Evil* (New York: Harper & Row, 1974), 1.
[61] Reno, 'Theology's Continental Captivity', *First Things* (April 2006), 29.
[62] Ibid. 31.
[63] See my critique of Sallie McFague and Jürgen Moltmann in Crisp and Rea (eds.),
Analytic Theology, pp. 76–84.

personal and corporate transformation, the latter expressed in ecumenism.

Epistemic Virtue and Analytic Theology

H. L. Mencken once complained that '[l]earning... is not esteemed in the evangelical denominations, and any literate plowhand, if the Holy Spirit enflames him, is thought to be fit to preach'.[64] By the same token, might Plantinga's epistemology undermine rigorous theology by reinforcing Christian intellectual complacency?[65] In the essay 'Religious Knowledge and the Virtues of the Mind' Linda Zagzebski critiques Plantinga's inability to ground epistemic virtue.[66] She notes that Plantinga, in keeping with his Reformed background, has a strong focus on the individual that extends to the warrant assessment of personal beliefs. Further, she contends that Plantinga's incredulity toward internal deontological requirements reflects in part a Reformed pessimism about the pervasive noetic/doxastic effects of original sin. Zagzebski charges that this Reformed influence contributes to Plantinga shirking epistemic responsibility and capitulating to individualism. At the same time, she seeks to defuse the danger that internalism poses unobtainable criteria by arguing that internalist requirements are primarily shouldered not by individuals but by the Church:

The possessor of warrant is fundamentally the Church, not the individual, so the conditions for justification of a belief are conditions that the Church must satisfy, not Francis or Jane or Edward. The criteria for justification of key religious beliefs and the conditions for knowledge in these cases are

---

[64] Mencken, *Mencken's America*, ed. S. T. Joshi (Athens, OH: Ohio University Press, 2004), 131.

[65] As Michael Lynch observes, '[it] is depressingly common for people to think they personally know what the truth is on any subject' (*True to Life: Why Truth Matters*, p. 34).

[66] Zagzebski, 'Religious Knowledge and the Virtues of the Mind', in Zagzebski (ed.), *Rational Faith: Catholic Responses to Reformed Epistemology* (Notre Dame, Ind.: University of Notre Dame, 1993), 199–225; cf. Zagzebski, 'Plantinga's *Warranted Christian Belief* and the Aquinas/Calvin Model', *Philosophical Books*, 43/2 (2002), 117–23.

not primarily a matter of an *individual* believer satisfying certain criteria independently of the Church.[67]

It would appear that Zagzebski is proposing a treasury of epistemic merit so that the Church doles out epistemic justification alongside soteriological justification. But how exactly does the *Church* meet these internalist requirements for individuals? There are at least three possible ways to interpret this claim: (1) warrant resides in Christ as head of the Church; (2) the ontological unity of the Church, and with it warrant, supervenes on the individual members of the Church; (3) warrant arises from each of the Church's members and is shared among them in a sort of commonweal.

For our purposes it is not important to discern which interpretation is correct, since each one entails an externalist view of warrant regarding the individual. According to (1), no believer need be aware of such evidence or defeaters; perhaps it is even possible that the evidence is *in principle* unobtainable to finite human knowers, so long as it is known by Jesus Christ (and since he knows every true proposition, this is not a problem). In the case of (2), there may be a defeater for a particular belief, but different people may know different propositions which, when combined, would defeat the defeater. Externalism also follows from (3). To illustrate, picture an atheistic philosophy professor who presents his class with a defeater for Christian belief; according to (3), a freshman Catholic in the class may retain his warrant for his Christian beliefs because there is, say, a Jesuit scholar in Poland who is able to rebut the argument. But if distance cannot prevent warrant transfer, then why think *time* is any limitation? If warrant transfer could be *diachronic* then the young student could retain his warrant because Augustine or Thomas Aquinas possessed the knowledge to defeat the defeater.[68] Whether or not any of these proposals is viable, it is important to note that each entails externalism regarding the individual.

Zagzebski raises the problem of defeaters, which, as I have argued, must be addressed by any adequate theological epistemology. It is

[67] Zagzebski, 'Religious Knowledge', p. 208.

[68] If warrant could come from the past, perhaps it could also come from the future. Indeed, it may be that an individual could be justified by their *own* eschatological knowledge!

important to keep in mind that defeaters are person relative, such that a particular argument or proposition may be a defeater for one individual relative to his knowledge base but not a defeater for another individual relative to her knowledge base. Ironically, when we take the role of defeaters into account, it appears that Plantinga holds a *stronger* internalist condition than does Zagzebski, for he has always maintained that Christians have an epistemic responsibility to rebut defeaters to Christian belief. In 'Reason and Belief in God' he observes:

Many believers in God have been brought up to believe, but then encountered potential defeaters. They have read books by skeptics, been apprised of the atheological argument from evil, heard it said that theistic belief is just a matter of wish fulfillment or only a means whereby one socioeconomic class keeps another in bondage. These circumstances constitute potential defeaters for justification in theistic belief.[69]

In *Warranted Christian Belief* Plantinga reiterates that the Christian's warrant is prima facie.[70] For Plantinga, individuals cannot simply turn defeaters over to the Church, for *they* must seek a defeater to the defeater, rather than merely taking someone else's word for it.[71] (It is possible that the testimony of a trusted authority could suffice as a defeater, but that would depend critically on the content and credibility of the testimony.) It is *precisely* these kinds of stipulations that are lacking in the non-foundationalist proposals of Lindbeck, Marshall, and Vanhoozer.

This raises an unsettling question: How do we know (individually or corporately) when our beliefs are no longer warranted? It is extremely difficult to answer this type of question, since for many beliefs there is an extended twilight of diminishing justification before one is plunged into the darkness of irrationality. As a general principle, however, Basil Mitchell is right to countenance a prima facie conservatism against defeaters: 'It is not sensible or, indeed, possible,

---

[69] Plantinga, 'Reason and Belief in God', in Alvin Plantinga and Nicholas Wolterstorff (eds.), *Faith and Rationality: Reason and Belief in God* (Notre Dame, Ind.: University of Notre Dame Press, 1983), 84.

[70] Plantinga, *Warranted Christian Belief*, pp. 366–7.

[71] For more on the internalist role of Plantingan defeaters see Michael Czapkay Sudduth, 'The Internalist Character and Evidentialist Implications of Plantingian Defeaters', *International Journal for the Philosophy of Religion*, 45/3 (1999), 167–87.

in this predicament, to be constantly changing our stance, because in that case we should not adhere to our convictions long enough to put them to the test, or to effect worthwhile changes in the world, or to develop for ourselves a consistent character'.[72] Such stability is necessary in order to evaluate one's beliefs adequately. Within a theological context, we must also factor in recognition of the inherent transcendent mystery of the subject matter.[73]

Given that a doxastic community is not simply a set of individual knowers, it is important to consider how one might develop a theory of communal warrant transfer. Stephen Wykstra has argued that an individual need not have evidence for his belief so long as someone in his community is aware of the evidence.[74] If this is correct, then it makes sense this role should primarily be shouldered by Christian intellectuals, including theologians. As Mitchell suggests, 'this obligation to respond to criticism is not laid upon all equally. It is a duty particularly of intellectuals and is one they perform on behalf of the community generally'.[75] For example, a few years ago I heard William Lane Craig present in a church arguments for the existence of God. While it was clear during the talk that many people did not follow Craig's arguments, it also seemed that for many the primary value was simply in being reassured that there are Christians with good arguments. Thus, the internalist demand to defeat defeaters is primarily communal and ought to be shouldered primarily by theologians and other Christian intellectuals.

With this attitude one commits to disambiguating the world of live options of belief for believer and non-believer alike.[76] The theologian has an important obligation to bring the Christian system of belief into dialogue with the world. We can summarize this process as

[72] Mitchell, *Faith and Criticism*, Sarum Lectures 1992 (Oxford: Clarendon, 1994), 37.

[73] For an excellent discussion of paradox in theology see James Anderson, *Paradox in Christian Theology: An Analysis of Its Presence, Character, and Epistemic Status* (Milton Keynes: Paternoster, 2007).

[74] Wykstra, 'Toward a Sensible Evidentialism: On the Notion of "Needing Evidence"', William L. Rowe and William J. Wainwright (eds.), *Philosophy of Religion: Selected Readings*, 2nd edn. (Fort Worth: Harcourt Brace Jovanovich, 1989), 426–37.

[75] Mitchell, *Faith and Criticism*, p. 44.

[76] On disambiguation see Terence Penelhum, *Reason and Religious Faith* (Boulder, Col.: Westview, 1995), ch. 6.

seeking theological consilience. The term consilience refers to 'a "jumping together" of knowledge by the linking of facts and fact-based theory across disciplines to create a common groundwork of explanation'.[77] This describes scientific and theological disambiguation alike. As with Marshall's concept of inclusive and assimilative power, theological consilience assumes that if Christianity is true, then it will be able to explain the widest variety of facts and defend its truth against all comers. As a result, while it is simplistic to say that Christians believe because of certain evidences, a range of evidences serve at innumerable points to reinforce Christian belief. For instance, Thomas Morris observes that he is a Christian because of the overall interpretative power of Christianity as it extends from abstract metaphysics to everyday experience.[78] This represents the best outcome of a Plantingan epistemology, one that is rich in doxastic virtue and strongly emphasizes the role of the theologian in cultivating it.

Finally, this epistemology should facilitate a process of intellectual development in which people move from immaturity to maturity,[79] or as Ernest Sosa says, from animal knowledge to reflective knowledge:

One has *animal knowledge* about one's environment, one's past, and one's own experience if one's judgments and beliefs about these are direct responses to their impact—e.g., through perception or memory—with little or no benefit of reflection or understanding.

One has *reflective knowledge* if one's judgment or belief manifests not only such direct response to the fact known but also understanding of its place in a wider whole that includes one's belief and knowledge of it and how these come about.[80]

---

[77] E. O. Wilson, *Consilience: The Unity of Knowledge* (London: Little, Brown, 1998), 6.

[78] Morris, 'Suspicions of Something More', in Morris (ed.), *God and the Philosophers* (New York: Oxford University Press, 1994), 17–18. While evidence may serve as an occasion for belief, it is typically not a *cause* of belief: 'It is not that the theist sizes up what the world appears to be like (including the existence of theistic belief itself) and then proposes the existence of God as the best explanation of these phenomena' (Plantinga, *Warranted Christian Belief*, p. 371).

[79] As Paul put it, moving from milk to solid food (1 Cor. 3: 1–2).

[80] Sosa, 'Knowledge and Intellectual Virtue', in *Knowledge in Perspective: Selected Essays in Epistemology* (Cambridge: Cambridge University Press, 1991), 240.

Animal knowledge is closely related to simple perception and thus provides our epistemic foundation. The challenge is to move from a primal experience of the world to true reflective (objectual, propositional) knowledge. It is part of the theologian's task to move the Church to a fuller objectual and propositional knowledge of the '[g]reat things of the gospel'. This knowledge includes awareness of and ability to respond to defeaters, even as we seek to disambiguate the world epistemically and to appreciate the consilience of Christian belief.

A final word. While we do not have direct control over our beliefs, we do have control over our attitudes, and thus the disciplines by which we form and hold beliefs.[81] Moment by moment, we have the choice to cultivate epistemic virtues whereby we seek evidence for our beliefs, are not unduly deferential to them, strive for objectivity, eschew dogmatism and our own inbuilt confirmation bias,[82] and so on.[83] Thus, our epistemic obligations entail the obligation both to respond to defeaters and to cultivate belief virtues to guide the pursuit of truth. This rigorous pursuit of truth differs markedly from the attitude of the theologian in C. S. Lewis's *The Great Divorce* who, after years of poor belief dispositions, ends up in hell:

Having allowed oneself to drift, unresisting, unpraying, accepting every half-conscious solicitation from our own desires, we reached a point where we no longer believed the Faith. Just in the same way, a jealous man, drifting and unresisting, reaches a point at which he believes lies about his best friend: a drunkard reaches a point at which (for the moment) he actually believes that another glass will do him no harm. The beliefs are sincere in the sense that they do occur as psychological events in the man's mind. If that's what you mean by sincerity then they are sincere, and so were ours. But errors which are sincere in that sense are not innocent.[84]

---

[81] James Beilby, *Epistemology as Theology: An Evaluation of Alvin Plantinga's Religious Epistemology* (Aldershot: Ashgate, 2005), 154.

[82] Raymond S. Nickerson, 'Confirmation Bias: A Ubiquitous Phenomenon in Many Guises', *Review of General Psychology*, 2/2 (1998), 175–220.

[83] For further discussion of virtue epistemology see Linda Zagzebski, *Virtues of the Mind: An Inquiry into the Nature of Virtue and the Ethical Foundations of Knowledge* (New York: Cambridge University Press, 1996); W. Jay Wood, *Epistemology: Becoming Intellectually Virtuous* (Downers Grove, Ill.: InterVarsity, 1998).

[84] Lewis, *The Great Divorce: A Dream* (Glasgow: Collins, 1946), 38–9.

Note that it was not the rigorous pursuit of truth that led the wayward theologian finally to yield to the force of defeaters and the decided lack of theological consilience. Rather, it was a lack of virtue that led him, step by step, away from the truth of the faith. It is a sad fact that this could serve as a parabolic description of the journey of many theologians who have gradually abdicated their essential role as epistemic exemplars for the community of faith whilst ending up as little more than tenured heretics.

'Timeless, Universal Propositions?'

Perhaps it is possible to maintain a rigorous theological virtue with proper-function foundationalism. But isn't it also true that a view of theology as the pursuit and systematization of interpretative frameworks with true theological propositions commits one to an untenable view of doctrines as timeless and universal systems? And once we admit such systems, don't they inevitably calcify into inflexible inhibitors of transformative ecumenical dialogue that threaten to oppress dissonant voices? While there are a number of issues behind these concerns, the short answer is that it is simply erroneous to think that cognitive-propositionalism combined with an analytic theological method commits one to timeless and universal propositions or epic theologizing. Perhaps the best way to allay these concerns is by deconstructing the central fear of 'timeless and universal propositions'. To that end I will argue two points. First, even if cognitive-propositionalism did entail timeless, universal propositions, this view would have no implications for oppression. Second, the non-foundationalist's central concern is really best understood as an objection to the view that the world is amenable to only one true description. But this concern is unfounded, for in fact cognitive-propositionalism is wholly congruent with a qualified, non-absolute anti-realism. I will close with a suggestion of how this might unfold in ecumenical discussion.

The worry about the link between cognitive-propositionalism and oppression is central for many non-foundationalists. For instance, Middleton and Walsh ask: 'How can we presume that our own worldview is so in touch with reality...that we can magisterially

pronounce on the truth or falsity of any other worldview?'[85] Note
that for them merely asserting the conviction that one's world-view
is true is necessarily *magisterial*; that is, domineering or oppressive.
Similarly, Vanhoozer warns that '[c]ognitive-propositionalist theology risks deflecting doctrine from its proper role of drawing us into
the drama by turning it into an ossified, formulaic knowledge that
will either wilt on the vine or, on another plausible scenario, be
used as a shibbolethic instrument of power'.[86] Thus, on this view the
Procrustean bed of doctrine will either become irrelevant or it will
assert its dominance. And so, the view of doctrines as descriptions
of reality rather than guides for transformation leaves them open to
being used as instruments of coercive power.

Given the influence of these views, it is surprising to consider just
how spurious these claims are. Keep in mind that the end of true
descriptive systems of doctrine only comes about by a public appeal
to evidence, a willingness to rebut defeaters, and other epistemic
virtues. This approach utterly repudiates any recourse to violence or
oppression. As Reno points out:

Totalitarian governments tend to silence reasoned arguments, not encourage
them as tools for domination. The equation of universal truth with violence
would strike them as absurd. In what sense does the principle of noncontradiction lead to colonialism or gender inequality? How does $2 + 2 = 4$
suppress religious differences?[87]

To ask these questions is to answer them. Logic does not oppress people; people oppress people. And it isn't logic's fault if it gets employed
to oppress people. After all, even a feather pillow can become a deadly
weapon, but that hardly warrants a campaign against pillows. Indeed,
the best way to avoid oppression is by setting all prejudices aside in the
singular pursuit of truth in dialogue. This singular pursuit of truth
is inimical to the influential contemporary conception of theology
as a perpetual, transformative, communal conversation. Ironically,
this view in which the value of theology comes in transformation
through conversation is in danger of perpetuating power abuses. In

---

[85] Richard Middleton and Brian Walsh, *Truth is Stranger Than It Used to Be: Biblical
Faith in a Postmodern Age* (Downers Grove, Ill.: InterVarsity, 1995). 30.
[86] Vanhoozer, *The Drama of Doctrine*, p. 88.
[87] Reno, 'Theology's Continental Captivity', p. 28.

the essay 'Theology as a Bull Session' I critique Jürgen Moltman's view of theology along these lines:

> Ironically, Moltmann's model of perpetual conversation may contribute to precisely what he repudiates: the abuse of power. Moltmann does not appreciate the pure discursive meritocracy that is secured by the analytic theologian's demand for rigor, concision, and clarity from all. Within this discursive culture the appeal of your rhetoric, impenetrability of your prose, and security of your reputation matter nothing if your arguments are poor. It is on this egalitarian and iconoclastic ground that upstart Bertrand Russell could write his famous 1903 letter shooting down Frege's Basic law V. Now try to imagine this dazzling exercise of analytic reasoning if Frege had written with Heideggerian obfuscation. In such a climate, Russell could easily be dismissed as a smarmy upstart whose temerity to challenge such a profoundly difficult thinker could only come from youthful ignorance. Hence, Moltmann's dismissal of carefully reasoned analysis as a hubristic power grab could easily become a means to indemnify the academic elite against criticism.[88]

Thus, once you deny the possibility of true theological description you effectively undermine the primary means by which we hold theologians accountable for the claims they make. Deference to reputation can set a dangerous precedent.

Let us grant that timeless, universal doctrines are not necessarily oppressive. Nonetheless, we might worry that whatever modest knowledge gains we might make would be overshadowed by a wider inhibiting of ecumenism. Is this a legitimate concern? In order to answer this question we must first concede that ecumenism ought to be a central task of the Church. Indeed, it seems to me that the credibility of the Church as a faithful witness of Christ may well depend upon significant ecumenical advance.[89] But why think that cognitive-propositionalism will threaten ecumenical discussion? Lindbeck explains the concern with respect to rigidity in doctrinal formulation and development: 'Each proposition or act of judgment corresponds or does not correspond, is eternally true or false: there

---

[88] See Rauser, 'Theology as a Bull Session', in Oliver Crisp and Michael Rea (eds.), *Analytic Theology*, p. 83.

[89] See Bruce Marshall, 'Who Really Cares About Christian Unity?', *First Things* (Jan. 2001), 29–34; Ephraim Radner, *The End of the Church: A Pneumatology of Christian Division in the West* (Grand Rapids, Mich.: Eerdmans, 1998).

are no degrees of variation in propositional truth'.[90] Similarly Grenz
claims that cognitive-propositionalism leads to the 'crystallization of
biblical truth into a set of universally true and applicable propositions'.[91] Once the theologian has caged herself behind the iron bars of
universal and timelessly true doctrines, she will find that this inhibits
any substantial ecumenical advance.

It does not take much reflection to discern that the real concern is
not with the eternal truth of doctrines per se. For one thing, virtually
every theologian affirms some doctrines (but not others) as universally and timelessly true. Consider:

(1) God is triune.
(2) God is omniscient.
(3) God is good.
(4) God is the creator.
(5) Human beings are made in the image of God.
(6) Jesus rose from the dead.

Surely most Christian theologians would affirm that (1)–(3) are
always true and further that (4)–(6) are not always true, since (4) was
false prior to creation, (5) was false prior to the creation of human
beings, and (6) was false prior to the resurrection. Even an eternalist
about propositions (that is, one who believes that propositions are
timelessly true) will recognize a modal distinction between (1)–(3)
and (4)–(6).

It would appear that the real concern is not simply with individual doctrines but rather with systems of doctrine. For instance, it
would seem likely that Lindbeck was reacting to the notion of one
true theological description when he developed his cultural-linguistic
theory.[92] Lindbeck sought to address the problem by marginalizing
doctrines, with the claim that they are second-order statements that
regulate communal practice; as a result, the only true description
occurs when the community conforms to true practices.[93] On this

---

[90] Lindbeck, *The Nature of Doctrine: Religion and Theology in a Postliberal Age*
(Philadelphia, Pa.: Westminster, 1984), 47.
[91] Stanley Grenz, *Revisioning Evangelical Theology: A Fresh Agenda for the 21st
Century* (Downers Grove, Ill: InterVarsity Press, 1993), 65.
[92] Lindbeck, *The Nature of Doctrine*, p. 35.   [93] Ibid. 51.

view, the only point of doctrines is to regulate behaviour.[94] Given the motivation of Lindbeck's theory of doctrine, it is ironic that it ends up looking much like the experiential-expressivism that he repudiates. (Perhaps the central difference is that Lindbeck accepts Wittgenstein's private-language argument and thus externalizes the ground of theology.) It should not be missed that this position follows experiential-expressivism in radically reinterpreting the nature and function of doctrines, and as a result it conceals a whiff of elitism by marginalizing the basic assumptions of most Christians: let the great unwashed pew warmers think their doctrinal ascriptions have a realist function, for *we* know that the *real* function of doctrine is ethical and regulative.[95]

Lindbeck and his epigones have offered the cognitive-propositionalist an ecumenical challenge. My response (couched in obstinately militaristic terms), will begin with an epistemological shot across Lindbeck's bow. The point here is that nothing of import for ecumenism follows from the fact that there is one true description of reality. On this point, note how Michael Lynch defines the one true description thesis: '[H]ypothetically at least, there is a theory waiting "out there" that *is* completely right, and the search for that theory is the point of metaphysical inquiry'.[96] Obviously a person could accept this view and remain uncertain as to whether (or to what degree) they had achieved that complete true description. In addition, one might believe that ecumenical dialogue provides an essential critical process through which we will come to grasp that one true description.

Let us grant for the sake of argument that the 'one true description of reality' view would frustrate ecumenism. But, then, why think that cognitive-propositionalism is even committed to there being only one

[94] Ibid.19.

[95] See Alister McGrath, *The Genesis of Doctrine: A Study in the Foundation of Doctrinal Criticism* (Grand Rapids, Mich.: Eerdmans, 1990), ch. 2; 'An Evangelical Evaluation of Postliberalism', in Timothy R. Phillips and Dennis L. Okholm (eds.), *The Nature of Confession: Evangelicals and Postliberals in Conversation* (Downers Grove, Ill.: InterVarsity, 1996), 23–44, esp. pp. 35–9. For a critical defence of Lindbeck see Chad C. Pecknold, *Reforming Postliberal Theology: George Lindbeck, Pragmatism and Scripture* (Edinburgh: T& T Clark, 2005).

[96] Lynch, *Truth in Context: An Essay on Pluralism and Objectivity* (Cambridge, Mass./London: MIT Press, 1998), 10.

true description of reality? In fact it is not. Although I would reject an unqualified constitutive anti-realist position according to which everything exists relative to a conceptual scheme, that fact does not exclude the possibility that *some things* exist or are constituted only relative to a conceptual scheme. And if that is true, then it may be that some of the doctrines that are currently disputed in ecumenical dialogue are among those that are relatively true, and that identifying them as relative is a vital key to ecumenical advance. Indeed, the identification of certain doctrines as relatively true could provide a powerful means to resolve a number of seemingly interminable and intractable theological disagreements.[97]

In order to set this position up we can begin by clarifying the distinction between the natural world and the socially constructed world.[98] The anti-realist errs in refusing to make this distinction due to the assumption that all objects of human thought are socially constructed. Our critique of unqualified conceptual-relative anti-realism in Chapter 6 illustrated the bracing problems with this position. Thus, we must first concede a very large class of objectively existent things (including mountains, stars, trees, rocks, and lakes) all of which would exist even of there were no (non-divine) minds. In addition to the class of objectively existent entities there is a class of socially constructed entities including money, dresses, chairs, and the law. For instance, speed limits clearly exist, but it is also obvious that a speed limit does not exist in the same way as a tree. Speed limits are dependent on the conceptualizing activity of human minds in a way that objective entities like trees are not. Thus, if human beings did not exist, the speed limit on California Highway 101 would not exist (neither of course would the highway), but California's magnificent General Sherman Sequoia would (or at least could) still exist (though of course it would not have been *named* 'the General Sherman'). While human beings name the tree and embed it within a cultural context (for instance, by granting it a certain romantic mystique and making it an object of pilgrimage and postcards), we certainly do not *create the tree*. By contrast, speed limits and other laws are

[97] This parallels Michael Lynch's argument for metaphysical pluralism based on 'the peculiar intractability of metaphysical debate' (*Truth in Context*, p. 16).
[98] See John Searle, *The Construction of Social Reality* (New York: Free Press, 1995).

wholly dependent upon human beings, for they are constructed out of human minds. Michael Lynch thus observes: '[P]ropositions of law clearly aren't true in the way that propositions about spruce trees are: they don't correspond to something concrete and mind-independent called "the Law" '.[99] But such propositions are nonetheless true.

Cognitive-propositionalists have no problem admitting socially constructed objects, events, or states of affairs into their catalogue of existence, but doing so does not immediately address the ecumenical problem raised by the one-true-description view of doctrine. In addition, what we require is that some socially constructed objects, events, or states of affairs that are central to doctrines are susceptible to two or more ecclesially centred constituting social constructions. Here I will focus on the event of baptism as a test case, since it is the subject of ongoing, interminable debate and as such is a solid candidate for ecumenical relativization. Indeed, reflection suggests a particular implausibility in the absolutist position on baptism, in so far as it entails that a large percentage of Christians throughout Church history have misunderstood and so not even participated in the central rite of initiation for the Christian Church. This surprising implication prompts a question: If the Spirit is leading the Christian community into all truth (John 16: 13), wouldn't he see to it that Christians were actually baptizing their members?

The relativized view of baptism proposes that there is not a single form of baptism, or group that ought normatively to be baptized (e.g. infant or adult). Instead, very different events, including infant sprinkling and adult immersion, both constitute the same rite of initiation. The function of each as baptism depends on the practice's cultural embedding within a particular ecclesial communion. Thus, within the Catholic community infant sprinkling might be constituted as a (normative) baptism while in a Baptist community adult immersion might be constituted as the sole legitimate baptism. In so far as one concedes the relativity of baptism to theological framework and religious community, one must abandon the notion that there is one true description of the normative practice of baptism for all Christians, since both Catholics and Baptists practice legitimate baptism relative to their ecclesial communions. I would submit that that

[99] Lynch, *True to Life*, p. 44.

which may be true for baptism may also be true for a number of other debated doctrines, including the real presence in the eucharist,[100] the relationship of justification and sanctification, and perhaps even the *filioque*. However, the primary point here is not to defend a list of doctrines that can be relativized, but simply to point out that cognitive-propositionalism is fully amenable to the denial of the one-true-description view of doctrine. The point is that there is nothing stopping cognitive-propositionalists who are staunch realists regarding doctrine from leading the way in genuine ecumenical advance.

CONCLUSION

The core problem with cognitive-propositionalism and orthodoxy may be more one of image than of substance. If so, then we must work to enable people to see the passionate excitement in a rigorous and committed theology. The cognitive-propositional view of doctrine is not naive, simplistic, Procrustean, or rationalistic. But it is rooted in the mystery of divine accommodation and revelation. And orthodoxy is not a dry set of beliefs, but rather 'a warm continuity of human experience—of grandmothers teaching granddaughters, of feasts and stories, of rites and dancing'.[101] If a warm piety is the beating heart of the living Church, orthodoxy is the skeleton. And, in the midst of it all, the systematic theologian has a truly staggering responsibility to spur on towards the health and flourishing of this living reality we call the Church as a proleptic community of truth.

---

[100] See my 'Ecumenism, Eucharist, and an Antirealism We Can Live With', *Canadian Evangelical Review*, 30–1 (2005–6), 23–41.

[101] Oden, *After Modernity... What?*, p.152.

Bibliography

Abraham, William, *Crossing the Threshold of Divine Revelation* (Grand Rapids, Mich: Eerdmans, 2006).

—— 'The Epistemological Significance of the Inner Witness of the Holy Spirit', *Faith and Philosophy*, 7/4 (1990), 434–50.

Adam, A. K. M. (ed.), *Handbook of Postmodern Biblical Interpretation* (St Louis, Miss.: Chalice, 2000).

Adams, Robert, *The Virtue of Faith: And Other Essays in Philosophical Theology* (New York: Oxford University Press, 1987).

Albert, Hans, and Rorty, M. V., *Treatise on Critical Reason* (Princeton, NJ: Princeton University Press, 1985).

Alston, William, *Divine Nature and Human Language: Essays in Philosophical Theology* (Ithaca, NY/London: Cornell University Press, 1989).

—— *Epistemic Justification: Essays in the Theory of Knowledge* (Ithaca, NY: Cornell University Press, 1989).

—— *Perceiving God: The Epistemology of Religious Experience* (Ithaca, NY: Cornell University Press, 1991).

—— *A Realist Conception of Truth* (Ithaca, NY: Cornell University Press, 1996).

—— *A Sensible Metaphysical Realism*, Aquinas Lecture 2001 (Milwaukee, Wisc.: Marquette University Press, 2001).

—— (ed.), *Realism and Antirealism* (Ithaca/London: Cornell University Press, 2002).

—— 'How to Think about Reliability', *Philosophical Topics*, 23/1 (1995), 1–29.

—— 'Back to the Theory of Appearing', in James Tomberlin (ed.), *Philosophical Perspectives, xiii. Epistemology, 1999* (Atascadero, Calif.: Ridgeview, 1999), 181–203.

—— 'Sellars and the Myth of the Given', at <http://www.ditext.com/alston/alston2.html>, accessed January 2009.

Anderson, James, *Paradox in Christian Theology: An Analysis of Its Presence, Character, and Epistemic Status* (Milton Keynes: Paternoster, 2007).

Aquinas, Thomas, *The Compendium of Theology*, trans. Cyril Vollert (London: Herder, 1947).

Aristotle, *Metaphysics*, trans. W. D. Ross (n.p.: NuVision, 2005).

Asimov, Isaac, *The Relativity of Wrong* (New York: Doubleday, 1988).

Asselt, Willem J. van, and Dekker, Eef (eds.), *Reformation and Scholasticism: An Ecumenical Enterprise* (Grand Rapids, Mich.: Baker, 2001).

Audi, Robert, *Epistemology: A Contemporary Introduction to the Theory of Knowledge* (London: Routledge, 1998).

Augustine, *Confessions*, trans. Henry Chadwick (Oxford: Oxford University Press, 1991).

—— *'Against the Academicians' and 'The Teacher'*, trans. Peter King (Indianapolis, Ind.: Hackett, 1995).

Ayers, Michael, 'Is Perceptual Content Ever Conceptual?', *Philosophical Books*, 43/1 (2002).

Bacote, Vincent, Miguélez, Laura, and Okholm, Dennis (eds.), *Evangelicals and Scripture: Tradition, Authority, and Hermeneutics* (Downers Grove, Ill.: InterVarsity, 2004).

Baillie, John, *Our Knowledge of God* (London: Oxford University Press, 1939).

—— *The Sense of the Presence of God*, Gifford Lectures 1961–2 (London: Oxford University Press, 1962).

Bainton, Roland H., *Here I Stand: A Life of Martin Luther* (London: Penguin, 2002).

Barth, Karl, *Dogmatics in Outline*, trans. G. T. Thomson (London: SCM, 1949).

Barth, Karl, *Church Dogmatics: The Doctrine of the Word of God*, i–ii, trans. G. W. Bromiley, ed. G. W. Bromiley and T. F. Torrance (Edinburgh: T&T Clark, 1975).

Barwise, Jon, and Perry, John, *Situations and Attitudes* (Cambridge, Mass.: MIT Press, 1983).

Bavinck, Herman, *The Doctrine of God*, trans. William Hendricksen (Grand Rapids, Mich.: Eerdmans, 1951).

Beale, G. K., *The Erosion of Inerrancy in Evangelicalism: Responding to New Challenges to Biblical Authority* (Wheaton, Ill.: Crossway, 2008).

Beilby, James, *Epistemology as Theology: An Evaluation of Alvin Plantinga's Religious Epistemology* (Aldershot: Ashgate, 2005).

—— (ed.), *Naturalism Defeated? Essays on Plantinga's Evolutionary Argument Against Naturalism* (Ithaca, NY: Cornell University Press, 2002).

Benacerraf, Paul, and Putnam, Hilary (eds.), *Philosophy of Mathematics* (Oxford: Blackwell, 1964).

Berger, Peter, *The Heretical Imperative: Contemporary Possibilities of Religious Affirmation* (Garden City, NY: Anchor, 1979).

—— 'Secular Theology and the Rejection of the Supernatural: Reflections on Recent Trends', *Theological Studies*, 38/1 (1977), 39–56.

—— 'Protestantism and the Quest for Certainty', *Christian Century*, 26 Aug.–2 Sept. 1998, pp. 782–96.

Bergmann, Michael, *Justification without Awareness: A Defense of Epistemic Externalism* (Oxford: Oxford University Press, 2006).

Berkhof, Louis, *Systematic Theology* (Edinburgh: Banner of Truth Trust, 1958).

Beversluis, John, 'Reforming the Reformed Objection to Natural Theology', *Faith and Philosophy*, 12/2 (1995), 189–206.

Blackburn, Simon, *Truth: A Guide for the Baffled* (Oxford: Oxford University Press, 2005).

—— 'Robert Brandom, *Reading Rorty*', at <http://www.phil.cam.ac.uk/~swb24/reviews/Rorty/htm>, accessed January 2009.

Blamires, Harry, *The Christian Mind: How Should a Christian Think?* (Ann Arbor, Mich.: Servant, 1978).

Blanshard, Brand, *The Nature of Thought*, ii (New York: Macmillan, 1941).

Blumenthal, H. J., *Aristotle and Neoplatonism in Late Antiquity: Interpretations of* De Anima (London: Duckworth, 1996).

Boffetti, Jason, 'How Richard Rorty Found Religion', *First Things* (May 2004), 24–30.

Boghossian, Paul, *Fear of Knowledge: Against Relativism and Constructivism* (Oxford: Clarendon, 2006).

—— and Peacocke, Christopher (eds.), *New Essays on the A Priori* (Oxford: Clarendon, 2000).

BonJour, Laurence, *The Structure of Empirical Knowledge* (Cambridge, Mass.: Harvard University Press, 1985).

—— *In Defense of Pure Reason* (Cambridge: Cambridge University Press, 1998).

Borg, Marcus J., *Meeting Jesus Again for the First Time* (New York: Harper-SanFrancisco, 1994).

Boyd, Gregory A., and Boyd, Edward K., *Letters From a Skeptic: A Son Wrestles with his Father's Questions about Christianity* (Colorado Springs, Col.: Chariot Victor, 1994).

Brown, Warren S., Murphy, Nancey, and Maloney, H. Newton (eds.), *Whatever Happened to the Soul? Scientific and Theological Portraits of Human Nature* (Minneapolis, Minn.: Fortress, 1998).

Brunsmann, John, *A Handbook of Fundamental Theology*, i, trans. Arthur Preuss (St Louis, Miss./London: Herder, 1928).

Buckley, Michael J., *At the Origins of Modern Atheism* (New Haven, Conn.: Yale University Press, 1987).

Calvin, John, *Institutes of the Christian Religion*, ii, ed. John T. McNeill, trans. Ford Lewis Battles (London: SCM, 1961).

—— *Institutes of the Christian Religion*, trans. Henry Beveridge (Grand Rapids, Mich.: Eerdmans, 1989).

Carson, D. A., *Becoming Conversant with the Emerging Church* (Grand Rapids, Mich.: Zondervan, 2005).

Chalmers, David J., *The Conscious Mind: In Search of a Fundamental Theory* (Oxford: Oxford University Press, 1996).

Charnock, Stephen, *The Existence and Attributes of God* (1682; Grand Rapids, Mich.: Baker, 1996).

Charry, Ellen, review of Bruce Marshall (ed.), *Theology and Dialogue: Essays in Conversation with George Lindbeck*, *Theology Today*, 48/3 (1991), 340–4.

—— 'Walking in the Truth: On Knowing God', in Alan G. Padgett and Patrick R. Keifert (eds.), *But Is It All True? The Bible and the Question of Truth*, (Grand Rapids, Mich./Cambridge: Eerdmans, 2006.

Chisholm, Roderick, *The Problem of the Criterion*, Aquinas Lecture 1973 (Milwaukee, Wisc.: Marquette University Press, 1973).

Chomsky, Noam, *Language and Problems of Knowledge*, Managua Lectures (Cambridge, Mass.: MIT Press, 1987).

Clark, David, *To Know and Love God: Method for Theology* (Wheaton, Ill.: Crossway, 2003).

—— 'Relativism, Fideism and the Promise of Postliberalism', in Timothy R. Phillips and Dennis L. Okholm (eds.), *The Nature of Confession* (Downers Grove, Ill: InterVarsity, 1996).

Clark, Kelly James, *Return to Reason* (Grand Rapids, Mich.: Eerdmans, 1990).

Clarke, Samuel, 'The Scripture Doctrine of the Trinity', in *Classics of Protestantism*, ed. Vergilius Ferm (New York: Philosophical Library, 1959).

Clayton, Philip, *The Problem of God in Modern Thought* (Grand Rapids, Mich: Eerdmans, 2000).

Clifford, W. K., 'The Ethics of Belief', in *Lectures and Essays*, ii (London: Macmillan, 1901).

Clouser, Roy, *Knowing With the Heart: Religious Experience and Belief in God* (Downers Grove, Ill.: InterVarsity, 1999).

Coffman, E. J., and Howard-Snyder, D., 'Three Arguments Against Foundationalism: Arbitrariness, Epistemic Regress, and Existential Support', *Canadian Journal of Philosophy*, 36/4 (2006), 535–64.

Cottingham, John (ed.), *The Cambridge Companion to Descartes* (Cambridge: Cambridge University Press, 1992).

Craig, William Lane, *Apologetics: An Introduction* (Chicago, Ill.: Moody, 1984).

—— and Moreland, J. P. (eds.), *Naturalism: A Critical Analysis* (London: Routledge, 2000).

—— —— *The Blackwell Companion to Natural Theology* (Oxford: Blackwell, 2009).

Crease, Robert P., and Mann, Charles C., *The Second Creation: Makers of the Revolution in Twentieth Century Physics* (London: Quartet, 1997).

Crisp, Oliver, and Rea, Michael (eds.), *Analytic Theology* (Oxford: Oxford University Press, 2009).

Crisp, Thomas, Davidson, Matthew, and Vander Laan, David (eds.), *Knowledge and Reality: Essays in Honor of Alvin Plantinga* (Dordrecht: Springer, 2006).

Cunningham, David, *These Three are One: The Practice of Trinitarian Theology* (Oxford: Blackwell, 1997).

Cupitt, Don, *Creation out of Nothing* (Philadelphia, Pa.: Trinity, 1990).

Darwin, Charles, *The Autobiography of Charles Darwin, 1809–1882: With Original Omissions Restored*, ed. Nora Barlow (New York: Norton, 1969).

Davidson, Donald, *Inquiries into Truth and Interpretation* (Oxford: Clarendon, 1984).

—— 'The Structure and Content of Truth', *Journal of Philosophy*, 87 (1990), 307–8.

—— 'Intellectual Autobiography of Donald Davidson', in Lewis Edwin Hahn (ed.), *The Philosophy of Donald Davidson* (Peru, Ill.: Open Court, 1999), 3–69.

Davis, Richard, 'Can There Be an "Orthodox" Postmodern Theology?', *Journal of the Evangelical Theological Society*, 45/1 (2002), 111–23.

Davis, Stephen T., *God, Reason and Theistic Proofs* (Grand Rapids, Mich.: Eerdmans, 1997).

—— ' "What Can Be Known about God is Plain to Them": A Meditation on Religious Unbelief', in Daniel Kendall and Stephen T. Davis (eds.), *The Convergence of Theology* (New York: Paulist, 2001), 253–69.

Dawkins, Richard, *The God Delusion* (Boston, Mass.: Houghton Mifflin, 2006).

Dekker, Eef, and Asselt, Willem J. van, *Reformation and Scholasticism: An Ecumenical Enterprise* (Grand Rapids, Mich.: Baker, 2001).

DePaul, Michael (ed.), *Resurrecting Old-fashioned Foundationalism* (Lanham, Md.: Rowman & Littlefield, 2000).

DePoe, John, 'In Defense of Classical Foundationalism: A Critical Evaluation of Plantinga's Argument that Classical Foundationalism is Self-refuting', *South African Journal of Philosophy*, 26/3 (2007), 245–51.

Descartes, René, *Meditations on First Philosophy*, trans. and ed. John Cottingham, rev. edn. (Cambridge: Cambridge University Press, 1986).

Derrida, Jacques, *Limited Inc* (Evanston, Ill.: Northwestern University Press, 1988).

Devitt, Michael, *Realism and Truth*, 2nd edn. (Princeton, NJ: Princeton University Press, 1996).

Diller, Kevin, 'Does Contemporary Theology Require a Postfoundationalist Way of Knowing?', *Scottish Journal of Theology*, 60/3 (2007), 271–93.

Dorrien, Gary, 'The Future of Postliberal Theology', *Christian Century*, 18–25 July 2001, pp. 22–9.

Dulles, Avery, *The Craft of Theology: From Symbol to System* (New York: Crossroad, 1992).

—— *A History of Apologetics* (1971; San Francisco: Ignatius, 2005).

Earman, John, *Hume's Abject Failure: The Argument Against Miracles* (Oxford: Oxford University Press, 2000).

Ehrman, Bart, *Misquoting Jesus: The Story Behind Who Changed the Bible and Why* (New York: HarperSanFrancisco, 2005).

Erickson, Millard, *The Evangelical Left: Encountering Postconservative Evangelical Theology* (Grand Rapids, Mich.: Baker, 1997).

—— *Christian Theology*, 2nd edn. (Grand Rapids, Mich: Baker, 1998).

—— *Postmodernizing the Faith: Evangelical Responses to the Challenge of Postmodernism* (Grand Rapids, Mich.: Baker, 1998).

—— *Truth or Consequences: The Promise and Perils of Postmodernism* (Downers Grove, Ill.: InterVarsity, 2001).

Euhling, T., and Wettstein, H. (eds.), *Studies in Epistemology*, Midwest Studies in Philosophy, iv (Minneapolis, Minn.: University of Minnesota Press, 1979), 73–121.

Evans, C. Stephen, *The Historical Christ and the Jesus of Faith* (Oxford/New York: Oxford University Press, 1996).

—— *Faith Beyond Reason: A Kierkegaardian Account* (Grand Rapids, Mich./Cambridge: Eerdmans, 1998).

Fackre, Gabriel, *The Doctrine of Revelation: A Narrative Interpretation* (Edinburgh: Edinburgh University Press, 1997).

Fales, Evan, *A Defense of the Given* (Lanham, Md.: Rowman & Littlefield, 1996).

Fee, Gordon, and Strauss, Mark L., *How to Choose a Translation for All Its Worth* (Grand Rapids, Mich.: Zondervan, 2007).

Flew, Antony, and MacIntyre, Alasdair, *New Essays in Philosophical Theology* (London: SCM, 1955).

Franke, John, *The Character of Theology: An Introduction to Its Nature, Task, and Purpose* (Grand Rapids, Mich.: Baker, 2005).

Frei, Hans, *The Eclipse of Biblical Narrative* (New Haven, Conn./London: Yale University Press, 1974).

French, Peter A., Uehling, Theodore E., and Wettstein, Howard K. (eds.), *Midwest Studies in Philosophy, xii: Realism and Antirealism* (Minneapolis, Minn.: University of Minnesota, 1988).

Fumerton, Richard, *Metaepistemology and Skepticism* (Lanham, Md.: Rowman & Littlefield, 1995).

—— 'Plantinga, Warrant, and Christian Belief', *Philosophia Christi*, 3/2 (2001), 341–51.

—— 'Foundationalist Theories of Epistemic Justification', in *Stanford Encyclopedia of Philosophy*, at <http://plato.stanford.edu/entries/justep-foundational>, accessed January 2009.

Geisler, Norman, *Explaining Hermeneutics: A Commentary on the Chicago Statement on Biblical Hermeneutics* (Oakland, Calif.: International Council on Biblical Inerrancy, 1983).

—— *Baker Encyclopedia of Christian Apologetics* (Grand Rapids, Mich.: Baker, 1999).

Geivett, Douglas R., and Jesson, Greg, 'Plantinga's Externalism and the Terminus of Warrant-based Epistemology', *Philosophia Christi*, 3/2 (2001), 329–40.

Gettier, Edmund, 'Is Justified True Belief Knowledge?', *Analysis*, 23 (1963), 231–3.

Goldman, Alvin, *Epistemology and Cognition* (Cambridge, Mass.: Harvard University Press, 1986).

—— *Knowledge in a Social World* (Oxford: Clarendon, 1999).

—— 'A Causal Theory of Knowing', *Journal of Philosophy*, 64/12 (1967), 35–72.

Goodman, Nelson, 'The Way the World Is', in Peter McCormick (ed.), *Starmaking: Realism, Anti-realism and Irrealism* (Cambridge, Mass.: MIT Press, 1996).

Greco, John, review of Alvin Plantinga, *Warranted Christian Belief*, *American Catholic Philosophical Quarterly*, 75/3 (2001), 461–6.

Grenz, Stanley, *Revisioning Evangelical Theology: A Fresh Agenda for the 21st Century* (Downers Grove, Ill.: InterVarsity, 1993).

—— *A Primer on Postmodernism* (Grand Rapids, Mich.: Eerdmans, 1996).

—— *Renewing the Center: Evangelical Theology in a Post-theological Era* (Grand Rapids, Mich.: Baker, 2000).

—— *The Social God and the Relational Self*: *A Trinitarian Theology of the Imago Dei* (Louisville, Ky./London: Westminster/John Knox, 2001).

—— *Rediscovering the Triune God: The Trinity in Contemporary Theology* (Minneapolis, Minn.: Fortress, 2004).

—— and John Franke, *Beyond Foundationalism: Shaping Theology in a Postmodern Context* (Louisville, Ky.: Westminster/John Knox, 2001), 50.

Griffin, David Ray, Beardslee, William A., and Holland, Joe, *Varieties of Postmodern Theology* (Albany, NY: State University of New York Press, 1989).

Griffiths, Paul, review of Bruce D. Marshall, *Trinity and Truth*, *Journal of Religion*, 81/1 (2001), 155–8.

Groothius, Douglas, 'Why Truth Matters Most: An Apologetic for Truth-seeking in Postmodern Times', *Journal of the Evangelical Theological Society*, 47/3 (2004), 441–54.

Grube, Dirk Martin, 'Religious Experience after the Demise of Foundation-alism', *Religious Studies*, 31/1 (1995), 37–52.

Grudem, Wayne, *Systematic Theology: An Introduction to Bible Doctrine* (Grand Rapids, Mich.: Zondervan, 1994), 1203–7.

Guinness, Os, *The Gravedigger File: Papers on the Subversion of the Modern Church* (Downers Grove, Ill.: InterVarsity, 1983).

Gunton, Colin, *The One, the Three and the Many: God, Creation and the Culture of Modernity*, 1992 Bampton Lectures (Cambridge: Cambridge University Press, 1993).

—— *Intellect and Action: Elucidations on Christian Theology and the Life of Faith* (Edinburgh: T&T Clark, 2000).

Hardcastle, Gary L., and Reisch, George A. (eds.), *Bullshit and Philosophy* (Chicago/LaSalle, Ill.: Open Court, 2006).

Harris, Sam, *The End of Faith: Religion, Terror, and the Future of Reason* (London: Free Press, 2004).

Hart, Hendrik, Van Der Hoeven, Johan, and Wolterstorff, Nicholas (eds.), *Rationality in the Calvinian Tradition* (Boston, Mass.: University Press of America, 1983).

Harvey, Van, *The Historian and the Believer: The Morality of Historical Knowledge and Christian Belief* (New York: Macmillan, 1966).

Hauerwas, Stanley, and Willimon, William, *The Truth About God: The Ten Commandments in Christian Life* (Nashville, Tenn.: Abingdon, 1999).

Hauerwas, Stanley, Murphy, Nancey, and Nation, Mark (eds.), *Theology Without Foundations: Religious Practice and the Future of Theological Truth* (Nashville, Tenn.: Abingdon, 1994).

Hecht, Jennifer, *Doubt: A History* (New York: HarperSanFrancisco, 2003).

Heil, John, *The Nature of True Minds* (Cambridge: Cambridge University Press, 1992).

Helm, Paul, *Faith and Understanding* (Grand Rapids, Mich.: Eerdmans, 1997).

—— review of Alvin Plantinga, *Warranted Christian Belief*, *Mind*, 110/440 (2001), 1110–15.

Heppe, Heinrich, *Reformed Dogmatics*, ed. Ernst Bizer, trans. G. T. Thomson, rev. edn. (London: 1861/London: Wakeman, n.d.), 530–2.

Bibliography   293

Heyer, Kristen, 'How Does Theology Go Public? Rethinking the Debate Between David Tracy and George Lindbeck', *Political Theology*, 5/3 (2004), 307–27.

Hick, John, *An Interpretation of Religion: Human Responses to the Transcendent* (New Haven, Conn.: Yale University Press, 1989).

Hill, Daniel J., '*Warranted Christian Belief* – A Review Article', *Themelios*, 26/2 (2001), 48–9.

Hitchens, Christopher, *God Is Not Great* (New York: Twelve, 2007).

Hodge, A. A., *Outlines of Theology*, enlarged edn. (London: Banner of Truth Trust, 1972).

Hoitenga, Jr., Dewey J., *Faith and Reason From Plato to Plantinga: An Introduction to Reformed Epistemology* (Albany, NY: SUNY Press, 1991).

Honderich, Ted (ed.), *The Oxford Companion to Philosophy* (Oxford/New York: Oxford University Press, 1995).

Hopp, Walter, 'Minimalist Truth and Realist Truth', *Philosophia Christi*, 10/1 (2008), 87–100.

Howkins, Kenneth G., *The Challenge of Religious Studies* (London: Tyndale, 1972).

Jackson, Frank, 'Epiphenomenal Qualia', *Philosophical Quarterly*, 32 (1982), 127–36.

—— 'What Mary Didn't Know', *Journal of Philosophy*, 83/5 (1986), 291–5.

James, William, *Pragmatism* (Cambridge, Mass.: Harvard University Press, 1975).

Jobes, Karen H., 'Relevance Theory and the Translation of Scripture', *Journal of the Evangelical Theological Society*, 50/4 (2007), 773–97.

Johnson, Luke Timothy, 'Explaining God Away', *Commonweal*, 123/22, 20 Dec. 1996, 18–20.

Joseph, Marc, *Donald Davidson* (Montreal: McGill-Queen's University Press, 2004).

Kant, Immanuel, *Critique of Pure Reason*, trans. Norman Kemp Smith (New York: St Martin's, 1929).

Keating, Karl, *Catholicism and Fundamentalism: The Attack on 'Romanism' by 'Bible Christians'* (San Francisco, Calif.: Ignatius, 1988).

Keifert, Patrick R., and Padgett, Alan G. (eds.), *But Is It All True? The Bible and the Question of Truth* (Grand Rapids, Mich./Cambridge: Eerdmans, 2006).

Kenneson, Philip D., 'Truth', in A. K. M. Adam (ed.), *Handbook of Postmodern Biblical Interpretation* (St Louis, Miss.: Chalice, 2000), 26–75.

Kenny, Anthony, *What is Faith? Essays in the Philosophy of Religion* (Oxford: Oxford University Press, 1992).

Kenny, Anthony, *Aquinas on Mind* (London/New York: Routledge, 1993).

—— *Frege* (London: Penguin, 1995).

Kerr, Fergus, *Theology After Wittgenstein* (Oxford: Blackwell, 1986).

—— Wood, Charles, and Marshall, Bruce, 'Book Symposium: Bruce D. Marshall, *Trinity and Truth, Modern Theology*, 16/4 (2000), 503–27.

Kilby, Karen, 'Perichoresis and Projection: Problems with Social Doctrines of the Trinity', *Blackfriars*, 81/956 (2000), 432–45.

Kirkham, Richard L., *Theories of Truth: A Critical Introduction* (Cambridge, Mass.: MIT Press, 1992).

Kornblith, Hilary, *Naturalizing Epistemology*, 2nd edn. (Cambridge, Mass: MIT, 1994).

Kulp, Christopher B. (ed.), *Realism/Antirealism and Epistemology* (Lanham, Md.: Rowman & Littlefield, 1997).

Küng, Hans, *Does God Exist?*, trans. Edward Quinn (New York: Vintage, 1981).

Kuyper, Abraham, *Calvinism* (Grand Rapids, Mich.: Eerdmans, 1931).

Kvanvig, Jonathan, *Warrant in Contemporary Epistemology* (Lanham, Md.: Rowman & Littlefield, 1996).

Larm, Terry A., review of *The Drama of Doctrine*, *Evangelical Review of Theology*, 32/1 (2008), 86–8.

Latourelle, René, and O'Collins, Gerald, *Problems and Perspectives of Fundamental Theology*, trans. Matthew J. O'Connell (New York: Paulist, 1982).

Lehrer, Keith, *Theory of Knowledge* (Boulder, Col./San Francisco, Calif.: Westview, 1990).

Lepore, Ernie, and Ludwig, Kirk (eds.), *The Essential Davidson* (New York: Oxford University Press, 2006).

Lewis, C. S. *The Great Divorce: A Dream* (Glasgow: Collins, 1946).

—— *Miracles: A Preliminary Study* (New York: Macmillan, 1947).

—— *God in the Dock*, ed. Walter Hooper (Grand Rapids, Mich.: Eerdmans, 1970).

Lewis, David, *On the Plurality of Worlds* (Oxford: Blackwell, 1986).

Lindbeck, George, *The Nature of Doctrine: Religion and Theology in a Postliberal Age* (Philadelphia, Pa.: Westminster, 1984).

Lindsell, Harold, *The Battle for the Bible* (Grand Rapids, Mich.: Zondervan, 1977).

Lints, Richard, *The Fabric of Theology: A Prolegomenon to Evangelical Theology* (Grand Rapids, Mich.: Eerdmans, 1993).

—— 'The Postpositivist Choice: Tracy or Lindbeck?', *Journal of the American Academy of Religion*, 61/4 (1993), 655–77.

Locke, John, *Essay Concerning Human Understanding*, ed. Peter H. Nidditch (Oxford: Clarendon, 1975).

Locke, John, *The Reasonableness of Christianity*, ed. John C. Higgins-Biddle (Oxford: Clarendon, 1999).

Long, Eugene Thomas (ed.), *Prospects for Natural Theology* (Washington, DC: Catholic University of America Press, 1992).

Loux, Michael, *Metaphysics* (London: Routledge, 1998).

Loux, Michael (ed.), *The Possible and the Actual* (Ithaca, NY: Cornell University Press, 1979).

Lull, Timothy F., 'The Trinity in Recent Theological Literature', *Word and World*, 2/1 (1982), 61–8.

Lycan, William J., 'Could Propositions Explain Anything?', *Canadian Journal of Philosophy*, 3/3 (1974), 427–34.

Lynch, Michael, *Truth in Context: An Essay on Pluralism and Objectivity* (Cambridge, Mass.: MIT Press, 1998).

—— *True to Life: Why Truth Matters* (Cambridge, Mass.: MIT Press, 2004).

McCormick, Peter J. (ed.), *Starmaking: Realism, Antirealism, and Irrealism* (Cambridge, Mass.: MIT Press, 1996).

McGinn, Colin, *The Problem of Consciousness: Essays Towards a Resolution* (Oxford: Blackwell, 1991).

—— *Problems in Philosophy: The Limits of Inquiry* (Oxford: Blackwell, 1993).

McGrath, Alister, *The Genesis of Doctrine: A Study in the Foundation of Doctrinal Criticism* (Grand Rapids, Mich.: Eerdmans, 1990).

McGrew, Timothy. 'Has Plantinga Refuted the Historical Argument?', *Philosophia Christi*, 6/1 (2004), 7–26.

—— and McGrew, Lydia, 'On the Historical Argument: A Rejoinder to Plantinga', *Philosophia Christi*, 8/1 (2006), 23–38.

Machuga, Ric, *In Defense of the Soul: What It Means to Be Human* (Grand Rapids, Mich.: Brazos, 2002).

MacIntyre, Alasdair, *Whose Justice? Which Rationality?* (Notre Dame, Ind.: University of Notre Dame Press, 1988).

—— *Three Rival Versions of Moral Enquiry: Encyclopaedia, Genealogy, and Tradition*, 1988 Gifford Lectures (London: Duckworth, 1990).

McKnight, Scot, *A Community Called Atonement* (Nashville, Tenn.: Abingdon, 2007).

Maier, Paul, *A Skeleton in God's Closet* (Nashville, Tenn.: Westbow, 1994).

Maritain, Jacques, *Reflections on America* (New York: Charles Scribner's Sons, 1958).

Marshall, Bruce, *Trinity and Truth* (Cambridge: Cambridge University Press, 2000).

—— (ed.), *Theology and Dialogue: Essays in Conversation with George Lindbeck* (Notre Dame, Ind.: University of Notre Dame, 1990).

Marshall, Bruce, ' "We Shall Bear the Image of the Man of Heaven": Theology and the Concept of Truth', *Modern Theology*, 11/1 (1995), 93–117.

—— 'Who Really Cares About Christian Unity?', *First Things* (Jan. 2001), 29–34.

Martin, Michael, *The Case Against Christianity* (Philadelphia, Pa.: Temple University Press, 1991).

Mascord, Keith, *Alvin Plantinga and Christian Apologetics* (Eugene, Ore.: Wipf and Stock, 2006).

Mavrodes, George, 'The Gods above the Gods: Can the High Gods Survive?', in Eleonore Stump (ed.), *Reasoned Faith: Essays in Philosophical Theology in Honor of Norman Kretzmann* (Ithaca, NY: Cornell University Press, 1993).

Mencken, Henry Louis, *H. L. Mencken on Religion*, ed. S. T. Joshi (Amherst, NY: Prometheus, 2002).

—— *Mencken's America*, ed. S. T. Joshi (Athens, OH: Ohio University Press, 2004).

Meynell, Hugo, *An Introduction to the Philosophy of Bernard Lonergan*, 2nd edn. (Toronto: University of Toronto Press, 1991).

Middleton, Richard J., and Walsh, Brian, *Truth is Stranger Than It Used to Be: Biblical Faith in a Postmodern Age* (Downers Grove, Ill.: InterVarsity, 1995).

Mitchell, Basil, *Faith and Criticism*, Sarum Lectures 1992 (Oxford: Clarendon, 1994).

—— 'Theology and Falsification', in Antony Flew and Alasdair MacIntyre (eds.), *New Essays in Philosophical Theology* (London: SCM, 1955).

Moore, Andrew, *Realism and Christian Faith: God, Grammar, and Meaning* (Cambridge: Cambridge University Press, 2003).

—— 'Philosophy of Religion or Philosophical Theology? A Review Essay of Bruce Marshall *Trinity and Truth* and Alvin Plantinga *Warranted Christian Belief*', *International Journal of Systematic Theology*, 3/3 (2001), 309–28.

Moreland, J. P., 'Truth, Contemporary Philosophy, and the Postmodern Turn', *Journal of the Evangelical Theological Society*, 48/1 (2005), 77–88.

—— and Craig, William Lane, *Philosophical Foundations for a Christian Worldview* (Downers Grove, Ill.: InterVarsity, 2003).

Morison, Frank, *Who Moved the Stone* (1930; Grand Rapids, Mich.: Zondervan, 1987).

Morris, Thomas, 'Suspicions of Something More', in Morris (ed.), *God and the Philosophers* (New York: Oxford University Press, 1994), 8–18.

Moser, Paul, 'Man to Man with *Warranted Christian Belief* and Alvin Plantinga', *Philosophia Christi*, 3/2 (2001), 369–77.

Murphy, Nancey, *Theology in the Age of Scientific Reasoning* (Ithaca, NY: Cornell University Press, 1990).

—— *Beyond Liberalism and Fundamentalism: How Modern and Postmodern Philosophy Set the Theological Agenda*, Rockwell Lecture Series (Valley Forge, Pa.: Trinity, 1996).

—— 'Introduction', in Stanley Hauerwas, *Theology Without Foundations: Religious Practice and the Future of Theological Truth*, ed. Nancey Murphy and Mark Nation (Nashville: Abingdon, 1994).

—— and McClendon, Jr., James William, 'Distinguishing Modern and Post-modern Theologies', *Modern Theology*, 5/3 (1989), 191–213.

Murray, Paul D., *Reason, Truth and Theology in Pragmatist Perspective* (Leuven: Peeters, 2004).

Naugle, David K., *Worldview: The History of a Concept* (Grand Rapids, Mich.: Eerdmans, 2002).

Newbigin, Lesslie, *Truth to Tell: The Gospel as Public Truth* (Grand Rapids, Mich.: Eerdmans/Geneva: WCC, 1991).

—— *Proper Confidence: Faith, Doubt, and Certainty in Christian Discipleship* (London: SPCK, 1995).

Nickerson, Raymond S., 'Confirmation Bias: A Ubiquitous Phenomenon in Many Guises', *Review of General Psychology*, 2/2 (1998), 175–220.

Nouwen, Henri, *Adam: God's Beloved* (Maryknoll, NY: Orbis, 1997).

Nozick, Robert, *Philosophical Explanations* (Cambridge, Mass.: Harvard University Press, 1981).

Oakes, Robert, 'Theism and Infallibilism: A Marriage Made in Heaven?', *Religious Studies*, 40/2 (2004), 193–202.

Oden, Thomas, *After Modernity ... What?* (Grand Rapids, Mich.: Zondervan, 1990).

—— *Systematic Theology, i. The Living God* (Peabody, Mass.: Prince, 1998).

Ommen, Thomas B., 'Theology and Foundationalism', *Studies in Religion/ Sciences Religieuses*, 16/2 (1987), 159–71.

Otto, Randall, 'Moltmann and the Anti-monotheism Movement', *International Journal of Systematic Theology*, 3/3 (2001), 293–308.

Padgett, Alan, review of Bruce Marshall *Trinity and Truth*, *Scottish Journal of Theology*, 54/3 (2001), 433–6.

—— ' "What is Truth?" On the Meaning of our Confession that Scripture is True', *Canadian Evangelical Review*, 29 (2005), 5–13.

Pannenberg, Wolfhart, *Jesus: God and Man*, trans. Lewis L. Wilkins and Duane A. Priebe (London: SCM, 1968).

—— *Basic Questions in Theology: Collected Essays*, trans. George H. Kehm, ii (Philadelphia, Pa.: Fortress, 1971).

298   Bibliography

Pannenberg, Wolfhart, *Systematic Theology*, i, trans. Geoffrey W. Bromiley (Grand Rapids, Mich.: Eerdmans, 1991).
—— *Systematic Theology*, ii, trans. Geoffrey W. Bromiley (Grand Rapids, Mich.: Eerdmans, 1994).
Pascal, Blaise, *Pensées*, trans. and ed. Roger Ariew (Indianapolis, Ind./ Cambridge: Hackett, 2005).
Patterson, Sue, *Realist Christian Theology in a Postmodern Age* (Cambridge: Cambridge University Press, 1999).
Pecknold, Chad C., *Reforming Postliberal Theology: George Lindbeck, Pragmatism and Scripture* (Edinburgh: T&T Clark, 2005).
Peirce, Charles, *Collected Papers of Charles Sanders Peirce*, ed. Charles Hartshorne and Paul Weiss (Cambridge, Mass.: Harvard University Press, 1931–58).
Penelhum, Terence, *God and Skepticism: A Study in Skepticism and Fideism* (Dordrecht: Reidel, 1983).
—— *Reason and Religious Faith* (Boulder, Col.: Westview, 1995).
Penner, Myron B. (ed.), *Christianity and the Postmodern Turn: Six Views* (Grand Rapids, Mich.: Brazos, 2005).
Perry, John. 'Dissolving the Inerrancy Debate: How Modern Philosophy Shaped the Evangelical View of Scripture', *Quodlibet Journal*, 3/4 (2001), at <http://www.quodlibet.net/perry-inerrancy.shtml>, accessed January 2009.
Peters, Ted, *God as Trinity: Relationality and Temporality in Divine Life* (Louisville, Ky.: Westminster/John Knox, 1993).
Phillips, Timothy R., and Okholm, Dennis L. (eds.), *Christian Apologetics in the Postmodern World* (Downers Grove, Ill.: InterVarsity, 1995).
—— —— (eds.), *The Nature of Confession: Evangelicals and Postliberals in Conversation* (Downers Grove, Ill.: InterVarsity, 1996).
Pitcher, George (ed.), *Truth* (Englewood Cliffs, NJ: Prentice Hall, 1964), introd., pp. 5–6.
Placher, William, *Unapologetic Theology: A Christian Voice in a Pluralistic Conversation* (Louisville, Ky.: Westminster/John Knox, 1989).
—— *The Domestication of Transcendence: How Modern Thinking about God Went Wrong* (Louisville, Ky.: Westminster/John Knox, 1996).
—— 'Postliberal Theology', in David F. Ford (ed.), *The Modern Theologians: An Introduction to Christian Theology in the Twentieth Century*, 2nd edn. (Cambridge, Mass.: Blackwell, 1997), 343–56.
Plantinga, Alvin, *God and Other Minds: A Study of the Rational Justification of Belief in God* (Ithaca, NY: Cornell University Press, 1967).
—— *God, Freedom, and Evil* (New York: Harper & Row, 1974).

—— *The Nature of Necessity* (Oxford: Clarendon, 1974).

—— *Warrant: The Current Debate* (Oxford: Oxford University Press, 1993).

—— *Warrant and Proper Function* (Oxford: Oxford University Press, 1993).

—— *The Analytic Theist: An Alvin Plantinga Reader*, ed. James F. Sennett (Grand Rapids, Mich.: Eerdmans, 1998).

—— *Warranted Christian Belief* (Oxford: Oxford University Press, 2000).

—— and Tooley, Michael, *Knowledge of God* (Malden, Mass./Oxford: Blackwell, 2008).

—— and Wolterstorff, Nicholas (eds.), *Faith and Rationality: Reason and Belief in God* (Notre Dame, Ind.: University of Notre Dame Press, 1983).

Plantinga, Alvin. 'Is Belief in God Rational?', in C. F. Delaney (ed.), *Rationality and Religious Belief* (Notre Dame, Ind.: University of Notre Dame Press, 1979), 7–27.

—— 'The Reformed Objection to Natural Theology', *Proceedings of the American Catholic Philosophical Association*, 54 (1980), 49–63.

—— 'Is Belief in God Properly Basic?', *Noûs*, 15/1 (1981), 41–51.

—— 'How to Be an Anti-realist', *Proceedings of the American Philosophical Society* (1982), 47–70.

—— 'The Foundations of Theism: A Reply', *Faith and Philosophy*, 3/3 (1986), 298–313.

—— 'Justification and Theism', *Faith and Philosophy*, 4/4 (1987), 403–26.

—— 'Positive Epistemic Status and Proper Function', in James Tomberlin (ed.), *Philosophical Perspectives, ii. Epistemology* (Atascadero, Calif.: Ridgeview, 1988), 1–50.

—— 'Augustinian Christian Philosophy', in Gareth B. Matthews (ed.), *The Augustinian Tradition* (Berkeley, Calif.: University of California Press, 1999), 1–26.

—— 'On Heresy, Mind, and Truth', *Faith and Philosophy*, 16/2 (1999), 182–93.

—— 'Internalism, Externalism, Defeaters and Arguments for Christian Belief', *Philosophia Christi*, 3/2 (2001), 379–400.

—— '*Warranted Christian Belief*: A Précis by the Author', 3/2 (2001), 327–8.

—— 'Historical Arguments and Dwindling Probabilities: A Response to Timothy McGrew', *Philosophia Christi*, 8/1 (2006), 7–22.

Polanyi, Michael, *Personal Knowledge: Towards a Post-critical Philosophy* (Chicago, Ill.: University of Chicago Press, 1958).

—— *The Tacit Dimension* (Garden City, NY: Doubleday, 1966).

Pollock, John, *Contemporary Theories of Knowledge* (Totowa, NJ: Rowman & Littlefield, 1986).

300 *Bibliography*

Putnam, Hilary, *The Many Faces of Realism*, Paul Carus Lectures (LaSalle, Ill.: Open Court, 1987).

—— *Reason, Truth and History* (Cambridge: Cambridge University Press, 1991).

—— *Renewing Philosophy* (Cambridge: Harvard University Press, 1992).

—— *Representation and Reality* (Cambridge, Mass.: Bradford, 1998).

—— *Jewish Philosophy as a Guide to Life: Rosenzweig, Buber, Levinas, Wittgenstein* (Bloomington, Ind.: Indiana University Press, 2008).

—— 'The Meaning of "Meaning"', in Keith Gunderson (ed.), *Language, Mind and Knowledge*, Minnesota Studies in the Philosophy of Science, vii (Minneapolis, Minn.: University of Minnesota Press, 1975), 131–93.

Quine, W. V. O., *From a Logical Point of View* (Cambridge, Mass.: Harvard University Press, 1953).

—— *Ontological Relativity and Other Essays* (New York: Columbia University Press, 1969).

—— and Goodman, Nelson, 'Steps Toward a Constructive Nominalism', *Journal of Symbolic Logic*, 12/4 (1947), 105–22.

—— and Ullian, J. S., *The Web of Belief*, 2nd edn. (New York: Random House, 1978).

Quinn, Philip, 'In Search of the Foundations of Theism', *Faith and Philosophy*, 2/4 (1985), 469–86.

Radner, Ephraim, *The End of the Church: A Pneumatology of Christian Division in the West* (Grand Rapids, Mich.: Eerdmans, 1998).

Rauch, Jonathan, 'Let It Be', *Atlantic Monthly* (May 2003), 30.

Rauser, Randal, *Faith Lacking Understanding: Theology Through a Glass Darkly* (Milton Keynes: Paternoster, 2008).

—— 'Can There Be Theology Without Necessity?', *Heythrop Journal*, 44/2 (2003), 131–46.

—— 'Ecumenism, Eucharist, and an Antirealism We Can Live With', *Canadian Evangelical Review*, 30–1 (2005–6), 23–41.

—— review of Stanley Grenz *Rediscovering the Triune God*, *International Journal of Systematic Theology*, 9/2 (2007), 231–5.

Raymo, Chet, *Skeptics and True Believers: The Exhilarating Connection Between Science and Religion* (London: Vintage, 1999).

Reid, Thomas, *An Inquiry into the Human Mind on the Principles of Common Sense*, ed. Derek R. Brookes (Edinburgh: Edinburgh University Press, 1997).

Reiser, William, ' "Knowing" Jesus: Do Theologians Have a Special Way?', in Daniel Kendall and Stephen T. Davis (eds.), *The Convergence of Theology* (New York: Paulist, 2001), 259–75.

Reno, R. R., review of Bruce Marshall, *Trinity and Truth*, *First Things* (Oct. 2000), 53–7.

—— 'Theology's Continental Captivity', *First Things* (April 2006), 26–33.

Reppert, Victor, *C. S. Lewis's Dangerous Idea* (Downers Grove, Ill.: Inter-Varsity, 2003).

Rescher, Nicholas, *Paradoxes: Their Roots, Range, and Resolution* (Chicago/LaSalle, Ill.: Open Court, 2001).

Richards, Jay Wesley, *The Untamed God* (Downers Grove, Ill.: InterVarsity, 2003).

Richardson, Mark W., and Wildman, Wesley J. (eds.), *Religion and Science: History, Method, Dialogue* (New York: Routledge, 1996).

Robinson, Howard, *Perception* (London/New York: Routledge, 1994).

Robinson, John, *Honest to God* (Philadelphia, Pa.: Westminster, 1963).

Robinson, W. D., 'Reason, Truth and Theology', *Modern Theology*, 2/2 (1986), 87–105.

Rockmore, Tom, and Singer, Beth J. (eds.), *Antifoundationalism Old and New* (Philadelphia, Pa.: Temple University Press, 1992).

Rorty, Richard, *Philosophy and the Mirror of Nature* (Princeton, NJ: Princeton University Press, 1979).

—— *Philosophical Papers, i. Objectivity, Relativism, and Truth* (Cambridge: Cambridge University Press, 1991).

—— 'A World without Substances or Essences', in his *Philosophy and Social Hope* (Harmondsworth: Penguin, 1999), 47–71.

Ruether, Rosemary, review of David Tracy, *Blessed Rage for Order*, *Journal of Religious Thought*, 33/2 (1976), 77–8.

Russell, Bertrand, *The Problems of Philosophy* (Oxford: Oxford University Press, 1912/1980).

Russell, Bertrand, 'Can Religion Cure Our Troubles?', in *Why I am Not a Christian and Other Essays on Religion and Related Subjects*, ed. Paul Edwards (New York: Touchstone, 1957), 193–204.

—— *My Philosophical Development* (London: George Allen & Unwin, 1959).

Sanks, Howland T., 'David Tracy's Theological Project: An Overview and Some Implications', *Theological Studies*, 54 (1993), 698–727.

Scott, Michael, 'The Truth Conditions of Christian Belief: A Critique of Bruce Marshall', *Journal of Religion*, 85/1 (2005), 43–57.

Searle, John, *The Construction of Social Reality* (New York: Free Press, 1995).

—— *Mind, Language, and Society: Philosophy in the Real World* (London: Weidenfeld & Nicolson, 1999).

Sellars, Wilfred, *Science, Perception and Reality* (London: Routledge & Kegan Paul, 1963).

Sessions, William Lad, *The Concept of Faith: A Philosophical Investigation* (Ithaca, NY/London: Cornell University Press, 1994).

Sherman, Steven B., *Revitalizing Theological Epistemology: Holistic Evangelical Approaches to the Knowledge of God* (Eugene, Ore.: Pickwick, 2008).

Shults, LeRon F., *The Postfoundationalist Task of Theology: Wolfhart Pannenberg and the New Theological Rationality* (Grand Rapids, Mich.: Eerdmans, 1999).

Sloane, Andrew, *On Being a Christian in the Academy: Nicholas Wolterstorff and the Practice of Christian Scholarship* (Carlisle: Paternoster, 2003).

Smith, James K. A., *Introducing Radical Orthodoxy: Mapping a Post-secular Theology* (Grand Rapids, Mich.: Baker/Milton Keynes: Paternoster, 2004).

Smith, Scott R., *Truth and the New Kind of Christian* (Wheaton, Ill: Crossway, 2005).

—— 'Post-conservatives, Foundationalism, and Theological Truth: A Critical Evaluation', *Journal of the Evangelical Theological Society*, 48/2 (2005), 351–63.

Sosa, Ernest, *Knowledge in Perspective: Selected Essays in Epistemology* (Cambridge: Cambridge University Press, 1991).

—— and Kim, Jaegwon (eds.), *Epistemology: An Anthology* (Oxford: Blackwell, 2000).

Sproul, R. C., Gerstner J., and Lindsley A., *Classical Apologetics* (Grand Rapids, Mich.: Zondervan,1984).

Stackhouse, John, *Humble Apologetics* (New York: Oxford University Press, 2002).

—— (ed.), *Evangelical Futures: A Conversation on Theological Method* (Grand Rapids, Mich.: Baker, 2000).

Stout, Jeffrey, *The Flight from Authority: Religion, Morality, and the Quest for Autonomy* (Notre Dame, Ind.: University of Notre Dame Press, 1981).

—— *Ethics After Babel: The Language of Morals and Their Discontents* (Boston, Mass.: Beacon, 1988).

Strong, Augustus, *Systematic Theology* (Valley Forge, Pa.: Judson, 1907).

Stroud, Barry, *The Significance of Philosophical Skepticism* (Oxford: Clarendon, 1984).

Stump, Eleonore (ed.), *Reasoned Faith: Essays in Philosophical Theology in Honor of Norman Kretzmann* (Ithaca, NY: Cornell University Press, 1993).

Stump, J. B., 'Christians and Philosophy of Mind: A Review Essay on *The Problem of the Soul*', *Philosophia Christi*, 5/2 (2003), 589–99.

Sudduth, Michael Czapkay, 'The Prospects for "Mediate" Natural Theology in John Calvin', *Religious Studies*, 31/1 (1995), 53–68.

Sudduth, Michael Czapkay, 'The Internalist Character and Evidential-ist Implications of Plantingian Defeaters', *International Journal for the Philosophy of Religion*, 45/3 (1999), 167–87.

——'Plantinga's Revision of the Reformed Tradition: Rethinking our Natural Knowledge of God', *Philosophical Books*, 43/2 (2002), 81–91.

Swenson, Robert, *More Than Meets the Eye: Fascinating Glimpses of God's Power and Design* (Colorado Springs, Col.: NavPress, 2000).

Swinburne, Richard, *Responsibility and Atonement* (Oxford: Clarendon, 1989).

—— *The Existence of God*, rev. edn. (Oxford: Clarendon, 1991).

—— *The Christian God* (Oxford: Clarendon, 1994).

—— *Providence and the Problem of Evil* (Oxford: Oxford University Press, 1998).

—— *Epistemic Justification* (Oxford: Clarendon, 2001).

—— *The Resurrection of God Incarnate* (Oxford: Clarendon, 2003).

—— *Revelation: From Metaphor to Analogy* (Oxford: Clarendon, 2007).

——'Plantinga on Warrant', *Religious Studies*, 37/3 (2001), 203–22.

Taylor, Daniel, *The Myth of Certainty: The Reflective Christian and the Risk of Commitment* (Nashville, Tenn:. W Publishing Group, 1986).

Thiel, John, *Nonfoundationalism* (Minneapolis, Minn.: Fortress, 1994).

Thiemann, Ronald, *Revelation and Theology* (Notre Dame, Ind.: University of Notre Dame Press, 1985).

Tillich, Paul, *A History of Christian Thought* (New York: Touchstone, 1972).

——'The Two Types of Philosophy of Religion', in Tillich, *Theology of Culture*, ed. Robert C. Kimball (New York: Oxford University Press, 1959), 10–29.

Tippett, Krista, *Speaking of Faith* (New York: Viking, 2007).

Tomberlin, James (ed.), *Philosophical Perspectives, i. Metaphysics* (Atascadero, Calif.: Ridgeview, 1987).

—— (ed.), *Philosophical Perspectives, ii. Epistemology* (Atascadero, Calif.: Ridgeview, 1988).

—— (ed.), *Philosophical Perspectives, xiii. Epistemology, 1999* (Atascadero, Calif.: Ridgeview, 1999).

—— and Peter van Inwagen (eds.), *Alvin Plantinga* (Dordrecht: Reidel, 1985).

Topping, Richard R., 'The Anti-foundationalist Challenge to Evangelical Apologetics', *Evangelical Quarterly*, 63/1 (1991), 45–60.

Torrance, T. F., *Theological Science* (Edinburgh: T&T Clark, 1969).

—— *God and Rationality* (London/New York: Oxford University Press, 1971).

Torrance, T. F., *Preaching Christ Today: The Gospel and Scientific Thinking* (Grand Rapids, Mich.: Eerdmans, 1994).

Tracy, David, *Blessed Rage for Order: The New Pluralism in Theology* (Chicago, Ill.: University of Chicago Press, 1975).

—— *The Analogical Imagination: Christian Theology and the Culture of Pluralism* (New York: Crossroad, 1981).

—— *Plurality and Ambiguity: Hermeneutics, Religion, Hope* (San Francisco, Calif.: Harper & Row, 1987).

—— 'The Necessity and Insufficiency of Fundamental Theology', in René Latourelle and Gerald O'Collins (eds.), *Problems and Perspectives of Fundamental Theology*, trans. Matthew J. O'Connell (New York: Paulist, 1982).

—— 'Approaching the Christian Understanding of God', in Francis Schüssler Fiorenza and John P. Galvin (eds.), *Systematic Theology: Roman Catholic Perspectives*, i (Minneapolis, Minn.: Fortress, 1991), 133–48.

Trigg, Roger, *Rationality and Science: Can Science Explain Everything?* (Oxford: Blackwell, 1993).

Tully, James (ed.), *Philosophy in an Age of Pluralism: The Philosophy of Charles Taylor in Question* (Cambridge: Cambridge University Press, 1994).

Turretin, Francis, *Institutes of Elenctic Theology*, ed. James T. Dennison, Jr., trans. George Musgrave Giver, i (Phillipsburg, NJ: P&R, 1992).

Vanhoozer, Kevin, *The Drama of Doctrine: A Canonical-Linguistic Approach to Christian Theology* (Louisville, Ky.: Westminster/John Knox Press, 2005).

—— 'Disputing about Words? Of Fallible Foundations and Modest Metanarratives', in Myron B. Penner (ed.), *Christianity and the Postmodern Turn: Six Views* (Grand Rapids, Mich.: Brazos, 2005).

Van Huyssteen, J. Wentzel, *Essays in Postfoundationalist Theology* (Grand Rapids, Mich.: Eerdmans, 1997).

Van Inwagen, Peter, *God, Knowledge, and Mystery* (Ithaca, NY: Cornell University Press, 1995).

—— *The Possibility of Resurrection and Other Essays in Christian Apologetics* (Boulder, Col.: Westview, 1998).

—— 'Some Remarks on Plantinga's Advice', *Faith and Philosophy*, 16/2 (1999), 164–72.

Walker, Ralph C. S., *The Coherence Theory of Truth: Realism, Anti-realism, Idealism* (London: Routledge, 1989).

Watson, Francis, *Text, Church and World: Biblical Interpretation in Theological Perspective* (Grand Rapids, Mich.: Eerdmans, 1994).

Webber, Robert C., *The Younger Evangelicals: Facing the Challenges of the New World* (Grand Rapids, Mich.: Baker, 2002).

Westphal, Merold, 'Taking Plantinga Seriously: Advice to Christian Philosophers', *Faith and Philosophy*, 16/2 (1999), 173–81.

Wilken, Robert, *Remembering the Christian Past* (Grand Rapids, Mich.: Eerdmans, 1995).

Willard, Dallas, 'How Concepts Relate the Mind to Its Objects: The God's Eye View Vindicated?', *Philosophia Christi*, 1/2 (1999), 5–20.

Williams, David, review of John R. Franke and Stanley J. Grenz, *Beyond Foundationalism*, *Journal of the Evangelical Theological Society*, 44/4 (2001), 752–4.

Williams, David, 'Scripture, Truth and Our Postmodern Context', *Evangelicals and Tradition, Authority, and Hermeneutics*, (eds.) Vincent Bacote, Laura Miguélez, Dennis Okholm (Downers Grove, IL: InterVarsity, 2004), 229–43.

Williams, John G., *Christian Faith and the Space Age* (Cleveland/New York: World, 1968).

Wilson, E. O., *Consilience: The Unity of Knowledge* (London: Little, Brown, 1998).

Wolfe, Alan, *The Transformation of American Religion: How We Actually Live Our Faith* (New York: Free Press, 2003).

Wolterstorff, Nicholas, *John Locke and the Ethics of Belief* (Cambridge: Cambridge University Press, 1996).

—— *Thomas Reid and the Story of Epistemology* (Cambridge: Cambridge University Press, 2001).

—— 'True Words', in Alan G. Padgett and Patrick R. Keifert (eds.), *But Is It All True? The Bible and the Question of Truth* (Grand Rapids, Mich./Cambridge: Eerdmans, 2006).

Wood, W. Jay, *Epistemology: Becoming Intellectually Virtuous* (Downers Grove, Ill.: InterVarsity, 1998).

Wright, Tom, *The Original Jesus: The Life and Vision of a Revolutionary* (Grand Rapids, Mich.: Eerdmans, 1996).

Wykstra, Stephen, 'Toward a Sensible Evidentialism: On the Notion of "Needing Evidence"', in William L. Rowe and William J. Wainwright (eds.), *Philosophy of Religion: Selected Readings*, 2nd edn. (Fort Worth: Harcourt Brace Jovanovich, 1989), 426–37.

Yolton, John, *Perception and Reality: A History from Descartes to Kant* (Ithaca, NY: Cornell University Press, 1996).

Yolton, John, *Realism and Appearances: An Essay in Ontology* (Cambridge: Cambridge University Press, 2000).

Young, William, *The Shack* (Newbury Park, Calif.: Windblown, 2007).

Zagzebski, Linda, *Virtues of the Mind: An Inquiry into the Nature of Virtue and the Ethical Foundations of Knowledge* (New York: Cambridge University Press, 1996).

—— 'Religious Knowledge and the Virtues of the Mind', in Zagzebski (ed.), *Rational Faith: Catholic Responses to Reformed Epistemology* (Notre Dame, Ind.: University of Notre Dame, 1993), 199–225.

—— (ed.), *Rational Faith: Catholic Responses to Reformed Epistemology* (Notre Dame, Ind.: Notre Dame University Press, 1995).

—— 'Plantinga's *Warranted Christian Belief* and the Aquinas/Calvin Model', *Philosophical Books*, 43/2 (2002), 117–23.

Zeglen, Urszula M. (ed.), *Donald Davidson: Truth, Meaning, and Knowledge* (London: Routledge, 1999).

Zizioulas, John, *Being as Communion* (Crestwood, NY: St Vladimir's Seminary Press, 1985).

Index